# A VERY ENGLISH HERO

# A VERY ENGLISH HERO

*The Making of Frank Thompson*

Peter J. Conradi

B L O O M S B U R Y

LONDON • NEW DELHI • NEW YORK • SYDNEY

First published in Great Britain 2012

Copyright © 2012 by Peter J. Conradi

The moral right of the author has been asserted

Images are from the Frank Thomson papers in the E. P. Thompson
collection held by the Bodleian Library, Oxford, reproduced by permission
of the late Dorothy Thompson, except where credited otherwise

Maps by ML Design

Every reasonable effort has been made to trace copyright holders of
material reproduced in this book, but if any have been inadvertently
overlooked the publishers would be glad to hear from them

Bloomsbury Publishing Plc
50 Bedford Square
London
WC1B 3DP

www.bloomsbury.com

Bloomsbury Publishing, London, New Delhi, New York and Sydney

A CIP catalogue record for this book is available from the British Library

ISBN 978 1 4088 0243 4

10 9 8 7 6 5 4 3 2 1

Typeset by Hewer Text UK Ltd, Edinburgh

Printed in Great Britain by Clays Ltd, St Ives plc

For E. P. Thompson (1924–1993)
and for Dorothy Thompson (1923–2011)

The only things that have any value today are love and courage

from a letter to Désirée Cumberledge, 19 November 1941

# Contents

# Frank Thompson's Theatre of War, 1943

UNION OF
SOVIET
SOCIALIST
REPUBLICS

Baltic
Sea

Leningrad
(St Petersburg)

Tallinn

Riga

*Volga*

■ Moscow

REICHSKOMMISSARIAT
OSTLAND

*Dvina*

•Smolensk

Königsberg
(Kaliningrad)

•Minsk

Berlin ■

Warsaw ■

GERMAN EMPIRE

REICHSKOMMISSARIAT
UKRAINE

Kiev•

SLOVAKIA

Lviv

*Dnieper*

*Don*

Stalingrad

HUNGARY

Odessa•

Crimea

ITALY

CROATIA

Frushka Gora

ROMANIA

Bucharest•

Ordzhonikidze

Black Sea

Caspian
Sea

SERBIA

Sofia•

Pristina•

BULGARIA

ALBANIA

Istanbul

Caucasus Mountains

Baku•

Rome ■

Bari•

Brindişi•

Athens•

TURKEY

IRAN

Sicily

MALTA

Avola•

Rhodes•

DODECANESE
ISLANDS

Hamadan
•

SYRIA

Beirut•

Zahle

*Tigris*

Mediterranean
Sea

PALESTINE

Damascus■

*Euphrates*

Baghdad ■

Tripoli
■

Benghazi•

Tobruk•

Alexandria•

Jerusalem•

TRANSJORDAN

IRAQ

El Alamein•

Cairo•

*Nile*

LIBYA

N

EGYPT

*Red Sea*

SAUDI ARABIA

| 0 | 100 | 200 | 300 | 400 | 500 miles |
| 0 | 200 | 400 | 600 | 800 kilometres |

*Prologue*

# 'The Story of a Great Englishman'

On 8 March 1945 the left-wing *News Chronicle* published a full-page account of the last days of Frank Thompson, headlined 'The Story of a Great Englishman' and garnered chiefly from a Bulgarian delegate to the World Trades Union Congress in London. Since no details were officially known, this 'eye-witness report' was significant.

Frank, 'brilliant 23 year old son of Mr Edward Thompson the poet', was a British liaison officer dropped into the Balkans to work with Bulgarian Partisans, who were fighting in hopes of overthrowing their government, which was Royalist, Fascist and pro-German. Captured in May 1944, he had been executed around 10 June after a mock trial at Litakovo, fifteen miles from Sofia, with four other officers, one American, one Serb and two Bulgarians. One arresting detail concerned the treatment meted out to the fifty-seven Partisans captured out of all those he had been sent in to liaise with: some had had their eyes gouged out before being shot. Here was a casual brutality shocking to readers schooled in the relative decencies of the war in Western Europe. Many of the executioners had themselves already been put to death.

———

The unforgettable and highly charged part of the *News Chronicle* article concerned Frank's demeanour during his trial. Attempts to stir the local citizenry to lynch the Partisans failed, and the village hall was packed with spectators when the brutal and as yet unnamed

Bulgarian Army captain started his interrogation. Frank leaned against a pillar, calmly smoking his pipe. He was asked for his name, rank and political opinions, and then: 'By what right do you, an Englishman, enter our country and wage war against us?' Frank astonished his listeners by answering without an interpreter, in fluent, idiomatic Bulgarian, replying that the war was much bigger than the battle of one nation against another, and the greatest thing in the world now was the struggle of Fascism and anti-Fascism. 'Do you not know that we shoot men with your opinions?' the captain said. Frank answered that he was ready to die for freedom and that he was proud to die with Bulgarian patriots as his companions. The crowd was deeply stirred and one old woman, passionately weeping, stood to denounce the trial, declaring that the whole village was on the side of the Partisans. Proceedings were brought swiftly to a close, after less than half an hour.

Major Thompson took charge of the condemned men and led them to the castle. As they marched off before the assembled people, he raised a clenched fist, the salute of the Fatherland Front which the Allies were helping. A gendarme struck his arm down, but Thompson called out to the people, 'I give you the Salute of Freedom!' All the men died raising this salute. The spectators were sobbing; many present declared the scene one of the most moving in all Bulgarian history, that the men's amazing courage was the work of the English officer who carried their spirits, as well as his own.

They were hurriedly buried in an unmarked grave. The article ended with part of a Christmas letter Frank had written to his parents in 1943.

My Christmas message to you is one of greater hope than I have ever had in my life before. There is a spirit abroad in Europe finer and braver than anything that tired continent has known for centuries and which cannot be withstood. You can, if you like, think of it in terms of politics, but it is broader and more generous than any dogma. It is the confident will of whole peoples, who have known the utmost humiliation and suffering and who have triumphed over it, to build their own life once and for all.

The *News Chronicle*'s 'scoop' created a stir, and gave credence to a version of Frank's end that endured until his 2004 *Oxford Dictionary of National Biography* entry. In Bulgaria too the story of Frank's fearless denunciations of Fascism at his trial and his confident bearing on his way to execution stirred readers to their depths: he stands to Bulgaria as Byron to Greece. Frank was posthumously decorated, a railway station near Sofia was named after him and a kindergarten; nursery rhymes are still sung about his adventures. A reliable if flowery Bulgarian biography of Frank was published in 2001, as yet untranslated.*

---

I first encountered Frank Thompson when writing Dame Iris Murdoch's authorised biography.† I was greatly attracted by his brilliant, warmhearted, brave personality, and moved by the remarkable tragedy of his early death. I was not alone in thinking that he seemed a good deal nicer than Dame Iris then was. At a celebration of Frank's life at the Bulgarian Embassy in the year 2000, one of his schoolfellows described him as having 'ten thumbs, a brilliant mind, and an enormous heart'. When the previous October I was invited by Professor Philippa Foot to accompany her on a trip to Bulgaria, Frank's Oxford friend Noel Martin, to whom I mentioned this forthcoming trip on the telephone, said lightly, 'Kiss the ground for me, won't you?'

Philippa shared a wartime flat with Iris Murdoch, where, in November 1944, she brought Murdoch the news that Frank was Missing Believed Killed and, as at no other moment in her sixty-year friendship with Philippa, Iris wept. In March 1939, when Frank first fell in love with her, Iris had persuaded him to join the Communist Party.

In Sofia Philippa and I met ex-Partisan General Slavcho Trŭnski, fourteen days before his death; he reminisced fondly about Frank, and shed tears. We travelled to Litakovo, where a group of five villagers

---

* Kiril Yanev, *The Man from the Legend: A Life of Frank Thompson*, Sofia, 2001.
† In 2010 I edited his and Dame Iris's surviving correspondence, together with another letter-run and journal, in *Iris Murdoch, A Writer at War: Letters and Diaries 1938–1946*, London.

including the Mayor showed us the hand-carved pipe Frank had smoked in captivity, and then we all progressed in silence to his grave. Philippa surprised me – not the only occasion – by opening a bag she was carrying and handing me a single red carnation to place there, as if from Iris.

Then we waited for some hours to meet Naku Staminov, who was delayed by a meeting about privatising land. Staminov's recollection contradicted the 'official' version of Frank's death. In June 1944, at twelve years old, he followed a group of a dozen Partisans including Frank, the tallest, handsomest and strongest, who was chewing something, and witnessed his execution. Frank wore a green jacket with a zip-fastener, and Naku later recognised his picture in the newspaper as that of the foreigner whose murder he had unexpectedly watched. (The last parcel Frank's mother sent him – I later discovered – was dispatched at Christmas 1943 and contained copies of *Life* magazine and a zip-up waterproof jacket, which he acknowledged by cable.)

The Partisans that day were surrounded by Gendarmerie but seemed calm. Later Naku learned they had been lied to and told that they were being marched to another village. There was complete silence while the killing took place. They were shot in a ditch. Frank half turned, shouting something furiously in English before being raked with fire. He was the last to stop convulsing. A ring was cut off his finger with a knife. Naku was sick with terror for months afterwards, and his mother gave him a lead bullet as a Balkan charm to counter its effects. We watched him, reliving that terror, develop a facial tic.

The contrast between Staminov's memory and the 'official' version could not be starker. On the one hand a national hero whose noble bearing in adversity inspired a whole nation; on the other a uniformed British officer duped before being shot in a ditch. This book is concerned with establishing the truth about how Frank died, and with what, in his short life, led up to and helped shape this fate. It also examines the nature of heroism itself: can a seemingly pointless death be accounted heroic?

When I was sixteen my grandmother took an overdose and died. This was in 1961. There is still family debate about how befuddled whisky had made her when she kept swallowing those sleeping pills, and how desperate she was. Despair began twenty years before when her favourite child, blond, blue-eyed and weeks shy of his twentieth birthday, was shot down during a so-called tip-and-run raid off the Lincolnshire coast and killed. That was his final trainee-navigator's flight, in November 1941. By extraordinary chance her grave-digger turned out to have dug her son's twenty years before, and asked, vividly recalling her grief, whether she had ever 'got over it'. In some sense she did not. She wore his 'wings', made up as a marcasite brooch, for her remaining days of good works, tippling and bridge.

About 1961 Frank Thompson's mother Theo, who had moved to Grange-over-Sands because it reminded her of the Lebanon where she grew up, also took an overdose. Her daughter-in-law Dorothy recalled that Theo wanted to quit while the going was good and before frailty overcame her; but the death of her favourite son Frank in 1944 may have played its part in weakening her will to continue. She survived and moved to live near her surviving son E. P. Thompson and Dorothy for her last years.

The Second World War casts long shadows, with some of which the final section of this biography is concerned. I was living in Kraków, Poland in 1990–2 when Russian troops were finally expelled and I vividly remember one journey from London. No London–Warsaw planes had been allowed to fly over fortified Berlin since 1945: each detoured instead over Danish Jutland before veering sharply south. On one such trip, despite our taking off late, it was announced that we were the first flight given permission to overfly Berlin, and so would land early. I (whose family originated in Dresden) was moved that another symbol of the Cold War had thus gone, a war that had caused much suffering, and whose first victim – or so his brother believed – was Frank Thompson himself.

———

I was not alone in finding Frank attractive or wishing to write his biography – the literary form in which the dead are invoked in order to teach the living. Five other British writers had the same idea. Dr Rod Bailey, arguably the best younger writer on SOE, arrived for tea with a file of Frank-related research papers gathered over years in Washington DC and elsewhere and generously handed them over without conditions. Rod has been a marvellous support, without whom (to take two examples) I should not have known what Expeditionary Force Messages were, nor what happened to the widow of Major Mostyn Davies, the officer Frank Thompson was dropped into Bulgaria to assist (see Chapter 14).

After my *Iris Murdoch: A Life* was published in 2001 I received a letter from Frank's sister-in-law Dorothy Thompson: she had joined the Communist Party in 1938 aged fifteen, her husband the historian E. P. Thompson had joined the CP in 1940 aged seventeen, and Frank had joined in March 1939 aged eighteen. Dorothy wrote to thank me both for sympathetically understanding and then also for 'explaining' the militant idealism of her generation to her children and grandchildren. And although the E. P. Thompson papers, which include all of Frank's, are in closed collection in the Bodleian Library until the year 2043 – because Dorothy thought that a biography of EP should not be written until fifty years after his death – she gave me privileged access without which the writing of this biography would not have been possible.

For a while Simon Kusseff, given permission to write a life of Frank around 1993, and I planned to co-write Frank's biography. Simon had in 1998 generously given me a bulky three-part 'Chronology' (in effect a quarry) of Frank-related documents when I was writing *Iris Murdoch: A Life*. In 2008 he added a collection of interviews conducted with Frank's friends.

Kusseff took the view that Frank's emphasis on our need for a 'new communal ethic' spoke prophetically to today's crises of financial meltdown and global warming. Now, after much further research – and for all that the world seems on the brink of another 1930s-style depression – this seems fortuitous, if not wrong-headed. Frank's outer circumstances are inevitably of their epoch and three examples suggest how remote these are. First, Frank's Colonel in the Royal Artillery in 1940 kept a handbook entitled 'Social Classification of Officers': Frank got bad marks for claiming to be a Methodist (an atheist, which is what he really was, would have been allotted menial tasks), but good marks for having been to Winchester. This was routine: his younger brother EP's friend the writer Robin Maugham, interviewed by a colonel in the 15th/19th Hussars, read the following marks (out of ten) that his answers had earned. What games did you play at school? – None [mark: *nought*]. Which school? Eton [mark: *ten*]. Do you earn a hundred pounds a week or a year? A year [mark: *nought*]. What's your father do? Lord of Appeal [mark: *ten*].

Then Frank's first flight was from Malta to Tripoli in July 1943. All his many pre-war travels – to the USA, to Syria, Brittany, Haute Savoie, Greece, Rome, Austria, Ireland, then to Egypt in 1941 – were by coal-powered train and/or ship. He knew that flying was the travel of the future. It scared him and he disapproved of it, too. 'Let me be earth-bound all my life,' he prayed.

Finally, when he arrived in Hamadan in Persia in November 1942 he was amazed to find the streets lit up – the first street-lighting (apart from Cape Town) he had enjoyed since 1 September 1939 when the blackout started on the day that he joined up, two days before the outbreak of war. Nowhere in Egypt, the Levant, London, Oxford or Glasgow had he strolled under illuminated street lamps since that date. Frank spent nearly five long years, from the age of nineteen to almost twenty-four, in a world literally as well as figuratively darkened, something hard for us today to imagine.

'When the lights go on again / All over the world / And the boys come home again': a sentimental Vera Lynn song thus expressed the yearning for conflict to be over; but light-and-dark imagery haunts W. H. Auden's wonderful 'September 1 1939' too, where waves of anger and fear circulate over 'the bright / And darkened lands of the earth, / Obsessing our private lives'. Frank was compelled by the suffering of his age and conceived himself at war with the powers of darkness too. I see him, to his fingertips, as a Popular Front intellectual, that loose alliance of progressives from the CP to anti-Fascist Tories who wanted

Hitler beaten so that a better world could be born. He none the less wrote, aged twenty-two, that 'there is no point in trying to hate men. We'd be wasting our time . . . Worse than that – we'd be losing our own virtue.' That too suggests something of his rare quality.

---

There are other reasons why Frank Thompson may interest us today. He is a figure in many different landscapes: Boars Hill; pre-war Oxford; the war, during which he served for nearly five years, and was a civilian-soldier in two 'private armies' – Phantom, then SOE; and not least a remarkable family, whose maternal forebears founded the American University of Beirut, while his own father, a missionary in Bengal, translated Rabindranath Tagore and was befriended by Nehru and Gandhi. His younger brother E. P. Thompson was both political activist and brilliant historian, among the first, in his *The Making of the English Working Class*, to enfranchise the voices of the poor. (EP was known by his second name, Palmer, until after 1944, when he changed over to Edward. As Edward was his father's name too, they are distinguished here respectively as EJ and EP.)

Frank was an apprentice poet who wished to speak for his remarkable generation – who had their youth stolen from them by the chance of world war – and in his best-known poem succeeded. He is representative as well as individual. Because he died at twenty-three, his papers, diaries and enormous correspondence were, in effect, frozen. This was due partly to delay in official notification of his death, partly to his parents' desire to commemorate him. His twenty or so boxes – many hundreds of thousands of words – provide for the strange and fascinating age through which Frank lived a picture of unparalleled depth and detail, a period of much intrinsic interest, now that its survivors are each year fewer. Juliet Gardner, author of *Wartime* and *The Blitz*, believes that the lives of no other Second World War soldiers are documented with this degree of detail.

On 13 January 1944, days before being dropped into occupied Serbia as a British liaison officer to work with the Partisans, Frank asked his brother EP to send him anything he had written 'these last three years'.

They were a family of writers. Frank rarely had enough time to write. His journals, he apologised, were written so hurriedly in such a childish style that they would only be valuable 'as raw material for more considered writing after the war'. That all his writings are work-in-progress does not lessen their value as fresh witness to a lost age.

It is moving to me that a half-dozen of his school contemporaries are still with us, aged around ninety, and have aided this research; and it is a strange thought that we might have had the pleasure of his company for the last sixty-odd years. Frank is still much mourned. And since we cannot enjoy his company in the flesh, a biography is one way of celebrating him in spirit.

In 1975 Stowers Johnson wrote a fanciful life of Frank that offended friends and family, entitled *Agents Extraordinary* (see Chapter 14). Johnson gives no sources, he supplies everybody's thoughts, and where a fact stated by him can be independently verified it often turns out to be false. Basil Davidson, who was dropped by SOE into the Balkans, characterised his book as 'unnecessarily ill-informed', naive and 'highly inaccurate'. This is frustrating, because not everything within it can be invented. For another account of Johnson and of Frank, the reader is referred to Alan Ogden's *Through Hitler's Back Door: SOE Operations in Hungary, Slovakia, Romania and Bulgaria 1939–1945* (2010). I made a tactical decision to base my own account on two first-hand narratives written in 1944, held in the National Archives in Kew: those of Major Mostyn Davies and of Kenneth Scott, two men who fought with Frank in Bulgaria and whose accounts are thus free from accretions of later Cold War legend.

---

A sense of communion with Frank continues today: he has been the subject of biographical chapters in recent books by writers as different as Freeman Dyson (1979), Fred Inglis (1991), Luisa Passerini (1999), Alan Ogden (2010) and the present writer (2001). Books about him in Bulgaria abound. He haunted his friend Iris Murdoch, who believed that had he survived she and Frank would have married, and colours a number of characters in her novels. Many of his letters survive because they were prized, and, like his best-known poem, retain their power to make us feel spoken to.

On 15 August 1945, the day of Victory over Japan, *The Times* published Frank's 'An Epitaph for my Friends'. It is his best poem, much anthologised:

> As one who, gazing at a vista
> Of beauty, sees the clouds close in,
> And turns his back in sorrow, hearing
> The thunder-claps begin
>
> So we, whose life was all before us,
> Our hearts with sunlight filled,
> Left in the hills our books and flowers,
> Descended and were killed.
>
> Write on the stone no words of sadness
> – Only the gladness due,
> That we, who asked the most of living,
> Knew how to give it too.

Frank Thompson was not a great poet. He died before he could turn himself convincingly into a minor one. Much that he wrote was in the nature of a first draft or quarry to be reworked after the war. Yet 'An Epitaph for my Friends' goes some way to suggesting what English poetry may have lost in June 1944. In the best collection of Second World War verse the editors single out this poem to represent the rest. It was read by Edward Fox on the fiftieth anniversary of VE Day before an audience including the monarch and the Prime Minister. Lines from Frank's poem are written on the monument at Netley on Southampton Water to commemorate D-Day.

The language is simple, the rhetoric stoical and prophetic. It is the poet's imagined adjustment to his own possible end that touches us, combined with his light-hearted willingness to embrace a very particular fate. Fewer than 500,000 British men and women died in that war, less than I per cent of the population. If you compare casualty rates to those in Poland (16 per cent), USSR (13 per cent) or Germany (10 per cent), British losses were very small. 'An Epitaph for my Friends' is Frank Thompson's bid to speak for his entire generation. It is both modest and boastful: modest in relinquishing his individuality, boastful in speaking for 'the few', and making 'the many' (including we who come later) indebted to his self-sacrifice. Its full title, 'Polliciti Meliora' – Latin for 'Having Promised Better Things' – implies that the poet may die in order to create a better world. A vision of progress inspires Frank, and his willingness to sacrifice himself is its warranty. Through his courage he also passes on to us his own burden of caring for the world we share. 'This' poem, too, is a device whereby the dead speak directly to the living.

The poem's 'books and flowers' are not soldierly weapons; and the two women who knew him best at Oxford in 1938–9 both thought Frank an improbable soldier: there is no record of his ever having fired a weapon in anger. Iris Murdoch told him that there was no bitterness in his letters; and after his death she wrote that 'He didn't seem in the least framed to be a soldier.' Nor did many others: joining up to be part of an amateur, civilian army also makes him typical of his generation.

---

Literature was one theme Frank and his parents corresponded about. Here, since few censors read Homer, was first of all a way of encoding information. Iris Murdoch could ask in 1943 whether he was 'anywhere near the precincts of the foam-born lady', knowing he would recognise the reference to Aphrodite's legendary birth out of the sea near Cyprus; while in his final letter to her in April 1944 he allusively implied his location on the Serbian–Bulgarian border. A dictionary he was carrying once stopped an enemy bullet and saved his life. And a volume of the great Roman poet Catullus was found on him after his death. But literature also enshrined all that he cared most about; he believed that the arts were the focal point of human living, and literature paramount. He fought a 'poet's war'.

He was that extremely rare combination, an intellectual with a heart, a brilliant man capable of emotion. Formidably clever and observant, he was, as he put it, 'more inclined to love than analyse'. One fascination of his story is watching the gentle scholar with his books and flowers evolve into an adventurous soldier. His poems, many letters and his journals talk to us still – as they did to his family – with a startling intimacy.

# PART ONE

## Between Two Wars
### 1919–39

# I

## The Missionary Position

Theodosia Jessup met the Methodist chaplain and English writer Captain Edward J. Thompson in the summer of 1918 in Jerusalem, where he was on leave and she was helping run the Mount Sion orphanage, teaching Arabic and French. The writer Margaret Storm Jameson recorded: '[Edward] married the one woman he should have married,

an American, the serenely beautiful child of American missionaries in Syria.' She was known for having hair of so golden a colour that 'you could lose a sovereign in it', for having numerous admirers, and for having extricated a donkey from a ditch, stubbornly pulling it by the tail. She had courage, intelligence and will power. He, at thirty-three, was seven years her senior.

Edward's courtship of Theo lasted six troubled weeks. She approximated to the ideal type he most admired: a graceful upper-class blonde seated on a horse. She had been educated at a patrician college in the US and was a skilled linguist, while his education had been hit-and-miss. It is likely that she mixed with grander people in Jerusalem than he did. While he had taught himself to enjoy riding, she had ridden well from childhood.

But there were difficulties involving friends and one past lover. She sometimes found him conceited; he thought her censorious. Not for nothing were they both children of missionaries, this chapter's topic. She disliked seeing him drink and he had to explain that he had never smoked till he was thirty, and nor had he during six long years in India adopted the habit of the *chota peg*. Only after his wartime breakdown when many friends and a beloved brother had been killed had his habit of a single evening 'sun-downer' started. Watching so many innocent men die in agony had left him drained, disillusioned and doubting God's goodness. Though her alertness to sin and ugliness sometimes made her 'a silly goose', he also told her that her poise, 'queenly self-control' and 'daintiness' (by which he meant fastidiousness) might in time redeem him. When she agreed to marry, he wrote, 'No English poet before me, save Browning, has been so lucky.' This flattered them both, implying that Theo had a poet's mind, too, worth weaning from harshness. Her love is not only to help him to fame – for which he pretends to care nothing – or peace of mind – which mattered 'a great deal' – but to help him back to God. He felt a misfit among the tribe of 'narrow, savagely self-righteous men' from which he came.

As for Theo, she married a penniless Methodist minister against the wishes of worldly-wise friends, some of whom – who knew the foolish

English social discrimination against non-conformists – were angry and horrified. Others declared themselves very sorry for her and disappointed that life should have closed down so suddenly. But she was attracted by the fact that he was a published writer, with two plays and five books of poetry to his name.* He sent her copies. Somehow they understood one another.

They married on 10 March 1919 in the classic and magnificent great inner court – *Da'ar* in Arabic – of the aristocratic Beirut house rented by Theo's missionary father William Jessup. Before the war the Jessup family believed James Elroy Flecker, an inefficient British vice-consul, had stayed there, writing *The Golden Road to Samarkand* with its perfumed Orientalism and being visited by an admiring T. E. Lawrence

---

* *Knight Mystic – Verses* (1907); *The Enchanted Lady: A Comedy* (1910); *Saul: A Drama* (1915); *John in Prison – Verses* (1912); *Ennerdale Bridge & Other Poems* (1914); *Waltham Thickets & Other Poems* (1917); *Mesopotamian Verses* (1919); *The Leicestershires Beyond Baghdad* (1919); *Vae Victis* (1919).

before starting to succumb in April 1913 to TB. The villa's palatial rooms stayed cool through the intense heat of summer.

This hall, sixty feet long and proportionately wide and high, featured many doors leading off into stone-built state-rooms, fine rugs cast over the black-and-white marble floor, and clerestory archways at each end to receive light, with panelled screens of intricately carved wood standing beneath. Edward's fellow officers of the 2nd Royal Leicestershires attended in full dress, and Edward wore the Military Cross he had been awarded for bravery in Mesopotamia. The palest apple-green taffeta gown a friend had sent for Theo she gave instead to her sister Faith, her only bridesmaid.

There was much to celebrate. The Great War, during which 10,000 had died locally of famine, had recently ended; the British Army had entered Jerusalem, overturning four centuries of Turkish rule, and were heroes of the hour. Ottoman suzerainty had been hard for Protestant missionary families like the Jessups. Perhaps the coming of the British heralded a brighter future? Edward was their triumphal representative. He was witty, ambitious, impatient and capable of heavy irony; she was less worldly than she appeared. When he joked about the limitations of the country he always waggishly called 'Amurka', she was not amused.

———

Theo's grandfather Henry Harris Jessup arrived in Beirut, after a wretchedly stormy voyage, on the sunny spring morning of 7 February 1856. He had sailed on a slow 300-ton bark – the *Sultana* – laden with a mixed cargo of New England rum-kegs destined for Smyrna and carrying eight teetotal Presbyterian missionaries who intensely disapproved of alcohol. They had embarked during a freezing Boston snowstorm, arriving weeks later into an early spring landscape of flowers and white almond blossom. The custom each anniversary of exchanging almond sprays as a thanksgiving offering was shared for decades by this closely interlinked American group, who resembled a large extended family.

Beirut then numbered 8,000 souls, and a church meeting convened on the day of arrival included a richly gifted Lebanese, the founding father of Arab nationalism, Boutros al-Boustani, whose family had been Maronite, a sect allied to Catholicism. Maronites and Greek

Orthodox, hostile to these Americans, anathematised those of their flock who became Protestant. Al-Boustani had a price on his head: the Maronite Patriarch had already had another Presbyterian convert killed.

Eastern Christians had grounds for hostility. The Ottomans had declared the conversion of Muslims illegal; one such convert had also been killed and others smuggled out of the country. When Jessup against the odds converted a single Muslim, the book he published about it was grandiosely entitled *The Setting of the Crescent and the Rising of the Cross* (1899). His sole convert – Kamil Ataini – died in suspicious circumstances in Basrah. Jessup longed for British rule in the hope that it would sanction the conversion of Muslims. Meanwhile the different Christian sects poached each other's adherents.

Henry Harris Jessup, the grandfather whom Theo knew well – when he died, a white-bearded figure in a frock coat, she was eighteen – is by any standards extraordinary. After graduating from Yale he lived for fifty-three years as a missionary in Syria – the name until 1920 of the territory encompassing both the Lebanon and present-day Syria. Here he taught himself Arabic well enough to preach and even to publish a

book of children's verse. He was a learned man – what the eighteenth century called a man of parts – with a breadth of knowledge from the classics to geology and world history that in Europe goes with tolerance. He knew his Gibbon and Voltaire – but if not a bigot he was certainly a religious zealot.

His many well-written books showcase his Syrian work, inveighing equally against Islam and non-Protestant Christians, whom he labelled 'Nominal Christians' only. Greek priests are rich, greedy, unscrupulous, ignorant and corrupt vagabonds adhering to false and superstitious doctrines, selling Absolution, idol-worshipping the Madonna and Saints, practising confession and offering Prayers for the Dead. Instruction in the Scriptures is virtually unknown: when the Americans distributed Bibles in Arabic, Greeks and Maronites collected and burned them. They have so many holy days they keep none, being too busy propagating 'a bitter feeling of [sectarian] party spirit', a phrase whose sheer double-think takes away the breath. He evidently held the Calvinist belief that he belonged to 'an Elected Few'.

Jessup estimates the number of Eastern Christians worldwide in 1910 at ten million, but he believes that God will help all these discover 'gospel light and liberty', after which all Islam will follow, because in the day-to-day piety of Jessup and his like they will actually see 'the Bible acted out in Life'. Statistics were massaged: a published 1882 statement claimed 3,894 Presbyterian Syrian converts, while an unpublished letter admitted only 1,542.

His books paint a picture of a Syria designed to alarm and to excite generosity – fallen from erstwhile greatness, plagued now by locusts and lies. A few examples will suffice. The local custom of rapidly interring the recently dead ran the risk that terrified Edgar Allan Poe: awakening to discover that you are buried alive. Then he claims a local doctor gave as one quack remedy, pulped into a liquid, some pages from the *New York Tribune* ('Do tell me how it acted?' its editor asked Jessup. 'Cathartic or Emetic?'). Here was a land in need of modern medical knowledge.

The treatment of women inspired him to write *The Women of the Arabs* (1873). The burial alive of female babies was an ancient tradition, and in 1857 the wife of one American missionary endured being routinely spat at. Muslims still condoled with each other when a daughter was born, names for girls including Just Right and This Is Enough. Arab women were subservient, forbidden to pray in mosques within sight of men, their state 'vile and degraded'. Traduced as greedy, unclean cowards, they cannot inherit and so live as a chattel of their husbands, who can divorce them at whim. Women are poisoned, thrown down wells, beaten to death and drowned at sea. The Qur'an promises a good Muslim in Paradise seventy-two houris or heavenly concubines, on top of his statutory four wives. Jessup hints at practices too barbarous to name.

Jessup's championship of the welfare of women was qualified in the case of his eldest child Anna, manipulated into staying at home after she had fallen in love. Jessup and his wife 'interposed' with 'various and sundry reasons'. Their trump card was to terrify her with her 'inherited predisposition to puerperal fever', to which they were mysteriously privy. In his magnum opus *Fifty-Three Years in Syria*, he accordingly thanks Anna for her 'invaluable aid'. Like other Victorian women Anna evidently became a cheap housekeeper, amanuensis and drudge.

Jessup tells one tale so obscene it recalls Fox's propagandistic *Book of Martyrs*. An Arab mother maddened by grief at the death of her son was taken to a quack Muslim 'Saint' for a cure. This Saint, in order – as he later claimed – to cast out her devils, hung her upside-down, used a red hot poker to jab out one eye, and then, setting fire to a gallon of pitch-tar, burned her alive. He was not brought to trial. One can imagine how this tale might help fund-raise for a mission presented as sole bulwark against such horrors.

Poisoning was one traditional way of settling disputes. Jessup proposed an antidote. His fellow missionary Dr Daniel Bliss in the 1860s founded the Syrian Protestant College to correct such barbarities. Its pathological laboratory tests identified poisons, bringing culprits to justice. It was renamed after 1920, to attract a larger constituency, the American University of Beirut (AUB).

The AUB also incorporated from its early days a seminary for wealthy young ladies. Jessup's claim that his was the sole mission teaching Syrian women reading and writing, nursing, domestic economy, cooking, sewing, geography, history and arithmetic would also have rallied support. In reality Catholics – especially the French – soon outdid them. During the 1870s Maronites and Catholics replaced the Orthodox as the Americans' chief rivals. Small surprise Jessup soon recorded that Papal beliefs were 'semi-barbaric', or that Theo later remembered Catholic priests in Zahle encouraging children to throw stones at the Jessup family.

The names of Jessup, Dodge, Leavitt and Bliss, all associated with the AUB, have been well known in the Lebanon now for a century and a half. E. P. Thompson, great-grandchild of Henry Harris Jessup, was informally sounded out after he graduated in 1946 for a post at the American college but made it clear that he was politically incorrect for such a position. The AUB was then starting to be seen by EP's mother Theo as an instrument of the State Department if not of the CIA. The family connection none the less persists. As recently as 1997 AUB founder Daniel Bliss's great-grandson David Stuart Dodge (1923–2009) was AUB head, despite having being kidnapped in 1982 for a

The American Presbyterian Community in Beirut, c. 1890.
H. H. Jessup is seated centre, with stick.

year by Shi'ite Muslims. The current President (2009) is another descendant.

These families, moreover, were related by kinship as well as denomination. After giving birth to three children Jessup's wife fell ill and died in Alexandria. Jessup remarried in 1869 Harriet Elizabeth Dodge, with whom he had five children before she too died in 1882. The 1890s in Syria have been called the 'age of the Jessups'. Henry was surrounded by numerous close and distant relatives in mission and college: 'discipline was tightened, conformity expected'. His eldest son William, another missionary, arrived from the USA in November 1890, with his new bride Faith Jadwin, whose family money came from patent medicines, as reinforcements. Henry advised William always to travel both with his own cook and with clean bedding, thus avoiding the risks of food poisoning, fleas, lice and bedbugs. William would ride out for a fortnight at a time into the plains of the Beka'a valley on Gypsy, his fine Arab mare.

Theo, eldest of William and Faith's five daughters,* was born fifteen months later. She was named after Henry Jessup's third wife, her step-grandmother Theodosia; it was a name she always disliked.

———————

Arab culture, language and traditions were despised and languished under 400 years of Turkish rule. Lebanese Christians played a well-attested role in agitating for independence; and the founding of the AUB – followed by an American Hospital and schools – remains the missionaries' main public achievement, helping a native and ecumenical Arab nationalism to blossom. In this they were more successful than the missions of other countries. The AUB's language of instruction in 1866 was Arabic, which helped raise confidence, and thus the AUB set in train a revival of the Arabic language and literature and with it 'a movement of ideas which was to leap from literature to politics'.

Theo's youngest sister Jo towards the end of her life wondered whether the Jessup influence on the Lebanon had been futile or even

* Theo (born 1892), Beth (1893), Helen (1894), Faith (1902), Marie-Josephine aka Jo (1911).

pernicious. This judgement seems harsh: the admirable paradox both about the Jessups in Syria and about Edward Thompson in India is that, arriving as apologists for Western culture, they stay on as champions of local customs and history, turning into anti-imperialists whose most devout wish is the political independence of those they once wished to dominate (India) or convert (Syria). To differing degrees both Edward and the Jessups, in the slang of the age, 'went native'.

Such an anti-imperialist legacy is all the more commendable in that vulgar racism hurt early Jessup efforts. An American citizen applying for missionary employment in 1854 was rejected because he was not of WASP descent but Armenian; while the great Boutros al-Boustani, then helping to translate the Bible into Arabic, was turned down for ordination in 1857, redirecting his huge energies thereafter into education, producing the first Arab-language encyclopaedia and dictionary, and starting up newspapers and a review. Though they came to establish a native Church, the pastorate of the first native Protestant Church in Syria forty years after its establishment continued to be held by Jessup, an American. Were mission funds, he demanded to be told, 'really to be at the disposal of irresponsible natives'? The mission indeed paid Syrian teachers $30 per month when American teachers claimed over $200 a month themselves.

The missionaries early established for themselves a tradition of spacious houses with servants and carriages, the Jessups decamping with their possessions by mule-train in summer from a beautiful house at Zahle in the mountains to another at Aleih high above Beirut. Henry Harris Jessup rebutted the charge that they were living in luxury.

Here in the biggest house in Zahle Theo and her four sisters were born and brought up, living with a second missionary family, stockaded all together, as it were, in an American frontier settlement. The Jabal Sannin, second highest peak of the Mount Lebanon range at nearly 9,000 feet, gives Zahle its fine stream, the Bardouni, one reason for its popularity: it brings down with it the cool air enjoyed by townsfolk eating mezze in the outdoor cafés or on their terraces, shaded by vines growing up trellises, and by mulberry trees for cultivating silkworm.

The town's hard-working inhabitants brokered the sale of Bedouin sheep to Beirut, Egypt and Palestine.

William, 'very formal when he talked to God', took morning and evening prayers, reading from the New Testament in Arabic so the servants could follow. His wife and daughters learned Arabic too and loved the Lebanon: it was 'a pioneer . . . close-to-the-country' way of growing up. Their mother Faith, a good seamstress, made clothes for her daughters on her novel American sewing machine; though the family did not much mix with natives, a lady from the prominent Shehadi family helped, squatting cross-legged on the floor.

During a typhoid outbreak in 1897 Faith gave birth to a boy, another Henry. Before long her husband, William, recovering from a forty-day delirium, learned that this baby son, suffering from Cholerum infantum, had died and was already buried. Although they were finally nursed back to health, his wife and daughter Beth sickened too. The family fought successfully thereafter for a good water supply by getting a reservoir constructed.

Not only Syrians ardently desired boys: Faith took the loss of her

only son very hard. Her fourth daughter was born in 1902 – a year
when, ominously, and despite the help of an American nurse, Faith's
sister Amy died in childbirth. Although Faith was warned that another
baby might kill her, she persisted in hopes of a son, suffering many
miscarriages. By 1911 she was pregnant once again, and Theo was
summoned home after her sophomore year at Vassar College in upstate
New York on fictitious grounds of her mother's 'kidney trouble'. She
returned instead to find her mother, while giving birth to her youngest
sister Marie-Josephine (aka Jo), on her deathbed. Arab women walked
shoeless over the mountains to attend her funeral, and much later, in
1965, a school named after her opened in Zahle.

The exaggerated sense of responsibility an eldest child sometimes
manifests had rational causes in her case: the nineteen-year-old Theo
interrupted her studies to come back and care for four half-orphaned
sisters and a grieving father during two hard years of loss and mourn-
ing. Theo's surviving diary makes clear her piety and her protective
anxiety about her baby sisters.

In 1913 the addition to the household of a demanding, old-maid-like
stepmother called Kate ended this episode. Later, going through her father's
papers, Theo saw that marriage to Mother Kate brought much-needed
money into the family. And Theo felt displaced by Kate – otherwise she
could have been the centre of the family and have brought up her sisters
herself. Kate, among other sins, burned their mother's diaries. Theo duly
returned that year to Vassar, where she was twice president of her class.

Theo's sister Faith once compared American young ladies' over-
protectedness with that of Arab women. Even after the Great War the
girls accounted themselves, in a happy phrase, 'harboured with rectitudes', inhibitions as much provincial as religious. They enjoyed card
games, albeit never in front of Syrians, and eschewing court cards. And
when the sisters danced the polka at home, it was not the indecency of
the dance that affronted their father William but the fact that some of
his daughters had donned men's trousers. The girls noted drily that this
was how Arab women dressed most of the time.

Of the Jessups Theo once recorded accurately that 'Ten branches (at least) of the family emigrated from England to America in the seventeenth century.' That 'at least' is both studiously vague yet boastful: the Jessups are an East Coast establishment family, Henry Harris's father having chaired Abraham Lincoln's nominating committee. Five of Theo's Jessup first cousins, all boys, were rich power-brokers. The middle child, Phil Jessup, who married Lois Kellogg, would be US representative to the UN under Harry Truman and later John Kennedy's candidate for the International Court of Justice. Their family's extensive property had been in the family 'about 300 years'. On the Jadwin side (Theo's mother's family) one aunt in 1964 left to Princeton what at the time was the biggest single bequest ever made – $27 million. When common people began to move into the part of Brooklyn Heights where two Jadwin widows lived they simply bought the surrounding houses and pulled them down. Theo's was a cadet branch, so that, though she had some money, there were always rich relatives on both sides to whom she and her sisters felt they should behave obligingly.

Kindness, courtesy and closeness to God, Theo later maintained, were Lebanese characteristics. High-minded and public-spirited families such as hers are much to be admired. Fadlo Hourani, father of the historian Albert Hourani, converted by Daniel Bliss, was impressed not by his Calvinist belief in predestination so much as by the admirable life-example these Americans set: sobriety in dress and conduct, avoidance of extravagance and ostentation, help to one's fellow man and good works. Such qualities Theo brought to her marriage, and – soon – to her two sons.

———

Art and music were 'all around' the Jessup girls as they grew up. Theo and three of her sisters wrote plays; one of their Beirut aunts ran a choral society; other aunts – and sister Beth too – painted. They had – so long as these activities were carried out in private, and not in front of Syrians – real scope and freedom.

Edward came into a very different inheritance. As a very little boy at a local pre-prep school he won a box of watercolours as a school prize. He brought them delightedly home where his father, the Rev. John Moses Thompson – in outrage and disgust – threw them on the fire. Born near Stockport (Hazel Grove) in 1886, he was the second of six children, four boys, two girls,* of a Wesleyan minister who took his family when Edward was one year old to live in Tamil Nadu, South India. Edward survived typhoid there; his father's pleurisy was more serious, necessitating their return in March 1892. In September that year they moved to live in the Manse at Colwyn Bay where the acute 1893 flu epidemic permanently weakened his mother's heart and triggered his father's final decline: on 7 April 1894, two days before Edward's eighth birthday, he died, leaving his widow in desperate straits. She had a family of seven with an annual income of £100 to try to subsist on.

In 1897 Edward was sent to Kingswood School in Bath, open to the sons of Methodist ministers, which had been founded in 1748 by John Wesley himself. It was in the process of 'normalising' itself as an

EJ in 1902, aged sixteen.

* Mollie (born 1882), Edward (1886), Alfred (1887), Anne-Margaret (1889), Arthur (1890), Frank (1893).

independent school, turning away from narrowness and joylessness, incorporating rugby football and a house system, and, in 1902, employing as English master Frank Richards,* who fed and encouraged Edward's intense and passionate love of literature. Edward won literary prizes, yet lampooned the school in one novel as a place of licensed bullying, flogging, a style of teaching given to catechism, and hated rice puddings. Edward's closest Kingswood friend George Lowther told him that his bitterness was baseless if not 'absurd'.

Edward's grievance was enhanced by the fact that, also in 1902 when he was just sixteen, with reasonable hopes of an Oxbridge scholarship, his beloved mother asked him to come home to support the family financially: they lacked food. He accordingly worked as a clerk in the Bethnal Green branch of Midland Bank in the East End of London where he earned – after five years and including overtime – only £80 per year. Work with the Boys' Brigade, a Christian organisation, Sunday school teaching and outdoor preaching (leading to sciatica) filled some leisure hours; he won occasional half-guinea prizes for his verses in *Westminster Gazette* competitions and often spent his lunch money of seven pence (worth a few pounds in today's money) on books. This recalled Dickens's nightmare childhood interlude in the shoe-blacking factory: here his hopes for self-improvement were thwarted.

His family fed this life-myth. One year after Edward finally escaped from the bank to train as a minister himself at Richmond Theological College, where he gained an external London University BA, his youngest brother Frank, aged fifteen, was summoned from Kingswood to work very long hours for the family with the publisher J. M. Dent, then starting the Everyman Library in Letchworth in Hertfordshire. Frank's health also suffered and he too hoped to attend evening classes to qualify for a better job. Yet it was Edward's sacrifice, not Frank's, that was remembered. Frank's nickname for Edward – 'big boy' – attests to his all-important seniority, and his sister Margaret wrote, 'we all owe a tremendous portion of our happiness to you'. Edward's sacrifice was, by implication, the significant one. His bank years from 1902 to 1907 amounted to a standing deficit.

* No relation of the Frank Richards who wrote the Billy Bunter stories.

EJ standing behind his mother, flanked by sisters Anne-Margaret and Mollie,
and by brothers Alfred, Frank and Arthur.

Not that Edward's hardship should be under-played. These five years
resembled an iron band around a growing tree: he suffered real poverty,
grinding work, insufficient food and exercise, no holidays, and a dearth
of friends. He watched Kingswood contemporaries' careers overtake his
own and started a spiritual/psychological *agon* that would not end till
1923 – a conflict between piety and poetry. Methodists regarded the arts
with vigilant suspicion, and Edward believed his twin vocations –
pastor and poet – to be in contradiction. The most important problem
of his life was reconciling his passion for poetry with his religious
urgings.

In 1904 he and Lowther were oppressed by a fear that the pleasure
they took in poetry (reading and writing alike) might be sinful. Edward's
'wrestling Jacob' experience lasted for months, and encouraged his
growing conviction that he should give up writing poetry. This passed,
but not without a shadow. In 1907 he funded publication of *Knight
Mystic – Verses* from a small inheritance and put up with misunder-
standing, rude questions and cheap wit from fellow ordinands. His

mother was sixty before she entered a theatre, finding much in Shakespeare to offend, while Edward was twenty-four when he saw his first professional Shakespeare – *The Taming of the Shrew* in 1910. Lowther, who believed in Edward's gift, paid most of the cost of the private printing of his mock-Elizabethan hotch-potch play *The Enchanted Lady*. The same year a group of Wesleyan ministers in Gloucestershire challenged 'the propriety of his writing poems of a personal nature'.

In October 1910 he was ordained minister, accepting a posting as a missionary teacher to Bankura School and College in Bengal. His motives included the desire to escape constriction, the hope of pleasing his mother and the prospect of teaching English literature. He also had happy childhood memories of long, slow South Indian afternoons with little green parrots flying from the tops of enormous trees, of palm-fringed beaches and of community life within the compound enveloping a child in warmth and security. He had been fluent in Tamil. He sailed on 21 November from Liverpool, on a four-week voyage to Madras.

Bankura was different. Edward arrived with no knowledge of the Bengali language or of Bengali history in a landscape he found monotonous. Bengal was politically restless after its recent clumsy partitioning, which was due to be annulled in 1911 after six years. During the durbar held at the end of that year to mark the coronation of George V, the capital of India was moved from Calcutta to New Delhi, causing further antagonism among Indians. The Swadeshi ('Own Country') movement urged the boycotting or burning of European goods, especially Manchester cloth.

The pupils put up good-humouredly with scripture lessons to acquire enough English for university entrance and white-collar employment. As with the Jessups in Syria, it was the missionaries' provision of education here that was precious and life-changing – not their evangelism. Indeed when the first local boy for ten years converted to Christianity, Edward thought him a fool. Edward quickly gained a reputation as a gifted teacher of literature, launching at least one student on a distinguished scholarly career, publishing an *Anthology of Verse for Indian Schools* (1915) and a *Handbook of English Prosody and Poetry-Writing for*

*Indian Students* (1924). He also liked teaching football and cricket, excelling at both.

Yet, for all his receptiveness to the charm and the comedy of Indian life, Edward felt 'absolutely alone'. Indians lived behind their own intrinsic colour bar; English Wesleyans offered little by way of companionship or intellectual challenge. In 1912 publication of his *John in Prison*, a collection of poems, led to a stupid, upsetting attack from a fellow missionary who appreciated Edward's ebullience but resented his conceit. Self-pity and an ineffectual attempt to move to South India followed. The real, consequential move he would make was a lateral one, into Bengali culture, which soon refreshed his spirits: by 1913 he was a fluent Bengali-speaker and starting to acquire a better knowledge of Bengali poetry than that of any other Englishman.

Edward, who had lost his father when he was seven and collected older literary mentors, travelled that autumn for a momentous meeting with the patrician Rabindranath Tagore, whom he believed the world's greatest living poet. Tagore spoke of the loss of his wife, son and daughter, Edward of Lowther's recent death by drowning in the Lakes. Edward's great gift was for empathy and friendship, and he recorded after meeting Tagore that he now felt more at home than ever before in India.

The sudden fame in the West of Tagore (1861–1941) – educator, poet, playwright and novelist – resulted from relentless campaigning by W. B. Yeats, Ezra Pound and William Rothenstein. During Tagore's recent, triumphal stay in London, they introduced him to the 'right' salons, magazines and patrons. Yeats's preface to Tagore's *Gitanjali*, lyrical prose-poems in praise of God, publicised the 'mystic' who, Yeats claimed, was famous throughout India. Tagore was in fact scarcely known outside Bengal.

Yeats also underplayed the fieriness of Tagore, whose essays, lectures and patriotic songs antagonised the British, whose best stories celebrated the lives of the poor, and who would firmly renounce his English knighthood after the 1919 Amritsar Massacre. The second time that Edward met Tagore, a sheaf of telegrams interrupted supper, announcing that he had won the Nobel Prize for Literature: the first Indian ever to do so. Sadly he remarked, 'I shall have no peace now, Mr Thompson.'

Edward's own conversion-experience had begun. He had started that night on the path that would lead eventually to Mahatma Gandhi calling him 'India's prisoner'. Among the fifty or so books he would write are two controversial studies of Tagore, novels set in India and notable histories of India, and he would spend over twenty years as lecturer in Bengali and Sanskrit at Oriel College, Oxford. Albeit not the bardic role he most desired, Edward would, through his vexed friendship with Tagore, find a vocation: as go-between or 'Friend of India' to the Indian press, explaining one culture to the other, an Alistair Cooke to the sub-continent. His younger son would eloquently call him 'a courier between cultures who wore the authorized livery of neither', an outsider wherever he went. This task, in the long run-up to Indian independence, was fraught with misunderstandings. With one exception, his books today in the United Kingdom are out of print and forgotten; in India interest in him, and in his publications, continues.

EJ (*second row, seated left*) with staff colleagues at Bankura, Wesleyan College, *c.* 1915.

Edward served with distinction as chaplain in Mesopotamia and
Palestine in 1916–18, an experience retold in three of his books, most
memorably in *The Leicestershires Beyond Baghdad* (1919) which was
reprinted in 2007. That Indians in Mesopotamia outnumbered British
soldiers three to one, fighting bravely for an empire not of their own
making, helped Edward further to sympathise with them; their generosity and gallantry touched him deeply.

EJ in 1918.

One incidental annoyance of the Mesopotamian theatre of war was
that, compared with Flanders, it was seen as a tiny sideshow in the
Great War, concerned more with oil than with territory. Edward's list
of the many other miserable small vexations is long and impressive: bad
water from filthy wells that sickened you, blinding dust-storms that
made your papers fly twenty feet into the air and had you fighting for
breath, and could even cause your rifle to fall and hit you on the head
as you lay in your tent. In certain seasons the dreadful heat, thirst and
flies of the day combined with penetrating cold at night to conduce to
a sense of 'insane wretchedness'. There were grass needles, sandflies,

mosquitoes, large black biting ants, snakes and scorpions; long footsore marches and the uncertainty for months at a time of mail getting through; and then also colitis and rheumatism and unspecified 'old troubles'. When Edward's physical and psychological health finally gave up he was sent back to India for a month to recover.

Great resentment was caused by Bedouin Arabs surreptitiously digging up the British dead to plunder their graves. Edward, reflecting on how sacrosanct graves are in Islam, sees that such tomb-robbers are, according to their own ethos, criminals. This scavenging of the dead – like the cruel murder of isolated wounded Britons for purposes of loot – causes burgeoning anger. Maddened by repeated desecrations, a British Tommy carefully digs dummy graves and mines them with Mills bombs (hand-grenades) whose pins he removes, employing a precarious weight of soil to prevent their immediate detonation. He and his friends then sit quietly by and watch with satisfaction the grave-thieves approach and duly dig with their fingers, before the booby traps find them Elijah's way to heaven 'fiery chariot-wise'. To these desperate people, Edward comments, even life and limb were worth risking for some small gain; their callousness, he notes, stems from hopeless poverty.

He has an ear for comedy, japes and practical jokes: camaraderie consoles him. Nature too: fresh fruit in season – mulberry, pomegranate, fig and date. He was already a gifted nature-writer whose spirits could be lifted by bird-life – crested lark, owl, sand grouse, stork feeding on grasshopper, a hawk or two and brilliantly plumaged roller, bee-eater and kingfisher.

Edward dedicated this regimental history to his brother Frank, an idealist who sang in the Alexandra Palace choral society and joined the Independent Labour Party. Frank felt unhappy about the war's aims, but the first Zeppelin raid over London in May 1915, 'the sight of an evil he had not imagined' – the bombing of defenceless women and children – drove him to enlist. He served the average for a second lieutenant in the Flanders trenches in the bitter winter of 1916/17, three months, before being shot and killed by a sniper's bullet on 15 January 1917. His fiancée had just lost her brother. Frank is buried at Ypres. Like his nephew, another Frank and another idealist, he was remembered as gay, selfless, courageous, beloved. Edward told Theo that, night after night for many

months, Frank's image crowded in upon his thoughts. He would return
to Frank's death on the final page of *These Men, thy Friends*, his 1927 novel
inveighing against the unparalleled stupidity and incompetence of
English generals and press hangers-on in Mesopotamia, while celebrating
the quiet patience especially of Indian soldiers. Chaplain Kenrick is
Edward, whose brother Frank appears as John. When Edward left
England in 1910 Frank was barely seventeen: on the last pages Kenrick/
Edward reflects that he never saw the man John/Frank became, and had
to intuit his newfound 'strength and poise' via his letters. The family at
home had learned to lean upon his courage and gallant cheerfulness, and
to one sister he was 'inexpressibly dear' – a phrase Edward would unconsciously recycle for his own elder son in 1944.

The painful fact is that Edward, longing above all else to write one
great poem, mistook his own gift. He was an old-fashioned, observant
nature-poet who went in for intense mystic questioning within a dissenting Christian tradition. But – and although his later poems are stronger
– it is as a prose-writer that he excels. His account of the random obscen-
ity and terror of modern warfare survives his own prettifications. He
recounts in horrifying detail his attempt to save a Turkish sniper who is
still alive despite his brains running down his face. Edward's attempts to
lift this heavy man simply result in his staining his clothes red with blood.
Later, this man has dug a hole in the thorns to bury his piteously tortured
face, his legs waving feebly like an insect's, and by the following morning
he has crawled some hundred yards before dying. Edward recorded the
death of another man, 'invertebrate . . . like an eel', and calling out in his
agony. Edward once shared an oil-sheet with a corpse.

Helping the doctors and purveying accurate news are jobs for chap-
lains. While Edward boasts of his own insouciance, he never mentions
that he was awarded the MC for bravery – taking two Turks prisoner,
nursing the wounded (the fighting at Istabulat and Samara, though it
cost 2,400 casualties, earned only a single line in a Reuters report). He
regards the Turks as worthy adversaries, brave and carrying themselves
like free men, loyal to one another: 'Johnny Turk' was a term of affectionate regard. He bandaged and rescued Turks as well as Britons.

You sense the author bravely trying to gain a perspective in all of

Theo's college friend Melanie Avery, Theo and EJ at Buckingham Palace for his
investiture with the Military Cross, 1919.

this, on what was inexpressibly horrible. He does not always convince.
He claims that Henry V's great speech before Agincourt was quoted by
the Leicestershires three times. Henry famously glories in an unequal
fight – 'We few, we happy few, we band of brothers' – but by Edward's
third citation you tire of this bravura and (even if true) find it literary
and improbable. Edward parades other antique sources – Xenophon,
Virgil – to dignify and console; it was a cultured habit of mind his sons
inherited. He shows off his learning: 'maniple', 'meinie' and the
Shakespearian 'maugre' are not common words.

Yet truth has a way of breaking through. A curiously prophetic
episode entails a press movie-photographer choreographing war scenes
with an eye to cinema audiences. He asks an ambulance crew to remove
from their vehicle a wounded Turk whose stretcher they have just
loaded, and then to drive up smartly once more towards the camera,
before again reloading this poor casualty a little faster. We have grown
used to the cynical press-manipulation of image into factoid; this same
photographer later stage-manages a shot of a gruesome dead Turk with

Edward and a doctor standing behind. Here are striking early instances
of pseudo-events or war as mass entertainment.

An unnamed witness in June 1919, watching the newly married
Edward climbing a hill through young corn near Jerusalem, noted
how carefully he moved – as if he feared damaging the crop – and
commented astutely, 'I rather suspect that thoughtfulness is typical of
him.' Like so many who survived the slaughter of the Great War, the
experience marked him for life. Thoughtfulness was one result, rage
against a world order that caused the disaster was another. And fear of
the future.

Like his wife Theo, Edward inherited from his missionary background an alarming high-mindedness and idealism. There were related
habits of priggishness and an exaggerated sense of responsibility. These
qualities – together with an impassioned anti-imperialism and internationalism – they duly passed on to their two sons, both of whom Storm
Jameson described as 'intransigent idealists'. Each – differently –
showed prophetic zeal and purpose, albeit in a secular and political
fashion. The Great War also inspired in EJ a theory that Britain's guilty

EJ by the Wailing Wall, Jerusalem, summer 1918.

imperial past required a cleansing sacrifice or atonement – and *Atonement* was the title of a play about India he wrote in 1924, revived during the Second World War. He could not know how literal-mindedly his elder son would listen to and act this thesis out.

# 'Stay away from Boars Hill': 1919–33

William Frank Thompson was born one month prematurely in Darjeeling, on 17 August 1920, and was piously named after his ailing grandfather William, who died that December, and after his recently killed uncle Frank. Obligation towards the family dead marked Frank from birth.

Theo stayed nursing her dangerously sick infant in the cool of the Darjeeling hills, while Edward 500 miles away in Bankura struggled

alike with the heat of the plains and his religious vocation. Both Theo and EJ were proud, unworldly and new to compromise. A prophetic note of financial alarm runs through their letters. Although Theo was lonely and depressed, with only her ailing baby for company, EJ 'can't afford the ghastly expense' of a month's leave to join her; he had declared a Victorian husband's willingness to ensure his wife's days were free from care and so shrank from relying on her American income. On a Wesleyan chaplain's salary they could not have everything, but Theo was unaccustomed to frugality. EJ begs her not to send her American relatives so 'glowing a picture of our feudal splendour, servants and meals'.

Meanwhile, his disenchantment with God and Empire grew. Theo later recorded that EJ in 1910 felt entirely conventionally about Indian 'sedition', arriving on the sub-continent with no preconceived ideas of Indian independence. That was changing fast. One powerful trigger was the 1919 Amritsar Massacre when around 380 peacefully protesting Punjabis were machine-gunned and killed and more than a thousand injured. Further insults followed, such as Brahmins being forced to do sanitary work and Indians being made to crawl on all fours along one street where an Englishwoman – before being saved by nearby Hindus – had been assaulted. The missionaries, aided by EJ, wrote a mild letter of protest that won them considerable hate-mail. Tagore, as we have seen, returned his knighthood.

Though EJ fondly hoped that 'English rule [was] still the sanest and fairest on the globe', his faith in Empire as a force for good and in Christianity was shaken. At Bankura preaching was to gain converts; and depriving an Indian of his Hinduism without amending his poverty or the race-prejudice that justified that poverty was doubly insulting. He increasingly abhorred Methodism's exclusive, macabre doctrine of conditional salvation, the record of every sin and wicked word chronicled in '[the] Dreadful Book'. He disliked its emotional blackmail sugared over with concern for the soul's eternal safety. As early as 1912 EJ had written to his pious, simple mother complaining of the cruel doctrine of hell-fire: 'If everyone who dies in a certain condition drops into a hot bath . . . it wd be wicked & the act of a fiend. Even if the Bible teaches it, it isn't true.'

His fellow missionaries were uncongenial and EJ sent in a letter of resignation to take effect in 1923. He spent time writing on Tagore. As well as explicating what he found marvellous in his work, EJ had the courage to criticise the cult of Tagore, who scolded the West for loving comforts even as he earned fat lecture fees in the USA, travelling with his secretary in his own private railway compartment. EJ's own powerful missionary impulses, increasingly homeless, henceforth went into questioning and trying to reform British imperialism in India, partly by explaining Tagore and Bengali literature to the British. After considering living in the USA, EJ was offered a lectureship in Bengali at Oriel College, Oxford, which Theo conceded the equal of Princeton. He sailed by himself on 23 January 1923 to look for family lodgings, while Theo and Frank waited four months in Beirut.

On her arrival in Oxford that May, Theo was thirty-one, having lived eighteen years in Syria, nine in the USA and four in India. When EJ told Theo he had met at Port Said another pretty, highbrow 'Amurkan' girl, evoking her 'comical, drawling' speech and shallow culture, his description stung: sharp letters ensued. Theo had been educated by governesses, two good, one bad, and then at two first-rate institutions (the Packer Institute in Brooklyn, and Vassar), but superficially. True, a Columbia year trained her to teach English, which she did at Smith College in 1917–18. But her Vassar BA split between fifteen separate subject-areas had given this highly intelligent young woman no deep or confident grounding in any. In later life she accounted herself fortunate that, so ignorant did she remain, there was always plenty to learn.

In London en route for India she asked her sister Faith to blindfold her in the British Museum, lead her slowly up to the Elgin Marbles and remove the cloth (neither knew that these were plaster-of-Paris replicas, the originals stored for safe-keeping against Zeppelin raids). Theo was enraptured, too, by London Bridge, the Tower, everything. The Thompsons furthered her education. Theo asked EJ's sister Margaret a hundred and one questions, 'about shops, room-rents, the best places to buy things, customs that are a bit different from American customs &tc . . . I am using her as a combination encyclopedia & traveller's

Guide.' And EJ continued Theo's education, starting with Boswell's *Life of Johnson*.

His high-sounding post in Bengali at Oxford University turned out to be part-time, teaching Indian Civil Service probationers vernacular Bengali. It carried no university membership, and the salary was £160 a year, plus £5 per student. Since he found only one student awaiting him, he was free, once he had mastered Sanskrit, to give time to literary studies and his own writing. But this salary did not even meet his rent – 'cruelly expensive' – for two Oxford rooms. After six weeks they moved to picturesque Islip, seven miles outside the city, with fishing rights on the river, down which some congenial neighbours, the poet Robert Graves and his energetic wife Nancy, together with their children, soon came to call in a canoe.

Graves wrote to his mother that the Thompsons were their closest educated neighbours, he a north-country man '& Wesleyan Minister, a very good man who plays football'. The two families met most days, sharing picnics, Christmas dinner, guests and children's parties. Few of Theo's Vassar friends could visit Oxford, but she and Nancy liked and admired each other and sympathised with each other's troubles, surviving such mishaps as Nancy driving Theo so hard into the pavement that a wheel of her car fell off. Both Nancy and Theo in their respective marriages 'wore the trousers'; both were devoted, headstrong and occasionally sharp-tongued; each directed a formidably intelligent, future 'Great Writer' in whom she believed. When Nancy had her fourth child, Theo and EJ looked after her previous three for some days.

Nancy was interesting. The wilful daughter of the painter William Nicholson, sister of the artist Ben, boyishly slim and stylish, she made all her own and her children's clothes, wore a land-girl's breeches instead of skirts, no wedding ring, and refused to go to church or have her children baptised. She assured Robert that the age-old sufferings of women exceeded the Great War traumas he would memorably chronicle in *Goodbye to All That*. House chores were accordingly shared and on feminist principles she and her two daughters kept her maiden name of Nicholson while her two sons used Graves: Virginia Woolf relished this provocation. Nancy made some of their furniture and bicycled around Oxfordshire smoking Woodbines, setting up stall and giving village women free – and illegal – contraceptive advice: something she had missed when producing her four children in four years (her health suffered as a result). Baths were communal, she and Robert always soaking together. Both Thompsons appreciated the Graveses' bohemianism.

Nancy wanted Robert and herself to be 'dis-married' so that they could live together without religious or moral obligation; Islip folk were not impressed by the contempt with which she treated her husband, as a 'representative male'. As for Graves, an eighteen-stone student at St John's College, patrician in manner and profoundly shell-shocked, he had a strong streak of masochism and a love of submission. He indulged Nancy in 1920 when she insisted on opening a traditional village shop on Boars Hill, an adventure that lost them both a great deal of money.

The friendship between Graves and EJ thrived: both were traumatised war veterans with progressive views, struggling to make their names as writers, though Graves was better connected, visited even then by T. E. Lawrence, Siegfried Sassoon, Edith Sitwell and the Asquiths. EJ was soon to edit the poetry of Graves – as of Masefield, Bridges and Tagore – for a sixpenny poets series published by Ernest Benn which sold well but was incompetently managed, a source of continuing aggravation. Graves sympathised. Meanwhile Nancy designed the cover for EJ's novel *An Indian Day*, among the few commissions she then received.

Soon they were no longer neighbours. In 1926 Graves and Nancy sailed to Egypt where Graves briefly took up an academic post that proved disastrous, together with a neurotic American poet called Laura Riding, so fierce a dominatrix that Nancy by comparison seems easygoing. Graves assured EJ with self-serving optimism that 'It's lucky that Laura and Nancy are each other's best friends . . . so there'll be no trouble.' Over the following three years, a painful and unstable *ménage à trois* evolved. 'It seems a pity that now the Turks have given up polygamy,' Nancy's father jested, 'Robert should have decided to take it up.' Shocked, he withdrew her allowance. Nancy largely brought up the four children herself, on little or no money. When her daughter Jenny wished to learn to be a dancer, Nancy, unable to afford a London rent, bought a hulk on the Thames near Hammersmith on which she built a Noah's Ark of a house, incurring only the costs of wharfage.

---

When the Thompsons moved to a rented cottage on Boars Hill,* EJ, who had recently won a London PhD for what became his *Tagore: Poet and Dramatist* – a book Tagore and other Bengalis found patronising – was in February 1925 elected an honorary Fellow of Oriel. Theo, emboldened, bought some land near by and commissioned an architect to build a comfortable residence with a large hall and big stairway of dark polished oak, set in two and a half acres of grounds. The back windows gave a splendid view of their land: a long broad slope wooded at the bottom with the Chilterns in the distance. They kept a mare whom they exercised. An idyllic setting in which to bring up two boys, they named it Scar Top after the Penrith farm where EJ's father had grown up. There were promising neighbours.

The archaeologist Sir Arthur Evans, short, thickset and imperious, invited the Thompsons to walk in his nearby sixty acres of grounds, bluebell-filled in May, and to swim and canoe in his two-acre lake – a privilege not extended to all. Youlbury, his vast, ugly, rambling twenty-two-bedroom mansion, had an elegant Siena-marble pillared entrance hall with a Minotaur mosaic on the floor. Evans was from 1894 also the owner, excavator† and in a real sense the lordly inventor of the equally fantastical Palace of Minos at Knossos in Crete. Its principal works of art were exhibited in London in 1903, and in spring 1938 Sir Arthur helped Frank to get to Crete to excavate there.

Evans's letter-cards to EJ, forty years after his wife died of TB in 1893, are still heavily black-bordered: 'protective colouring', his half-sister Joan suggested. He had at the age of seventy-three been charged with an act of public indecency in Hyde Park with a young man – possibly an aberration – and he reputedly preferred boy-visitors to girls, but

---

* Judging from a letter from Graves, they were at this cottage by August 1924.
† Together with the British School of Archaeology at Athens.

neither prevented his Twelfth Night parties for children being a high-light of the calendar. Evans danced with all and sundry and held the Thompsons in evident affection, calling round repeatedly at Scar Top during the summer of 1939 – despite approaching ninety years old – in fear of missing the right moment to wish them farewell.

Evans's telephone number was Boars Hill 10. Boars Hill 1 meant the Greek scholar Gilbert Murray and his wife Lady Mary, at Yatscombe, where they had retired in 1919 for the last decades of their long lives. Strictly vegetarian, teetotal and non-smoking, they personify Matthew Arnold's famous dictum about Oxford as 'home of lost causes . . . and impossible loyalties'. Lady Mary during the May 1926 General Strike was seen, aged sixty, pushing her pram the eight miles round trip into Oxford to collect her shopping rather than pay a scab (blackleg) volunteer bus driver. She had inherited Castle Howard from her father the Earl of Carlisle, before exchanging it for a consideration with a brother. George Bernard Shaw caricatured Murray as Adolphus Cusins, and his dictatorial mother-in-law as Lady Britomart in *Major Barbara* (1905), while Major Barbara's own passionate idealism was directly based on Lady Mary's – Shaw's working title being 'Lady Mary and her Mother'. Lady Mary inherited a large measure of her battle-axe mother's monstrous bossiness, censoriousness and humourlessness.

Lady Mary was essentially kind-hearted too. But her odd upper-class mix of high-mindedness and high-handedness was on display when EJ arrived with his second, younger son EP for luncheon one day. She had insisted on this call, even though it was highly inconvenient, so call they did. She petted EP, who played the role of guileless little angel, remarking on his goodness but, soon switching to hauteur, was also outrageously rude. The worst outburst happened after EJ said he hoped the Labour Party would, if they got in, tackle Britain's problems and not tie the country up with irrelevant experiments as in Russia. She flared up at any criticism of the Bolsheviks. Murray, embarrassed and keen to put things right, later explained on a walk that, like many Labour people, Lady Mary had a fierce emotional feeling about Russia: 'My wife thinks the Bolsheviks are a kind of Quaker.' Murray was once asked in an American questionnaire whether his marriage was 1) happy, 2) very happy, 3) very, very happy,

4) unhappy or 5) disastrous. But – despite prolonged reflection – he confided to EJ that he had not yet arrived at a suitable answer.

Murray, who was the Regius Professor of Greek, lived halfway between the great world and the academic world, at home in neither. Visitors eating his nut cutlets and sipping his orangeade included Bertrand Russell (a cousin by marriage), H. G. Wells and Julian Huxley. This Murray confraternity with progressive intellectuals may be one reason why, in Evelyn Waugh's *Brideshead Revisited*, Charles Ryder's cousin Jasper gives him early the memorable life-advice: 'Stay away from Boars Hill,' home to the smart Fabian-socialist movers and shakers whose influence Waugh feared and hated. Lady Mary's rebellious son, Basil Murray, Waugh acknowledged as a model in two novels for the attractive, caddish Basil Seal.

Lady Mary influenced Theo. Alert to the differences between what later would be termed U and non-U behaviour and wanting to do the right thing socially, she took seriously Lady Mary's say-so that in England children of good families 'never have butter *and* jam on their bread'. And Theo never fully recovered from the shock of learning from her that in England you cannot be both Methodist – as, by marriage, was Theo – and upper class at the same time. Forty years later Theo still pondered this conundrum. Of course England and the USA differ profoundly: there have been five Methodist presidents of the USA and no Methodist prime ministers of England. Lady Mary became a Quaker in 1925, and after the Second World War Theo emulated her.

Gilbert Murray, courtly, idealistic, shy and with an innate revulsion from cruelty that unfitted him for modern life, was working with his friend Robert Cecil from 1918 for the League of Nations Union. In case such duties left him insufficient time for his academic responsibilities, Murray typically offered up half his salary to fund a readership in Greek. He was another of EJ's mentors, who read some of EJ's drafts and wrote encouraging him in a tone of gentle and good-humoured teasing and ironic badinage. EJ had only a toehold in the academic world, and little hold at all on the great world: Murray's friendship flattered him.

Robert Bridges and John Masefield – two successive Poets

Laureate – were other close neighbours whom EJ, wishing to make his own name as a poet, did not neglect. Both are old-fashioned, pre-modern, nature-loving and, like EJ himself, largely forgotten today. EJ, collecting signatures during the General Strike in favour of compromise or mediation, found both neighbour-poets too conservative to sign.

EJ visited Bridges in 1914 when explaining the new Laureate to the Indian press and first encountered his bright eye and abrupt, challenging manner. Bridges would enter Scar Top unannounced to read books in EJ's library and complain if a book were not where he expected to find it. After playing whist with him EJ noted that 'the old man [was] at his worst, a selfish battening pig whose pose of being bored by, & superior to, everyone you cd mention, was tiresome'. EJ thought Graves not far wrong to call Bridges a 'silly old man'. Such acerbity did not prevent EJ writing Bridges's biography.

EJ's acquaintanceship with Masefield, with his shy morning smile and love of Chaucer, was kindlier. Like EJ, Masefield had had to leave school to work (at sea) from the age of sixteen, was therefore self-taught and had suffered during the Great War. He built a private theatre in his garden. Here the Thompsons, with other neighbours, casually acted, and EJ later recalled 'the nightingales singing all about us' while they were rehearsing Masefield's play *Good Friday*. The Thompsons' cat Pushkin appears as the black cat Nibbins in Masefield's children's story *The Midnight Folk*, and Masefield inscribed on the flyleaf of the copy he presented to Scar Top 'To Frank Thompson from John Masefield 1928' together with the author's drawing of a witch.

———

Frank's youthful head was too large for his body, so that Robert Graves later remembered him as 'that imperturbable top-heavy child of 1924' and witnessed him, aged only three, dividing his chocolate into four to share with the Graves children: perhaps altruism might be an aspect of his character? That year, 1924, Theo gave birth to her second boy, Edward Palmer, named after both EJ and a long line of Palmers on her side of the family; Palmer was a name he increasingly resented and the

Private Collection

Frank and 'Little Ma', EJ's mother, 1924.

cause of many family rows.* Another neighbour when the Thompsons first came to Boars Hill, meeting Theo wheeling round a baby with curly blond hair, thought it was called Pamela and a girl. The brothers got on and were 'best friends'. Sibling love, unlike sibling rivalry, is not a fashionable topic nowadays, but these boys none the less loved each other. Late in life Edward still relished Frank's clowning: 'Frank, you're sitting on a cheese sandwich.' 'No I'm not: it's a tomato sandwich.' A simple joke to charm a younger brother, and a charm still operating sixty years later.

Frank asked questions endlessly from a brain working every minute, and soon there was education to ponder. Theo considered Dora

---

* The naming of children (later of grandchildren) was a battlefield and, if there were a struggle of wills here, EJ won with Frank, and Theo with Palmer – her younger son given a name he hated, because of its impeccable Jessup pedigree. EP probably got teased at Kingswood for having a name that reminded boys of a popular cheap scent, Parma Violet (according to Dorothy Thompson). Disliking her own name of Theodosia did not render Theo any more understanding.

Frank and his brother EP, *c.* 1928.

Russell's newly opened progressive Beacon Hill School in Sussex but, when she took Edward down, in the same room where Dora interviewed them were also several young pupils straining thoughtfully upon their potties. Theo couldn't get away fast enough. She opted to send both her boys to the already fashionable Dragon School on the Bardwell Road in North Oxford. Dragon alumni include Hugh Gaitskell, John Betjeman and EP's classmate John Mortimer, who fictionalised it as 'Cliffhanger School' in his play *A Voyage Round my Father*. Three other Boars Hill families sent their boys there, all making their turbulent way in together by bus – unaccompanied in those safer days by any adult. Each of the fathers of the Boars Hill gang, as they became known, was an Oxford don.

The father of the two neighbouring Gardner boys* was a bacteriologist at University College who ended up as Oxford's Regius Professor of

---

* Michael (born 1919) and Andrew (1922). Their father was Arthur Duncan Gardner (1884–1978), who married Violet Newsam.

Medicine. There were Rex and John Campbell Thompson – known always as the 'Cannibal Thompsons' and no relation – whose mother was descended from William de Morgan, friend and acolyte of William Morris, and whose home – full of de Morgan tiles – was an education in Art Nouveau. Reginald Campbell Thompson, an Assyriologist at Merton College, had with T. E. Lawrence in 1911 excavated Carchemish, an ancient city on the border between modern Syria and Turkey. Frank later accounted Rex and Brian Carritt, 'my only two friends of life-long intimacy'. He and Rex went together for the first time to the Dragon in summer 1928, and Brian, youngest of the Carritts, followed soon after, and excelled at both sport and lessons, becoming head boy. Each family lost children to the war.*

The Carritts at Heath Barrows were closest to the Thompsons. Edgar Carritt lectured in Philosophy and was a Fellow at University College with a troubled marriage: his beautiful wife Winifred was an exceptional musician, frustrated not to have had a career. Their son Gabriel believed that Edgar 'admired the bodies of young men more than those of young women'. Edgar and Winifred separated for a time after her lover – who had sired Anthony, one of her five sons – was killed in the Great War.† There were two girls in addition to the boys, an expensive cohort to maintain. The Carritt children famously ran naked around their seven acres of wild garden shared with three goats, two pigs, hens, ducks and bees in their hives; they painted themselves in bright colours, believing that everyone did. The cooler months found them in roughly patched and darned hand-me-downs. Food and blankets were scarce and W. H. Auden, in love with Gabriel, was notorious for taking up the Carritt stair carpet to put on his bed in an attempt to stay warm, then raiding the larder at night to wolf cold potatoes and leg of lamb. Auden wrote poetry inspired by Gabriel's physical beauty and athleticism and found his company

* Anthony Carritt was killed in Spain aged twenty-three, the same age as Frank in Bulgaria. Brian Carritt, Rex Campbell Thompson and Andrew Gardner died at twenty-one.
† Arthur Derbyshire, Boars Hill neighbour and Research Fellow in genetics.

restful. Guests were an event. Stephen Spender, who was being tutored by Carritt *père* and who, like Auden, fell in love with Gabriel, visited, as did Richard Crossman, later a Labour Cabinet minister, who sarcastically called his set 'the golden boys'.

Frank, too, came to stay, his best friend being Brian Carritt, one year younger and, like his brothers, at the Dragon School. Brian, aka 'Tow', blond, clever and good-looking, swam with Frank in Evans's lake, and they made up games of lurkey (kick-the-can) in the shrubbery and 'chaotic and murderous charades': no other outsider apart from Brian was so much a part of the Thompson family. One Carritt sister, Penelope, died of anorexia in 1924 and Gabriel put her virtual suicide down to family unhappiness, something to which her five brothers and their musical mother Winifred found a quite different solution: all six joined the Communist Party.

These Oxford dons' intellectual-bohemian families in their Betjemanesque villas – the Thompsons at Scar Top, the Carritts at Heath Barrows, the Gardners at Chilswell Edge and the Campbell Thompsons at Trackways, together with another new friend, the artist Hilda Harrisson at Sandlands – recall John Betjeman's spoof poem 'Indoor Games near Newbury' with its evocation of well-to-do Berkshire families between the

EP, EJ, Theo and Frank: Thompson family picnic, *c.* 1933.

wars (Boars Hill was then in Berkshire) living at Bussock Bottom, Tussock Wood and Windy Break and giving off a sense of social advantage.

Michael, eldest of the Carritt children, analysed this Boars Hill world further: such Oxford dons and their families, he believed, represented a small but influential sub-group of the upper-middle class – the academic intelligentsia – who lived in and were encouraged to absorb the rarefied atmosphere of a self-conscious elite. This coterie, set apart by their 'cultural excellence', accepted the duties, and claimed the privileges, of that pre-eminence. Egalitarian yet elitist, here was one pre-war forerunner to champagne socialism or 'radical chic'. Everyone knew everybody else worth knowing.

EJ and Theo took the view that there were 'top people', artists, intellectuals and great political leaders, who shared an atmosphere above politics and nationality. Perhaps Boars Hill might provide entrée.

———

John Mortimer depicts the Dragon School as progressive and engagingly dotty. Schoolchildren had to address Dragon masters by their nicknames such as 'Shem', 'Ham' and 'Japhet'. (This mode of speech of 'Noah the Head' – A. E. Lynam – mingling Kipling and the Old Testament, was soon borrowed by EJ in his letters to his sons, which contain facetious injunctions like 'Rejoice therefore!') Pupils could bicycle round town and take boats on the river. At concerts where the boys drank cider-cup, the masters sang 'Olga Pulloffski the Beautiful Spy', 'Abdul the Bulbul Ameer' and 'Gertie the Girl with the Gong'.

The Dragon had a pre-school that took children from the age of six, and Frank, with all his fierce inquisitiveness, was there by 1928, aged seven and a half, Edward following in 1930. On arrival Frank was not merely top of his class, but so far ahead of his age group that he had to be moved up two forms by that September. In this new class, though the youngest by two years, he still came second. He soon won prizes for Classics, French, appreciation of English, Recitation and Reading, and at twelve won the Fitch award for 'one of the best essays ever produced' on the topic 'Our civilisation is no better than that of the Greeks and Romans'. Precociousness dogs his story: aged seventeen on Crete in

1938 he would be asked where his wife was, and aged twenty-two in Egypt would take command of troops ten years his senior.

From 1930 to 1933 Frank and Edward overlapped at the Dragon and experienced contradictions in their relationship. Young EP, wrongly thought a dimwit, was awed by Frank's brilliance. EP, however, excelled at sports while Frank, ill as an infant, did not catch up on his own strength till he was twenty-two. Robert Graves's reminiscence – Frank as 'top-heavy' with a large head too big for his tall, thin body, uncoordinated and accident-prone – was accurate. Frank had private lessons to correct his lisp. He was forever breaking things or knocking them off tables, and as late as May 1943 wrote home, 'Thompson is not popular in the mess at the moment – last night I broke a chair while telling a Russian joke.'

A maladroit, lisping child may attract bullies; and Edward would intervene with flailing fists and tears to try to protect his elder brother. But Edward, aged only six or seven, was too small to help – hence his tears. Here is a central motif in their relationship. Frank had a reckless disregard for his own safety that afflicted Edward with intense protective anxiety. That later in 1944 he inspired a deeper anguish through the manner of his death no doubt intensified Edward's recollections of early woe, and Frank's end rendered Edward's protective anxiety about him permanent. The theme colours their childhood. Around 1935 Theo and EJ sent the boys to the Norfolk Broads to learn to sail. Instructed to splice two ends of rope together Edward succeeded while Frank, after five minutes, failed miserably and was – to Edward's chagrin – heavily rebuked. Edward hated his own success being used to humiliate Frank. But both Frank's brilliance and his ungainliness set him apart. Frank accepted his clumsiness stoically and learned to turn it to comedy, exploiting it to buy popularity.

It is striking that Edward recalled the Dragon as 'robust, brutal and nasty'. His exact contemporary John Mortimer enjoyed it, and (unlike Frank) simply evaded uncongenial sports. Young Edward, by contrast, excelled at both sport and drama, those twin Dragon specialities. Mortimer recalled Edward at nine, his socks round his ankles, rushing after a ball while Mortimer shivered miserably near the touchline. Each

year a Shakespeare play and a Gilbert and Sullivan operetta were put on
and cast democratically – by popular vote rather than by audition.
Frank rose only to the walk-on role of a mariner in *The Tempest*,
while Edward was elected to play John of Gaunt to John Mortimer's
Richard II. Both Edward and John Mortimer adored acting, but
Edward's popular success evidently did not attenuate the more potent
memory of Frank's loss of face.

A few girls – if daughters of an Old Dragon or staff member, or
sisters of a boy already in school – were welcomed: the future writers
Naomi Mitchison and Antonia Fraser were two such. Girl Dragons had
a reputation for succeeding at whatever they set their mind to do,
rugby included, but numbered at any one time out of the whole school
of 140 only between six and twelve. Girls, generally, were in short
supply. EJ had two sisters: Margaret was married to Charles Pilkington-
Rogers, a headmaster in Retford with one daughter, Barbara (aka
'Tubsie'), with whom they spent Christmas; Mollie married Charles
Vivian, a doctor and a kindly British Israelite living in Leighton Buzzard,
who, knowing that his poorest patients could not in those pre-NHS
days afford to pay him, simply neglected to charge them. He had three
children: Trevor and Graham became professional soldiers, and the
charming and witty Lorna Vivian, with a congenital heart condition,
helped introduce Frank and Edward to pony riding. Those two girl
cousins apart, the Thompson boys' childhood world was largely masculine; it was Theo, however, who ruled the roost and administered
punishments when needed.

---

EJ, that lifelong outsider, yearned to belong in Oxford and yet found
its rituals ossified. Meanwhile he continued to educate the British
about India. Apart from books on Tagore and poetry, he wrote plays –
*Atonement* (1924) and *Three Eastern Plays* (1927) – *A History of India*
(1927), a study of suttee or Hindu widow-burning (1928), two novels
– one fictionalising his time in Bengal, *Indian Day* (1927), another
fictionalising his war in Mesopotamia, *These Men, thy Friends* (also
1927) – and *Crusader's Coast* (1929), a study of the Levant from which I

learned that two of the murderers of St Thomas à Becket are buried under the Al Aqsa Mosque in Jerusalem (Frank would travel the Middle East during the war with his own copy). It was a prolific but uneven output.

Most notably in 1925 he published his first work of history, *The Other Side of the Medal*, which created a scandal. Here was a pioneering study of the so-called Indian Mutiny of 1857 from the Indian point of view. It made no bones about British chauvinism or cruelty, and demonstrated a continuity of stupidity and bad faith between 1857 and the 1919 Massacre at Amritsar. EJ expounded many Indian grievances – not merely the sepoys famously having to bite open the ammunition for the 1853 Enfield rifle greased with lard, unclean to Muslims, or tallow, anathema to Hindus.

He itemised the massive British revenge-killings, with rebel sepoys tied to the cannon muzzles (a traditional Mughal punishment for rebellion) and blown apart. This was a brave book, and justly made his name. Since he was partly funded by the India Office, he had also risked his livelihood. Robert Graves was not alone in congratulating him on his courage and success – though EJ must have envied the huge sales Graves enjoyed with his best-selling biography of T. E. Lawrence, *Revolt in the Desert* (1927), which was followed by *Goodbye to All That* (1929) and the Claudius novels (1934 and 1935). EJ was now an India pundit. The publisher J. M. Dent soon wrote asking him to write a book telling ladies outward bound for India how to get servants and what the correct etiquette was for each occasion. He begged with due irony to be excused as 'unqualified to advise on these high problems'.

On the 150th anniversary of the Mutiny in 2007 a British publisher declined to republish *The Other Side of the Medal* on the grounds that it looked today insufficiently radical. EJ did not call for British withdrawal from India but wished to restore the confidence of Indians in the Empire. Especially in the UK today there is a tendency to patronise EJ as an outmoded liberal believing against the odds in the British Empire as a potential force for good, from which Indians were wrong to wish to separate themselves. Yet his emphasis throughout his life on the need for a spiritual reconciliation between Britons and Indians was entirely appropriate for a man who saw himself primarily as a poet with religious promptings, rather than a politician.

To some degree EJ has been the victim of his own success. The reconciliation he so passionately favoured has come about, and so now belongs to history.

———

What of Theo? At this point she interests me more than EJ. In a report to her old college, Vassar, she lists as occupations 'Keeping in touch with friends and events in India and the Near East. Writing. Gardening. Producing children's plays.' She wrote a touching one-act play about Miriam – Hebrew name for Mary Magdalene – co-publishing this with EJ as one of their *Three Eastern Plays* in 1927, and collaborated with EJ in writing one other play in the 1930s. But if she saw herself as a writer, she was a frustrated one. Theo's diary-notes from 1925–31 manifest dissatisfaction. The first year at Scar Top was a tiring business.* For three months early in 1926 she was ill in bed getting what she called 'heart attacks' – possibly panic attacks. She saw a specialist on 5 March. EJ's mother helped with the children while Theo spent two weeks in the Acland Hospital on the Banbury Road. 'Miserable time,' she writes. 'Dr Good tried to "analyse" me. I hated the idea of meeting clever people – was afraid of the ladies of the Hill – all except the most domestic and helpful ones. Felt a fool with good talkers . . . Dreaded coming back to entertaining & any social life . . . Palmer developed a horrid mouth sore – pronounced impetigo – think rather it was due to nervous trouble.' On a photo of herself holding Frank she scored through her own face; she later destroyed a commissioned portrait of herself by a fashionable painter, finding it unflattering.

Her isolation comes across: no mother to advise or back her up. She had mothered her own younger sisters Faith and Jo, while neither Little Ma (EJ's mother) nor Mother Kate (Theo's disliked stepmother) offered much support. Theo belonged to a generation of educated women who lived the lives of their husbands more than their own, only half aware of their anger and resentment.

---

* They moved in a few days before Christmas 1925.

By Good Friday 1926 she has recovered enough to visit the kindly Masefields, and by the end of May starts having a friend or so in to tea. Her diary-notes – 'Lunch with the Murrays . . . Sir Arthur [Evans]'s reception . . . Tagore calls . . . Storm Jamesons for weekend . . . Frank given a boxing lesson or two by Dr Campbell Thompson . . .' – suggest a resumption of social life, and she occupies herself that summer with 'Jam making (strawberry, blackcurrant), cake making, hay making'. Yet a twice-repeated phrase 'plagued with woodlice' sounds the note of estrangement. Each aspect of her environment evidently had to be managed: even woodlice, not normally thought of as constituting 'plagues' unless to someone with a remarkable love of control?

Two visits from Nancy Nicholson, the first with her children, the second with Laura Riding and Robert Graves, provided food for thought. Trapped in a triangular relationship resembling the one depicted in Noël Coward's 1933 play *Design for Living*, Nancy even ran up on her sewing machine in 1926 a trousseau of dresses for Laura Riding to take to Austria, effectively on honeymoon with Robert

Graves, while she – Graves's wife Nancy – stayed behind looking after their children. Nancy was victim to her own instinctive iconoclasm, her ideals forbidding expression of jealousy.

———

Theo was one of a rapidly growing audience to a notable tragicomic scandal but also an unusual friend with the rare good sense to proclaim sexual jealousy a natural emotion. The Graves *ménage à trois* became a *folie à quatre* when Laura declared the Anglo-Irish poet Geoffrey Taylor a fourth player. The latter vacillated, however, and Nancy agreed on Laura's behalf to go tamely to Ireland to entice Geoffrey back, only to find him falling in love with Nancy himself; she reciprocated.* Her marriage finally at an end, Nancy, her four children and Geoffrey moved to Sutton Veney in Wiltshire, where she started the Arts and Crafts Poulk Press from a house she and her family built out of Baltic pine. Frank's 1941 reference to Graves as 'that man' accurately records his family's view of the matter: Nancy remained a good friend to Theo.

Compared with Nancy's dramatic problems, Theo's, however painful, must have seemed small beer, domestic and bourgeois. Among her comforts was a handsome dwarf manservant named Albert who had been with the Thompsons since Islip days, part of the furniture in that first house they rented when they came to Oxford. Theo scaled down the Scar Top kitchen to fit him. Albert was handy with clothes-making, running up 'a second pair of small grey flannel trousers' for EP, bringing Theo breakfast in bed, caring for funny good-tempered little Sandy the dog – half poodle, half Scots terrier – and daily weighing Pushkin the family cat. From time to time Albert would send his photograph – head and shoulders only – to marriage agencies, looking, unsuccessfully, for a partner.

---

* Laura duly threw herself out of a fourth-floor window of Robert Graves's Hammersmith flat, breaking her pelvis and some vertebrae, following which Robert opted to leap out of a window on the third floor; the ensuing scandal won in 1929 huge international newspaper coverage. The crippled Laura and the twice-born (so he claimed) Graves, after bitter words with Nancy, adjourned to Majorca. See Richard Graves, *Robert Graves: The Years with Laura 1926–1940*, London, 1990, ch. 3.

Albert's acquisition of a motorbike during the General Strike was useful as the Thompsons possessed neither telephone nor car. Trips as a result seemed a great effort, life 'a dragging affair'. To go anywhere – Wantage, the White Horse, Burford – meant 'catching buses, carrying bags &tc & was a tiresome business'. Theo was mainly housebound, the garden heavy and hard going despite help. While never openly questioning her 'wifely' role, Theo felt secretly thwarted. She did not have her friend Nancy's resourcefulness or ability to reinvent herself.

Then there were headaches – and rows – about money. In 1927 Theo noted 'V. depressed Jan 23 & wonder if we can afford to stay at Scar Top or shd try for job in America'. They spent 1929–30 in Poughkeepsie, New York State, where EJ lectured at Vassar for $4,000 a year, the boys going to a public school and Theo catching up with her family. It was a year plagued by ill health, all four Thompsons sick with different ailments; EJ – whose mare had kicked and broken his leg – travelled on crutches and was in and out of operating theatres and hospitals for years afterwards. American condescension towards British difficulties in India irritated EJ: it came with no acknowledgement of the many unpunished lynchings of blacks happening each year in the American South or of their own race-based caste system. The boys returned with temporary American accents and Theo built in the Scar Top garden a Baalbek summer house, expression of her longing for elsewhere.

EJ had no inherited wealth of his own and got by on his teaching and writing. By marrying Theo – who came, in his own charged phrase, from 'Moneyed People' – EJ was marrying out of Methodist puritanical poverty. A stylish, scented grande dame whose clothes, food and furnishings were elegant, a social mover with ambition and occasional assurance – keeping house by itself scarcely exhausted her abilities.

What Theo required in order to pay for her custom-made clothes alone was redoubtable. Like Kingsley Amis and John Osborne in a later generation who both 'married up', socially speaking, what attracted EJ also affronted him. Scar Top was paid for from Theo's family money and she later said that she thought it very snobbish of the English to look down on a husband who used his wife's money for a house. He resented both Theo's spending and his own dependence on her capital. When Theo, her two sisters and the two boys went out to the Lebanon in 1927 EJ provided a sum of money which Theo mistook for 'pocket money', buying them all new bits of clothing and small luxuries only to discover too late that it was the money for the whole long journey. After she had paid the fares there was nothing for food or extras.

In 1933 EJ told Masefield that Scar Top was for sale. In the event they stayed another six years, but anxiously. Edward later recalled either lying in bed and hearing his parents fiercely quarrelling, or weeping at the top of the stairs at the emotional storms beneath – mainly, he thought, about money. His parents kept separate bedrooms, a common practice then among educated people, without necessarily signifying a *mariage blanc*; but Theo was frustrated and unfulfilled. Moneyed assurance combined with intellectual self-doubt. She quarrelled with a succession of maids, as with her husband, who was doubtless impatient, impetuous and sometimes pompous and sardonic. She was bossy and controlling with her boys, who loved her but feared her moods of needing to organise others.

A big change was getting the first family car – an old Austin – in 1930. Theo alone drove the first year, hating it, 'an agonizing business'. In the beautiful summer of 1932 Edward learned to drive and took the family nearly 100 miles towards Devonshire. Soon an open-topped Morris replaced the Austin before giving way in turn to an old Armstrong Siddeley.

In early June 1933 Theo, young Edward and Sandy the dog walked in Sir Arthur Evans's woods with Frank's Winchester scholarship exam schedule so that they could calculate exactly when he finished his Greek exam ('which we think was easy') and began Maths 2 ('which we think was hard'). Such strenuous attempts to guess at the lives elsewhere of those you loved would, when war came ten years later, be a national pursuit. Theo and EP imagined Frank scanning the questions . . . and indeed it is startling to find from his Bodleian papers that Frank was that afternoon giving each question his personal grade, from 'Good', 'Fair' and 'Hard' to 'Easy' and then – quite often, and showing no lack of chutzpah – 'Potty'.

Theo had sent Frank detailed instructions on how to behave if

Frank and Theo.

summoned for a Viva: 'Recall you are only 12 years old, which will count in your favour, and . . . say to yourself "In three hours or so it will all be over and I shall be on my way home."' Frank won a scholarship to Winchester. The headmaster of Rugby, his school of second choice, sent his congratulations, making clear Rugby would also have welcomed him. 'Wonderful school,' Theo jots on this letter. 'But not quite up to Winchester.' Her elder son was to be enlisted into the British ruling class: Theo always accounted this the happiest day of her life.

3

# A Class Apart: 1933–8

A year ago, in the drowsy Vicarage garden
We talked of politics . . .

from 'To a Communist Friend', Frank's epitaph
for Anthony Carritt, December 1937

Frank, echoing his mother, accounted his Winchester time 'some of the happiest days in my life' and when required one family Christmas to sing one of its school songs – 'Dulce Domum' – fought back tears. His housemaster Monty Wright sent Theo in 1933 a vignette of his appearance on arrival: '[Frank] . . . throws his head & limbs about & blurts out remarks with an engaging but unusual simplicity. But we are used to odd people in College [as the scholars' house is known], and his seems a very likeable kind of oddness.' At Winchester Frank discovered clowning and the ability to make people laugh – exaggerating his ungainliness to excuse his brilliance, sometimes deploying his brilliance to pardon his lack of coordination. Frank learned how to secure affection. He gained popularity through imaginative obscenities, of which one very mild one survives. Once when a Jewish contemporary ran 220 yards fast, Frank was roundly told off for shouting from the touchline, 'Well buttocked, Hebrew!' Such clowning underlay Wright's warning one year later 'not in any way [to] trade upon the fact that he is "odd" or mistake notoriety for distinction'.

Since these years had a profound impact on him, it is striking to hear Frank's troop commander in March 1940 echoing this 1933 judgement: 'A very big man who sometimes seems to have little control over either the movements of his body or the expression of his thoughts.' Frank had then just got into a 'catastrophic row' after drawing 'cats all over some official report I'd filled out, thinking it was finished with'. Cat-faces decorate Thompson family letters, even on occasion Theo's – an apt emblem of privacy and independent-mindedness. If Frank courted popularity, there was also an attractive streak within him of devil-may-care nonchalance, unconventionality, a cat-like ability to find his own direction.*

In this spirit Frank made fun of the stammering Bible Revision teacher apropos Ur of the Chaldees. Frank asked him mock-innocently to name that place in the corner of the biblical map: 'Er . . . er . . . *UR.*' Wright noted that Frank should learn to confine his frivolity to suitable occasions. His mind constantly active and alert, he had to 'grow out of baby ways and discipline some of his restless energy' to realise his excellent promise. Restlessness and frivolity were in evidence when Frank tussled about the lighting of a dorm fire, chipping one of John Dancy's front teeth and necessitating a replacement.†

College was the medieval religious community of seventy scholars founded by William of Wykeham in 1394, with the longest unbroken history of any school in England and one dedicated to the Virgin Mary, to whose statue over Middle Gate Frank and his peers were expected to doff their hats as they passed. In 1933 its buildings had scarcely changed over nearly 600 years. Upstairs chambers or dormitories were partly lit by candlelight. Within the huge stones of the four-foot-thick walls, the great Seventh Chamber seemed to stretch upwards into limitless darkness as electric lightbulbs hung down thirty feet from the smoke-blackened ceilings. In a vast fireplace

---

* In the Western Desert in 1942 he, yet again, caused raised eyebrows when a visiting officer found he had drawn cats all over his route-map.
† 'That tooth', said his dentist in 1961, when Dancy took up the Marlborough headmastership, 'might do for Lancing. It will not do for Marlborough.'

burned fires lit by bundles of twigs named, after a woodsman, 'Bill Brighters'. Here, at first, all seventy scholars were taught, among walls with marble tablets recording the names of previous scholars over the centuries. Within these great cool rooms it is said that a 1985 snowman lasted indoors for nearly a week. Present scholars sat in 'toyes' – partitioned cubicles with very dimly lit (albeit by electricity) working surfaces and bookshelves smelling of ancient polish – wearing a black gown of medieval design with puffed-out sleeves over a waistcoat and pinstripe trousers, together with black ties and straw boaters ('bashers') on weekdays, on Sundays stiff wing-collars, white bow ties and black top hats.

There were no boys at Winchester – all, from arrival, were called men. Each was examined on his Notions book, a pamphlet perhaps thirty pages long, bound in dark-blue paper, listing the many odd turns of phrase and tradition the school had accumulated since the foundation (for example, 'to thoke': to be idle). Insider jokes abounded. In the middle of Chamber Court, where scholars lived, were two drains for rainwater. Each drain was called Hell and the stone runnels leading to them were called Good Resolutions. The most remote of the several separate chambers in which they lived and worked by day was called Thule. In the middle of the east wall of Chamber Court was a drinking fountain called Moab (from the psalm: 'Moab is my washpot; and over Edom will I cast out my shoe'), so of course there was also a shoe closet called Edom. Here was a private code designed to repel outsiders.

Winchester could help anglicise you and render you acceptable. Frank's contemporary the half-Prussian Wolfgang von Blumenthal later changed his name to Charles Arnold-Baker, while the Jewish Seymour Schlesinger, whose father was chairman of the merchant bank Keyser Ullmann and whose long-established family did not know where in central Europe they originated, changed his name in 1942 to Spencer in case he got taken as a prisoner of war. Schlesinger – known at Winchester as 'The Hebe', short for Hebrew – experienced some isolation. He behaved on arrival to Frank and others in a way he himself thought 'spikey'; Frank was unusual in claiming him as 'My very dear friend'. Such an appellation evinced Frank's freedom and his warmth of heart. In one 1938 letter Frank addressed his boon companion Tony Forster as 'My beloved Antony'. They walked arm in arm around cloisters in the evenings, a habit encouraged and known as 'tolling'. They were not lovers, and quiet, gentle, genial Forster was seen by others as an also-ran, a planet revolving around Frank-as-the-star. Frank, vibrant and imposing, made friends more easily than did his brother.

─────────

Two years after Frank went up to Winchester Theo referred to him in his absence as 'a decent chap'. EP answered fervently and with what his mother recognised as – for him – an unusual display of emotion, 'He's more than that.' The boys, so different, were none the less devoted to one another. Edward hated his sporting successes being used to humiliate Frank and generously forgave Frank's intellectual successes being used as a whip for his own back.

Edward minded never getting into the top form at the Dragon School where, his mother chillingly observed to EJ, the masters were 'far from despairing' of him. 'We can't expect him to be as book-brilliant as Frank – and he doesn't work badly, as a rule. He has his points and we don't want to break his spirit as we were in danger of breaking Frank's. Frank was at times, for his age, absurdly patient, apologetic and philosophical, don't you remember?' They had, Theo recorded, presumably out of misplaced puritanism, failed to praise Frank sufficiently.

EP concurred with Theo's judgement in 1926 that 'nervous trouble' contributed to the impetigo he first suffered then, a contagious skin complaint recurring over twenty years. Awaiting posting to North Africa he was in March 1943 in hospital with impetigo, the blisters on his face covered in purple iodine; and two years later in March 1945, after the stress of the battle of Monte Cassino and the subsequent liberation of Florence and waiting to be demobbed, this old ailment brought him back to hospital in Tuscany. The comical ad for a clear complexion EJ glued on to one October 1940 letter is intended to cheer EP up: 'Use Pendle Creams* faithfully and your skin, like Lady Normanton's, will look smoother, clearer, lovelier than it ever did before – and with less trouble on your part.'

Theo knew that she had mythical standards of perfection; others saw her as too controlling. How far did her non-stop, bossy, detailed commands, rebukes, injunctions and corrections contribute to her children's nervous tension? Her letters often compare her two sons invidiously, rarely to EP's advantage. He was, he later agreed, the 'duffer' of the family, not least to himself.

He grew up considering himself – like Winnie-the-Pooh – a Bear of Very Little Brain. Although he was his father's favourite son, this did not stop EJ colluding in Theo's lifelong campaign for their younger son's betterment, once at a Retford Christmas shocking the Pilkington-Rogers family – the daughter Barbara feared her Thompson cousins, finding them intimidatingly intelligent – by publicly calling young EP

---

* 'Creams' is crossed out: EJ has written 'soap'.

a fool. It is unsurprising if his strongly left-leaning handwriting suggested a lack of confidence.

Theo found EP self-satisfied, unserious and unsocialised, and lacking Frank's great talent for friendship. In September 1936, EJ wrote shrewdly to EP, then applying to public school, 'Remember, this year is of tremendous importance. I am sure you have plenty of brains, if you were not such a slack little beggar. No, it isn't exactly that; only a slowness to "react".' Probably criticism made EP retreat into his shell. In November 1938 EJ issued the barbed remark that on a skiing holiday in Val d'Isère EP might learn some French 'if you care to take the trouble'. But EP had none of Frank's love of and ease with languages. In July 1939 EJ advised, 'Look up the spelling of repetition,' quipping heavy-handedly in 1941 about EP's misspellings of 'meat' for meet, 'ake' for ache, and during EP's first year at Cambridge was facetious about his writing 'Desert spoons and medecine [*sic*]'. As late as April 1944 EP started a letter, 'I don't think I've wrote you since I changed my address.' Ability to master grammar and spelling does not necessarily equate with intelligence, something his

EP, *c.* 1940.

parents never grasped. EJ once described EP's letters with the damning word for a Thompson: 'Adequate'.

All four Thompsons regarded themselves as writers in the making and read and commented on each other's poems, and one of the last times they were together (Alfriston in May 1940) argued fiercely about poetry. It was thus also a natural Thompson habit to appraise one another's style. As the Count de Buffon put the matter: 'The style is the man'; so in evaluating one another's habits of expression the Thompsons were always criticising character too. Theo in February 1938 started by praising EP's school essay and the brevity and terseness of his letters, noting that he is not – unlike her – wordy: perhaps her verbosity resulted from fear of not being listened to? But her praise was often prelude to a bruising and she moves on swiftly to attack him for pomposity. Some daft comments on her part follow.

EP's use of such inoffensive words as 'derive', 'erect' (for build) and 'respite' reminds Theo of early Victorian essayists. To cure him she proposes that he read some really modern writer like Max Beerbohm (born in 1872) or Aldous Huxley (born 1892), commending Thackeray (1811–63) and Gibbon (1737–94) as well. True, she also extols Cyril Connolly, Auden and Isherwood's 1936 play *The Ascent of F6*, Auden's recent poem *Spain* and Hemingway, whose subjects are 'pretty crude & beastly, but his bare plain style is currently influential'.* She disapproves of Latinish words like 'despite' and recommends instead a future regimen of words like 'baste, morticed, laced, knit, sown, sprung, larded and furrowed'. One boggles at the Mrs Malaprop-like work of art that combining Theo's preferred words might elicit. Edward's essays, she adjures, ought to sound like him; yet her appeal itself sounds artificial.

During EP's final year at school, EJ cut out and glued on to the top of a letter to him another ad, headed 'DOES YOUR ENGLISH

---

* Frank had 'outgrown the pompous and declamatory, at first even to the point of "bad form" – it "isn't done" to talk like an orator. But he is much better now, quite terse and pithy and *much* more natural . . . You start with an advantage over him in that you *naturally* are brief and direct' (Theo to EP, 14 Feb. 1938, Bodl. d 2701).

EMBARRASS YOU?' Then, in successive smaller strips, 'Are you content with the way you speak and write? Are you sure that you are not making mistakes that cause people to underrate you?', and at the bottom, 'Many ambitious people are handicapped in this way; they cannot depend upon their English not "letting them down".'

EJ's intention was at least half humorous, and father and son had on the whole an excellent understanding. But both parents agreed that schoolboy EP had a habit infuriating to Theo of using words with a special top-spin or meaning of his own. EJ addressed this directly in 1940: 'People have complained that you are a terrible sea-lawyer – that you force words & phrases to carry your own meaning and – yes, you have a rude manner on occasion.' A 'sea-lawyer' is someone who attempts to shirk responsibility or blame through trivial technicalities or, alternatively, questions all orders and rules.

Both boys rebelled against the values of their parents, most obviously in joining the CP. But their rebellions differed. Even at the age of thirteen Frank picks up all references in his parents' letters, saying something to let them know that they have been carefully listened to. Through attending closely to their concerns, he occasionally shook free of his parents, exercising independent choices of his own. This knack came less easily to Edward.

In a sense both bear the marks of Theo's and EJ's conflicts – Frank condemned to the role of victim doomed to understand everyone in every dispute, EP to playing a different kind of victim who does not. Indeed he acquired an unfortunate and lasting habit of misreading others on occasion.

---

EP resented Winchester for dividing the brothers. It had the highest and most rigorous classical training of any English school, a training Frank loved, internalised and made his own. EP by contrast attended Kingswood, a school 'with no elite pretensions and no classical ambitions'. He disliked Winchester's self-satisfied sense of its own excellence, its cult of eccentricity and affectations, and the ruling-class manners and arrogance of one or two of Frank's friends. Frank too could communicate an unconscious sense of insidership, as when, skiing in France, he accurately identified by manner and accent alone a fellow public schoolboy as having attended Charterhouse. Did EP and Frank inhabit different social classes?

In fact Winchester scholars' sense of entitlement was as much intellectual as social. Some scholars paid nothing, not even extras, a source of notable tension between scholars and commoners. College was still notionally for the poor, and considerable school wealth dating from the compulsory sale of land under Cardinal Wolsey subsidised scholars' education; Frank's parents paid only thirty guineas per year inclusive, for board, tuition and lodging combined. Considering that commoners paid £200 (from 1937, £220), this was a significant remission. Yet if poverty did not exclude you, this was middle- or upper-class poverty: even to be considered for Winchester you needed to have attended a prep school teaching you Greek. That Frank's education cost their hard-pressed parents a good deal less than Edward's no doubt added to his popularity.

Edward – by contrast – was sent to Kingswood, his father's school, where the sons of laymen were charged £115. Why was he sent there? EJ had after all felt cheated at Kingswood of the rounded education major public schools afforded; and Theo once remarked that Edward's teeth began to go bad when he went to 'that dreadful Methodist school', adding brightly and foolishly, 'If only we had sent him to a nice *ordinary* school *like Eton or Rugby*.' The fact of the matter seems to be that, wrongly believing Edward too dim to get into the foremost schools, Kingswood appeared to his parents a safe bet. He none the less won an exhibition and found to his surprise and pleasure that he was on arrival nearly two years ahead of his year in Latin and Greek; he matriculated at fourteen, one year later joining the sixth form.

EP would later provide a terrifying account of Kingswood around 1748 when Wesley's ferocious, cruel-to-be-kind intentions in founding it were all too evident; he famously castigated Methodism as 'a ritualized form of psychic masturbation'. Since EP had received little religious education before, Kingswood probably constituted a shock.

The sons of lay people had first been admitted in 1922, but around 50 per cent of boys were still sons of ministers and missionaries, the remainder children of 'honest hard-working poor tradesmen'. While Winchester cultivated leadership and turned out company directors, dons and MPs, Kingswood produced accountants, lower-ranking civil servants, scientists. There was a strong emphasis on serving the community, and religion's more puritan and repressive forms were important – the world's problems discussed in religious terms. Methodism was 'all pervasive' and the headmaster given to one-to-one homilies.

On the outbreak of war the school was evacuated to Uppingham in the East Midlands. Kingswood's historian sagely records that the head-masters of Uppingham and Kingswood 'wisely' chose not to amalgamate schools 'so different in size, clientele and ethos' but preferred 'to co-exist'. This meant that although they lived cheek by jowl they were almost totally separate. For four whole years, and despite wartime 'solidarity', most boys never addressed one word to their peers in the other school.

Uppingham – the senior, solidly Anglican foundation – evidently feared pollution. In his seminal history *The Making of the English Working Class* (1963) EP presented Methodists – beginning under the aegis of the Church of England – partly as cowardly lickspittles urging appeasement of the rich and powerful. Kingswood was certainly the more 'aspirational' of the two schools, with which Uppingham refused to play rugby matches at 1st XV level: EP wrote that they feared losing caste if beaten by the socially 'inferior' school. George Orwell noted the many small yet intractable gradations of the British class system, and apartheid between different parts of the great British middle class would interest EP the future historian. He made no Uppingham friends.

After a brief, unserious flirtation with the Oxford Group (caricatured as a 'Salvation Army for snobs' and supplying one Kingswood house-master) EP campaigned first for the inclusion within chapel services of Blake, Whitman and William Saroyan, later forming an actively anti-chapel committee that wanted church attendance made voluntary. EP considerably upset the partly liberal, one-legged head Dr A. B. Sackett (he had lost the other leg at Gallipoli) by demythologising Christianity to the History Society, citing both Karl Marx and Sir James Frazer's *The Golden Bough*.

Kingswood, for all that he deplored about it, gave him friendships with other radically minded alumni that mattered for life: the future publisher Adrian Beckett, the poet-academic Geoffrey Matthews and the writer Arnold Rattenbury, two years older, with whom EP half-unhappily fell in love and who exercised a profound influence. EP was reduced from the rank of prefect for smoking or for his Marxist politics or both. He, Rattenbury and Matthews, who had all joined the CP, began selling the Party's newspaper the *Daily Worker* in the dormitory. When they tried to join the Young Communist League their letters of application were intercepted and they were interviewed by the police in the headmaster's study, an event that did little to discourage revolutionary fervour.

EP felt mixed about Kingswood. There were two flourishing literary societies and a library rich in modern books; there were also annual plays, and in one religious drama he acted the Archangel Michael. He was always very keen on acting. And he liked the school's virility, variety and independent-mindedness. Then, in 1940, a year when Theo encouraged him to think of attending RADA to become an actor, an essay of Christopher Hill's on the Levellers – the political movement during the English Civil Wars which emphasised popular sovereignty, extension of suffrage and equality before the law – electrified him. Thus was born in him that famous urge to 'rescue the ordinary person from the vast condescension of posterity' that would famously inspire his life-work. Condescension and disempowerment were topics his upbringing had schooled him in, as were exclusion and unfairness. He was sensitive to slights to others as well as to himself.

When EP was at Cambridge EJ observed to him that 'your inherited danger is to be a bit of a prig' – someone who parades moral superiority to compensate for the want of other kinds of excellence. EP agreed: 'I have seen Kingswood turn out prigs'; and he acknowledged his own 'annoyingly serious attitude to life plus certain puritan strains'. His drive was moralising, demotic, even Methodistical. One of Frank's

Winchester friends, borrowing terms made famous by Matthew Arnold, contrasted EP's 'Hebraism' with Frank's 'sweetness and light'. Frank's apprehension of the world, EP noted in his turn, was more aesthetic, EP's own more earnest and moralistic.*

Boys about to leave Kingswood spent hours in discussion with the school chaplain. The contrast with Winchester is striking. Donald McLachlan, who taught Frank Divinity, was a free-thinker, and gave out Plato and even Voltaire. Unsurprisingly, in a school debate shortly before he left Winchester Frank claimed that he was no puritan and lacked any form of 'non-conformist conscience'.

---

What EP termed Winchester 'eccentricities and affectations' are plain. Its dandy delinquencies included staying up late eating 'exquisite anchovy toast and scrambled eggs which challenged Boulestin', ending up at half-past two with the gramophone playing Paul Robeson's 'Little Man, You've Had a Busy Day' ('You've been playin' soldiers, the battle has been won / The enemy is out of sight / Come along there soldier, put away your gun / The war is over for tonight'). Or absconding to the library roof to pipe-smoke Three Nuns or Classic Curly Cut. Frank noted on leaving 'The numerous and glorious societies', formed by himself and his friends – '[the] brown shoe soc, pyjama top soc, evening trouser soc . . . Self-Expression Soc with its blaze of red shirts, yellow pullovers, lumber jackets, overcoats, umbrellas, berets, glassless spectacles & odd stockings'. Together with some friends, Frank also formed the Philology Society whose members – it was unfairly claimed – liked to exchange insults and obscenities in obscure languages or scripts such as Glagolitic.† Winchester dandyism could appear

---

* EJ described EP to Frank (23 Sept. 1943) as 'saturated [at Kingswood] with moral earnestness . . . the earnestness stuck only too well'.

† Peter de Wesselow, Hallett, Frank, Peter Wiles. The annalist recorded that its object was the dilettantish study of useless languages so as to establish a superiority complex. De Wesselow knew a little Dutch; Wiles a little Italian and Russian plus what might have been Danish; Hallett knew Spanish; Thompson some Russian and a very little Italian; Thompson also presented Russian newspapers and a stolen Dutch hymn book to the society. In addition they all knew Latin, Greek, French and German.

Frank 'absconding to the library roof'.

irresponsible, exclusive and conceited, and make Frank sound like a brainy member of the Brideshead set. But he also learned Russian at the school.

Edward once argued that Frank was strongly influenced by the 'rather easy cynical philosophy of Winchester . . . together with its lazy all-embracing humanism'. Frank agreed. In 1943 he argued that levity and superficial cynicism marked Wykehamists (as ex-pupils are known) for life. While the school paid lip service to civic duty, and he could imagine a Wykehamist willing to die so that a public building survived, he believed that, despite such aestheticism, the school inculcated 'next to no idealism but a strong intolerance of folly' instead. He joked that when he started drinking less in 1943, this was not from moral principle – he was 'too loyal a Wykehamist to be guilty of harbouring a conviction' – but from disinclination. Its whole method made one into a private person. Winchester was therefore a typical major public school, which he thought turned out officers frivolous to the point of nihilism.

Yet Frank retained the irritating habit of *liking* more people than

Edward, so that when EP complained of the self-conceit of an Old Harrovian in his regiment, Frank remonstrated, 'It's a mistake to hate people because of their class.' As for Frank, he has only generous things to say of his younger brother, accounting Edward in 1941 'what I would like to have been – an honest, warm-hearted witty & imaginative Englishman with no illusions. He writes poetry with signs of genius – at 17.'

---

In the autumn of 1936 Frank underwent a crisis. His friend the future historian M. R. D. Foot had been confirmed into the Church of England by the Bishop of Winchester, Cyril Garbett. Should Frank follow? In the event Frank followed his own star and was never confirmed. But on 24 October that year he and a visiting Theo walked down College Street, she unaware since it was dark that he was silently choking back sobs, his cheeks tear-stained. Theo remonstrated, thinking him bored. 'She's very unhappy about me.' What good would confirmation do? It would make him ten times more unhappy. His diary records self-flagellation, refusing to entertain 'thoughts of suicide . . . From what a nice family I come, to think how nice I really am myself, and how foully I behave at school. I am noisy, bumptious, foul-mouthed and foul-minded. It is not my life at home that is hypocrisy (even there I'm often vile) it is in the life here that I am true to myself. It is depressing.' Contemporaries recalled how his ribaldries kept everyone amused. He was growing up so big and uncoordinated he was nicknamed 'Ban' for Caliban.

A prefect penned comments on the other scholars with a very Wykehamical mixture of urbanity and malice (never dreaming that biographers would later root among them). Peter Wiles, brilliant, short and waspish, a future Fellow of All Souls and Sovietologist at the London School of Economics, recorded Frank as the Chamber Poet. 'Hates to put his feelings into words: hence his only safety valve is poetry & that not very effective . . . even after his most brilliant eruptions [Frank] remains a mass of unrelieved uncomfortableness.'

Poetry and clowning were safety-valves. Meanwhile Wiles goes on cattily to describe Frank's physical clumsiness as irritating 'even though partly not affected', and he saw that his rumbustiousness, being partly a pose, concealed as much as it put on display. It was later observed that, if Frank didn't like or trust you, he did not break his reserve. Wiles sketches Frank's insomnia, constipation, tendency to embarrassment, prudishness, sleepiness, 'abominable' cleverness, his mix of cynicism, Falstaffian *joie de vivre* and high moral earnestness.

Frank, 1936.

The painful quarrel within Frank between high-mindedness and low motives – common among adolescents – is here shrewdly caught. It fuelled his confirmation crisis, about which he wrote to EJ, then on a four-month trip to India. EJ replied memorably from Calcutta on 2 November 1936. He had lost his own faith, and knew that most boys get confirmed automatically, meaning little by it. Because EJ's own difficulties and sufferings have arisen from the 'unconventionality' of his upbringing, he wants his sons not to repeat these mistakes. He honours Frank's scruples but undercuts the exaggerated sense of responsibility that underlies them. Frank had expressed to his father a concern that he might one day become a Catholic. EJ, after dismissing this point, continues:

I will tell you what I believe. Nothing matters except character, which as the years pass is its own increasing reward. There is a mind in the universe, some kind of personality that seeks to get into touch with the spirit of man . . . The 'worship' sought is not adoration of some super-mortal sultan, but the spontaneous rushing-out of our wills into selfless action. And here again comes in one of those truths by which we are saved. 'He that saveth his soul shall lose it, and he that loseth his soul shall save it'. These swiftly passing earth-days are ours, not to develop an aggressive 'personality', a noisy individuality – but to lose what we are, to get rid of ourselves so that we may rise into a self that is greater & purer & nobler than we can ever imagine.

We have got to lose our soul, our self. Why not? There is a nobler soul waiting to be ours! It is hard to explain but it happened – that men and women do get gripped by something that fills their lives with personal communion, & gives them a sense of destiny which makes them fearless.

The credo Frank lived and died by owed much to his father's alarming courage, inspired by his Christian belief and *Boy's Own*-like bravado. One should, EJ believed, 'face the music' as he had himself done during important crises. He gives an example from the Mesopotamian campaign in 1917. After his 'very dearly beloved brother' was killed, a period of desolation and physical weariness followed. In April came heavy fighting, which at first appalled him. Then, suddenly, on a day of grim battle something 'took hold of' him, and 'without even knowing what fear was' he won a reputation with brave men for bravery. He does not mention gaining the Military Cross; Frank would take this as understood. Despite being very ill afterwards and lying sick in Basra, EJ had all that summer lived in 'a serenity of destiny and fearlessness. It was a wonderful experience . . .'

EJ also wrote about how periodically an English hero redeems his country's bad faith. He had in mind Byron, who 'died encouraging the Greeks still firing at their Turkish oppressors'. He asked rhetorically, 'Can one man today achieve anything that matters by a gesture?' – a provocative question to the impressionable Frank. No doubt the sacrifice EJ intended was less extreme than the one Frank, in the event, found himself making. During the next war Frank would echo his father's beliefs in the heroic virtues of selfless action, of nobly losing one's soul in order to gain it, and inhabit his own serenity of destiny and fearlessness.

Winchester had many ways of endorsing these codes of chivalry and gallantry. Some streets away from College was Winchester Castle Great Hall, in which hung the eighteen-foot Arthurian Round Table created around 1290 in solid oak for Edward I, designed for royal tournaments and decorated with the names of twenty-four Arthurian Knights including Sir Galahad, Sir Gawain and Sir Lancelot. Then in June 1934 a College library copy of Malory's *Morte d'Arthur* (later identified as the book used by its first printer William Caxton) was discovered, and scholars were set Malory as a topic for the English prize. Malory's knightly sentiment and the horrible end meted out to villains captivated Frank and contributed to his winning the Gillespie Prize in 1935. He won many other prizes – for poetry, Latin verse and archaeology. Scholars were intensely competitive. Winning prizes mattered.

———

Frank would later claim that he was converted to belief in Communism by Iris Murdoch in the second week of March 1939. Yet among the leading questions about confirmation that he put to Theo in 1936 was 'Suppose I should want to be a Communist after a few years?' Why might Frank have predicted this?

First there is the case of John Hasted's conversion. Frank in 1933 took Hasted, whose widower father had fought with EJ in Mesopotamia, under his wing. Hasted acknowledges that after having first thought Frank 'rather an ass' he later changed his view. M. R. D. Foot, closely observing this friendship, believes Frank influenced Hasted while both were still at Winchester to become a libertarian Bolshevik. Hasted, whose political commitment connected with his love of popular song, later became Professor of Chemistry at Birkbeck, where he did much to foster folk music, and stayed on in the CP after 1956.

Then there was the mock election in College to coincide with the

1935 General Election, when Robert Conquest – later pioneer unmasker of Stalin's Great Terror – stood as a Communist candidate. Although the Conservatives won, the CP gained an astonishing fifty votes. Agitprop featured, as did red scarves, clenched-fist salutes and cries of 'Red Front!' (meaning Popular Front) ringing round the old school building, all tokens of the temper of the times. Only two years before, a school election had been cancelled when two young gentlemen turned up wearing red ties. Conquest joined the CP for one year on leaving Winchester in 1937. During this 1935 mock election Frank deputised for Conquest and the CP and, when asked why he had shaved off his eyebrows, Frank said he hoped they would grow back bushy like Uncle Joe's. (They failed to do so, and meanwhile he bought an eyebrow pencil to make good the deficit.)

There were also radical left-wing teachers like Eric Emmet, by whom Frank was taught maths, and Donald McLachlan, who had been *The Times*'s man in Warsaw. In Berlin the night of the Reichstag fire in February 1933 McLachlan wrote a dispatch so good that he was summoned to London to write leaders. (Frank and M. R. D. Foot had read the *Times* reports of the Dimitrov trial to each other that autumn. Dimitrov would play a part in Frank's 1944 downfall.)* Bored with journalism, McLachlan arrived in Winchester in 1936 to teach Russian, German and current affairs. He was a stimulating teacher, encouraging his pupils to think for themselves, and sharing with them a first-hand knowledge of European personalities. When the Spanish Civil War started in July 1936, he hung a map of Spain in class with the battle fronts marked daily so as to keep up to date. Frank followed the *Times* reports every morning: the pro-Franco stance of Spanish Catholics soon helped wean him from a flirtation with Anglo-Catholicism.

Another influence was the Carritts, close neighbours and friends. All five Carritt boys like their mother were in the CP, even young Brian at Eton where he raised money for twenty hunger marchers to be fed at

---

* Georgi Dimitrov (1882–1949), Bulgarian Communist politician, from 1934 General Secretary of the Comintern, and from 1944 leader of the Bulgarian CP, was in 1933 on trial charged with complicity in setting the Reichstag on fire.

Windsor and invited leading CP theorist Palme Dutt to speak. His elder brothers, suspicious of his choice of school, gave Brian an annual interrogation. 'Shades of Karl Marx! A communist in a top hat!' quipped Frank. 'What will Gabriel have to say?'

What Gabriel Carritt – who proletarianised his name to Bill – said was that left-wing politics seemed an absolute answer for his psychological problems. Joining the CP for your own needs was, Bill thought, nothing to be ashamed of: for the Carritts revolutionary social change was connected with personal growth. Bill's own problems were completely buried under this energy and enthusiasm, the 1930s being the 'most marvellous time to [be] alive . . . a happy time among all those friends! . . . We believed . . . we could change history.' Among Frank's 1937 poems is one dialoguing with Brian, another with Anthony Carritt, with almost identical titles.

Lines to a Communist Friend

Here, in the tranquil fragrance of the honeysuckle,
The gentle, soothing velvet of the foxgloves,
The cuckoo's drowsy laugh, – I thought of you,
The ever-whirring dynamos of your will,
Body and brain one swift, harmonious strength,
Flashing like polished steel to rid the world
Of all its gross unfairness. – But the grossest
Unfairness of it all is that, tomorrow,
When both of us are gone, my sloth, your energy,
The world will still be cruelly perverse.
– Why not enjoy the foxgloves while they last?

July 1937

'Body and brain one . . . strength' mirrors Brian's famed sporting prowess, a synchronisation now dedicated to his egalitarian politics. The poem weighs this politics against fleeting beauty, sceptical about the chance of ameliorating life's cruelties. Frank had written in his diary of the sense of futility College could instil: 'the old grey walls frown down & say, "We know. It is not worthwhile. Before you, there were

Private Collection

Brian Carritt, *c.* 1938.

many others who wrote poems here. They have all gone, some to oblivion, some to glory, but the world runs on without them.'" Thus he pits the fugitive foxgloves of English pastoral elegy, endorsed by Winchester, against activism.

The theme of being a trapped, conscience-ridden spectator recurs in another July 1937 poem, 'Suave Mari Magno', its title a tag from Lucretius meaning that it is sweet, during a tempest, to witness from the safety of landfall the perils of those at sea: that is, the jeopardy entailed by those committed persons fighting for and against Fascism, ready 'to perish, even to kill'. Within the frame of a love letter Frank enquires into the political passion that would inspire three Carritts to go to Spain. The poet prays for their faith and inspiration. The 'my darling' of the poem need not refer to a given woman, but other poems do invoke a specific, unnamed beloved who might be Tony Forster's 'wacky' sister Felicity/Fifi or Robert Graves's daughter Catherine Nicholson, green-eyed, red-haired, to whom Frank was attracted, and whom Theo at some point hoped he might marry.

At the start of the Spanish war Gabriel Carritt together with the secretary of the Young Communist League walked over the Pyrenees to find out what aid was needed. He co-founded the British Youth Foodship Committee, collecting food and clothing for the Republic. When Gabriel returned, two of his brothers set out. His middle brother Noel arrived in Albacete in December 1936, having informed their parents by means of a note scribbled on the back of an old cheque sent as he left via Victoria that he was joining the 2,700 Britons in the International Brigades: 'Darling Mother and Father, I hope you're not too furious with me . . . sorry not to have seen you but I thought you'd probably try and stop me.' A teacher in Sheffield, he gave his school no notice. Anthony joined him. Their mother and Brian collected for Spanish Medical Aid in Oxford and at Eton respectively, Brian also raising £200 to commemorate an Old Boy and friend (Lewis Clive) killed with the Brigades.

Anthony and Noel trained at Madrigueras. In February 1937 at the battle of Jarama an enemy bullet hitting his rifle broke Noel's wrist; later as an ambulance driver during the battle for Brunete he was wounded in the head. Here Noel's brother Anthony, two years older than him, was also badly wounded in an air attack; Virginia Woolf's nephew Julian Bell was killed in the same battle. Noel scoured hospitals and field stations exhaustively before accepting that Anthony must be dead.

It would be surprising, given his closeness to Gabriel and Brian, if Frank did not learn of one trigger for Anthony's Spanish odyssey: distress at discovering his parentage. He had recently asked Amy, the Carritt family housekeeper, of a photo of Arthur Derbyshire, his mother's lover killed in the Great War: 'Is this bastard my father?' Amy – fond of Anthony – could only admit that she believed he was. This recalls Gabriel's view that Communism helped his generation solve psychological difficulties, of which Anthony's illegitimacy was a case in point. His family offers further case histories: Penelope committed suicide, Betty rebelled, Michael in the Indian Civil Service cooperated clandestinely with Indian nationalists, Noel often fell into apathy and isolation.

In December 1937 Frank addressed Anthony's ghost in a second poem

Private Collection

Noel (*left*, in Spain) and Anthony (*right*) Carritt, both 1937.

entitled 'To a Communist Friend', a sonnet whose careful half-rhymes underscore the seriousness of its writer's engagement with its themes.

> A year ago, in the drowsy Vicarage garden,
> We talked of politics; you and your tawny hair
> Flamboyant, flaunting your red tie, unburden'd
> Your burning heart of the dirge we always hear –
> The rich triumphant and the poor oppress'd.
> And I laugh'd, seeing, I thought, an example
> Of vague ideals, not tried, but taken, on trust,
> That would not stand the test. It sounded all too simple.
> A year has pass'd; and now, where harsh winds rend
> The street's last shred of comfort, – past the dread
> Of bomb or gunfire, rigid on the ground
> Of some cold stinking alley near Madrid,
> Your mangled body festers, – an example
> Of something tougher. – Yet it still sounds all too simple.

Anthony impressed Frank by putting his ideals to the test, not merely of action, but of martyrdom. The poem's painful dispute between scepticism and belief no longer recalls an historical disagreement between friends but a conflict within the present moment that haunts Frank, experiencing the urgent summons of the new politics: 'The rich triumphant and the poor oppress'd'. Anthony, in the words of this poem, had indeed 'stood the test'. Frank later wrote that 'Spain was so real, that it hurt.'

———

A Winchester contemporary of Frank's, the noted physicist Freeman Dyson, opposed Frank's martyrdom in the Balkans to the Allied firebombing of Dresden, known for its pre-war beauty as Florence-on-the-Elbe. News of both would break early in 1945. Dyson deplored the obscene horror and waste of Dresden's destruction as wicked and counter-productive; he spent his war in Bomber Command, involved in a technological war at a distance that seemed to him corrupt and futile. By contrast Dyson envied and revered Frank as someone fighting for a 'clean' cause, in hand-to-hand combat.

Dyson's admiration for Frank started at their first meeting in September 1936 when he arrived in College, three years younger than Frank, another scholar sharing the same Chamber. There was no privacy but a constant and cheerful uproar with verbal and physical battles raging unpredictably. Frank was the largest, loudest, most uninhibited and most brilliant of Dyson's new schoolfellows. He wrote: 'I learned from him more than I learned from anybody else at that school, even though he may have been scarcely aware of my existence.' He recalls Frank coming striding into the room after a weekend away, singing, 'She's got . . . what it takes'.* This set him apart from the majority in their cloistered all-male society.

The reasons for Dyson's admiration were many. First, Frank loved learning new languages with a passion, especially at this point Russian,

* More likely 'You've Got What Gets Me' from Gershwin's *Girl Crazy* (1932). 'You've Got What It Takes' dates from 1960.

which he and his friends, together with one master, decided after a talk by Bernard Pares to put most energy into learning. They had lessons twice a week, and Frank was before long translating Gusyev and Mayakovsky.

Then Frank, sensitive enough to feel the enchantment of Winchester and – to take a trivial example – to address his women-friends after leaving the school as 'Madonna', was also strong enough to react against it. In June 1935 he had called the Middle Ages 'one of the best ages the world has ever had . . . the most interesting. Such a peculiar mixture of learning, superstition, cruelty and beauty.' In 1943 by contrast he wrote that 'the culture one imbibed at Winchester was too nostalgic. Amid those old buildings and under those graceful lime trees it was easy to give one's heart to the Middle Ages and believe that the world had lost its manhood along with Abelard. One fell in love with the beauty of the past, and there was no dialectician there to explain that the glory of the past was its triumph over the age that came before it; that Abelard was great because he was a revolutionary.'

At fifteen Frank had already won the title of College Poet, was a connoisseur of Latin and Greek literature, and was interested in Silver (late) Latin and soon modern Greek too. He was more deeply concerned than the rest of them with the big world outside: with the civil war then raging in Spain, with the world war he saw coming. From him Dyson caught his first inkling of the great moral questions of war and peace which were to dominate all their lives thereafter. Dyson knew what had happened to the English boys who were fifteen at the start of the First World War and arrived in the trenches in 1917 and 1918. M. R. D. Foot also wrote: 'In all probability I had not many years to live.'

Listening to Frank talk, Dyson learned that there was no way rightly to grasp these great questions except through poetry. For him poetry was no mere intellectual amusement. Poetry was man's best effort through the ages to distil some wisdom from the inarticulate depths of his soul: there was no deeper way to grasp the great questions of the day. He envied Frank, fighting 'a poet's war' – and meeting (though Dyson never exactly says so) a poet's death.

Frank could no more live without poetry than could Dyson without mathematics, and Dyson quotes Frank's 1940 poem 'For the Sake of

Another Man's Wife', which relates Dunkirk to the Trojan Wars: for Frank (Dyson felt) it is natural and obvious that the grief and hatred of these Greeks 3,000 years ago, made immortal by a great poet 700 years later, should mirror and illuminate our own anguish. The essentials of war – the human passion and tragedy – are the same. So he weaves the two together. It is interesting that it was exactly this account of Frank by Dyson that reconciled young Edward – prejudiced against the great public schools – to what Winchester had meant to Frank.

Frank was that rare combination, a soldier-poet and scholar-soldier. The great human problems are for him problems of the individual, not of the mass.

On his final night at College evening prayers Frank burst into tears when Loyola's famous prayer was read ('Teach us, good Lord . . . to give and not to count the cost, / to fight and not to heed the wounds, / to toil and not to seek for rest, to labour and not to ask for any reward / save that of knowing that we do your will') and continued weeping (again) through the school song 'Domum'. He feared he might never

*Seated left to right*, Frank, David Scott-Malden and Roddy Gow (killed at Arnhem 1944); *standing*, Hugh T. Morgan (left) and unidentified. Sunday wear, 1937.

again share his lunacy with men so spontaneously inspired. On the library roof after half a pint of sherry afterwards, and while he and his friends reeled about pretending they were being funny, Frank made two resolutions: '1) however many women I may go to bed with, never to marry until I meet one with whom I am in poifect [*sic*: Brooklynese] sympathy, – to whom I can tell all my vices and who will know how to laugh at the same. 2) to leave the world somehow better than I found it. I don't know how, but I'm buggered if I won't do it somehow.' He also recorded that he was a little drunk. High-mindedness, like the writing of poetry, ran in all the Thompsons.

# 4

# Laughter in the Dark: 1938

Laughter and sleep were all I loved on earth;
And now I find the latter far the best.
from 'My Epitaph', February 1938

Frank, aged seventeen, secured a scholarship at New College, Oxford, to start in the autumn of 1938 to study classics (known as 'Mods and Greats') and left Winchester for good in early April. His father would later say that Frank's taking himself off thus, in the middle of the academic year, was symptomatic of his fatal restlessness. But he passionately wanted to visit Greece. While there he sent home fifty-plus pages he had written 'in the form of Mass-Observational Diaries' and he also wrote poems. The contrast between the prose and the poetry is instructive. The last of his Greek poems, 'The Norman in Exile', evokes his homesickness: 'Here in this land of blue, unclouded sky, / This languid land of death, I long for home.' While this poem is a typical lament exploring melancholy, nostalgia and foreboding, his letters at the same time evoke him 'laughing himself sick' in Crete.

Frank had a happy temperament. The low spirits he suffered with jaundice in Hamadan in 1942 are remarkable for being the only time in his life when he sounds genuinely downbeat and unresourceful. Iris Murdoch wrote accurately to Theo in 1941 about his seeming to have 'a genius for finding all experiences fascinatingly interesting'. He was the least despondent, most effervescent and exuberant of men, his curiosity about the world always on display. Comedy and tragedy are two ways of exploring this curiosity and – increasingly – two halves of one whole. Frank's prose is happy and given to what John Pendlebury, with whom he excavated on Crete, termed Frank's 'puppyish lunacy', his letters and diaries conveying a comedic delight in life's details. His verse, by contrast, is sad, his poems enshrining sturdy pessimism and the sense of his generation's fragility. Poetry is his way of mythologising his real difficulties into a half-pleasurable gloom and melodrama, prose (diarising and letter-writing) his way of obtaining a very different kind of release through clowning.

Had Frank survived the war – he could well have – his poems might have seemed to his older judgement immature, a source of embarrassment to be disowned or forgotten. Since he did not survive, their interest remains as lyrical attempts to negotiate the pain of growing up in a time of exceptionally dramatic public events which they reflect; and they have the gloomy added value – since so many take the form of epitaphs – of appearing prescient, and foretelling his fate.

Death and dying attract immature poets. Keats – whose grave Frank visited in 1938 – in his 'Ode to a Nightingale' wards off the anguish he had witnessed five months earlier when his brother died of TB with wishful thinking about an 'easeful death' for himself. Tom's death had not been 'easeful' and indeed heralded Keats's own. Conjuring with the idea of death can be a secret talisman against it happening for real. Keats's romantic *Schwärmerei* in the famous lines 'Now more than ever seems it rich to die / To cease upon the midnight with no pain' is a prayer for escape from the real suffering all the Keatses underwent, the poet himself soon included. And his marvellous ode is great because it contrives to evoke death and immortality in equipoise, in an intensely moving dramatisation.

Frank, too, flirted with his own Keatsian death-wish. More than his Winchester contemporaries he was – as Freeman Dyson saw – marked by certainty that his generation was to be drastically culled by war. Poetry was, as Dyson understood, his dramatic means to explore and develop this understanding. His first surviving poems date from 1935 and conjure with death. 'Death of a Dryad' is mere adolescent emotionalism about transience. 'Death in the Mines' is socially and politically aware. 'Death in the Mountains' concerns the necessary nobility of courage. 'Pythagorean Love' in March 1936 asserts the permanence of love against death, but not yet persuasively.

In 'War so Jung und Morgenschön' ('[He] was so young and lovely as the morning'), written in December 1936, we hear for the first time his own fluent voice. This is not at all modernist: there is little that he wrote that would have surprised W. S. Landor (1775–1864). But he is developing lyrical strength and confidence, expressing the theme with which we most associate him – the strange happiness of those who risk an early death, unsullied by the cares of age. Its first stanza starts:

> Spring on his brow – and in his heart was spring:
> He left us in the April of his years.
> He does not ask for sighing or for tears
> Who left when it was still worth lingering . . .

Lawrence Binyon, too old to fight at forty-five and so a spectator when he wrote his 'Ode of Remembrance', famously envies the invulnerability of dead soldiers – 'Age shall not weary them, nor the years contemn . . .' Frank at sixteen, by contrast, elegises his generation who are to die young while identifying with the insouciance of bravery himself. The title, from Goethe's 'Heidenröslein', showcases his already devout internationalism. His poem titles from German, Latin, Greek, Russian, French and Silver Latin have today the unfortunate effect of distancing Frank. He belongs to that remote age when all gentlemen were presumed to share familiarity with the classical canon, and other languages too. His internationalism was one way of demonstrating anti-Fascism.

That a time is coming when every man's mettle will be tested is the theme of the 'Democrat's Defeat' (May 1938), with its strangely scanned long third line:

> Some will gutter and faint in an hour,
> Some will crash at last in the flames
> Having blazed for a while on the sky and men's hearts' amazement
> At the radiance of their fame.

Though the next and last verse asserts that 'the gulf between glory and silence is minute', this qualification seems polite, rather than persuasive. The poem reflects EJ's belief in war dividing the men from the boys.

'When Lovely Woman Stoops to Folly' compares a woman friend's unhappiness on surrendering to a handsome man with a moth burning its wings in a candle:

> Last evening, as I sat reading in the twilight,
> A moth came whirring in, graceful and velvet-sleek,
> Batter'd her soft brown wings against the curtains,
> Half-terrified and brush'd against my cheek.

Although purporting to concern the woman friend with whom, together with her sisters, he had been staying, the thought that really inspired the poem was 'what a shame it wd be if they were all killed in a war'. Without obvious logic, this somehow prompted Frank's simile of the moth's singed wings. The connection between the casualties of love and those of war is not self-evident: the apocalyptic fears of the time dictate it.

'Farewell to Fame' (spring 1937) is a successful lyric gracefully comparing – in a partly Audenesque way – his soul to an aeroplane that crash-lands. Its use of language is witty, its handling of feeling dexterous:

> Stretched out in cool green fields of clover,
> Heart beating hard with earth,

I found it was not stars but flowers
Presided at my birth.

All these poems set the personal against the political, aware that public affairs threaten soon to extinguish the personal.

'On the Extinction of Austria', a poem written the same month as the *Anschluss* (March 1938), has the lines:

The time for resistance is past.
Not a cause but an aeon is dead.
An age, not a nation is plunged in the final darkness
Of the storm-cloud's smothering dread.

For all their immaturity and occasional woodenness, one sees why Frank deserved the title of Chamber Poet. Frank's death-consciousness played another and paradoxical role: that of intensifying his sense of the preciousness of life. He was to remember the 'invasion summer' of 1940 as the most beautiful ever. The sense of jeopardy, which his poems repeatedly explore, always heightened his happiness, like a mountaineer experiencing a rush of elation.

'My Epitaph', of February 1938, sketches his extinction in the spirit of a light-hearted epigrammatist, who – it should be noted – invites not grief at his demise but the mirth, if not applause, of future Wykehamists to whom the cloister belongs. Its cheerful and upbeat treatment of the theme of extinction looks forward to his best-known poem, 'Epitaph for my Friends'.

Here in the sunlit cloister let your mirth
Blend and suffuse my last and sweetest rest.
Laughter and sleep were all I loved on earth;
And now I find the latter far the best.

This jokes about two notable aspects of Frank's character – his love of fun and his laziness ('laughter and sleep') – but above all manifests *sprezzatura*: that pose of studied carelessness valued as typically patrician since Castiglione wrote *The Courtier* in the fifteenth century.

*Sprezzatura*: a form of defensive irony; the ability to disguise what one really feels, thinks and intends behind a mask of apparent reticence and nonchalance. It is brave performance-art, invoking a courage that one might not merely ape in a poem, but live and die by, too, and displaying an easy facility in accomplishing difficult actions which hides the conscious effort that went into them. The difficult action about which Frank nonchalantly teases is dying. He wrote many epitaphs for himself.

---

Both major structures of feeling – comic and gloomy – Frank inherited from his father. Theo believed that EJ's County Wicklow great-grand-mother gave him that 'Irish pessimism' that occasionally disheartened her. But she thought Irishness also the source of the wit and humour he and both their boys shared, leavening the pessimism and making it bearable.

What was Frank's father EJ, that lifelong outsider, doing in the 1930s? His many attempts to find a more secure position finally bore

EJ (*seated fourth from left*) with Oriel Fellows.

fruit when a Senior Research Fellowship at Oriel College was founded for him in 1936, and for three years earned him £250 per year. A string of well-reviewed books had also established his name, and Scar Top became a watering hole for writers, liberal dons and Indian nationalists. He was better off financially, yet continued to look elsewhere. A photograph of him with other convivial Oriel Fellows shows him seated alone and apart. EJ regretted never being elected to the Athenaeum in London: 'English affairs of every kind are run from two or three clubs, and the Athenaeum is where you meet everyone.' It might, he thought, have purchased him more influence.

The title of one poem, 'Repentance for Political Activity', gives a potent clue to his state of mind. Could he have read his own obituaries in 1946, little would have hurt more than the one dismissive sentence, 'He also wrote poetry.' EJ passionately wished to be remembered as Thompson-the-poet. In reality he was known sometimes as Thompson-the-writer but more often as Thompson-the-writer-on-India and political activist. Though in 1932 he published an anthology of religious verse, *O World Invisible*, and in 1935 *A Life of Sir Walter Raleigh*, followed by a biography of Robert Bridges, India was still his main – partly involuntary – focus. When despondent EJ would quip that the mere mention of the word 'India' was enough to empty the smallest hall in Oxford. He was none the less in increasing demand to speak and write about India, often on stage in public debate, importuned alike by literary editors and campaigners of all political hues.

In 1931 he published a sequel to *An Indian Day* entitled *A Farewell to India*. Gandhi himself noted the unconscious irony of this second title. Within a day of landing for the Round Table Conference on India in London in September 1931, Gandhi came to Boars Hill with his famous spinning wheel. A photograph of him at Scar Top survives; whether the pet goat with whom he also travelled was in attendance is not recorded. After Theo had served breakfast to his three followers, she discovered Gandhi-ji himself asleep in front of the drawing-room fire, exhausted from a punishing schedule. Gandhi interrogated EJ as follows:

'They tell me, Mr Thompson, that you have published a book entitled *A Farewell to India?*'

'That is so, Mahatmaji.'

'Well, it seems to me that you have been wasting your time again. How do you think that you are ever going to say farewell to India? You are India's prisoner.'

Gandhi in the Thompsons' garden at Boars Hill during the 1931 Round Table Conference.

'India's prisoner' is apt and eloquent. EP later remembered the hushed, reverent atmosphere in the normally boisterous household when Gandhi visited. The young EP did not doubt but that Indians were their most important visitors: the sideboard laden with grapes and dates plus the exotic postage stamps to be cadged off Indian visitors both attested as much. As for EJ, although he liked and admired Gandhi this did not stop him depicting him in *A Farewell to India* as acting more out of instinct and passion than reason, and later he would sometimes despair of Gandhi's common sense.

Gandhi was none the less accurate in pointing out that EJ's

valediction to India was premature. Following publication of *A Farewell to India* EJ revisited India three times aided by grants from the Rhodes Trustees – in 1932 to survey the vernacular literatures of several provinces; in 1937 to access unpublished material relevant to his book *The Making of the Indian Princes* (1943); finally in late 1939 to report on the political situation on the outbreak of war. His output on India in the 1930s was prodigious, an obsession explored in many different genres.*

In 1935 EJ wrote to Frank: 'On Tues I saw Jawaharlal Nehru who was President of the National Congress in 1929, when they passed their Independence Resolution. A v. tired embittered man, just out of prison and having left a dying wife in Germany.' (Nehru's wife Kamala died weeks later in Lausanne of TB, aged only thirty-seven.) Nehru told EJ he had done an autobiography 'in which he attacks me' and sometimes he launched savage tirades. To soothe him EJ took him to meet that 'old India hand' Herbert Fisher, Warden of New College, who had served as Royal Commissioner in India in 1912–15, and with whom Nehru chatted happily about histories and other books. EJ naively reported to Frank that 'It was what [Nehru] wanted, as an old Harrow & Cambridge bloke who went to India to find the British clubs shut against him.'

The implication that Nehru's deepest resentment in the 1930s was of mere social exclusion says more about EJ than it does about Nehru, whose grandly patrician relatives were fully aware that missionary families like the Thompsons were 'scarcely top-drawer'. Nehru went to prison nine times for agitating for full independence for India, while EJ

---

* His *Reconstructing India* was timed to coincide with the 1930 Simon Report; soon *A Letter from India* (1932), a report on the crisis, was followed by *So a Poor Ghost* (1933), which he termed a seditious pot-boiler. EJ wrote with a new soulmate and India hand, Geoffrey Garratt, *The Rise and Fulfilment of British Rule in India* (1934), an admired history of India since the East India Company's founding in 1599, showing British rule as a succession of unhappy improvisations. And he followed this with two novels drawing on his own family and experience as a Bengal missionary, *Introducing the Arnisons* (1935) and *John Arnison* (1939). Finally he wrote *The Life of Charles, Lord Metcalfe* (1937) about the Liberal Governor-General of Bengal who served 1835–6.

Nehru (*second left*) and EJ (*right*).

held out for Dominion status. So any emollient effect from visiting the
pompous, long-winded Fisher – whose first cousin Virginia Woolf
recorded him as 'so distinguished yet . . . so empty' – can scarcely have
been long-lasting.

Nehru's affection for EJ and his family was none the less real, and
EJ's lifelong gift for friendship and empathy overrode much. On the
Thompsons' backyard cricket pitch Nehru gave EP batting lessons,
doubtless with tips picked up at Harrow and Cambridge. Over the
succeeding years Nehru, even when in prison for sedition against the
Raj, corresponded with the Thompsons, who long held that when
Nehru's daughter Indira Gandhi married, she did so in a sari belonging
to Theo. When EJ published *You Have Lived through All This: An
Anatomy of the Age*, his dedication ran 'To Jawaharlal Nehru: In
Friendship'.

There was always passionate discussion at Scar Top of international
and domestic politics, all the Thompsons appearing formidably intelligent and well informed. Seriousness was none the less leavened with

humour. The family's 1933 Christmas charade featured Hitler in the year of his accession to power, and joked that Pushkin the family cat feared the Nazis might take away his mice. And even during solemn intervals when distinguished Indians visited, EJ also played practical jokes on all his guests – balancing untoward items over doors and planting others in beds.

The in-jokes typifying Thompson home-life were never intended for public scrutiny. Family was 'Fambly', EJ was 'Dadza', and Theo 'The GM' or 'Great Muvverkins' or 'Mwonk', about whose 'terrifying fierceness' many jokes circulated. Talking Cockney and American were staple drolleries. The GM hailed from the United States of 'Amurka' via missionaries in 'Soorya'. Theo herself would ape a strong NY accent when quoting one of her rich aunts on the possibility of cutting Theo's hair: 'What, cut Theo's hair? Why she'd be the ugliest girl in Brooklyn.' Perhaps Theo's fierceness came out of her own womanly unconfidence and exclusion – from Oxford, from Indian affairs.

All Thompsons wrote 'pomes' (many do so today). Frank and EP as teenagers picked up the note of clowning, Frank writing to his younger brother 'To Ugliface from Handsome', 'Dear Ship-mate' and 'You horrible Beast', signing off 'wiv plenny of lurv' and, once, 'Hippopotamus'. EJ's punning could be heavy-handed: Robert Graves was the 'Sepulchral Bob', to distinguish him from Robert Bridges the 'Pontine Bob'. More embarrassing are his inept attempts to claim friendship by referring to Betjeman as 'Jack' Betjeman, Churchill's son Randolph as 'Randy', and the film-maker Michael Powell, with whom EJ hobnobbed during the war (when Powell's partnership with Emeric Pressburger made both famous), successively as 'Mick Powell' and then as 'Mike Powell', making painfully clear how threadbare such acquaintanceships really were. Hopkins, to whose poetry his boys were partial, becomes 'Gerry' Hopkins. On meeting Lady Ottoline Morrell's husband Sir Philip to discuss Lord William Bentinck, he 'wangled' a tea at Garsington, the Morrells' Oxfordshire house, for Theo.

Of course what Victorians termed EJ's tuft-hunting (social

climbing) is easy to mock.* The insecurity behind name-dropping probably fuelled his boys' compassion; they were a close family and understood EJ's particular, painful struggle. He was also a good father, was a tireless friend to India, tried to be a kind husband and was generous to other talents. Both Frank and EP were powerfully influenced by their parents' interests and attitudes. Albeit that in politics they would soon part company, both shared their father's passionate love of literature. Both loved their father while seeing that the liberal synthesis he represented was in worldwide crisis.

During 1938 EJ spent time cultivating Alexander Korda, who wished to film EJ's novel *Burmese Silver* and, before departing for Hollywood that Christmas, offered EJ a one-year retainer. They thought of moving to a large rectory at Lewknor, midway between Denham film studios and Oxford, with a grass tennis court ruined by local lads using it for cricket. There was a five-acre paddock – 'it's all very large & will cost a lot to run'. Little came of this.

———

Frank finally left Winchester during the Easter break to join an Aegean tour, with lectures from Hugh Casson – a Greek odyssey EP would repeat one year later. Though only seventeen Frank seems older: fellow Brits ask him where he is teaching, and Greeks (as we have seen) where his wife is. He writes home, independent-mindedly, 'Some people are going to dig in Crete in May and I may go with them. Not sure how I will get back to England, but will let you know.' He fancied he might want to be an archaeologist. Or a diplomat. He left the tour group behind in Athens and was away in the end for three months. His sheer irresponsible, infectious love of life, and

* As against this reading, Frank's niece Kate writes (letter to author): 'His use of familiar names . . . [is] more likely to be facetious than ingratiating . . . He idolised no one. His criticisms of people, particularly of those who were believed to be above criticism, often got him into trouble. Although in some ways he took himself extremely seriously, he also had the ability to laugh at himself, and to tell stories against himself (often misunderstood), and no one who came into his orbit was beyond the same treatment. (Viz. the door traps set on visiting Indian dignitaries etc.)'

ability to turn his adventures to tough-minded comedy, is everywhere in his letters home.

After contriving an empty carriage much of the way to Venice apart from one 'bloke' opposite 'with a face like a rather lewd haddock', they crossed the Alps where the Italians behaved with their usual inefficient bravado. 'They collected everybody's passport three times . . . gave us tremendous documents to sign, and then handed them back stamped, without bothering to look at them.' He could not take the Fascist Italian seriously as a systematic viper: more as an elemental, misguided clown.

On their first day in Attica Frank and company were much struck by the fierce Greek arguing. 'It seemed so new & strange' to them, and they were 'convulsed with laughter'. Laughter recurs. In Athens he stayed on a camp-bed in the British School library and during the magnificent Easter processions bought a Roman candle which the vendor assured him could safely be held in the hand. On igniting this of course backfired immediately, knocking Frank flat, then 'slithering venomously along the road and exploding across the street where it nearly killed two women and a policeman . . .' At Delphi 'We laughed at everybody and everybody came out and laughed at us.' At Pergamon in Turkey there was 'uneasy laughter' too. His trip continued in this vein; he claimed never to meet a Greek peasant over forty who didn't make him want to 'laugh himself sick'.

Frank uses the phrase 'laughing himself sick' perversely to betoken laughing *with*, never laughing *at*, something that implied a sense of proportion, and sympathy. It was a token of shared humanity, a high compliment. The premium Frank put on laughter is remarkable. When one friend wrote after his death that laughter followed Frank 'as closely as his shadow', this was more than conventional condolence. It was not only his own jokes that mattered: he enjoyed others' too. Laughter combined for Frank the gratifications that the religious get from celebrating the Mass, with a sense of almost physical release, fellowship, close communion. This helps explain some of the intensity of his feelings for Greece, which twice influenced his choice of unit during the war. He longed to return to the land of joyous laughter that reflected

– as he saw it – free and courageous spirits; he never felt so happy as among Greeks.

Frank's humorous ease with others went with groundedness. He discerned that a Greek ex-filmstar they uncovered on board, travelling incognito nominally because she was famous, in reality simply feared revealing her age – in Frank's words 'A cattier reason' for dissembling. Then, accosted by some very intense Brits, and before understanding that they are 'enemies' – evangelistic Oxford Groupers on a mission – he 'hands over most of my key-positions'. When they require his name he blurts out, in a sudden rush of insanity, 'Michael Foot'* – another Wykehamist going up to Oxford. Finally in Athens he finds it hard to shake off '10 grinning Greeks' who have already exchanged addresses with him. But this feat he managed.

Love of nature travelled with him too, just as it did his father and brother. Outside Basle he records cowslips and gentians; at the Lion Gate at Mycenae a kind of bee orchid (a species beloved by his father) quite new to him. Near Corfu he 'arrested a flower under strong suspicion of being a red helleborine and detained it for closer examination'. At Delphi he records the great profusion of fading blue squills, vetches and Compositae, and much more.

That he mostly felt at home in Greece – among its flowers, people and monuments – is clear. He was an adherent of the Philhellenism that has ornamented British life for centuries. One of its premises was that the ancient Greece of Pericles and the modern Greece of the dictator General Metaxas are – if not identical – continuous. Though his passionate wish to serve in Greece was frustrated, this hypothesis fascinated Frank. His final letters in 1944 to and from his brother touch on modern Greek.

The question was primarily linguistic. Frank pointed at objects and tried out the ancient Greek word in modern pronunciation, which worked nine times out of ten – though not for common things such as house, flower, bird. He noted the same nebulosity about special names

---

* Michael Foot is throughout not the politician but his distant cousin M. R. D. Foot, at Winchester and New College with Frank, and later a leading expert on SOE.

Parthenon 1938, Frank in foreground (*right*).

that the Greeks had in Pericles' time: every flower and bird named not by its species name but only as 'flower' and 'bird'. Then a Greek employed in the American excavations of the Agora told him they had found a bottle of wine from the first century BC, and – with a wink – that when he drank some it was (improbably) 'very good'. Athens was a second-rate modern city, Frank thought, but with its Parthenon still belonged to the ancient Greeks.

There were other and unexpected reminders of the ancient Greek past. He gives comic descriptions of modern life aboard ship, with two men in his cabin vomiting from sea-sickness from around Samothrace to the Negropont and Artimisium until he recalls that precisely here the whole Persian fleet was wrecked. At Olympia he sees that the ecstasies of Pindar – that beloved 'mercenary hack-journalist' – about its beauty are not exaggerated. The high point is Cape Sounion: wonderfully clear blue water, calm and deep immediately you left the rocks – an ideal spot both for bathing and for the ancient temple to Poseidon, dazzlingly white against the fine panorama on all sides: to the north-east the mountains of Euboea and the islands of Andros and Tinos, and to the south-west the Argolid and the Saronic Gulf.

For much of May he worked hard digging on Crete with John Pendlebury, an athlete who had lost one eye but like Frank a Wykehamist, free spirit and would-be writer. Cretans, Frank decided, were a fine set of men, unspoiled by tourists, tough, kind, humorous. On the voyage there Frank had twenty sailors dancing round shouting while he selected some chocolate and 'had the satisfaction of holding up the whole boat'. Frank was charmed especially by the old men in their grey mustachios, craggy breeches, with huge tail pockets to keep parcels in, thick top-boots, large purple cummerbunds, neat blue embroidered jackets – sometimes even turbaned heads: they had expelled their Turkish overlords only in 1898. He liked the dialect and put up with the squalor of village life: few drains, many cattle, cats, chickens, pigs, goats and donkeys all billeted in the street. Despite Mrs Pendlebury's best efforts, his lodgings were ineradicably verminous. The bug-bite swellings itched for three days.

The Palace at Knossos, he aptly quipped of his neighbour Sir Arthur Evans's famously fantastical reconstructions, was less Cretan than Concretan. Evans had recommended Frank to Pendlebury. Pendlebury told Frank funny stories of Sir Arthur and they exchanged light verse and 'a lot of happy memories' of Winchester. Pendlebury noted that Frank's puppyish lunacy combined with 'a good deal of common sense. His father is the writer on India.' (To take one example of Marx Brothers humour: Frank had decided that he had about as much chance of a good Balliol scholarship 'as a whelk winning the Men's singles at Wimbledon'.) Pendlebury also noted Frank's rapid clipped speech, a symptom of nervous intensity.

Frank helped Pendlebury at Karphi dig the city where Cretans fled the invading Greeks, with its sumptuous cemetery on the slopes below; here Pendlebury had found Minoan goddesses and Geometric vases. Excavation gave Frank joy – watching a wall work itself out, washing special vases in acid, cleaning and (less thrilling but more restful) sorting and fitting shards into whole pots. Frank boasted that he acquired a varied if shallow view of Greek archaeology. He also boasted

that Pendlebury left him for some days in undisputed command over-
seeing six remaining workmen – one of whom he saved twice from
scorpions. Here at the house down in the plain they uncovered a terra-
cotta dolphin-and-rider, red-figure duck vases and over one hundred
loom weights. Ancient mod cons at the house impressed Frank: a stone
corner seat, stone terraces, tetragons resembling modern Greek slaugh-
tering troughs that might have been for washing.

Though they worked a long day from 6 a.m. to 6 p.m. they made
time, too, for a pilgrimage to Zeus' birthplace – the Dictaean Cave at
Psychro. The motor car had been unknown in this part of Crete until
two years before. Despite the 'inevitable' fig tree and wild roses decorat-
ing the huge dark cavern, Frank quipped that Zeus on the whole had
better taste than he expected. The mountains were still snow-capped
when he left in early June.

Pendlebury's snapshot from behind of a hatted Frank leaving the
village on his last day shows a primitive village street. On his last night
Frank prepared brandy butter especially so that Pendlebury and he
could enjoy an Old Wykehamist dinner with tinned plum pudding.

John Pendlebury Papers, BSA Archive. Reproduced
with the permission of the British School at Athens

They drank the toast 'Stet Res Wiccamica', but Pendlebury couldn't remember the words to 'Domum' nor Frank the tune. Frank liked Pendlebury, finding him forceful, excitable and magnanimous – qualities he shared.

Pendlebury confided that he had had a forlorn face from birth 'exactly like the archaic smile one finds on early Greek statues'. Connoisseurs of dramatic irony might think such sadness fitting, and Pendlebury predicted to Frank his own role in the coming conflict. He would make a conscious decision to risk his life, training in a British intelligence section which was a precursor of SOE before returning to Crete, where he would famously be shot dead working heroically for the Resistance, aged thirty-six, in May 1941. Frank noted admiringly soon after: 'It is difficult to think of a higher crown for human achievement.'* He is buried in the Allied war cemetery at Souda Bay.

After visiting the graves of Keats and Shelley (and much else) in Rome Frank arrived back on 24 June wearing a blue coat and trousers in which he had slept, eaten, drunk and dug for the best part of twelve weeks, much stained and looking the worse for wear. He hoped to get to an Eton and Harrow cricket match the following day, at which event – he reassured his parents – he had always been as faultlessly attired as a member of the Drones Club. That same week, however, he threatened EP that he would visit Kingswood School, where EJ was to preach, sporting an orange tie and purple jacket, so that the whole school got a chance to admire the beauty of his colour scheme: 'LAUGH THAT OFF!'

---

* 19 November 1941: 'A bad piece of news. I'm afraid John Pendlebury is almost certainly dead. If so, he died performing a task which he prophesied to me three and a half years ago, and which will be revealed to his everlasting credit when the war is over . . . As the Cretans are the toughest kindest and most humorous people I have ever met, it is difficult to think of a higher crown for human achievement.'

# Oxford in the Age of Heroes: 1938–9

Even Patroklus died and I must die,
Morning or evening or at blazing noon . . .
from 'Death of Lykaon', written August 1938

If you should hear my name among those killed,
Say you have lost a friend, half man, half boy . . .
from 'To Irushka at the Coming of War', written 10 July 1939

On his final night in Rome in June 1938, after a farewell dinner in a
Jewish restaurant with plenty to drink, Frank next day could not recall
how he had got back to his hotel. He overslept and missed the train to
London. He was still seventeen, and tales of his getting fighting drunk
and passing out would continue until he left Britain for good in March
1941. At Oxford that autumn he failed to turn up to read the lesson in
morning chapel.* On 19 November 1938 he wrote to EP (whose own
release from tension came from cigarettes, not from drink)† with a
perfectly intolerable headache after the previous night trying to teach

---

* At New College scholars were required to read the lesson; both M. R. D. Foot and
Frank declared themselves agnostic; Frank, as if to make doubly sure, got drunk
and overslept.
† EJ to Frank: '[EP] is almost a Puritan in many ways. He never touches alcohol except
an occasional cider, detesting beer and keeping off spirits. His constant cigarettes are
rather a sign of nervousness seeking release' (5 Aug. 1943, UNC).

the New College porter to box, before a mixture of whisky and martini made him violently sick.

Instances accumulate. The first time Iris spotted Frank he was very drunk and lying flat on his back in the entrance hall of the Union with his head inside the telephone box. Referring to the bad beer likely to be served Frank in Egypt, Iris in 1941 wrote to his mother, 'But I suspect that he couldn't tell one drink from another.' This appears to have been more than commonplace youthful rebelliousness: his parents feared that Frank might become alcoholic.*

M. R. D. Foot had accepted his grandmother's bribe of £100 – over half his £180 annual allowance – if he neither smoked nor drank. This may account for the sober clarity with which he recalled Frank's undergraduate pub crawls, and the frequency with which he was called upon to rescue him. You were allowed to drink in college – four pints in an evening was not unusual – but not in pubs. Frank drank often none the less at the Nag's Head in Hythe Bridge Street by the canal. One night he had had more than enough and leaving the Lamb and Flag on St Giles at 11 p.m. with Michael, he saw the traffic lights on the Broad were at stop. Frank said, 'That damned bloody red I'll smash his face.' As he climbed the traffic light it changed to green; he collapsed in the quad and had to be carried to bed. It may have been the same evening Frank recalled Michael pouring a stream of cold water over him to sober him up, while next day the university Proctor, after rebuking him for being considerably the worse for wear, tried to swear him to temperance. When he and a friend were thrown out of a cinema because of Frank's cat-calls it is possible that Frank was in his cups. In June 1939 during his final week in Oxford he was certainly drunk.

He had a *nature riche*, from which some instinct for self-preservation seems missing. There was the Junior Common Room meeting that Michael asked to have adjourned on the grounds that 'On a point of order, Mr Chairman, Mr Thompson is on fire.' He had put his lighted pipe into his left-hand jacket pocket, a trick he pulled off again after

---

* He noted as much in 1943, saying his vice was more likely to be girls.

visiting his Oxford friend Leo Pliatzky at his family home in Bow. Leo
last sighted him on that occasion pausing during his run for the tram,
thumping vigorously at his smoking jacket.

Laddish antics apart, *why* was Frank self-destructive? Partly exhibi-
tionism, while something too was owed to his prophetic certainty about
what the political tensions of the times portended for him. His poems
continue to record political catastrophe – the extinction first of Austria,
then of Spain – and remain grimly visionary. In 'Death of Lykaon' he
imagines a Homeric hero who, remembering the laughter of boys in
meadows where last year he played, is simultaneously Frank himself:

> Even Patroklus died and I must die.
> Morning or evening or at blazing noon,
> With pointed spears or skilful archery,
> My fate will come, is coming, all too soon.

What pains or disturbances does this public surrender to 'fate'
attempt to escape? Theo's offhand remark about having nearly broken
Frank's spirit is haunting and horrible. 'Stop apologising,' his friends
would tell him, and when on a Cairo tram some drunken soldiers broke
Frank's finger his comment – 'Can't say I blame them' – seems over-
forgiving. (His attempt to discipline them was rewarded by their trying
to pitch him through the tram window.) Family tensions played their
part in his willingness to embrace suffering. When Frank playfully signs
off a humorous letter to Forster 'Life is hell,' he is being half-serious
too. But if there were rows at home about his drinking, no evidence
survives. From March 1939 there were in any case new matters to argue
about at home. He had fallen in love with a wholly unsuitable young
Irishwoman called Iris Murdoch and, during the same week, she had
talked him into joining the Communist Party.

---

There were many Wykehamists up at Oxford with him. Michael Foot
and Frank were both at New College, on different staircases and reading different subjects. In a malicious memoir of his time at Winchester

Frank indicates that he and Michael – known because he was pretty as 'Tootles' – had not at school been really sympathetic. Frank liked to appear lazy and shabby, his belongings always in a mess; Michael, energetic, tidy, staid and aloof, kept everything sorted and docketed, including one file labelled in large letters 'Own Works', and had edifying quotations pinned above his desk. One July Frank turned out to watch a thunderstorm, until a rhythmic tap-tap from an upstairs window made him understand that Michael was by contrast typing a poem in the heat of inspiration. Moreover Michael at school championed the learning of German and it would become fluent enough to assist him when captive in 1944. Frank, while he learned German too, preferred the freedoms of Russian. The implication is both clear and unkind: Frank perceives himself as wild, bohemian and authentic, Michael as conventional and hidebound. Moreover Frank believed that Michael stimulated his emotions deliberately to make melodramatic capital out of them, a charge to which Frank's poems are not immune.

Michael in his turn thought Frank a romantic ass of the most engaging kind, gauche and tactlessly direct without being shy, but lacking social experience. Something about him connected less with the real world than with a private dream-time; and Frank felt he had a duty to correct the misapprehensions of others. This clash was partly political. Frank, according to Foot, believing in the USSR's 1936 Constitution, became a libertarian Bolshevik who missed the clause that gave the Party power to override everybody else – even the Constitution – and so set up the Gulag. Tony Forster, by contrast, less troubled by Frank's further left-wing swing at Oxford, thought Frank got on well with others and wasn't dreamy.

Frank and Michael in their first term at Oxford marched from the British Museum down to the Spanish Embassy, which was then in the south-east corner of Belgrave Square, each holding one pole of a banner marked 'Arms for Spain'. They wanted to persuade the Government to sell anti-aircraft guns to the Republic for the defence of Barcelona, saying defensive weapons were not covered by the prevailing British policy of non-intervention. Then both were tellers in statutory white tie and tails at the Union debate on the motion 'That this House would go to war for Danzig', which was comfortably carried by four to one – an outcome unreported in the press. Hitler remembered the notorious 1933 Union debate instead: 'That this House will in no circumstances fight for its King and Country', passed by 275 votes to 153.

———

Jimmy Porter in *Look Back in Anger* in 1956 would famously lament the post-war lack of Good Causes to live or die for. Those at Oxford in 1938–9 suffered no such privation: rarely has any generation been so passionately and intensely engaged. The Spanish Civil War did not end until April 1939 and was, Frank wrote, 'so real that it hurt'. He attended in one week a farcical meeting in the Town Hall with Stafford Cripps, where £150 was raised to help feed Spanish refugees, and a Spain Social organised by the Peace Council, Frank making, then selling for three-pence, lemonade that cost a farthing a glass. They 'made a lot of money for Spain'.

The mystique and glamour of that final year of peace is not simply a product of retrospective nostalgia. Hope and fear, dread and anxiety all raised the temperature of life, lending to love, friendship and politics alike a rare intensity. Here were students who knew their chances of surviving to twenty-five were slim, who – as Iris would write to Frank – were 'master of their fate and captain of their soul', living 'vividly, individually, wildly, beautifully'. The Munich crisis made war for some weeks seem imminent, until its last-minute postponement. Not for long. The first apocalyptic air war was widely expected, with millions of casualties.

Neville Chamberlain had just betrayed the Czechs, abjectly surren-dering to Hitler's bullying ultimatum at a meeting at which Czechoslovakia was not even represented. Nehru, then in Prague himself, wrote to EJ warning him about the crisis. Within weeks of Frank's arrival the famous Munich by-election was called in Oxford, seen as a vote of confidence in the Prime Minister and his policy of appeasing Fascism. Quintin Hogg, flamboyant and ill-mannered, stood for the Conservatives against the Popular Front candidate 'Sandy' Lindsay, Master of Balliol and the first confessed socialist to head an Oxford college. Passions ran high.

Frank pretended to be a press reporter (he represented a student paper called *Living Newspaper*), mass-observing North Oxford people's attitude to the crisis and noting the look of hatred that came into people's eyes when you announced that you were a journalist. Like Ted Heath, Roy Jenkins, Denis Healey and Iris Murdoch, he canvassed for Lindsay; he got booted out from more than one house exhorting people to vote. He also addressed envelopes, delivered handbills, acted as sandwich-man for two hours advertising a trades union demonstration, and secured Sir Arthur Evans's signature for a protest letter to the *Oxford Mail*. Theo, until stopped by a policeman, drove round Oxford in procession with 'Save Peace, Save Czechoslovakia' pasted over the family car. 'A vote for Hogg is a vote for Hitler' read another placard. EJ was writing letters to everyone 'ticking them off', and addressing sometimes empty meetings. Frank wrote to EP a cod letter purporting to be from Lord Beaverbrook, so-called first baron of Fleet Street, to Sir Samuel Hoare, pro-Appease-ment Conservative politician, ending up with a cartoon of a cat in a scrum-cap and joking that 'The Thompson family have made their attitude clear from the start.' (He had been playing a bit of everything – hockey, soccer and rugby. He had grown to six foot with broad shoulders and thick hammy hands, tall, clumsy, still physically a buffoon. But even though big and gangly and 'with ten thumbs', his coordination was evidently improving: he scored two tries for the 2nd XV and even played on occasion for the 1st XV.)

Hogg won by a small majority of 15,797 to Lindsay's 12,363. The defeated Lindsay supporters with their tattered red and yellow rosettes, Frank recorded, confronted the Conservatives in St Aldate's in their horsey tweed coats, with their carnations and rolled umbrellas, who, they felt, rushed to sneer and crow at them 'as if after a day's beagling, or a night in London'. Frank always identified political reaction with blood sports. That not all his friends were like-minded was forgiven: Gabriel Carritt used once to ride to the Berkshire Hunt; Rex Campbell

Saunders Close, Bledlow.

Thompson shot grouse near Oban. But those dearest to Frank – as to his father – were at least in principle herbivorous. His parents had that August moved to a smaller house in Bledlow, a Buckinghamshire village chosen in part because of its relative absence of the hunting fraternity.

Lindsay's by-election defeat was a bad omen. 'What depressed us was that obscurantism had triumphed.' On the Lindsay side were 'the creative, the generous, the imaginative. In the other we saw only selfishness, stodginess and insincerity.' 'A friend bitterly remarked, "I hope North Oxford gets the first bombs, but it would be rough on the Pekinese."' Michael Foot added presciently that there were only two alternatives now – to join the Communist Party or abdicate from politics – and Michael could not swallow Communism.

They were still brooding on the by-election defeat in winter 1939 when Frank got involved in co-writing and putting on a play entitled *It Can Happen Here*, set in an imaginary concentration camp in Christ Church Meadow, where Jews and dissident liberals were interned, with flashbacks, one to the Lindsay Committee Rooms at the by-election.

There were six hectic weeks of brainstorming, script conferences and rehearsals. On 28 February Frank wrote: 'Our play is picking up. It may just shamble into shape in time.'

He collected information on Dachau, which had opened in 1933, and Buchenwald, in 1937. The gassings would not begin for two more years: inmates were starved, tortured and worked to death. The premise of the play was that Fascism had come to Oxford. Learning Anglo-Saxon to emphasise a shared Aryan race-mythology was now compulsory for all: an imaginative touch. The petty law-enforcing Proctors had their own stormtroopers, and the 'Noes' door at the Union was blocked up because free speech had been abolished. The play was put on at 8.15 p.m. on 6 March 1939, admission price 6d, in St Michael's Hall to a (largely) Labour Club audience, and was well received. Although futuristic and intended to be more grim than farcical, the play elicited laughter too. Frank had a dialogue with a girl saying something like 'You never give me any encouragement: how can a man be expected to do anything?' Everyone laughed: that sort of line suited Frank. The Labour Club

The Oxford University Labour Club

**DRAMA GROUP**

presents

═══ "IT CAN ═══

HAPPEN HERE"

at

ST. MICHAEL'S HALL

(Main Hall, New-Inn-Hall Street)

on Monday, March 6th, 1939

at 8.15 p.m.

Admission by Programme, 6d.

was reputed to have the best women, with whom temporary 'line-ups' might sometimes develop into an affair.* Frank hoped to find a girl, and within days was acting out this role of lover-frustrated-by-his-muse in real life.

———————

Frank had noticed and been impressed by Iris at a Labour Club meeting at Queen's College in November, listening to Stephen Spender give a woolly speech about Spain and 'the poet in politics'. Munich, he wrote, 'still filled us with a deep restless anger'. The hall which Spender described, foolishly, as a 'glorified railway station' was packed and steaming. Students were sitting on the tables and the floor. Frank managed to squeeze on to a bench against a wall where, possibly in drink, he fitfully dozed. When he awoke he noticed at the table in front of him a girl leaning on her elbow. She wasn't pretty and her figure was too thick to be good.

> But there was something about her warm green dress, her long yellow locks like a cavalier's, and her gentle profile, that gave a pleasing impression of harmony. My feeling of loneliness redoubled. Why didn't I know anyone like that? I saw her again at a Labour Club Social, dancing, – perhaps 'waddling' is a better word, with some poisonous-looking bureaucrat. It wasn't until the middle of next term that I got a chance to speak to her.

There is a welcome absence of rhetorical afflatus in this first impression. Iris's absence of prettiness, tendency to plumpness and 'waddling' dance are all calmly recorded. Yet there is also a 'pleasing impression of harmony', one that struck him again when he finally met her the following March, and the affinity he felt between them was put to the test.

———

* Denis Healey recounts the fury caused in the OULC (Labour Club) by Tom Harrison, founder of Mass Observation and then at Cambridge, with his savage essay on what he called 'Oxsex', which Healey thought 'not unfair' (*The Time of my Life*, London, 1989, p. 32).

Frank (who acted 'Dennis Fairlie' in *It Can Happen Here*) and Leo Pliatzky (poor, cynical, good at insolence, who wrote but did not act) went on a pub crawl that night of 6 March 1939, ending up with a 12s 6d bottle of whisky in the producer Doug Lowe's rooms in Ruskin College. Leonie Marsh (who also acted) had seen to it that Iris, 'the dream-girl to whom I'd never spoken', was with them. Leonie had a double interest in bringing Frank there: she found him attractive, and she had told Iris the previous term, 'There's Frank Thompson, a most remarkable man. We must get him into the Party.'

Frank learned just before meeting her that Iris was a classicist, something he had 'never dared to hope'. Lowe now informed Frank that Iris was 'a nice girl, and *pretty easy too*, from wot I 'ear': Lowe conceiving himself an expert, boasting 'Oi never tike a girl to the pichers, unless its definitely understood that she wants penis afterwards and Oi said to m'self, *there's a short trip for the SS penis there.*' Frank, too, delighted in bawdiness. But such boasting was wishful thinking on Lowe's part: Iris's promiscuous period came later, after she left Oxford. For now, with icy determination, she was set on hanging on to her virginity until after she had gained a First.

Doug Lowe, on one side of the bed in Ruskin College on which Iris reclined, started to 'paw' her. Frank, on the other, wanted to stroke her too. 'Anyone would want to stroke Iris.' Indeed a 'witty liberal' was trying to edge Frank out. But as Frank could see that Iris did not wish to be pawed, and wanting to make a good impression first time despite being pretty drunk, he grew solemn and started on politics.

EJ's left-leaning liberalism had hitherto influenced Frank. Their painter-neighbour Hilda Harrisson had taken the Thompsons to meet Lord Asquith in retirement at Sutton Courtney, and EJ, though he would vote Labour in 1945, still considered himself a Liberal of sorts. Frank first sighted Iris on the day he became College secretary of the Liberal Club, while he met her in the flesh in the week that he resigned on the grounds that the Liberal Club was 'too frivolous', while the Liberals thought Frank too socialist. But he had no use for the Labour leaders either. Iris asked provocatively, 'What about the Communist Party?'

Iris's question astonished him. Frank's comment after attending a CP tea party during his first term* – 'I think that English Communists are really rather sweet' – resembles a Mitford girl's, while a College row that February between Trotskyites and Communists seemed 'as barren and fatuous as schisms within the early Christian church'.

> I was dumbstruck. I'd never thought of it before. Right then I couldn't see anything against it, but I felt it would be wise to wait till I'd sobered up before deciding. So I said, 'Come to tea in a couple of days and convert me.' Then I staggered home and lay on a sofa . . . announcing to the world that I had met a stunner of a girl and was joining the Communist party for love of her. But next morning it still seemed good. I read [Lenin's] *State and Revolution*, talked to several people, and soon made up my mind.

By the time Iris came to tea, in his very untidy room with, typically, Liddell and Scott always open on the table, and a large teddy bear and a top hat on the mantelpiece and 'Voi che sapete' all too aptly playing on his gramophone ('You know what thing is love, ladies – See whether I have it in my heart'), there was no need for a conversion. 'My meeting her was only the point at which quantitative change gave place to change in quality.' Frank pondered: 'maybe I needed to meet her, to realise how gentle and artistic communists can be. Or maybe I needed to be drunk, so I could consider the question with an open mind.' Leonie welcomed him into the Party with a 'dramatic gesture, saved by a wicked smile'. Frank wrote to Tony Forster a long jocular letter with some crucial sentences thrown away at the end: 'Incidentally I've met my dream-girl – a poetic Irish Communist who's doing Honour Mods. I worship her.' 'Worship' was the mot juste, implying the distance that renders a *princesse lointaine*, however attractive, ultimately safe.

Much linked Frank and Iris, not merely youthful inexperience and the unusual simplicity friends observed in each. Both were apprentice writers who that April of 1939 wrote bad poems on the fall of Spain to

---

* Addressed by Abe Lazarus (a friend of the Carritts) who in 1937 just missed being elected as a Communist to the Oxford City Council for the Cowley ward.

Franco. Both took a bohemian and romantic view of the world, and both loved those lines from *Julius Caesar* – 'If we do meet again, why, we shall smile; / If not, why then, this parting was well made' – resonant lines in the run-up to a world war. Both were pantheists with a belief in little local gods and both contested imperialism. Iris had been briefly at school with Nehru's daughter Indira Gandhi, and in a piece in the university newspaper *Cherwell* noted English condescension towards both Irish and Indians.* Frank, whose father frequently compared India's struggle for independence with Ireland's, and who spent August 1938 in Ireland with his family, will have sympathised.

Iris identified fiercely with Irish nationalism and claimed Anglo-Irish ancestry through her Richardson mother's family, with its erstwhile big houses in County Tyrone. Her family had come down in the world. Her maternal aunt Gertie Bell was an alcoholic married to a Dublin car mechanic, three of whose sons worked as fitter, storeman and long-distance lorry driver for Cadbury's, and Iris was the first of her family to acquire higher education. She believed – unreliably – that she had lived in Ireland for her first two years and the brogue she affected was borrowed from her parents. She was given to unlikely imprecations for an Irish Protestant such as 'Holy Mother of God'. Iris Murdoch was a tough-minded woman whose enemies claimed she was coated with ice.

---

The group associated with *It Can Happen Here* took to 'knocking about together': Frank, Leonie Marsh, Leo, Iris and also Michael Foot. 'That was a bad passage, the first fortnight of the 1939 summer term,' wrote Frank:

> Like something in rather poor taste by de Musset. I was pining green for Iris, who was gently sympathetic but not at all helpful. Michael was lashing himself into a frenzy for Leonie [Marsh] who would draw him

* The Irish, she claimed, came of older, darker and holier stock than the English and possessed a sense of tragedy, while the Englishman had only a sense of propriety; so Shakespeare and Keats, she light-heartedly contended, were of course both Irish. See 'The Irish: Are They Human?', *Cherwell*, June 1939, collected in Yozo Muroya and Paul Hullah (eds), *Iris Murdoch: Occasional Essays*, Okayama, 1998, pp. 12–16.

on and then let him down with a thud. In the evenings we would swap
sorrows and read bits of Verlaine to each other.

There is something willed about all such infatuation, as well as something involuntary. When Frank wrote in one poem to Iris ('Himeros')
of wishing to lay his head in her lap and weep away his troubles, or in
another to her ('Defeat') 'To feel your hair caress my cheeks, and rest /
Til death on the soft fullness of your breast', he is invoking a Keatsian
beloved whose alarming remoteness recalls his mother's. Both Iris and
Theo could express warmth in letters; neither did so easily in person. A
retrospective 1943 poem Iris drafted but never sent to Frank contains
the lines 'folded in your room, your story and your arms' while her
quietly beating heart judged 'the long distance' between them. Probably
a chaste embrace was all he achieved. Intensity like Frank's can repel.

Frank spent three whole days that May walking round and round
New College gardens, observing the chestnuts bearing their white
candles, the pink tulips and blue forget-me-nots, in intervals between
writing Iris letters and tearing them up. He wrote her bad poems
expressing 'calf-love'.* Iris 'with her gentleness and her simplicity' was
the person from whom he wanted to hear good news about himself.
'But Iris never told a lie yet, so I got worse and worse.' His friends
watched in baffled unease. He stopped sleeping, started talking to
himself, gardening, going for walks, climbing trees. Michael hid Frank's
cut-throat razor from him. Leo, less melodramatic, more down-to-
earth and sexually confident, invited him to dinner. When, one evening,
Iris disappeared into Doug Lowe's rooms in Ruskin, Frank was in such
a bad way that he escaped to spend a week at home. On the practical

---

* For example, 'Himeros' (the god of uncontrollable desire): 'Putting down my pen, I
looked out into the garden / At the chestnuts thoughtfully budding; the tired wall /
Exulting silently in the evening; the grass / Still like a pool beneath a waterfall. / A white
cat ambled along the wall and vanished; / In the quadrangle someone was laughing;
once again / It hopped up to bask in the sunlight. Nothing would answer / The scum of
anger simmering in my brain. / Then suddenly something cracked. My heart went
numb. / My rage, frustration and hate all dropped asleep. / I thought of you. I knew that
you would not come. / And I longed to lie with my head on your knees and weep.'

advice of Theo, who had ambitions for her sons' marriages, he dug up an entire bed of irises as a counter-charm. Other things cheered him. There was the 'big joyous world of his friends, not only political ones'. He found comfort in the idylls of Theocritus, especially the tenth, 'The Reapers', which features a lovesick youth, and in the love-poets Bion and Moschus, whom he quoted to Iris 'exuberantly'.

Michael Foot was crazy about Leonie, who adored Frank, who was hopelessly in love with Iris. If Iris had then loved Michael, which happened later, that would then have made a perfect quartet of frustrated desire, like that in Act III of *A Midsummer Night's Dream*, and doubtless one blueprint – there would be others – for the love-vortices of her novels. Of this unhappy love quartet, Frank joked in a parody of Marxist-Leninist Newspeak: 'It's not shortage of resources that's the problem, comrades. It's maldistribution of supplies.'

Scarcity of resources, however, played its part. The ratio of men to women at Oxford at that time exceeded six to one, so that girl undergraduates regularly received attentions disproportionate to their charms. Among those paying court to buxom, fresh-faced, dirndl-clad and still very blonde Iris Murdoch were Leo Pliatzky, his gentle, dopey friend Noel Martin, kind, warm-hearted, undiplomatic Hal Lidderdale and – once he had recovered from Leonie – Michael Foot. Iris played the role of Zuleika Dobson in Max Beerbohm's famous 1911 novel of that name: men fell in love with her seemingly on sight, while she stayed impervious.

Frank was a front-runner. A schoolfriend of Frank's, never in love with her, believed that it was her spiritual quality that gave Iris her appeal; she had, all her life, an extraordinary quality of stillness and attentiveness.

---

Frank had suffered two *coups de foudre* together. He fell in love during the same week with Iris and with Communism: two flights of irrationality, it might be said, and two simultaneous conversion experiences. Sexual frustration played its part in the first, political frustration in the second. The Conservative Party, containing some who were actively pro-German, was irretrievably sullied by appeasement, the Labour Party by pacifism until 1935 and by resistance to conscription thereafter. Any undergraduate determined to stop Hitler was easy game for the Communist Party.

The extent of Communist penetration at Oxford is remarkable. The Labour Party in 1935 had permitted fusion of the Communist and Socialist societies at the universities and there were close links between the OULC and the CP headquarters on Hythe Bridge Street. The Labour Club, dominated by Communists, had over 1,000 members; nearly all its committee members were in the CP. But then all of the committees of the League of Nations Union, of the Liberal Club and of the Student Christian Movement, two of the five Conservative Club committee members and even two of the ten members of the British Union of Fascists committee were also in the CP. It helps give the atmosphere of the times to point out that Robert Conquest, while an open Communist, was a member of the university's Carlton Club, with the full approval of both bodies, and that the CP included John Biggs-Davison, later Chairman of the right-wing Monday Club.

Idealism, romanticism and a passionate anti-Fascism came together to move the best of a generation left-wards, into the Popular Front of all progressive forces opposed to appeasing Fascism, that famous 'Stage army of the Good'. The Oxford by-election was just such an anti-appeasement, Popular Front campaign, the Labour and Liberal parties agreeing not to field rival candidates against their Tory opponent. Some CP members still wanted a genuine alliance of left/radical opinion within the Popular Front that included the CP, rather than a secret recruiting ground for committed membership into the CP.

Frank himself often noticed that the Party appealed to opposed psychological types: the 'uncontrolled romantic and the cold blooded theorist'. He classified Leonie Marsh – over-sexed and over-emotional – together with himself in the first category. On the way back in January 1939 from Val d'Isère, where he had skied, made friends, practised his good, idiomatic French and read four books of *The Iliad*, he wondered what territories had lost their freedom to the Fascists while he was abroad. He then recorded a need to weep 'to think of the many good friends whom I have known for a few days and then left'. He was an eighteen-year-old sentimentalist, inexperienced and immature. The approach of war heightened emotions too.

His pull towards Communism lay in its promise of universal brotherhood, an imaginary politics of kindness, caring and compassion, and the belief in a utopian future to stand against the evident bankruptcies of capitalism and the nightmare world of Fascism. EP would later invent a brilliant phrase – 'the chiliasm of despair'* – to help explain Methodism's appeal around 1790. The phrase implies that a final conflict between good and evil is about to occur, an end of the world as prophesied in the Book of Revelation. It has its aptness to 1930s Communists. Book after book – Spender's *Forward from Liberalism* (1937) and John Strachey's *Why You Should be a Socialist* (1938) – announced that liberal democracy and capitalism were in their death throes, and mass unemployment, hunger marches and the rise of Nazism all symptomatic of final collapse. The belief that a better system must exist and could be born out of the coming apocalyptic struggle, while irrational, is not hard to understand.

To be a CP member was moreover to belong to a European-style intelligentsia, opposed to the narrow racist and nationalist ideologies of the far right. This appealed. Lastly, when Iris showed Frank 'how gentle and artistic communists can be' he was discovering another forgotten aspect of 1930s Communism: that it sanctioned creativity. Many painters and writers were CP members or sympathisers.†

Frank was soon preaching the new gospel. There were fierce

---

* From the Greek *chiliasmos*, meaning 'a thousand years': the essence of this teaching tells us that Christ will once again return to earth, defeat the Antichrist and establish a kingdom on earth in which the righteous will reign with Him for a thousand years, enjoying all the good things of temporal life.

† As Arnold Rattenbury (EP's friend) pointed out, listing painters, composers and many writers: 'Around *Our Time* and *Theatre Today*, the journals on which I worked, were [plenty of independent-minded Communists such as] the happily idiosyncratic... Sylvia Townsend Warner, Edgell Rickword, Patrick Hamilton, Montagu Slater, Randall Swingler and, around them, particularly in nearby pubs, such friends as Nancy Cunard, Lennox Berkeley, Roy Fuller, John Minton, Dylan Thomas, Julian Trevelyan and so on...' See 'Convenient Death of a Hero', *London Review of Books*, vol. 19, no. 9, 8 May 1997, pp. 12–13.

arguments, especially with his father at home, where Frank attempted to sell the *Daily Worker* in nearby Princes Risborough. He started to study and discuss dialectical materialism with those to whom he felt the future belonged, and to understand European history better; he benefited from its intellectual toughness. Yet although he recorded later that he spent that 'undistinguished year studying Greek and Socialism', Frank never became a dogmatic theorist. He left behind him no body of Marxist theorising to compare, for example, with the writings of John Cornford, that martyr of mythic power who had died in Spain aged only twenty-one and who at Cambridge spent fourteen hours each day on politics. Frank's scattergun interests are the exact opposite of Cornford's 'fierce single-mindedness of thought and action'.

Listening to the General Secretary Harry Pollitt give a rousing speech at a CPGB (Communist Party of Great Britain) youth camp that summer, Frank wrote to EP (addressed jokingly as Lev Davidovich – that is, Trotsky) remarking how nice it was to hear a spot of idealism 'because Communism tends to be a cold rational creed'. Frank always placed a high premium on human 'warmth', and, if his generation was of course ludicrously, grievously deluded about Stalin's Russia, it was a generous error.*

In 1936–7 alone two million had died in Stalin's purges, facts not hidden at the time: Malcolm Muggeridge and George Orwell observed accurately and testified. The appeal of Communism has been often discussed by those wishing to expose Communists as dupes and fools (from Orwell to Martin Amis's *Koba the Dread*) or traitors (Alan Bennett's *A Question of Attribution*). And yet we inevitably read this heroic generation through the distorting lens of the Cold War; and 'heroic' seems the right word.

---

* Little demonstrates the giddy lack of realism and the gullibility of Frank's and Iris's generation more than the contempt they shared for 'bureaucrats' and 'bureaucracy'. This referred to CP members who used administrative procedures to frustrate initiatives or to avoid making firm decisions, as well as to full-time Party workers whose job was to watch and report on the rank and file. They evidently swallowed Marx's make-believe about the withering away of the state.

With a duty of judging comes the challenge of understanding. Iris, who joined the Party as soon as she came up to Oxford, had been prepared by the ethos of her dotty Badminton School headmistress, who gave sermons on the sanctity of Lenin, Gandhi and Sir Stafford Cripps, and whose mistresses familiarly addressed one another as 'Com' for Comrade. Beatrice Webb rightly described 1930s Communists as 'those mild-mannered desperadoes'.

An attractive feature of Frank's generation of idealists is their willingness to get their hands dirty, to step out and help. His parents trained him to be civic-minded and public-spirited. Between April and July 1939 he helped with New College Crown Boys Club in the slums of Hoxton in north-east London, of which he was Secretary and for whose boys he acted in a pantomime as cannibal King Umballuna in his father's battered top hat. The poverty of the East End shocked him. He then taught at a school for Jewish refugees in Kent, followed by a fortnight in a camp for the unemployed in Wales, returning home flea-ridden, and finally attended CP summer school. This in addition to reading ten books of Virgil, six of Homer, and Hesiod's *Works and Days* and all his duties as an Oxford undergraduate. Small surprise that Frank found classics, which he had gone up to study, irrelevant to the political crises obsessing them all. He regretted not studying Russian instead.

During Easter 1939 Frank went in response to an urgent appeal for help to New Herrlingen School at Otterden in Kent. No official notice was at first taken of him until the headmistress, whom he called 'Tante Anna' ('cylindrical and with a squint'), looked sternly at him saying, 'Are you interested in this sort of work or have you come merely because you want somewhere to stay in the hols?' Frank gave a strangled gurgle. His programme, she explained, was to talk English with the German pupils, and play games with them in the afternoon on his own initiative. He was to look out for three adults, fresh from concentration camp, who might teach him German.

Headmistress Anna Essinger, that remarkable woman, founded her progressive boarding school near Ulm in 1926. When in 1933 Hitler came to power she soon realised that there was no future in Germany for her and the children, many of whom, like her, were Jewish.

Accompanied by some seventy pupils she refounded the school in Kent. A committee of Quakers and others helped Essinger rent and then buy Bunce Court, a large country house with extensive grounds. So many refugee children arrived in the UK in 1939 that she organised an emergency programme to help them through the Jewish Refugee Committee and the Quakers, even when no fees could be paid. Her school provided a home particularly for those children whose parents perished in the camps. They received not only a good and stimulating education but in the absence of domestic staff took on the tasks of cleaning, cooking, growing vegetables, repairing furniture, converting stables into dormitories and more. Pupils included the painter Frank Auerbach and the artist, musician and humorist Gerard Hoffnung.

Frank looked without success for the three fresh from a concentration camp to teach him German. He took classes and play-reading and discovered that he liked teaching, finding these children much more intelligent than average. He got permission to attend a Seder evening on the Friday night of Passover with its Haggadah service, and, since Jewish men wore hats both before and during the supper, he from respect donned his green beret. He worked out that the order of service probably dated from the fourteenth century and wondered whether its references to 'Next Year in Jerusalem' were in that century already Zionist – a sensitive question for pro-Arab Jessups like Theo. He heard first-hand accounts of German troops a few weeks earlier on 15 March marching into Prague, which the Luftwaffe, its aeroplanes visible overhead, threatened to bomb. When a Jewish child of nine with large eyes looked up at Frank and pleaded with him to obtain a permit to get his parents out of Germany, he was profoundly unsettled.

The do-gooding of 1930s left-wing intelligentsia is a source of satirical fun in stories by Angus Wilson such as 'Such Darling Dodos', yet their altruism is surely preferable to cynicism or despair. Iris would later, accurately, call the 1930s a time when many felt themselves to be trapped witnesses of history or 'conscience-ridden spectators'. That is well said and, although Iris also attended CP summer school in Surrey, no evidence of her doing welfare work survives. She spent the last weeks of peace in the Cotswolds with a group of touring actors called the

Private Collection

Iris Murdoch and Joanne Yexley on the Magpies' Tour, Bucklebury, 22 August 1939.

Magpie Players. But Frank did more than spectate; the sense of belonging to a bigger cause lent his life new sweetness and meaning.

He hated government inertia in the face of social hardship. Depicting himself as lazy, he in fact liked work: and if he was, in the jargon, 'slumming', he intended to do so thoroughly. At the Unemployed Camp in Carmarthenshire that July he disliked not being made to work hard enough and wished he could sign up for a week and work arduously and straight through, rather than in shifts. When it rained they had to waste time indoors playing whist while listening to the bad sentimental songs the unemployed liked to sing at the top of their voices about mill-streams and 'the one I love': his nerves suffered. But, often hungry himself, he recorded an attractive piece of dialogue, with two men saying, 'Hungry, whateffer? . . . I could eat a dead horse between two bloody bread-vans.'

He also recorded that he got drunk. His breakages included two tables and, he claimed, one chandelier.

The cleverest man they knew, Frank's friends thought, had fallen hook, line and sinker for tommy-rot and believed Stalin wonderful. The appeal of the CP was quasi-religious: Raymond Carr's ceremony of induction at Queen's College resembled a religious service, 'with candles and oaths'. Cecil Day Lewis reported that his generation had lost their Christian faith, despaired of liberalism as an outworn creed, and greeted Communism for its romantic, crypto-religious appeal, its radiant illusion that the world could be put to rights. Frank agreed with his father, who wrote to Nehru that year that religion was 'the greatest pest in the world'. The idea that he had joined a new religion would have dismayed Frank, and he would have protested.

Communism was certainly authoritarian and possibly dictatorial, demanding that its members 'sink their egos' for the higher good; and both the police and the Special Branch accordingly took a great interest in its activities. CP recruits were expected to toe the Party line, attend Party meetings, organise, speak, sell Party literature, join outside bodies and 'front' them. Philip Toynbee recorded that 'the Oxford CP practised dishonesty almost as a principle. It was indelicate, authoritarian and possessive . . . [displaying] a crudity of judgement which . . . extended to a bluff insensitivity about love affairs . . . There was a "line" for love; there was almost a line for friendship.' In this light Leonie Marsh's injunction to Iris that Frank was a remarkable man whom they 'must get in' to the Party sounds cold and sinister.

———

Frank and Iris processed together in that year's May Day parade over Magdalen Bridge and up the High Street, Frank, not yet nineteen, in emotional turmoil. This came at the beginning of his final term. In late June Frank's Oxford career ended rather as it had begun, in a drunken night with friends:

> In Corpus [Christi College] everyone stands one drinks and I was pretty whistled . . . After I had eaten two tulips in the quad and bust a window, they dragged me into Leo's room and sat on me. I calmed down and they thought I was safe enough to take on the river. The red

clouds round Magdalen tower were fading to grey, when we met two people we didn't like. We chased them and tried to upset their canoe. We got slowed up at the [punt] rollers, and then I dropped my paddle. With the excitement all the beer surged up in me. Shouting the historic slogan, 'All hands to the defence of the Soviet fatherland!' I plunged into the river. They fished me out but I plunged in again. By a series of forced marches they dragged me back and dumped me on the disgusted porter at the Holywell gate. After bursting into 'an important meeting of the college communist group' Comrade Foot, by a unanimous vote, was given 'the revolutionary task of putting Frank to bed'.

That was probably the only CP meeting Michael attended; and sixty years later Sir Leo Pliatzky, by then a retired permanent secretary, remembered both his alarm when Frank that night disappeared below the water and his relief at the rescue. Frank's account turns recklessness, once more, into high farce. His chief audience and muse alike was Iris. (Later they switched roles.)

As well as, doubtless, letters now lost, Frank wrote many poems dedicated to her. You can sense in his 'To Irushka at the Coming of War' written in July 1939 that he is using the sonnet form half-deliberately to stoke up his emotions, like Romeo with Rosaline, getting the maximum possible dramatic return out of his situation:

> If you should hear my name among those killed,
> Say you have lost a friend, half man, half boy,
> Who, if the years had spared him might have built
> Within him courage strength and harmony
> Uncouth and garrulous his tangled mind
> Seething with warm ideas of truth and light,
> His help was worthless. Yet had fate been kind
> He might have learned to steel himself and fight.
> He thought he loved you. By what right could he
> Claim such high praise, who only felt his frame
> Riddled with burning lead, and failed to see

> His own false pride behind the barrel's flame?
> Say you have lost a friend and then forget.
> Stronger and truer ones are with you yet.

('I liked the poem because it was like you: simplicity tinged with melodrama. You're a darling,' Iris astutely commented; to these qualities we return later.) His *sprezzatura* here concerns the conceit that Frank is inviting Iris to forget him while he yet lives – a rhetorical strategy recalling Shakespeare in Sonnet 73, inviting his beloved to take pity on him because of his expected early demise: 'This thou perceivest, which makes thy love more strong, / To love that well which thou must leave ere long.'

Frank's sonnet is entitled 'On the Coming of War'. On the momentous morning of Sunday 3 September when war was finally declared Tony Forster, visiting Bledlow, said, 'Whatever happens, we're going to have an interesting time.' Frank drily reminded him of the Chinese curse, 'May you live in interesting times.' By that Saturday, one crucial day before, Frank had joined up. Just turned nineteen and thus underage, he quarrelled furiously with his parents. Theo rang 'a large number of Generals' and also the College authorities and, on the grounds of youth and uncompleted studies, got the War Office to rescind his enlistment. Stormy scenes lasted for days before Frank prevailed. Not all parents could have managed that, nor all sons.

Other Winchester contemporaries signed up – John Hasted unsuccessfully; but the Winchester scholar David Scott-Malden joined the RAF. The second of two short stanzas Frank dedicated to David runs:

> You went, my friend,
> To spread your wings on the morning;
> I to the gun's cold elegance; and one
> – Did you feel the passing of a shadow
> Between the glasses? – one will not return.

What made Frank predict that one of them would not come back, when the likelihood must have been that neither would return? Scott-Malden, Battle of Britain fighter pilot commanding a fighter sector station by the age of twenty-three, DSO, DFC and Bar and Norwegian War Cross, was to die an air vice marshal on 1 March 2000, at the age of eighty. Frank would be killed at twenty-three in Bulgaria. His prescience, not for the first or last time, is unsettling.

Family portrait, 1939.

# PART TWO

# A Professional Murderer
## 1939–43

# Lessons in Gunnery: September 1939–July 1940

But if you're asked by anyone,
I can't quite think who would –
Tell them I got a bullet in the lung
When we charged Ilya's wood
Tell them how lousy our doctors are;
And say I send greetings to the old fatherland.

Epitaph from Lermontov's 'Youth's Testament',<br>as translated by Frank in February 1940

Stand to the barricades beside us!
Then I would die today and hardly care.

from Frank's 'To Irushka', July 1940

Frank wrote to Forster: 'My beloved Antony, My father . . . is very depressed. In fact he is nearly worn out. One can't go through two wars in twenty years, and remain a carefree optimist.' EJ, still exhausted from the Mesopotamian campaign and praying that war might never come again, realised that during this new conflict it would be his ironic duty to represent the civilisation 'for which the other poor buggers are fighting'. The ironies were multiple. The civilisation he was to represent had broken down: he listened to ill-informed critics blaming the war on his friends Gilbert Murray and Robert Cecil, both associated with the failed League of Nations, and felt personally implicated in this bankruptcy. Moreover the poor buggers who would fight on his behalf included his own sons. His generation had let them down.

The young had come to identify 'democracy' with reactionary self-indulgence on the part of the rulers and mass poverty and unemployment on the part of the ruled. Hitler, who had done away with German unemployment, might achieve the same elsewhere. While fearing and detesting Hitler, EJ none the less saw how profoundly unjust and weak democratic nations seemed. 'The Nazis and Fascists have demanded of their young people sacrifice, & so have lit a devouring flame'; but that Communism appealed to both his sons because it too demanded noble sacrifice and austerity he will not admit. His pessimism is on view when, speaking of the coming night-time of civilisation, he writes: 'We are sorry that you two boys (and how many other boys!) have been given a world so grim. I never dreamt it could happen again . . .' EJ then added movingly, 'I wish it were night and all well. It will soon be the one [night], but will it be the other [all well]?'

Old Edward's was the war of a writer mesmerised by India. Shortly after the outbreak he flew the five days it took from Poole harbour by hydroplane (Rhodes-funded) to meet up with Gandhi, Nehru and the Muslim leader Jinnah and then reported back to London on the readiness of India to join the war effort. Despite Viceroy Lord Linlithgow's gross ineptitude in informing the people of India that they were at war with Germany without consulting any Indians and despite the pro-Hitler politics of the nationalist leader Subhas Chandra Bose (whom Edward also met), India in the event provided two and a half million troops, the largest volunteer army in history. Edward played his part in all this, contributing *Enlist India for Freedom* (1940) for Gollancz's Victory Books.

His love for India and for Indians was passionate and never shallow. He confided to his family what it was like to travel in trains soiled by defecation, and the incompetent speeches given by Indians at an Emergency Conference on India called by the Fabians dismayed him: 'It is so easy to accept the case for Indian independence – until you hear Indians actually talk about it.'

*From left to right*: Peter Wright, Andrew Ensor, C. Seton-Watson, Frank
and T. L. R. S. Dickin

While EJ was in India, a letter with a railway warrant instructed Frank
to report to Larkhill for artillery training on 5 October 1939. Although he
boasted to friends that he was now to be schooled as a professional
murderer, Larkhill was not his first taste of army discipline. The above
photo survives of him in July 1936 at OTC (Officer Training Corps)
summer camp on Salisbury Plain near Tidworth (not far from Larkhill)
where Winchester boys marched, polished their buttons and turned out
on parade. Frank had problems getting his equipment clean and putting
on his uniform, and was found by a visiting general improperly dressed
in puttees. As today, OTC training provided a constructive grounding in
military skills: a War Office letter dated 23 December 1938 told Frank
that his name had already been registered in the Officer Cadet Reserve
for commission in the Royal Artillery in the event of mobilisation.

He was surely the least militant or military of men, and the most
rebellious. His horror of violence was real. And yet, when he and John
Hasted opted out of the OTC after one year, for a quieter life in the
Scouts, as they were entitled to do for their final two Winchester years,

this was emphatically not from anti-militarism. In April 1939 he and M. R. D. Foot marched in London against conscription exclusively because they thought a prime minister as bad as Chamberlain might misuse a standing army to break strikes; they were by no means against conscription as such. Frank went to OTC from New College for two weeks in July 1939, observing how the old-school-tie network dominated, and learned about motorised transport.

The war's first three years saw defeat after defeat for the British, notably at Dunkirk in 1940, then on mainland Greece followed by Crete in 1941, and finally the disastrous Dieppe raid of August 1942. The fact that Britain's was an amateur army, while the German war machine was highly professional, played its melancholy role. If Frank was unprepared, so was the country at large.

Larkhill was chaotic, with building work unfinished and much improvisation in evidence: a general camp, with all sorts of courses going on, in the midst of which the OCTUs (Officer Cadet Training Unit: Frank joined the 122nd) had their own huts and bits of parade ground while communal buildings housed lectures. Frank and his fellow cadets were billeted in Nissen huts during the coldest winter since 1895. Snow fell for weeks, trees and telegraph posts were encased in an inch of ice, and washing and shaving, after you were woken at six, happened outside. When two orderlies mistakenly hit and damaged both frozen boilers, there was no hot water for a fortnight; Frank's hands were raw. He appreciated the beauty of the frost more than he enjoyed marching a mile to church parade on black ice or, as a maintenance signaller on exercises, crouching behind haystacks with a bottle of rum to try to stay warm.

Beds were very narrow and one night Frank – so burly he was known as Tarzan – turned over in his sleep and fell on to the floor. Everything seemed in short supply – ammunition, guns and matériel – severely limiting firing practice. Their guns were in any case not yet the new 25-pounders but a standard Great War field gun, the Mark IV 18-pounders first tried out in 1916. There were bicycles to get around on. No exercise with vehicles was possible until civilian transport came in, when you practised loading everyone training for gun positions into, for example, a baker's van, which then proceeded to the mini-ranges.

Frank's Larkhill months throw light on why the British Expeditionary Force in France soon suffered disastrous defeat and evacuation. An Oxford don and Great War veteran taught the mathematics of gunnery, badly. A needlessly complicated, long-winded drill for getting guns into action entailed stages one, two and three during which Command Post Officer and Assistant transferred data from optical instruments to and fro for up to three hours, so that, by the time you were ready to fire, the Blitzkrieg might well be over. Here was one of many things wrong with the artillery. After June 1940 new procedures meant guns could be put into action much faster.

Much time was spent on ranging exercises with smoke drill. You surveyed at eye level a sand and canvas table model simulating rolling countryside. You had to calculate line, elevation, angle of sight and range and finally give your order to fire. There were deceptive false crests of sand, and someone with a smoke bottle represented your fall of shell-shot with a puff of smoke. No smoke at all meant a dud round, after which you had to work out what to do with your next fire orders. The highest degree of ranging was fifty yards, called a short bracket, while a verified short bracket meant two shells the other side, and two shells just short: the best you could achieve. Though it is difficult to imagine, Frank was none the less reported first in the mid-course gunnery examination.

The other cadets Frank dismissed as the same easy-going, humorous, mildly lecherous men you find wherever English public schoolboys herd together with wild northerners and Scots. The future gallery owner David Wolfers and Frank, both so bad at maths that they became soulmates, attempted their sums together. Frank seemed a lost boy to David, who being three years older mothered him. Their talk mainly concerned books: Frank read Virgil's *Aeneid*, Ovid's *Metamorphosis* and Browning's *The Ring and the Book* in bed for distraction, and both David and Frank wrote poetry. They wore battledress and sent up the customs of the army. They did not discuss politics. It seemed to them that they were accomplishing a practical one-year course in gunnery within five months. To compound the pressure, a second lieutenant's pay after tax was only

14 shillings a week, a private's 10s 6d, while a steak at the Red Lion cost 7s 6d.

Army customs were new, plentiful and disagreeable. You learned to give orders over the radio without superfluous words – for example, you should never say '*enemy* machine guns or tanks' since you would scarcely try to shoot friendly ones. There was plenty of 'bull': kit inspection, room inspection with all blankets dressed by the right, and dress inspection, all to Guards standard, with no bootlace allowed out of place. You used a hot spoon and then a toothbrush to spit and polish your boot toes. The idea behind such 'bull' was to help increase *esprit de corps* by making you feel proudly superior to sloppier units. Fresh from college, wild of hair and foul of pipe, Frank would not have lasted a week had he not had the unconscious ability to deflect criticism. When he stopped shaving for one day the Sergeant Major took pity and tried to reform him. But Frank riposted: since God had made him a tramp, who was he to tamper with His handiwork?

———

You were taught not only to talk as little as necessary but to put the well-being of your vehicles and men first. You (the officer) came second. Assessment happened quietly by Sergeant and Commander, after which those few who failed had the shame of telling their family, and the units to which they were returned. This happened twice, once with an officer whose voice could not carry: if the Tannoy was knocked out you had to be able to bawl. Frank by contrast was informed that he was gazetted for a commission with effect from 2 March 1940, his demeanour recorded as 'keen and intelligent'.

Kitting out as an officer followed: his murderer's kit, Frank called it. Military tailors laid out their wares and you chose your uniform as a private purchase on your small allowance, supplemented in Frank's case by £30 from his father. Sam Browne belt with its diagonal strap. Brown boots. Officer's greatcoat and cap. Officer's valise. Swagger stick for carrying under the right arm, with silver top bearing regimental insignia. When in 1943 EP joined the smart 17th/21st Lancers Regiment, Theo insisted he have at least one decently tailored uniform, and not – as

some were doing – buy his officer's outfit off the peg. Thus kitted out you went home on leave and awaited the telegram that told you to which unit to report: 259th Field Battery of the 118th Field Regiment, Royal Artillery, in Eastbourne in Frank's case. His pay had risen to 11 shillings per day.

One reason Frank would record even in 1942 that his bloodstream was still 'all Winchester and Horace' was that his transformation from student into soldier was so rapid. By April 1940 he was rising at 06.45 to check his men's breakfast (an earwig in the men's potatoes once prompted wide-eyed contemptuous stares).

He also with some thirty men and no other officer constructed road-blocks in East Kent to delay an invading army. He was wholly untrained as an engineer. Each night he had intensively to study army textbooks to keep ahead of his NCOs before an architect without military exper-tise came in to inspect his handiwork: small wonder he thought Britain's defences sleepy and uncoordinated. He wrote to Theo looking forward to a time when he could be a civilian again and live a life more consistent with his inclinations. Home leave for one night was bitter-sweet. Parcels containing (variously) maple syrup, ankle boots, tennis whites and racket, Oxford blazer, a whistle, torch and even a camp-bed, plus foods, his two books of Russian verse, books from the London Library and *Life* magazine, all helped.

Meanwhile – still nineteen – he wished he were a little older than a few of his colleagues and, above all, his men, a recurrent complaint: he had throughout his war somehow to impersonate the conviction of an officer in order to command men much older than he was. Pipe-smoking (Balkan Sobranie) won him gravitas. He liked the Bombardiers, disliked his Colonel, who kept a handbook entitled 'Social Classification of Officers', and rejoiced in his last English spring. Being out of doors every single day meant that he saw more of it than he ever could have done in Oxford: bluebells, early purples (orchids), galaxies of wind-flower (wood anemone). The inability of the other subaltern in his troop at thirty years old to distinguish blackthorn from hawthorn won Frank's tart rebuke that he did not deserve to be an Englishman. The subaltern explained that, as a Londoner, he had seen his first bird's nest only at twenty-three.

His younger brother soon repeated this swift metamorphosis. At Cambridge in 1941 the first time EP drilled a squad he covered up his ignorance with a fierce military manner. He enjoyed working with the Royal Armoured Corps (RAC), getting excellent instruction on how engines work and on practical maintenance. One afternoon they had driving instruction. When he sat at the wheel of a lorry, the Sergeant asked if he had ever driven before. 'No.' 'Well, these are the gears. You have to double-declutch when you change down. Now drive off.' Within half a minute he was driving a fifteen-ton lorry at 30 mph.

---

Frank had deplored the USSR and Germany signing their infamous August 1939 non-aggression pact just before both invaded Poland, even though he accurately saw that Marshal Piłsudski's was scarcely a liberal regime: 'next to the Fascist regimes it's the worst in Europe'. The CP, after days of in-fighting, declared that the war was between two kinds of imperialism and so to be boycotted. Some Communists excused Molotov, the Soviet Foreign Minister, by saying he was no worse than Chamberlain at Munich, parleying with Hitler to buy time. But a friend since childhood days severely shook Frank's confidence in the inevitable and absolute purity of Soviet intentions. Indeed Frank wrote to Forster, 'My father wins about Russia, but he has the grace not to be cocky about it.' And so his politics did not make Frank a reluctant soldier and he wrote rebelliously to Iris, then dutifully toeing the pacifist Party line, as 'Madonna Bolshevicka':

> Sure, lady, I know the party line is better.
> I know what Marx would have said. I know you're right.
> When this is over we'll fight for the things that matter.
> Somehow, today, I simply want to fight.
> That's heresy? Okay. But I'm past caring.
> There's blood about my eyes, and mist and hate.
> I know the things we're fighting now and loathe them.
> Now's not the time you say? But I can't wait.
>
> Maybe I'm not so wrong. Maybe tomorrow
> We'll meet again. You'll smile and you'll agree.
> And then we'll raise revolt and blast the heavens.
> But now there's only one course left for me.
>
> Autumn 1939

Complementing this poem is his later 'To Irushka' (July 1940) which ends by invoking the image of Iris herself arousing Frank from reverie: 'You with the peaceful eyes and soothing hair / *Stand to the barricades beside us!* / Then I would die today and hardly care.' Iris would refuse his invitation to stand on the barricades beside him (metaphorically speaking) until Hitler invaded the USSR in June 1941 and the CP – shamefully late according to its critics – declared the war effort legitimate. Meanwhile Frank wrote 'Bilge' over his first poem and 'Hooey' on his second, rejecting the poor poetry more than the political line.

Russia's invasion of Finland on 30 November – with three times as many soldiers as the Finns, thirty times as many aircraft and a hundred times as many tanks – was a severer test. Frank felt 'hit in the kidneys'. In uniform and very upset, he burst into Leo Pliatzky's room in Corpus: 'Right now how do you explain this going into Finland?' Leo, a fellow-traveller, tried to bluster some excuse. Evidently Frank allowed himself once more to be persuaded not to break faith with the USSR. And such loyalty as he felt to the tortuous reasoning of the CP seems not to have compromised his army career.

The bulk of the Oxford University Labour Club, sickened by this Winter War, split off in 1940 to form a new Democratic Socialist Club. Roy Jenkins wrote often to his Stalinist co-Treasurer in the tiny rump OULC 'Dear Miss Murdoch' to sort out their assets, while her replies started always 'Dear Comrade Jenkins'.

Iris thus stayed obediently pacifist in public while exploring private doubts only in some poor verses. Frank's meeting with her in Oxford over Christmas 1939 sounds to have been a peaceful one. Probably his joining up impressed her and they met as equals at last. Iris Murdoch is nevertheless the 'fighter and mystic' of 'Camilla' (January 1940) for whom he feels 'sick desire'.

EJ for his part observed these antics from Bledlow with a contemptuous eye and thought that the CP leadership's 'somersaultations', as he called them, in 1939 and again in 1941, lost the Party credibility. If Hitler was the enemy in 1941, why was he not the enemy when overrunning France? But by then Frank had left England for good.

---

The careers around 1940 of the family closest since childhood to Frank, the Carritts, all four surviving boys in the CP, contrast with his own. Once the Blitz started Frank dined regularly in the Carritts' Dolphin Square flat, with Bill's beautiful first wife Margot, Secretary of the National Union of Students, also present. Frank read Communist literature there that he could not easily access in the army, and probably learned the Party line. Although Bill Carritt excelled in his OCTU he was never made an officer; other blacklisted CP members never rose above the rank of sergeant or were never called up in the first place. The CPGB's backing of Stalin while he supplied the oil that may have helped Luftwaffe planes bomb London played its part here. An erratic and inconsistent government campaign against 'dangerous Reds' saw the *Daily Worker* banned between January 1941 and September 1942.

Brian Carritt, Frank's age and a close friend, was also at those dinners. Frank and Brian had been rivals for the affections of Robert Graves's daughter Catherine Nicholson, to whom Frank wrote as 'Katya aux yeux verts' (sometimes 'Madonna of the Green Eyes') just as he Russianised Iris to 'Irushka'. Catherine later berated herself for having preferred blond handsome feckless Brian to Frank, the solider of her two suitors. She visited Brian at Eton on 4 June 1939, his straw hat flower-garlanded for Founder's Day. He had set up an Eton CP cell, plotted to escape to fight with the International Brigades in Spain (he was too young) but joined CP meetings in Slough. In 1940 he spent two terms at Queen's College Oxford reading Modern History and wrote to her of 'people whose entire life is politics, and mine must be too'. When he failed to talk her into joining, he told her 'in despair' to stay away or his political friends 'would kill her'.* 'Some friends you've got!' Catherine reasonably retorted, promising to wait for him for two years.

Her story that Brian was required by the CP to filch papers from his father's desk is believable; such rifling was common and Kim Philby did the same. Though Professor Carritt's desk might offer little of interest, the fathers of other Etonians Brian recruited might have supplied richer pickings. Brian's complaint to Catherine of living in two worlds in conflict rings true.

Brian's middle brother Michael Carritt, still in the Indian Civil Service, in 1940 suffered a visit from senior police officers. Unfazed by his mother's protests they marched through the rambling Boars Hill

---

* Catherine met her future husband Clifford Dalton late in 1941 and they married at the register office in Aldershot on 31 January 1942. Since she alleges that he – a nuclear scientist who died of cancer – was in 1961 'murdered by the Australian secret service, who then killed others as a cover-up', she is no stranger to conspiracy theories. See Catherine Dalton, *Without Hardware*, Towamba, NSW, 1970, 3rd edn, 1980, *passim*.

house and triumphantly unearthed in a copse outside two tin chests of government papers and incriminating correspondence between Michael, the Indian independence movement and (probably) the CP of India. As well as advising the Indian underground of impending police raids, Michael had been able to import, through diplomatic channels, quantities of banned nationalist literature. Michael was neither sacked nor prosecuted but forfeited his pension of £12 per month.

The CP required you to drop your membership on joining the army but some continued in secret as so-called closed or clandestine members. Did Frank filch papers, or threaten the lives of friends? Although he was actively involved in CP business in Iraq in 1943, his Communism always seems less fanatical than Brian's or Iris's. Since he – unlike them – refused the Party line on the war in 1938–41 and also thought the French CP wickedly defeatist, it is unlikely that he then had opportunities to work for the Party.

In a March 1940 letter to EP Frank none the less twice asks him at home to play down Frank's political commitment – one EP already shared. This might have been from a desire to minimise further domestic disturbance. The best evidence against Frank's having been compromised is that he was so soon to be recruited to work for Military Intelligence and to rise in the army up to the rank of major. The question needs revisiting when in 1943 some British Communists like Frank were deliberately groomed and recruited for work in the Balkans. Meanwhile it is likely that in 1940 the common sense tempering his political zeal was clear to all.

———

Such common sense is clear from the copious letters he wrote to Désirée Cumberledge, reading English at Girton College in Cambridge, whom he had met in Wales at the Camp for the Unemployed the previous summer. That he poured his heart out to her so often in 1940–2 may owe something to Iris retreating into Pre-Raphaelite isolation while working towards the First she eventually won, and to Frank cooling in his pursuit of her. And Catherine, as we have seen, was occupied with

Brian. Désirée meanwhile made an excellent sparring partner, foil and confidante, before whose affectionate scrutiny he could define himself anew. His restless confusion in 1940 is mainly visible in his poetry and in his letters to her.

They differed on religion and politics, Désirée having abandoned Communism for Christianity and pacifism. Not a pacifist, Frank also thought that there was no God or afterlife – 'I damn well hope there isn't because they spoil and soften everything, take the meaning out of this life and lower human dignity.' He was also as baffled by Christ's celibacy as by his claims to be the Son of God. Frank preferred the pagan cult of Apollo, god of music and song and – because sexually libertine – more rounded than Christ. Some remarks of Gilbert Murray influenced Frank at school to pore over the obscure lexicographer Hesychius of Alexandria before having 'great fun' evolving his own theory in an essay about Apollo's origin as god of apples, and making ingenious parallels with non-classical gods from India and elsewhere. In fact the Apollo-as-apple-god theory had long been in the public domain. Frank also had a Wykehamist's conceited cult of the Virgin Mary, addressing Catherine, Iris and Désirée as 'Madonna', rather as Feste in *Twelfth Night* in courtly-comical style addresses Olivia, yet implying an ideal of womanhood too. Mary and Apollo are thus also private emblems for him of a stiffly traditional dichotomy between male and female.

His letters come alive when he defends his idea that there are matters worth discussing more than politics. Art and literature, he insists, are paramount, and those who cannot see this he believes damned. He returns to the argument more than once: the arts are not just the focal point of human living, but the only things that give any real point to it. War, he insists, is tolerable at all only because Horace, Marvell, Aeschylus, Homer in *The Iliad* and Tolstoy in *War and Peace* all knew that, despite its evils, the men who have to fight wars are in themselves none the less good. He has – or so he claims – almost abdicated as a politician. What better can a man do than create something beautiful, striking, interesting or inspiring, unless it be to live inspiringly? (This was a belief relating to the *sprezzatura* that he shared with his father.)

And it was exactly this faith in human values as enshrined in literature – in the heights as in the depths – that, he says, kept him sane while learning for months at a time at Larkhill the 'multiform details connected with the killing of men'.

---

Learning to ride a motorbike eased travelling. He returned to Oxford in October 1939 to sit an emasculated Honour Mods and met Denis Healey, who sixty years later recalled Frank's vivid spirit, and went to Winchester (thirty miles from Larkhill) in November, and to New Herrlingen in March 1940. He was looking for traces of his earlier civilian selves but found that while the places stayed the same they had forgotten him already. He drafted two poems on the theme of 'Le Revenant', the dead man who cannot break the habit of returning and who knows, like a ghost, his 'utter emptiness'. He was, as he half joked, revisiting the haunts of his more innocent schoolboy and undergraduate personae, poorly disguised as a professional murderer. He considered submitting a poem for the Newdigate before remembering that Oxford had suspended that prize for the duration.

He felt the contrast with his present army life 'rather bitterly' and wrote home about its pointless waste of energy. He reported that he had been woken in Eastbourne around 06.30 to reconnoitre together with another officer, quartermaster and battery clerk a small inland village with insufficient billets for their entire battery (perhaps one hundred men) who were to move there the following night. They knocked up the police force – one constable plus pushbike – then the Wesleyan minister, and finally the President of the Women's Institute. They also earmarked the two village pubs for the officers' and sergeants' messes. Villagers were rushing to the door with ready-made excuses about evacuees expected that very weekend and Frank's party was slowly gearing up to a state of smooth if slightly ruthless efficiency when a dispatch rider arrived with a terse note: 'Move cancelled. Return to Eastbourne forthwith'. (Evelyn Waugh's account of such futile military orders and counter-orders made EP smile with recognition when he read *Brideshead Revisited*.)

Frank's regiment had been given in succession three different places to move to and had dutifully packed and unpacked, yet met all this being 'messed abaht' with admirable patience and stoicism. The good humour and the incoherent cockney goodwill his men showed towards newcomers and new situations alike were sources to Frank of 'evergreen joy'.

They were on home defence, which he found almost as tiring and potentially as dangerous as 'the real thing' – joining the British Expeditionary Force in France – though far less glamorous. Jobs included relearning to ride a horse and to canter, trying at 1.30 at night vainly to pull a broken-down lorry with guns up a one-in-seven hill, a week's map-reading course and whizzing up and down at about 35 mph on a motorcycle guarding Beachy Head, plus six other 'Vulnerable Points' he was in command of, near Dover. When once his motorbike was dangerously grazed by a passing lorry he wrote a poem – of course – on just escaping death.*

He entertained his parents and EP, all of whom came to stay at the George in Alfriston, and the three men to Theo's distress – probably because it excluded her – discussed poetry. 'Three quite separate standards of performance & criticism, all most sincerely held, all with a lot to be said for them,' she remembered later.

He also had time each night to study an hour's Russian, to write another poem about Gogol starting 'I shall laugh my bitter laugh', read Gogol's *Inspector-General* in the original and some Turgenev and translate Lermontov's ironical, touching poem 'Youth's Testament', whose narrator – once again – is of course a romantic hero on his deathbed. He enjoyed medieval Latin verse too, especially secular love poems like 'The Nun's Complaint' and 'The Lover in Winter' that gave to love a graceful charm.

---

* The theme continues in a 'Nervous Monologue', ascribed by Kusseff to October 1939, in which he addresses Death: 'Okay Death. Now we're at shooting distance. Let's have a look at each other . . . What do you see? A young man, rather frightened, biting his lip and trying hard to smile, his throat all dry, his muscles cold and tightened, telling himself Life never was worthwhile . . . What good are folks like us to you, who take a hundred before breakfast every day? And I? Some seaweed on the shore, a cloud on the horizon, nothing more . . .'

At an Eastbourne dance four decorous young sirens tried to teach
Frank to jitterbug. Frank and a Balliol friend at an Oxford Labour
Club social had the previous year done a jitterbug walk in unison which
'did not make [them] exactly popular', and he recorded the jazz names
for well-known musical instruments – high hotlick suitcase, liquorice
stick, dog house, slush pipe and mud hook. The girls now tried to teach
him 'trucking and swinging', waving his right index finger in the air
while shuffling and kicking his heels – without much success.

Fifth columnists were thought to have been responsible for the falls
of Norway and of France in 1940, and the consequent rounding-up,
care and transportation of enemy aliens that spring absorbed him
briefly as a sideshow, German Jews and Nazi sympathisers alike being
subject to the same order. Frank was proud to count many Jews as
friends – 'so alive, so intelligent, so generous . . . they have a queer
fascination for me' – and enjoyed this new contact with his 'dearly
loved Israelites'. He felt an awful ass when picking up loaded rifle and
bandolier to converse with his group of pathetically friendly, dishev-
elled and unathletic Jewish refugees. He won good marks for being the
only officer in the battery who could pronounce their names correctly.

Summer 1940 abounded in fears about spies parachuting in, followed
by invasion: road signs were accordingly removed or painted over
(replaced only in 1942 to orientate GIs). 'Dear Shipmate', EP now
sixteen years old wrote to Frank in a letter by turns witty and inventive
in the Thompson manner. Taking a short cut one morning from their
new Bledlow home to visit a friend, along a beautiful overgrown country
lane, EP got arrested when he stopped to rest in a barn. A vigilant
farmboy who spotted him summoned a 'whiskered gaffer' in plus fours
who remarked 'narthenyungfeller showmeyerhidentitycard'.

EP produced it out of his rucksack, in which unfortunately a map
and telescope were suspiciously on view. The gaffer examined the identity card, saying 'mfraidshllhaftdetainyer'. Up the rickety lane came a
police car with a constable and another official. They took his name
and address, looked through his telescope the wrong end, examined his
map for red and green circles, went through his rucksack looking for
parachutes and bombs, cross-questioned him at length and ordered

him back to the road. As they had to back their car two miles down an unvisited green lane, EP got there faster than they did. Bledlow village, evidently fearing that he might have knocked the police on the head and be making a getaway, turned out in force to watch the execution. 'Which all goes to show that these bolshies jest wont have a chance . . . I hear a thundering on the door; I shall have to change the wave length . . .'

EP signed off: 'Daddy has applied for 18 jobs, and been accepted by the only one that isn't paid.' Money remained a hot topic. EJ, who cycled to Risborough to join the Home Guard that May, had been informed over the garden hedge on his return that – as an air-raid warden – he was ineligible. Theo and EJ were annoyed that they could be found nothing more positive to do; they seemed only to be asked not to do things. Not to travel. Not to spend. Not to use this or that. EJ was asked to help feed refugees in the London Underground, but Theo vetoed this: he would do better 'talking rot to the troops'. Sick of doing nothing, EJ volunteered as YMCA welfare/education officer attached to the Royal Artillery and went to Larkhill, where he was offered the rank of captain and lectured five times a week on such topics as (he joked) 'Can Germany stand the strain?' On one occasion the camp was bombed and there were seventeen deaths; luckily EJ was weekending at home.

One of his audience there, Peter Wright,* attested later how grateful he was for the lectures and discussions EJ offered on poetry, music, politics, cinema and much more. EJ offered human warmth and friendliness, intellectual stimulation and a way of understanding how and why it was that all their lives had been so grievously uprooted. He combined deeply liberal opinions with a remarkable breadth of mind. EJ mentioned to these men that he had a son in the army who was a Communist with whom he argued vehemently. While seeming perturbed by this, he was pleased that points he had argued out with

---

* This Peter Wright, recalled by EJ as 'an excellent chap who looks like a sulky lioness' and recurring later in Frank's story, is unrelated to the author of *Spycatcher* of the same name.

Frank could also be addressed at Larkhill. Even though the *Daily Worker* would shortly be banned, there was in the army itself still considerable freedom of expression.

Theo meanwhile kept busy tearing round the village helping with Bledlow's new fruit-preserving centre, watching out for enemy parachutists, attending first-aid lectures and collecting salvageable aluminium that might during the coming Battle of Britain be turned into Spitfires ('*such* a marvellous way to get to know the village'). She especially liked dawn patrol from 5.30 to 7.30 (as she pointed out, because of Double Summer Time adopted during the war, this period was really 3.30 to 5.30), and she thus enjoyed the summer dawn. The news at home was turned on 'about 23 times per day' and she lectured the WI on 'If the Invader Comes', where her demonstration of Rescue of Unconscious Person from Burning Room won 'Much Applause'. Civilians were instructed to 'deny food' to German troops and parachutists. 'Just exactly how is *that* done?!' Theo asked mordantly and, ever practical, suggested various places to hide food instead. She practised putting out fires with a stirrup pump and decided that incendiary bombs, though they sounded menacing, were manageable affairs; she also knitted for the army. In March 1941, after months of separation, she would let the Bledlow house and move down to join EJ in lodgings in Amesbury, on a main road so noisy with night traffic that sleep suffered, by day serving buns and tea in the canteen and offering Arabic lessons. Sandy the dog languished with a Bledlow neighbour, looking out each day from the drive for the return of the Thompsons and partaking in the general condition of separation and anxiety.

When the Dunkirk evacuation began in late May 1940 Frank was at Northiam in East Sussex, only thirty miles from the anger of the Wehrmacht, surrounded by Great War 4.5-inch howitzers with their dark-green muzzles, and by wood violets. He noted that as danger approached impressions grew more vivid. The Sussex oatfields had masses of flowering cow parsley that his troops stuck in their helmets as he marched them down the peaceful honeysuckled lanes. Later he thought that that 'invasion' summer had been gentler and the hedgerows greener than they had ever been before or would ever be again.

Danger intensified the glorious pleasures of the season: he had never felt so intensely alive.

On Sunday 26 May the King and Archbishop Cosmo Gordon Lang had requested prayers for miraculous delivery. There were false alarms when some fool by mistake set the church bells ringing, suggesting that invasion or some other disaster was under way. Then, in the nine days from 27 May to 4 June, 338,226 men from the beleaguered British Expeditionary Force wonderfully escaped from northern France to (mainly) Sussex and Kent, aboard 861 vessels. In fact – though this news was censored at the time – another 30,000 were also killed or wounded together with a similar number missing or captured,* and among these were so many linguists that, within a very short time, new and unforeseen calls would be made on Frank's abilities.

* Churchill's 4 June speech mentioned only 30,000 killed, wounded and missing – 50 per cent of the real total; and the sinking of the *Lancastria* with between 3,000 and 6,000 on board on 17 June was not acknowledged (*The Sinking of the Lancastria*, BBC Radio 4, July 2010).

# An Officer and a Gentleman: July 1940–March 1941

For my epitaph as good a line as any is [Ivan] Krylov's . . . 'He sometimes found it sad, but never boring.'

Frank's will, *c.* February 1941

Wartime Britain had many so-called private armies, each hush-hush,
many suspicious of and hostile to one another.* A War Office memo
told Frank on 6 July 1940 that he had been appointed to fill a vacancy
for a subaltern (Intelligence Section), at GHQ Reconnaissance Unit,
Lechlade, in Gloucestershire. The appointment took effect as from two
days earlier: this letter put an official stamp on a private deal.

The retreat from Dunkirk made clear how much a general in battle
needs a swift, accurate and steady flow of reliable information; the
usual channels were too slow. The GHQ Liaison (Secret Intelligence
and Communication) Regiment, code-named Phantom, answered this
need, performing well in Belgium in May. Phantom listened in to
German conversations between tank and unit commanders, accurately
predicting German attacks and where they could be thwarted.
Information was also provided on casualty rates and the condition of
roads and bridges. Phantom helped pre-empt so-called friendly fire too.

---

* Military Intelligence – remembered today chiefly for MI5 and MI6 – had in reality so
many branches that Frank's schoolfriend the SOE expert M. R. D. Foot gave up when
he heard of an outfit called MI27: nothing concrete could be discovered about it.

Frank would spend much of the next three years with Phantom in the Near East on individual patrols monitoring front-line radio traffic – both British and the enemy's. Phantom had its own private cipher system, good radio equipment and frequencies. It comprised volunteers of outstanding personality plus exceptional linguistic and motorcycling skills, the last of which Frank would acquire only with difficulty.

As early as the Munich scare in September 1938 his parents had made enquiries about Frank working in Military Intelligence. In March 1940 he and Theo had another stormy passage when she threatened once more to ring up generals on his behalf: she doubtless thought she could help him do better than become a Royal Artillery officer. On 18 May Frank thanked EJ's friend General Jack Collins for trying to get him a job worthy of his intelligence, but he was reluctant to move. He wrote home with a sketch of a cat-bombardier firing a 16-pound howitzer: 'I don't [mind] gunnery, I like guns & I'm very fond indeed of gunners. I don't want to leave them now unless I could get something *really* interesting.'

Private Collection

On 28 May, however, the *Aboukir* leaving Dunkirk was torpedoed and sunk. Among those killed were ten out of the then total of only fifteen Phantom officers plus twenty-two other ranks. Frank soon travelled to London to be interviewed by Lieutenant-Colonel

G. F. Hopkinson ('Hoppy') and his hard-pressed intelligence officers.

Hoppy was small, frighteningly tough, cheerful, energetic and lonely. A war-related injury to his shoulder that he refused to have treated meant he saluted left-handed; he later fractured his spine. He believed that fear of death was essential for strengthening men and tried to persuade all his officers to have their appendixes taken out. He himself had done this in the Great War, thus entirely avoiding the disappointment of missing future battles. Only the company of women frightened him and he actively forbade wives as security risks and strongly disapproved of his officers marrying. He spent one of his own leaves on a daylight RAF raid over Germany acting as tail-gunner. He was exactly the kind of professional soldier whose spirit and bravery Frank came increasingly – and against what he believed his 'better instincts' – to admire. Leading his men into an attack at Taranto in Italy late in 1943 Hoppy was killed.

Hoppy's team tested Frank's competence in four languages. Theo noted that there was a written exam and that Frank impressed his examiners by preparing one language that was beyond them. Probably he chose Russian, French and German with modern Greek as the maverick. Hoppy astutely promised Frank 'dare-devilry', danger and adventure. Romantic intellectual that he was, the prospect of danger interested and attracted Frank. That he disliked the unfairness of his RA officer-in-command played a role. That Phantom would prove open to the idea of sending a squadron to Greece, the country Frank felt passionate about, may have clinched the deal: the 'something really interesting' that he sought.

After Dunkirk Hoppy was skilful at making Phantom grow. Including the magic word 'Secret' in the name of his force he rightly believed would make scarce items of equipment easier to obtain. He requested an establishment of a thousand, confident that this would land him exactly half that number; in summer 1940 Phantom grew to eighty officers and 600 men largely by word of mouth: personal introductions avoided poor-quality material. Hand-picked officers recruited family and friends, mostly cavalry types like Hugh Fraser, son of Lord

Lovat and first husband of Lady Antonia Fraser, and the actor David Niven, who on film often played the part he enacted within Phantom. They were based in extreme comfort in Pembroke Lodge, a fine period house in a well-tended garden atop Richmond Hill with majestic views over the Thames from the veranda, where white-jacketed mess waiters served officers drinks. Bertrand Russell had grown up here, the house lent by the Crown to his grandfather Lord John, the Victorian Prime Minister.

Soon Frank paraded on his arm an embroidered white 'P' (for Phantom) on a black ground, which he noticed other troops imagined to signify a kind of Gestapo. The prevalent suspicion that he was checking up on errant colonels and brigadiers accounted for the mix of deference and caution with which Phantom officers were treated at HQs. It was partly true: reporting obvious inefficiencies or bad work within the Higher Command belonged within their brief and led naturally to unpopularity and friction. But their main work was front-line reconnaissance and communication.

Driving competence apart, Frank was an ideal recruit. Very young and innocent-looking liaison officers proved best at acquiring information from their French and Belgian counterparts. Frank, not yet twenty, looked the part and had charm. Junior officers were given considerable freedom to enter operations rooms to question their seniors, where they could be greeted with 'Who are you to ask me that sort of thing and what the hell is Phantom anyway?' Brigade and division HQs were often angry that they were not made privy to the information Phantom was collecting about them and passing on higher up the food chain. Significant tact was required, not least when, in 1942, these HQs could be American. Frank's being half-American – as also his Winchester training in smooth diplomacy, in making everybody feel at home – came to his aid.

Leaving his old unit made Frank emotional. On his last day with the RA he went round patting the guns on their smooth cold muzzles and chatting with the sergeants about their equipment and ammunition, concerned that some had had no leave for five months.

He had work to do to feel at home in the new officers' mess, with its

embargo on talk of shop, politics or money, its stilted life of bridge and
poker in the evenings together with 'a jump, a ride, a screw, a roger or
a rattle': these were, he noted like an anthropologist, the terms officers
and gentlemen used for their drinks. Frank, who had little small talk,
found conversation about horses of limited interest, sometimes skip-
ping dinner and escaping to central London on the Green Line bus
or tube.

Reading provided another escape: Tolstoy's *War and Peace* for the
second and third time; Sholokhov's *And Quiet Flows the Don*; the
*Oxford Book of French Verse*, which prompted after half an hour's
reading the snap judgement that most French poetry between du Bellay
and Verlaine was dire. Three writers he read in Russian and commended
to Désirée Cumberledge were the poets Blok and Yesenin, who died
early, and the fabulist Krylov. Frank also admired Bernard Pares's
romantic affection for the Russian people (in his 1941 book *Russia*) and
took note of Pares's condemnation of Stalin's Terror, much joked about
also in Ernst Lubitsch's comic film *Ninotchka*, starring Greta Garbo,
which he watched twice that year and which has lines such as 'The last
mass trials were a great success. There are going to be fewer but better
Russians.'*

Though Hoppy was not a zealot, discipline mattered, and Frank
soon complained that among the lesser evils of Phantom was that he
had to look smart: 'They might as well tell me to take up ballet-
dancing. It would come just as easily.' He ended mournfully, 'I'll write
again when I feel more cheerful.'

———

In late June he had written to Theo, 'I hope your argument with Miss
Murdoch didn't grow too heated.' Although EJ would joke in 1943
about both his sons' 'atrocious' taste in women, he would not have

---

* And also Anna: 'Oh, that Burganoff. You never know if he's on his way to the washroom
or the secret police'; and a Russian visa official to an unseen caller: 'Hello! Comrade
Kasabian? No, I am sorry. He hasn't been with us for six months. He was called back to
Russia and was investigated. You can get further details from his widow.'

invaded his wife's territory. Theo's curiosity had probably prompted a meeting with Iris Murdoch on some pretext or other at an Oxford coffee house, where the row happened.

Theo had two friends with views about their children's suitors – Winifred Carritt and Nancy Nicholson. Winifred, possessive about her sons, intervened in their love lives. Despite her own CP affiliation, she broke up a relationship between Brian and a young 'intellectually inadequate' working-class girlfriend and later encouraged the break-up of Bill's first marriage. Nancy offered a kinder model of motherhood. Theo – despite twice going on the warpath where EP was concerned, in 1943 and again 1945, eliciting information from third parties about successive girlfriends, the second his future wife – stood somewhere in the middle. Moreover, while tolerating Nancy Nicholson's bohemianism, Theo disapproved of Iris Murdoch's, especially when after 1942 Murdoch frequented the pubs and clubs of Fitzrovia, the artistic neighbourhood of north Soho.

The likely crux of heated debate between them was Iris Murdoch's doctrinaire unconcern as to whether Nazi Germany or Britain won the war, both being equally wickedly 'Imperialist'. While Iris was publicly toeing this Party line she was in private neither a fool nor a zealot, but probably Theo provoked her before discovering her to be a formidable debater. Yet Theo was also careful not to make an enemy of Iris who, she knew, did not then return Frank's passion. And Frank, aware of his mother's doubts, ended his June 1940 letter diplomatically, 'I still love her like a sister, although I haven't had time to write her for two months.' He had survived the passionate storms of the previous year, and to reassure his mother possibly exaggerated his present disengagement.

The week that Frank joined Phantom, aware that Iris's twenty-first birthday was coming up, he wrote to 'Dear Muvverkins' asking her to forward a letter together with his poems to Irushka to reach her at her parents' address. The ring-binder survives in Kingston University's Iris Murdoch archive; age has rusted its metal rings and its hard canvas cover is no longer straight or true. In it are twenty-five of his poems specially typed out on her behalf, many with their date of composition.

On the title page he wrote 'Mere Breaths of Flutes at Eve, Mere Seaweed on the Shore' from Kipling's poem 'Survival', modest words by which he deprecates both himself and what his verse addresses. His brother EP early saw Frank's constant impulse to perceive himself as nothing but 'seaweed on the tide of history' as a deliberate pose: it was a pose of heroic simplicity, and an identification that was growing. Lying loose-leaf on top is 'To Irushka' in Frank's own hand, written out that 5 July:

> When I can find the time between sleep and working,
> Between hard earth and [the] cold morning air,
> Or a longer rest in the sunlight basking,
> I like to remember the gentle things that were.
>
> The tireless novelty of age-grey cities,
> The tabby cat asleep with folded paws,
> Cornfields too conscious of their beauties
> – All these bring sense and freshness to my cause.
>
> But one things taunts me out of all this kindness;
> You with the peaceful eyes and soothing hair:
> Stand to the barricades beside us!
> Then I would die today and hardly care.

'To Irushka' has Brooke's 'The Great Lover' behind it, with its artful transmutation from the erotic into the domestic: 'These I have loved: / White plates and cups, clean-gleaming, / Ringed with blue lines . . .' The trajectory of Frank's poem, from the homely toward the heroic, is slighter, indeed adolescent. The propensities Iris accurately identified in an earlier poem – 'simplicity tinged with melodrama' – were his stock-in-trade and proved hard to outgrow. Meanwhile she declined his invitation to join him on the barricades or back the war effort, for one further year.

Both flirted at different times with Anglo-Catholicism, and together they once visited Westminster Cathedral where, with its candles flickering before the saints, he lit one to the Virgin Mary. Around her twenty-first birthday on 15 July Frank also dropped in on Iris's home at 4, Eastbourne Road, Chiswick. He had the polite habit of ringing beforchand, but the Murdoch telephone had been cut off because they were moving to Blackpool in two days with the Ministry of Health where her father worked. Ministries were being moved out to escape the coming Blitz.

Feeling lonely and low, Frank wanted someone to talk to, and her kindly parents fitted the bill. Iris herself was out. He studiedly arrived at a time that he thought would be after tea – 5.30, but found them just about to start – precisely the joke-misunderstanding Iris wrote into *The Sea, The Sea* when Charles calls on Hartley at a time that he hopes is between meals, having forgotten the lower-middle-class habit of eating the evening meal early.

Murdoch's father, thin, spectacled and with a slight Irish accent, told Frank about his career as a trooper in the last war. He had served in a yeoman cavalry regiment, the 1st King Edward's Horse – real cavalry then, before mechanisation. Frank called Iris's mother a 'pretty, blonde Dublinoise with much the best accent of the lot of them' and saw that she was miserable about going to Blackpool. He joined in their meal with zest and stayed till after seven; they invited him to linger, but seeing all the packing they had on their hands he didn't have the face to.

That same week Frank called on Leo Pliatzky's family in Bow in the Jewish East End. The Pliatzkys, having read some of EJ's books and a recent *Daily Herald* article, and heard him speak on the wireless, were in some awe of Frank as son of the 'Famous Author'. They were waiting out on the streets to greet and hustle him indoors with great delight and central European accents – 'we vont you to be at home' – and Frank took off coat and tie and ate a first-rate meal of cold beef and pickled cucumber. Leo had been called up one week before as a private in the Ordnance Corps. Visiting these two families who were currently connected neither to the cavalry nor to the Brigade of Guards cheered him up considerably.

Iris Murdoch would later publicly commemorate Frank's quietness, while privately making a journal reference to his 'torrent of restless talk'. Both were true. He acknowledged in his 1939 poem dedicated to her that he was 'uncouth and garrulous his tangled mind / Seething with warm ideas'. But none of his letters to her before June 1942 survives. Shakespeare's Ages of Man distinguishes the young lover from the older soldier; the many letters Frank wrote Iris in the former idiom – 'Sighing like furnace, with a woeful ballad / Made to his mistress' eyebrow' – Iris very properly kept to herself. Those he wrote in the idiom of the professional soldier 'seeking the bubble reputation / Even in the cannon's mouth' she by contrast rescued and, after his death, lent to his family at their request for their commemorative volume of his writings.

---

After the fall of France in summer 1940, when Britain and its empire stood alone, the mood of the war – at first fraught with shame and foreboding – made its first decisive shift. Frank and his father alike greeted the Battle of Britain and the Blitz with exhilaration. EJ predicted accurately that 'the time of waiting is nearly over and Ragnarok would now clash on our shores'. Ragnarok in Norse mythology is the terrifying, apocalyptic end of the old world, and the necessary overture to the beginning of a new one.

There was a Christian sub-text: what survived of EJ's Methodism included his belief in the value of redemptive suffering and sacrifice. Somehow the 1940 prospect of invasion and the first battles for centuries on English soil excited him, offering a chance of expiating the sins of imperialism. His 1924 play *Atonement* championed an English hero willing to renounce further violence against India and Indians, and adopt a passive and self-sacrificial role instead. 'I will pay the price myself,' he announces. During the war EJ developed these ideas further. Byron came to exemplify the recurrent type of Wandering Englishman who redeems his country's historical guilt and bad faith through symbolic self-sacrifice.

After Churchill had replaced Chamberlain as prime minister on 10 May 1940 EJ observed that the country 'by a miracle and at infinite cost' had recovered moral leadership of the world. Dread times were afoot, the Thames estuary and Kent would soon be under heavy air bombing and artillery fire, yet EJ's rhetoric is upbeat. 'Our cause gets daily cleaner . . . This country with all its sins is the world's moral front line.' He claimed to envision a new England and a new Commonwealth of Nations, worth fighting for and living to see. After the inertia of the 1930s he welcomed at last the prospect of action; even the prospect of suffering in and for itself was cleansing. Thus he shared the widespread disapproval of Auden's 'cowardly' 1939 emigration to the USA. He believed – at least with one part of his mind – that young men should stay to be tested in war, commenting bloodthirstily that it should cost 'everything a man has, to face the breaking of body and mind'.

Frank echoed this rhetoric of noble sacrifice. For all his atheism, he admired Christ's dictum that 'he that loseth his life for my sake shall find it' and thought Christ's death 'an even more splendid gesture than Socrates's'. In all of this he owed much to EJ. He, too, was somehow energised by Britain's isolation, jesting about the growing chances of Spain, Japan and Vichy France all coming in against Britain and jokily transferring the lexis of imperialist insult – coon, wog, wop, dago, nigger – from so-called inferior races to Fascists, whom he considered to have an inferior and hence dangerous philosophy ('We might as well take on all the niggers at once').

Starry-eyed Frank was inspired by belief in a never-never-land USSR, where hunger and unemployment had been banished, all had equal rights and all stories of Stalin's brutality were mere propaganda. EJ disagreed. Although he softened his rhetoric after the USSR and Britain became allies in 1941, he criticised the CPGB for sloganising and for failing to see that, despite all their apathy and ignorance, the mass of the British were dead opposed to the CP. He joked that listening on the wireless to the inanity of American crooners on *Workers' Playtime* was sufficient antidote to belief in any benign Dictatorship of the Proletariat.

There was an excellent teasing understanding between father and son, and many shared jokes. Frank let EJ ramble on with his peculiar mixture of acute observation and witty shallowness, not showing his own political hand. EJ inscribed Frank's copy of his inter-war memoir *You Have Lived through All This* with the words 'God help thee, poor half-witted boy.' Frank liked his father's outlook on life, his willingness to risk unpopularity by truth-telling, notably about India. Among those benighted liberals who rejected Communism, there was no one whose outlook on life he liked more, or to whom he listened more attentively: as late as 1943 his father's idle criticisms wounded him. He commended to his brother their father's facetious and burlesque humour, his sense of beauty and his steel-hard honesty.

What linked them was greater than what divided them: again and again Frank echoes EJ, on the evil of blood sports, the nobility of self-sacrifice, America and cats, aka 'tibs'. A November 1940 poem of Frank's entitled 'Loneliness' identifies cats with independent-mindedness: 'Learn like the cat / The stately cat, soft-prowling through the grass, / Silent and proud, to stalk and think alone.' Cats were free spirits to be emulated. Frank was thrilled to discover that Alexander Pushkin once romanced in an early poem that all his stories were told him by 'a learned cat whom he met in fairyland'.* Perhaps the Thompsons' name-sake cat Pushkin would be pleased at this discovery? But soon after Frank sent this poem home, translated into English, Pushkin was poisoned. EJ eloquently mourned: 'Never again will he sit, angry and dignified, batting an indignant paw at a shut window; or yowl on the buttress above the pear outside my window . . .'†

Both Frank and EJ understood American hostility to British imperi-alism and hoped that the war offered a chance to build a better world, not defend an outmoded status quo. If EJ had been twenty years younger he would have taken out Dominion or American citizenship post-war so as to be in with young nations and away from 'our own outmoded world of *Punch/ Tatler/ Sporting Times*'. Frank too intended to become an American citizen post-war: 'I get more homesick for America every day.' While the English were 'bloody fine people with virtues of self-criticism and humour that Americans lack, they're too old and lifeless'. Frank was willing to accept American bumptiousness

---

* Frank made this discovery reading Mikhail Pokrovsky (1868–1932) in February 1941 and wrote, 'Pushkin-the-family-cat will be pleased to hear his poetic namesake was evidently a great tibophil . . .'
† EJ mentions this without vouchsafing how their beloved cat met this end.

and stupidity 'so long as there's warmth and vitality too'. The plea for 'warmth' is eminently Frankish, a quality everyone agrees that he possessed. It is something he looked for and found in groups as unlike and distinct as Americans, Jews, Greeks, Slavs and fellow Communists.

---

Phantom officers indented for their ample army rations at depots and used their green forms at will to requisition billets near by at 3s 6d per night. By January 1941 Frank calculated that since joining the army he had slept in fifty-two different places. These included the last, a very comfortable pub where he had played darts with his genial batman Trooper Trollope* and then discussed Abelard with a staff captain researching medieval history; a three-ton lorry touring the Norfolk coast with sleeping bags on the floor during the invasion scare; the outhouse of one unnamed stately home that had had 120 bombs dropped on it, jettisoned on a Kent flight-path; and Cliveden. If the vagrant soldier's life suited his restlessness he was none the less relieved when Theo opted not to let out his room in Bledlow. He liked to think that there was a room somewhere which 'expressed' him in some measure, where the books, pictures, furniture and oddments were all to some extent of his own choosing. (After Frank died Theo tormented herself with the fear that his spirit had never found a home on this planet. 'Not even Iris was enough,' she wrote, to anchor him into this existence.)

In Bledlow the small swimming pool near the 'oddish' tennis court had been drained and converted to a makeshift air-raid shelter for aged neighbours. Frank reported the Famous Author spending most of one afternoon walking patriotically round the village inappropriately dressed up in khaki together with a grey trilby hat. Near by were cornfields, meadows, downs, beechwoods, deep lanes, a juniper copse.

---

* Frank's affectionate paternalism towards his batmen – Trollope, then Lorton – is notable. Trollope was a London house-painter from Finchley. 'Likes lighting fires, climbing trees, making jam . . . sleeps 14 hours a day and would like to spend the other 10 eating and drinking – graced with the slowest and best-humoured smile I have ever seen' (FT to his family, 23 Jan. 1940, UNC).

Butterflies abounded and from every part of the small Bledlow house
EJ could hear skylarks sing; sighting woodcock and whitethroat also
cheered him. And partridge and hare visited. Moreover that first spring
he heard a nightingale, and he waited in subsequent years for its return,
in vain. He feared that in the Chilterns nightingales, like his beloved
bee orchids, must be dying out.

Frank painted a troubled portrait of home life. Theo was unhappy.
In Boars Hill she had led a busy social life before they sold up and
moved to Bledlow, which was more economical to run but socially
speaking cheerless. She missed Boars Hill friendships and could not
admit that this move, on which she had insisted, probably throwing the
odd tantrum, was a failure. When Frank rebuffed her attempts to ring
up generals on his behalf, she tried out: 'If I died tonight I don't think
anyone would care.' When EJ offered her a six-month trip to America,
where she claimed all her real friends lived, she complained that they
wanted to be rid of her. She fell back on worrying and organising
others. Yet Frank defended Theo against EP's criticisms. Theo entertained too much, but this erred on the side of generosity. Her fantasy
of escaping to Syria was innocent. She was better on care and kindness
than on imagination. Her requests for her sons' help with odd jobs
around the house were often maladroitly timed: she loved organising
others but was also a talented person trapped in domestic arrangements
(not least the laundering, mending and darning of her sons' clothes,
which both sent home by mail). It was then that Frank discovered that,
aged twenty, she had pulled a donkey in Jerusalem out of a ditch by its
tail: no wonder they found her fierce.

EP had confided to Frank about the crush he had on Arnold
Rattenbury, who had, he believed, led him on then pushed him away
when he got close. Frank, who had endured a bad crush or two himself
at Winchester, was understanding. 'Panseatic' – the jokey Thompson
family code-word for 'gay' – suggests a civilised tolerance.* After talking

---

* It also suggests an awareness that homosexuals sometimes network with one another,
on the analogy of the Hanseatic League: not as good a joke as the similar 'Homintern'
sometimes ascribed to W. H. Auden.

EP's difficulties through with EJ, who had never experienced sexual feeling for men, he surmised that the sensual strain must come from Theo's side of the family. Frank hoped EP would outgrow this phase and encouraged him to do so.

Frank addressed EP's concerns, then moved on to his own problems, among the chief of which was looking for a woman. He needed one badly in lots of ways but thought the task of finding one in wartime when the balance of all one's thinking is so disturbed that 'one can't tell which of one's emotions are genuine and which are not' pretty hopeless. He had had friendships with several girls 'like my beloved Iris' but they never got very far. He tended to fall for women who were, like him, idealists – 'and if a woman's not an idealist I don't want her' – but such idealism prevented them going to bed together. 'Enough of this muck,' he concluded. 'A few months in the army's bound to lower my standards.'

---

When Frank moved from Phantom to the Special Operations Executive in Cairo in 1943 he arranged for his old Wykehamist friend Tony Forster to replace him: a classic piece of Phantom insider dealing. Forster noted that, despite mystification, many of Phantom's activities were humdrum and pragmatic. Moreover Phantom finally proved its usefulness only in 1944 after Frank had left, trusted by generals, its reputation such that Canadians, Americans, Free French and even the SAS wanted Phantom detachments working for them. It had some success in Italy (mostly due to luck and the Italians' eagerness to surrender), and was useful on and after D-Day, but by then it was a different sort of set-up with more emphasis on wireless and codes, and less on the derring-do motorcycling Frank had, in 1940, to learn.

But that Phantom always had a maverick side is also clear. Its spirit was partly ad hoc in a very English way, and it engaged from the start in extra-curricular activities. In spring 1940 Phantom reported accurately on the psychological state of the Belgian King Leopold III and of his commanders-in-chief and predicted their reactions as the Germans advanced and occupied their country. It also had one squadron trained to move behind enemy lines in battle, sometimes by parachute, an adventure we know that Frank once shared, though no details of this incident survive.

One early historian noted that among the virtues Phantom's founder Lieutenant-Colonel Hopkinson valued was 'criminality'; another calls Phantom wildly unorthodox; a 1946 War Office letter numbered Phantom among the bands of pirate-adventurers that mushroomed during the war – SAS, SOE, Commandos among them. The 'P' on Phantom's vehicles gave them priority over all other traffic on the road. From Cairo Phantom would have its very own dedicated telephone line to Regimental HQ in Richmond, a direct link used not for official purposes but by all ranks sending messages home. That such a line was known to exist added to Phantom's mystique.

Unorthodox too was Hoppy's insistence that officers undergo the wireless, Morse and motorcycle training that in 'normal' regiments was enjoyed only by other ranks. So in early August 1940 Frank rode a motorbike 160 miles, 'which is probably', he wrote home, 'why I sound so depressed'. (Two years later he recalled how his hands lost all feeling.) The same week he was teetering over Amberley Downs in Sussex in an armoured car pursued by maniacal New Zealanders in Bren-carriers, then bivouacking in the grounds of Arundel Castle with these same savages: 'great fun though hair-raising moments . . . Our [that is, Phantom's] job is to get to places like a whirlwind & send back vital information like lightning.' By October, when he was helping reconnoitre the South Wales coast and sleeping *à la belle étoile*, Frank could manage with Morse to encode and decode ten words per minute: Hoppy's aim was that everyone should achieve a speed of twenty to thirty words.

Since battles could begin at any time Hoppy became famous, too, for turning night into day, getting his men up at midnight to start a full day's work, to the puzzlement and anger of other formations. Frank was up all night during the first week of August on a day-for-night exercise, wrestling with wireless atmospherics on the Purbeck Hills. During bombing raids Hoppy also vetoed occupation of slit trenches on the grounds that hiding made men cowards. Frank was standing perilously to attention in a well-turned-out company of thirty being inspected by a visiting general when a German bomber flew over and dropped two bombs. No one told them to stand easy or dismiss. Hoppy's diktat prevailed.

In September 1940 when the Blitz started, a false alarm declared a German invasion imminent. The unit deployed to the east coast. En route on the night of 7 or 8 September Private Holding following too zealously crashed his truck into the back of Frank's scout car: a rare accident for which Frank was not responsible. B Squadron HQ stayed at Thelveton Hall near Diss in Norfolk and Theo sent biscuits and foodstuffs for the mess.

They found a farm for the vehicles, whence patrols went round the coast to report weather conditions and contact local military commanders. Frank, gazing out from the Suffolk coast, feared dawn might reveal the thousands of flat-bottomed German boats predicted by Erskine Childers in his novel *The Riddle of the Sands*. He passed some time stewing blackberries and roasting a partridge which his driver Trooper Jones, with country skills, had killed with a brick. Among the equipment with which Phantom then patrolled East Anglia was a large stock of theatrical disguises for use under the expected German occupation. David Niven, who joined at the same time as Frank, fancied dressing up as an Anglican parson. Another Phantom officer at this time explored the possibilities under occupation of sending secret messages using Asdic (sonar) on the pipes of the London sewerage system. Hoppy settled for carrier pigeons instead, and Phantom's pigeon loft in St James's Park with its 500 birds was tended by the political philosopher Michael Oakeshott.

When it was realised that the Germans were not coming, Frank's unit went back to Richmond, where the Blitz was in earnest. From Bledlow the night sky was red with flame as London burned forty miles to the south-east and gunfire was audible, but the Thompsons suffered little. Frank wrote that though the homeless people in the tube stations were a public scandal, by and large London was not such a shambles as EP might think from the papers. The nearest bomb by January 1941 was a 'good 200 yards away', merely splintering the Colonel's window at

Pembroke Lodge. Frank in the mess was smoking his pipe with a glass of whisky in his hand and dived between two sofas when the bomb went off, his pipe landing in his whisky glass. He found that a belly well lined with Younger's ale was a 'surefire ticket to the land of Nod'.

He minded more being locked with Désirée into a basement of the National Gallery during an air raid, forbidden to leave or stay with the Paul Nashes and Stanley Spencers upstairs. Half an hour sweating in a stifling basement gave him the horrors, a time 'dyed with claustrophobia'. Dive-bombing by Stukas in the Libyan Desert in 1941 would remind him of the feelings of a schoolboy awaiting physical punishment, but this episode in the basement during the Blitz is the only time he acknowledges a panic attack.

---

Theo was capable of referring without irony to what 'the best people' thought or said. That Phantom officers were better connected than RA ones would not have escaped her attention; belonging in England to the best people went with being 'in the know', with that entitlement to circulate intelligence that was Phantom's raison d'être.

At Richmond Frank met fellow Phantom officers Michael and Jakie Astor, younger sons of the redoubtable Nancy Astor, whom he at Oxford had dubbed with mock severity an 'arrant wanton'. The Astors had presented the mess with an ace radiogram which one day struck up EP's favourite Borodin symphony. Michael Astor turned it off 'in horror' (so Frank claimed) and they were treated to a commercial number. Frank tried to tolerate the purple depths of swing but complained that there was not one officer in this group who cared a damn for music. The philistinism, political reaction and anti-Semitism of the officer class were his running themes.

Frank watched Michael Astor take his patrol out as beaters when shooting pheasant, and stay with the Duke of Buccleuch while waiting for his patrol to recover from flu: 'Trust an Astor.' Relations between Lady Astor and her sons were famously impossible. That Christmas Phantom spent two weeks training and celebrating at Cliveden, the Astors' home, where officers stayed in the house, men in the stables (for which Frank apologised). One evening Lady Astor's second, 'Red' son David, the future *Observer* editor, had an argument with his mother about the unemployed. 'At one point the room was so full of shouting that several people on the fringes were yelling complete gibberish at the top of their voices so as not to be left out.'

Frank retreated into a corner with his copy of Marriott's *History of the Balkans*, bought with Christmas money from EJ, and devoted himself to the far more profitable subject of the Bulgars. 'I do *love* reading about Bulgars. My next book after my biography of Kosciuszko* will be a study of the Bulgar revolutionary movement of the 1860's and 1870's. The Bulgars are the most admirable of all Slavs – bucolic, hard-working, frugal and amazingly simple. The best phrase I have come across in this book is where he describes the population of some town in Macedonia as "terriblement Bulgare".' He also wanted to write a book on Alex Battenberg, first ruler of modern Bulgaria, whose Bogomil heretics attracted him too: teetotal and vegetarian, they rejected marriage, social contracts, rights of property and all the other established laws of God and bourgeois man – not bad for the tenth century. 'Why are Slavs such funny people? Or do they only seem funny to me? Like this to Dadza?'

This contrast is instructive: the Astors represented the England he hoped was doomed; the Slavs – especially Bulgarians – represented escape into an idealised elsewhere. There are pages in his letters commending the Slavs. From Sheering in Essex in September 1940 Frank wrote: 'From the start, the Slavs were *big-hearted and full of pity for their victims* [my emphasis] . . . Ivan the Terrible built an extremely decorative monastery on the walls of which he asked for prayers for the souls of his 3470 victims, citing some by name.' This is not ironic and scarcely sounds like a grown-up judgement: some solace to the victims! His view of innate Slavic virtue endangered his life in 1944.

The mess also included Lord (Toby) Daresbury, who took two horses, a valet and a groom with him wherever he went and claimed to

---

* Tadeusz Kościuszko (1746–1817), Polish national hero and leader of the 1794 uprising against Russia.

have jumped a fence every day of his life, and the Falstaffian Lord Banbury of Southam, who, when commanded to improvise a road-block out of whatever means lay to hand, instead summoned a builder from his feudal estate. Frank's Major, Tony Warre, uneducated but bright and efficient, had bought from a gypsy two hideously thin Norfolk lurchers that came into the mess each night with snouts scarlet from hares' blood. Warre was very hurt when Frank refused to go cours-ing with him. He advocated acquiring a pack of terriers too, with which each time they stayed in a rat-infested barn they could enjoy 'colossal sport'.

Frank believed: 'Get rid of blood sports & we should have made a big step at getting rid of Fascism and war.' He none the less charmed Major Warre so thoroughly that he was immediately forgiven the considerable damage he did to the squadron's vehicles, by mistaking the pedals at the critical moment or refusing to pass through gates in an orthodox manner. He once caused a head-on crash between his armoured car and a civilian saloon, and often landed his scout car in a ditch. (When his Scottish batman politely declined to ride his own motorbike any more – 'I just said to masel I wid na get on one agin' – Frank was glad that though incarcerated he was dealt with leniently.)

Major Warre won Frank's affection one night by admitting to an affection for poetry, albeit Kipling's *Barrack-Room Ballads*. And he used a phrase that summed up the small-mindedness of the Tory case for fighting the war and fascinated Frank for years: his ambition was to *re-establish the lunch tent at Ascot*.

---

Frank made no secret of his CP membership: his fellow officers took this in their stride. He confided in one of them, Norman Reddaway, that he was horrified by the blinkered, class-conscious attitudes of the British establishment; he opposed capitalism as the wave of the past and looked to Communism as the wave of the future. Reddaway accu-rately saw Frank as 'an emotional idealist, not like Eric Hobsbawm a theorist nor like EP a tough apparatchik'.

Although Frank praised the materialist interpretation of history as an intoxicating weapon – 'I feel as if I cd play with it endlessly. And only after one has wielded it for a long time can one appreciate its strengths and weaknesses' – in practice his natural instinct was to suspend ideological judgement and love his fellow men. He enjoyed the humour and companionship of these brave, decent 'but hardly imaginative' officers whom he termed 'good cards'. His own tolerance worried him. He wrote at length to Désirée about how governed he was by 'illogical things' like gallantry, loyalty and friendship that induced in him conflict, and wondered 'when, if ever, I shall get a chance to integrate my life'. His tolerance was one sign that he was growing up, while his untidy handwriting manifests unformed, contradictory energies.

Was this liking for his often Tory fellow officers because, being so young, every new experience was welcome to him? Maybe he should abandon politics after the war and confine himself to humanitarian work? He was not fit to be a politician, he told Désirée; he was a romanticist, not a materialist.

———

Inevitably Frank's study of what he termed the parasitical sub-species 'Officer-and-gentleman' involved some special pleading. EP, unhappy at school, would leave Kingswood in March 1941 to help on Biddesden Farm in Hampshire managed by the journalist Desmond MacCarthy's son Michael,* following which he thought of applying to a Scottish university. Frank was thoroughly alarmed: might not a Scottish university be dull or narrow-minded? He protested firstly to EP – 'Don't imagine England's a kind-hearted classless democracy, where merit's all you need. Irrelevant things like Oxford degrees and friendships are going to come in handy for many years to come . . .' – and he rebuked their parents for allowing EP to countenance the second-rate: 'Won't he bear a life-long grudge if he follows Kingswood by a Scottish University?'

* See Bruce Arnold, *Derek Hill*, London, 2010, for an account of Biddesden Farm in the Second World War.

When EP applied for a Cambridge scholarship instead, Frank was delighted. The father of a fellow Phantom officer, William F. Reddaway, Fellow of King's College and founder member of the *Cambridge Historical Journal*, telephoned through to Richmond a running commentary on EP's performance. On 18 December 1940 he vouch-safed that, although EP's languages were weak, the Thompson family would probably be pleased with the result; and Frank was relieved four days later to learn from the same source that EP had won a Mawson history scholarship to Corpus Christi College. Thus Frank both commended and exploited the usefulness of the old-school-tie network himself.

Frank's stereotyping of Michael Astor as a young blimp also reads oddly today. Astor left one of the most intelligent – and funniest – of the half-dozen post-war accounts of Phantom. So far from being the upper-class philistine of Frank's imaginings he longed to be a painter, trained at the Slade and under Victor Pasmore at Camberwell but was too impatient and dilettantish to persevere. He saw how war drove part of your personality into the deep-freeze, and hated and dreaded the monkish claustrophobia, tedium and sheer loneliness of life in the mess quite as much as did Frank. Shooting was his way of contriving time on his own, like Frank's imaginative escape into reading about the Balkans. He longed for respite, missed female company as ardently as did Frank and married in 1942.

Phantom – though technically a regiment, he terms it a mere 'outfit' – charmed Astor precisely because it was so English: irregular, eccentric and amateurish. Frank agreed that if the Allies ever won this war, it would be through valour, never efficiency.* A comical photograph of the mess

---

* Astor's story of debonair cavalry officer Major Warre's attempt to discipline his second-in-command – the genial, portly, cosseted Lord Banbury – is telling. Warre, in new riding breeches, matching top boots and a recent MC, was attempting to drill four rows of Phantom men, some recent recruits, in front of a small manor house near Lechlade. They were brought to attention, standing in line, while Major Warre went into whispered conference with his sergeant major. The air of expectant silence was suddenly rent by his tapping his boots and letting out a piercing scream: 'Lord Banbury, you will come out here and stand in front of the men!' After a moment the sash-window into the

that Cliveden Christmas, shows (left to right) Rupert Raw, Norman Reddaway, Lord Banbury, Major Warre, Frank and Michael Astor standing in a row. Frank, at nineteen and a half, looks shockingly young and innocent. He also seems slightly sheepish. Probably he has just been asked to brush his hair.

———

Frank decried what he – quite mistakenly – called Wilfred Owen's 'sickening self-pity' in his sonnet 'Anthem for Doomed Youth', for he was, after all, learning to transmute his own self-pity into intelligible public rhetoric. In March 1941 he sent Désirée a poem he had written whose English title is 'They Died in a War of Others' Making', quoting lines from Aeschylus's *Agamemnon* that moved him. Written the previous

---

dining room was raised sufficiently for Lord Banbury, wiping some breakfast from his moustaches, to answer in his fruity voice, 'All right, Toby [*sic*]; *but don't shout.*' The sheer Bertie Woosterish amateurism of this moment, its distance from German military professionalism, delighted Astor.

August, it starts 'Between the dartboard and the empty fireplace / They are talking now of the boys the village has lost; / Tom, our best bowler all last season . . .' It moves in its second part to the whisper that goes up against a war that is the fault of Helen of Troy's treachery, the Chorus evoking the intense grief of mothers seeing that their beautiful sons will come home, if at all, only as ashes. Its intention to dignify the Second World War by comparing it with the Trojan is audacious and touching, but not wholly satisfying.

Frank alerted Désirée to the presence of 'grecisms' in this poem and warned her that if his body were to be cast in the role of fertilisation (recalling Rupert Brooke's line 'In that rich earth a richer dust concealed') it would nourish not English daisies but deep red anemones and wild blue irises – thus indicating his destination in a manner censors could not blue-pencil. Similarly he gave his parents the easy clue that 'after a break of three years', that is since his trip to Crete, he had been offered and eagerly seized the chance once more to sight brown spider orchids.

Frank judged Italy's invasion of Greece in October 1940 the cruellest incident in this contest of empires. 'Never was there a people possessed of such boundless good nature.' Greece's only fault had been to put up with Dictator Metaxas's rotten government. The invasion also provided Hoppy with his first opportunity since Dunkirk to send men into battle. He created a new group and sent the first echelon out from Liverpool to Cairo, arriving in Athens under the leadership of Miles Reid in late December. Reid communicated directly with Phantom in Richmond via the wireless mast at Leith Hill. Here was exactly the promise of adventure Hoppy had tantalised Frank with when he recruited him.

Only one in fifty volunteered, joining the second echelon and sailing from Gourock that March, and Frank was among this small band. He would later say that he 'went for love of the scented hills'. He took Désirée and later Theo out to supper at a Greek Cypriot restaurant called Lefkos Pirgos (White Tower) to practise his modern Greek; he was excited about leaving but anxious. One night not long before his departure his echelon were staying at Wotton House near Aylesbury, restored by Sir John Soane, and he went out and got fighting drunk. Rupert Raw, whom he found sympathetic, together with Reddaway, helped undress him and get him to bed.

He had one week's embarkation leave before his eve-of-departure letter on 17 March 1941 instructed 'fambly' on how to get urgent messages of less than twenty words encoded in cable to him. He knew their anxieties. He had been writing home twice each week until, on the eve of Dunkirk the previous May, an unexplained ten-day gap opened. To Theo's reply-paid wire 'ARE YOU WELL?', Frank replied, 'Robust but occupied. Writing.' Now he tried to reassure them that if a battle started, 'you must reckon with hearing nothing till it is ended . . . no news of me is most definitely good news – (*nasty laugh from Bad Dadza*) – we have equipment to make bad news travel extremely fast'. That no news of him would necessarily signify good news was of course a lie. Not his last.

The will he left claimed that to die at the age of twenty represents getting a good deal from life: further and typical *sprezzatura*.

Dear Fambly

As this is a death-letter, there isn't much to say. I did enough talking while I was alive. Now I want to thank you for a score of interesting and enjoyable years. In other words a much better deal out of life than most people get.

You can read anything that I wrote, now. You may find one or two poems that amuse you in the bigger book. You might send the one entitled 'To Irushka at the Coming of War' to the lady it invokes, and Madonna of the Green eyes to Catherine [Nicholson]. For my epitaph as good a line as any is Krylov's . . . 'He sometimes found it sad, but never boring'. But you can probably think of something better yourselves. My dirge must be 'Proshchoi moi Tabor' which more or less sums things up [a popular Russian song 'Goodbye my Gypsy Encampment'].

I didn't believe in any form of after-life, so shan't get one. But any time one of you breaks something or trips over something, you will know that I am with you in spirit. Lots of love. Frank [cat's face]

Frank on leave in Bledlow, 1941.

The reference to breaking things and tripping up is a standing joke about his Prince Myshkin-like clumsiness. He told Reddaway he believed he would not survive the war.

# Cairo Frustrations: March–December 1941

*I shall be burned out at 23. I must seek an early death to keep my flame untarnished and immortal.*

Frank writing to Désirée in April 1941

The HMT *Pasteur* left Gourock on the Firth of Clyde on 19 March 1941. On board this former luxury liner built to carry a few hundred passengers and crew on the South America run were around 3,600 men; some had travelled eighteen hours prior to embarkation and all wartime trains were unheated. Phantom H Squadron contributed to this huge draft its fifty-one men and five officers, with Captain Peter Forshall, a former stockbroker, taking command and Frank, a former undergraduate, his acting second-in-command. Three other officers had joined Phantom only two days before sailing. Phantom H was headed for Greece via Cairo but, to minimise risk, the ship took the long route, towards Canada, doubling back via Sierra Leone before rounding the Cape and sailing for seven weeks in all.

After pelting rain and an air raid had detained them in Glasgow, they had boarded the *Pasteur* from ferries up a wet rope ladder – an interesting climb when trying to balance rifle, haversack, steel helmet, gas mask and bulging kitbag.

As the ship pulled out Frank noticed snow veining the hilltops, and watched a train slowly pass, before the Clydeside women and children waved and cheered – from filthy tenement balconies where linen was drying, from windows and from warehouse doors – for all that they were worth. Since meetings and processions were forbidden, opportunities for fraternisation were rare, and as scarcely one in a hundred was waving a Union Jack, Frank took their cheering for a show not of jingoism but of solidarity with all who suffered the indignity and servitude imposed by war. The troops on board in their turn hit back with a roar that shook the houses. This exchange of sympathy gladdened his heart.

Frank's diary makes a fierce indictment of this ship, embodying all that was wrong with Britain. Officers enjoyed luxurious six-course dinners, with printed menus on every table even at breakfast, and unrationed butter and sugar, while the long queue for other ranks to reach the canteen took three hours: 'Shop early for Christmas' they joked good-naturedly. Conditions below deck were dismal. The smell of 300 tons of rotting cabbage from the swimming pool pervaded everywhere; there were only four cells to accommodate the 120 men handcuffed because they had gone absent without leave (none from Phantom). The washrooms provided no baths, few showers, latrines that stank even before the sea-sickness of the voyage began and twenty basins only, some shared by up to 400 men. Water, moreover, was turned on for only four hours each day, and there were no laundry facilities. Floors and even meal tables were solid with sleeping men, while hammocks slung from the roof reminded Frank of bats roosting in an attic. Troops stared dumbstruck through the door of the opulent officers' mess at the spectacle 'as wondrous as the drinking scene from Gounod's *Faust*', where two boys from the Black Watch danced arm in arm, the room black with noise, excess of drink and tobacco. Frank wondered if it would ease the appalling congestion below deck if the troops took over the sergeants' and officers' lounges.

The men's satirical good humour was meant to be overheard by the officers – 'I say old chap I think I'll take my tea in bed this morning' – and impressed Frank. His fellow officers did not impress. One officer, unable to stand up straight himself, arrested five men for drunkenness. Some never went below deck at all, making no attempt to organise programmes for their men during their two months at sea, preferring with the padres to chat up nurses in the lounge, or dance with them on a deck where men were trying to sleep.

Frank, whose identity disc now proclaimed him 'Atheist', saw no priest of any denomination venture below deck nor even talk to the men above deck. Only the Catholic and non-conformist padres appeared to care – and even then only in theory – about their jobs. The Anglican padres he found mostly selfish, dirty, time-serving, petty-minded and '*cabotin*' – French for ham-actor. One wished chiefly to discuss sodomy; another on church parade, imagining that the troops shared the same living conditions as he did, fatuously thanked God for 'this luxury cruise'.

Forshall was confined to his cabin with sea-sickness, then sunstroke, then earache. The twenty-year-old Frank deputised, acting commander to fifty men, facing Britain's systemic rottenness and inequity. How should he help? He frequented the lower decks and fraternised with the men. Since the *Pasteur* lacked 'rolling chocks' (bilge keels) and, when sideways to a large wave, tilted alarmingly, drill – with the floor alternating between planes forty-five degrees each side of horizontal – was impossible. But Frank and an old Oxford acquaintance offered their men a grounding in modern Greek.\* The diary he kept on board was published in 1947 and has been referred to by historians since. None of his diarising was enough to assuage his sometimes murderous fury and indignation, but it was better than nothing.

———

A nurse he met on board charmed him; he asked her what it was like to have a man with TB for whom she had fallen die on her hands. Captivating, too, was an olive-green-eyed girl from Yorkshire who pronounced his name 'Frunck'. But, though there were couples necking

\* This was one Private Philip Schapiro, Phantom intelligence clerk, 4 foot 3 inches tall and from Merton College. Popular belief in the regiment was that Frank and Schapiro had between them so many languages that one or other of them could have acted as interpreter all the way from Athens to Oslo, including Budapest: R. J. Hills, *Phantom was There*, London, 1951, p. 54.

shamelessly and, as they headed into warmer weather, copulating on deck, he considered a troopship no place for romance. His recurrent complaint over the next three nomadic years was that intimacy could only be snatched at: you were never in one place long enough to let it grow.

Yet in some ways the nomadism of war suited him. He eagerly anticipated travel and new sights. He wrote a story about the mythical Hyperboreans who worshipped Apollo because they enjoyed his seasonal migrations to visit them in winter. Frank hymned Apollo as god not only of apples but of the singular virtues of restless travel.

Frank had space in his officer's quarters to read, think, keep a journal, write poetry. Letter-writing, he acknowledged, was his 'katharsis', buying him purifying release from inner turbulence. He claimed that his letters to Katya (Catherine Nicholson) and Irushka (Iris) were wasted on them: he flattered his mother that she remained his best audience.

He argued furiously with a right-wing pro-Franco opponent while appreciating this man's passion: he liked 'anyone who cares'. His reading on board stayed eclectic. He was trying to patch up his 'tattered and threadbare' – that is, truncated – education. Marriott on the Balkans (started at Cliveden) taught him something new about Bulgarians – that they were late-coming non-Slavs who adopted the indigenous language after arrival.

To Désirée he wrote a classic piece of Frankish *sprezzatura*. He had been reading Shakespeare and identified with Hamlet, that other young man rebelling against a rotten ruling-class background, and claimed that Hamlet's 'I am but mad north northwest' in Act II provided him with a 'new epitaph'. Frank also identified with Hamlet's death-wish and continued, 'I am if anything too brilliant. I am afraid that this my precocity will prove a flash in the pan. I shall be burned out at 23. I must seek an early death to keep my flame untarnished and immortal.' This mixture of boastfulness ('too brilliant'), self-deprecation ('flash in the pan') and melodrama ('early death') is further romantic self-dramatisation.

When they crossed the equator, he had to change his shirt twice daily. He maintained that to enjoy life fully one must always be learning a new language. He compared it to fiddling with the innards of a dormant car engine, or to Pygmalion breathing life into a statue. 'If the gods were clement' to him – a recurrent prayer – he would do a lot of translation. Regretting that he had never asked Theo to tutor him, he started on Arabic. Landfall in Cape Town, where they docked at 11 a.m. on 16 April for four days, offered many delights: his first glass of milk for one month, his first ever persimmon; sightseeing by droshky with two Cameron Highlanders; shopping; dancing and – despite pro-Nazi Afrikaners in the Broederbond – much hospitality. He thought he cut a fine figure in shirtsleeves.

During the first week of May they entered Suez, where Frank records without explanation that a provost sergeant major died, and after due rites was tipped overboard. By the time H Squadron had disembarked and made their way to Mena Camp in Egypt near the foot of the Great Pyramid of Cheops, Greece itself had fallen. They were no one's child: a bad thing to be in any army.

Graham Bell sailed with Frank in March 1941, and stayed with Phantom throughout the war; note the sand mat to extract the vehicle when bogged down.

Creating a private regiment like Phantom, based on the need for fast and accurate front-line communication, was one thing. Convincing others to integrate it into their plans was another. Hoppy had not adequately consulted the War Office about his plans; when the first Phantom group (which Frank's was intended to reinforce) had sailed to Greece in November they met with a blank or actively hostile reception in Cairo before making their way to Greece. There Miles Reid, commanding the group and wearing a tam-o'-shanter, travelled with his party improbably disguised as American journalists. As in Belgium, Phantom's fate turned out to be to communicate accurately from a battle zone during a massive rout. Eleven thousand British troops together with much valuable equipment were captured by the Germans, but the Phantom formation proved its worth by bravely and accurately communicating from the front line before most were killed or captured. The twelve survivors slowly made their way to Mena in Egypt to join up with Frank and his second group, together with ten tons of stores, wireless sets, now redundant parcels for the detachment in Greece, and some new shirts for King George of the Hellenes.

H were now the only Phantom squadron on active duty anywhere. They took the news from Greece badly. Their camp occupied a shallow wadi behind the Mena House Hotel with its welcoming swimming pool. One unnamed man who joined them found 'a rather gloomy little party with little idea of their purpose in life and quite unable to explain it to him'. Phantom was an 'unbadged' regiment, a small symptom of their not being wholly accepted by the military establishment and thus suffering a deficit of status and recognition. They wore their previous regimental insignia, their cap badges having a misleading diversity, a few choosing badges they simply fancied, without any entitlement.

Early June was disturbed by a 'vile piece of news . . . the worst I ever had'. His childhood and Dragon School friend Rex Campbell Thompson, acting flight commander on a bombing raid over Brest that he radioed home as 'successful', was killed when his returning plane crashed on Dartmoor in fog. He was twenty-one. Childhood memories connected them more than Frank's recently acquired politics divided them: Rex in his pushchair blowing bubbles, diving in the Evans lake, playing scrum-half at the Dragon, witness to Frank's first

Rex Campbell Thompson *c.* 1941.

pipe and first girlfriend, driving his battered Austin round Boars Hill. Separated by schooling – Rex went to Cheltenham – their friendship rekindled in the single year they were together at New College after which both joined up the same month. The lightness of touch of Frank's accomplished elegy – one long quietly half-rhymed single sentence of remembrance, with its shock final word 'buried' – is moving:

> Rex
>
> A word from England brought you back to mind,
> Oldest of friends, and how we walked together
> From Foxcombe round by Cumnor in the kind
> Celandine season or in harebell weather
> When haws glow crisp from hedges – dogs that were lost
> In long grass hunting rabbits, solemn talk
> Of school and coming college, till the last
> Visit to Sunningwell, when we tarried,
> Liking the churchyard and its yew-dark grass,
> Where, if they tell the truth, you now lie buried.

Rex was one of 'my only two friends of life-long intimacy'. The other was Brian Carritt, who was to die in 1942. Rex came from the same bourgeois world as Frank and shared its inhibitions. In 1938 Frank had prophetically recorded that over-protective parents had not helped Rex decide for himself 'what risks he is prepared to take about his own life',* while a eulogy written about Rex for the Dragon School recorded his 'desperate shyness'.

———

During this confused time, when not training, reading or learning languages, Frank sought out fugitives from Greece to piece together a picture of the 'elephantine stupidity' of this all too British retreat, during which transport was being unloaded on one part of Piraeus dock, taken for a short drive up the quay, then set on fire. In late June, too, the future writer Paddy Leigh Fermor, 'a classy captain who eyed the other ranks with disdain', and who had known Miles Reid in Greece, praised to Frank the quality of Phantom officers there. Others acclaimed Miles's work blowing bridges in Monastir, reconnoitring the Vardar Valley and 'triumphantly' touring the Peloponnese. 'A fabulous party', Frank commented excitedly, with an ominous hint of admiration for such heroic escapades and *Boy's Own* adventure tales. Frank also heard praise for the humour, hospitality and honesty of the Greeks, who put their own lives at risk to guide the retreating British soldiers to safety, with no bitterness about their own defeat or coming occupation.

Cairo was nightmarish in the heat of summer, and Egyptians hostile to the army of occupation. Expatriate Greeks Frank ran into in clip joints and watering holes made the city endurable, partly because he knew their language. On a memorable July outing with his unit to see St Catherine's Monastery in Sinai, a Fr Alexandros waived all fees for entry, food and lodging because they were British: 'unconsciously all Greek exiles identify George VI with George II [of the Hellenes] and

---

* Rex's parents 'increased his inferiority complex by letting him do things then stopping him at the last moment' (letter to his family, 20 Apr. 1938, UNC).

speak as if Greece were part of the Commonwealth'. Sinai also helped inspire a good poem, 'Soliloquy in a Greek Cloister'. He treated Alexandria – where Greek had after all been the main language for nearly 2,000 years – as a Greek city, eating only in Greek restaurants, going to the Greek theatre and talking Greek even to the Egyptian tram-conductors.

Greeks and English were allied politically. But Greeks also knew that life is funny, and that you and they are – there was nothing quite like a Grecian grin 'with its frank admission that everyone, oneself included, is a bloody fool: but what does it matter?' Where Brits embarrass one another and blush, Greeks simply shrug off awkward questions and laugh them off together. Apropos the learning of modern Greek Frank commented tellingly that 'one always feels embarrassed by emotion in one's own language'. As an 'emotional Englishman' he preferred his feelings safely distanced from him, lost in translation. 'I can only flirt in a foreign language,' he would add later.

Frank's strange list of Noble Savages – those idealised races born to transcend British middle-class inhibition – keeps growing. To Americans, Jews, Greeks, Slavs he now adds cockneys with their jaunty humour and – interestingly – sergeants. Frank envied what he termed the 'Homeric laughter' of the sergeants' mess compared to the chilliness of the officers' mess: as soon as sergeants gathered each evening to start on their superior beer, wall-to-wall wisecrack volleys started up, and they never finished the evening sober. He envied them both their better beer and deeper laughter and thought their humour 'ideally subversive of authority'.

A sense of carnival haunts this picture, and on the sea voyage to Cairo Frank had been enjoying Rabelais, whom the Russian critic Mikhail Bakhtin famously celebrated for his joyous subversion of authority and whose claim to write while drunk Frank thought credible. Indeed Frank asked his parents to send him a book by 'my old friend Bakhtin', which arrived disguised in a parcel of socks. Pretty as it would be to imagine Frank experiencing in Egypt the riotous ideals of Bakhtinian carnival, this Bakhtin was Mikhail's brother Nikolai, who worked at Birmingham University and in 1935 published *An Introduction to the Study of Modern Greek* – the book Frank in Egypt devoured 'at one gulp' in the desert on Christmas Day 1941.

Young Frank admired these sergeants because they by day enforced the traditions of the army, and then at night mocked them, with a double conviction he could not rise to. Alcohol was everyone's escape but had its dangers. One upstanding infantry officer with a weakness for ale who travelled out with Frank on the *Pasteur* he saw degenerating over fifteen months at a desert office desk into 'the bleariest and bloat-edest thing' seen outside a circus; coming adrift from his regiment, he lost all sense of purpose. Frank when disheartened thought such purposelessness ran through the British army from top to bottom, but the 'civilian soldier England is so good at producing' helped him keep faith: the 'best type in this diverse unit'. He was after all a prime example of this civilian soldier himself.

Frank early noted the contrast between the officer on campaign in the desert eager for a drink and a woman, contrasted with his desk-bound cousin surfeited with both. He believed that everyone had 'the right to get bottled' but celebrated in theory the 'quiet dignity of the British soldier' – always genial even when drunk – contrasted with the unattractive arrogance of drunken officers. His Marxism sentimental-ised the downtrodden. In practice he ran out that August as orderly officer without hat, belt or even pips on his shirt, a none too genial bottle whizzing past his head, to help incarcerate 'with pleasure' six British bombardiers who were breaking up the Naafi. Not too much 'quiet dignity' in practice adorned this scene, which reminded him of a Chicago-style brawl.

Being tall, rangy, handsome and weighing in at some thirteen stone, he was mistaken more than once for an Australian, and so took a keen interest in their doings, finding Australians sober to be warm-hearted, humorous and democratic, but drunk both 'charmingly child-like' and 'disgustingly brutal'. Those he met in Cape Town in April were beach-combing after missing their ships, having orgies of drunkenness, smashing cars and throwing pianos. A story from 1940 made him laugh: two aged Italians in their underclothes kept protesting vociferously after the capture of Bardia that they were generals. They were politely disbelieved until the police two days later picked up two drunken Australians dressed in full ceremonial kit as Italian generals. And six weeks in the Australian Hospital in Damascus that autumn would offer further opportunities for research. One Aussie orderly there, continuously drunk for three consecutive days, offered Frank brandy; Frank, noting that it was dangerous to decline an offer from a drunken Australian, none the less drew the line when this orderly sank to his knees.*

———

Even the Roman Empire under Hadrian had never flooded Egypt with such a cosmopolitan horde. Within days of arrival he counted fourteen nationalities on the Cairo streets including Palestinians, Czechs, French, Sikhs, Gurkhas, 'Negroes' [sic] and Maoris. He believed he could detect strength in the air. This note recurs. The following August after he had been posted far further afield, he thought the cavalcade of nationalities provided an epic spectacle: Greek and Yugoslav officers preening themselves on the streets of Alexandria, diminutive Iraqis in khaki among the white hollyhocks on the Persian frontier, Russians close-cropped and grinning, giving the V for victory sign, the Arab Legion, Poles, French Meharists in red-white headdresses, mounted on camels, and impressive Indian soldiers everywhere. He came to the conclusion that troops who had been out one year started to become denationalised, thinking of themselves less as Englishmen and more as Middle Easterners, even the ranks becoming to a certain extent declassed. Doubtless foreigners offered picturesque copy for letters home, but, besides that, this war was demonstrating beyond any hope of refutation, he felt, the unity of man.

On 22 June 1941, a corporal informed H Squadron that the USSR had that morning been attacked and was now Britain's leading ally. Frank observed this news – coming so soon after the most recent disaster of the fall of Crete – being greeted with cautious optimism. He met

* In his Libyan journal Frank praises the outstanding efficiency and courage of the Australian sappers, without whom Bardia would never have fallen so swiftly.

that evening at Cairo's Turf Club with Christopher Seton-Watson, whom he had known at school and New College, and Hal Lidderdale, an Oxford acquaintance and rival suitor of Iris's. Egypt of course was full of old friends and acquaintances: everyone you had ever heard of passed through at some point in the war. They searched vainly for a wireless to listen to Churchill's speech that night ('The Fourth Climacteric'), declaring Hitler crazy and wishing on him Napoleon's 1812 fate. Hal later recalled Frank ringing him up jokily in Cairo to propose a meeting: 'Hallo: Joe Stalin here.'

It was not that he thought Stalin's crimes mystically mandated by history: he refused to believe that the USSR could be such a corrupt and tyrannical regime as the papers said; and now he awaited impatiently a change of heart towards Britain's new ally. He listed its virtues to his family. The government of the USSR – 'whatever we say about its methods' – was uniquely concerned with the welfare of its people. Goodwill rather than selfishness governed all its social relations. Working people were accorded honour and security and the talents of the arts and sciences were combined for public benefit. Russians enjoyed better entertainment than Hollywood, and their young were brought up with less jazz-addled minds. He read the now forgotten play *Distant Point* by Alexander Afinogenev (1904–41) set in Siberia in 1935. Its dialogue – trite and sentimental as it now reads – almost made him weep: 'Tell them things are alright there – as they should be with Soviet Railwaymen' and 'Now let's sit down comrades, – but in an organised way.' It inspired him to write verse.*

There was mysteriously little sign of his brother-officers coming round to his point of view. Even one year later in July 1942 he met British officers who openly declared they loathed Russians more than Germans; and on entering a senior HQ to ask about publications on the Russian Army he was brusquely told to look under the Enemy Section.

He felt a deep emotional sympathy for what it must be like to be

---

* 'Red Gladiolus', ending 'Death is the end. But life goes on for ever.'

invaded by a ruthlessly cruel foreign army and he also felt an admiration that many shared, Churchill included, for the huge, self-sacrificial courage with which Russians were fighting. This went with a withering contempt for the Britain-can-take-it line: the best thing the English could do about the war was to keep quiet about it. While he sympathised with Britain's bomb damage and food shortages, he did not think that, in comparison with what the peoples of occupied Europe and of Russia were undergoing – with the enemy on their own territory, starving, shooting and hanging their citizens – the British had much to complain about, and believed that their smug desire for self-preservation would make them unpopular after the war. The British were (at this stage) rotten propagandists, and Frank's perspective was always pan-European and internationalist.

He longed to meet his first Russians but had to wait one further year and had meanwhile to make do with a subscription to the *Slavonic Review*, improving his Russian and translating Russian poetry, listening to Russian music – 'one has not known sadness until one listens to Russian music' – and cross-questioning 'renegade' Russian émigrés he met in Palestine who had left the Soviet Union in 1930, relieved to discover from them no flaws whatsoever in the country they had so mysteriously fled: 'When [Russians] laugh it breaks your heart.' He read *War and Peace* many times.

He praised all Slavs for suffering with such patience and courage, throwing their bodies between Europe and destruction. The Poles had suffered more than any other nation in Europe. Czech students had been shot in the street in cold blood; he tried to imagine that happening in Oxford. He had also read on the boat for the first time Marx's *Das Kapital* and claimed that, so brilliant and polymath was it, Marx must have been the name of a syndicate: no single man could have been so erudite. He claimed that every word made him homesick for England – Marx's classic land of industrial capitalism.

Frank's relations with his batman for more than two years, Fusilier George Lorton, belong here – his closest and most representative 'common man'. Only nineteen, a garage apprentice before the war, good-looking but anaemic, he drove while singing out of tune; Frank

'Fus. Lorton: for two years a faithful retainer,' reads Frank's caption.

did not know how politely he could get him to stop. When Frank asked him while shaving whether he was looking forward to seeing Jerusalem, Lorton replied, 'No, Sir.' Frank lost his temper and told him he was a fool: it was a waste of government money ever taking him to the Middle East. Lorton reasonably replied that he had never asked the Government to do so. How was it that war enlarged Frank's horizons, while narrowing Lorton's? (As for Frank in Jerusalem, he thought that any other European people would have ruined Palestine quite as effectively as the Jews had, but, while disliking Zionism, he liked Jews.)

Frank considered that Lorton on the whole bore his dull lot with quiet dignity, 'lacking the background that officers had' to help sustain him. He admired his mute ox-like endurance and in 1942 depicted him in the heat of Iraq, a rolled towel under one arm, fishing rod under the other, trundling Pooh-like to the river. In the evenings he shambled over to Frank's tent to engage him in conversations about prop-shafts and differentials; his sole and entirely reasonable interest was improving his knowledge of mechanics against the future. Officer–servant friendships were doubtless the stronger for the many hardships shared. For his part Lorton would remember that he used to scold Frank for his untidiness, adding, 'But I would have followed him to the end[s] of the world.'

Frank, so passionate and emotional in his advocacy, could be equally emotional in his criticisms, for even *his* naivety had limits. He thought Gorki's political essays shocking pieces of newspaper propaganda. He once again wanted a generous and humane Communism of the heart, not a cold one of the head: 'the only things that have any value today are love and courage'. He championed the 'friendliness and warm sentiment' without which socialism was cold and mechanical.* So while he admired Sholokhov's *And Quiet Flows the Don* he also regretted that a certain passion and irrationality were missing from Sholokhov's materialistic picture of life. Though he told Désirée that, if non-cooperative, an individual should lose his rights, he also believed that only individuality keeps man immortal.

Above all, and despite all his hypothetical hatred of the British officer class, in practice his admiration for their courage and efficiency continued to grow. The theme gets into letter after letter. The Sassoonist attitude was plain wrong: blue-blooded officers, those fighting 'to save the lunch-tent at Ascot', were often the bravest of all. When he first saw copies of the Communist-inspired periodical *Our Time*, in which EP was involved, he scorned its predictable portrait of a high-ranking officer as a stereotypical ass. Frank, by contrast, had long strolled, straw in teeth, down a winding English lane of impulse and instinct, but very rarely found himself 'wandering down the stream-lined autobahn of his socialist theory'.

---

Phantom feared that it might be disbanded as a white elephant, but slowly came instead to be understood as something between a commando and a signals unit, brought up to a strength of eight officers

---

* This was apropos learning German, an important language for the future, a language Frank liked, and the language of socialist tradition.

and eighty other ranks. They started with a six-week IWOS course (Irregular Wireless Operations School), which provided four motorbikes on which Frank's men happily pulled on gloves, goggles and revved up, but which was rumoured to have 'nasty ideas' about desertworthiness and to be training them for a forty-mile walk with only one halt and no water. The squadron was short-staffed and Frank wrote home in June: 'Don't laugh now, but I'm our maintenance & transport officer' (or MTO). Though he put on his best big act in a pair of filthy overalls, a less technically minded MTO is hard to imagine.

At least in Egypt he came to enjoy motorbiking. On 27 June he celebrated some of the sights he and his bike had encompassed: 'the delta in the evening with mixed choirs of frogs and crickets and blackwhite birds that fly like snipe or curlew; the desert at night, sweet and clean and dry and fathomlessly silent'. Some weeks later he found that in six days he had covered 1,100 miles, starting off with the morning sun peeping gingerly over the desert, singing lustily while the engine drowned the noise, and dead tired by evening: 'the more I travel the more it intoxicates me'. By August he accounted himself a dual personality, being more suitably employed as intelligence officer as well as MTO.

Frank confided to his diary that 'after two months of fucking around' his squadron retrained through much of 1941. They were divided into five or six long-range signals reconnaissance patrols, each consisting of one officer and five men carrying a fortnight's rations and 1,000 miles' worth of petrol in two eight-hundredweight wireless cars and one fifteen-hundredweight truck carrying no. 11 wireless sets, which had a range of thirty-five miles. The arts of desert survival included the use of sand mats to extract your vehicle when bogged down, a canvas watersack to keep the radiator cool, and navigating by prismatic compass and angle of the sun.

One ex-Commando officer who joined Phantom that August was Monty's future liaison officer Lieutenant Carol Mather, by whom Frank at first felt cramped, but warmed to when he obligingly 'mucked in'. This was not untypical: he had started by loathing his commanding officer Peter Forshall but grew very fond of him, and similarly with his successor Major Dermot Daly, whose friendship with Evelyn Waugh interested him. Frank was not unique in growing to like his opponents – including his political adversaries, if they evinced enough 'heart': no tales survive of his falling out with old friends.

Mather found Frank a delightful companion on a joint patrol to the Red Sea hills, camping out on the Gulf of Suez in which they swam naked, with the mountains of Sinai on the other shore, and speeding down the sparkling gulf next morning to the fabled Coptic monastery of St Anthony – the oldest active monastery in the world. Here he and Frank spent two nights in tiny whitewashed cells, their men outside with their vehicles. The monks fed them pigeon pie, and Frank and Mather got permission to swim in the cistern within the monastery's five-acre enclosure. It was a gentle baptism into desert life and their last escape from reality, remembered by Frank as 'one of the loveliest drives . . . ever' and sixty years later by Mather for its complete otherworldliness.

Mather knew that Frank claimed to be a Communist, with a strong attachment to the war aims of the Soviet Union, but accounted it all light-hearted, and doubted whether he were a paid-up member. He thought Frank essentially a patriotic Englishman in love with the English countryside, and noted that his extraordinary scruffiness and untidiness of dress, through which he expressed contempt for the conventions, never stopped his being an excellent officer.

His parents fretted about how he might stay healthy in the Middle East, where Theo grew up and EJ served in 1916–18. A scare about bubonic plague at Mena closed the camp for days but happily proved unfounded. Frank sickened by other means. On 2 June '500, 000 devils chose my stomach as their battleground'. He spent 4–11 July in a long, curved and corrugated Nissen hut hospital in Ismailia with sandfly fever, debilitating but not serious, and his head like a turbine, appreciative of the nursing he got from the 'thoroughly pleasant' sisters. 'Women are bloody marvellous, really, the way they manage to keep clean and neat and cheerful in an awful country like this.' He tried to learn Arabic but it did not grip his imagination. A Cypriot and he competed to see who could swat more flies, Frank averaging a bag of 230 per day. Officers in hospital had the task of censoring the letters of all the other patients. Most communicated their wretched homesickness in ways that were second-hand and trite: 'Cheer up Darling . . . We'll meet again.' But occasionally he found a Welshman – or someone who had read Shakespeare – and their eloquence in expressing the condition he too shared moved him to tears.

His sandfly fever was in July. That September his unit crossed into Syria via Palestine to gain wider experience in mountain country and ready themselves fast for desert warfare by October. Frank's finger was throbbing, septic and swollen to the size of a banana; the squadron Orderly Sergeant Frank Jacobson lanced it for him. (Since Jacobson's Communist opinions were known, the Sergeant later recorded that Frank didn't associate with him too openly. But they knew each other well, did things together and he comes into this story later.)

Soon acute septicaemia affected his leg too. He wrote to EP, newly arrived at Cambridge to read history, that the tale of this trouble was 'quite amusing'. He was up doing a job 'in Muvver's country' when he noticed some nasty poison spots on his leg. He dropped into a field ambulance and came over queer with a temperature. First they suspected measles, then jaundice, then his leg ulcerated. The doctors themselves were falling ill with sandfly fever and jaundice and evacuated Frank by ambulance to the Australian Hospital in Damascus, which had a skin specialist.

Frank wrote a short story, 'Picnic in Galilee'; and he claimed to EP to be working on a poem about the sufferings of Job, afflicted like him *inter alia* with boils, but the poem did not progress. Not till early November would they release him. Frank requested a bit of home news, the most fatuous jokes Dadza made in September or any outstanding example of Muvver's fierceness. The Middle East was hopeless politically – no public-spirited middle class – and he jokily glossed the heading 'MEF' (for Mediterranean Expeditionary Force) as 'Men England Forgot'.*

---

* Signing off as 'Kościuszko', the eighteenth-century Polish nationalist hero.

PICNIC IN GALILEE *by Frank Thompson*

It was a patient's outing to Tiberias. Thirty of us, two sisters, five officers and twenty-three assorted "other ranks," bumped and rocketed in a gray Arab bus across the twisty road from Nazareth, until we swung round onto a view of the lake, breathlessly blue with a reflection of red hills on the further side. Then a raucous descent through the town, cheering and whistling at every girl we passed, and a peaceful two-mile drive between eucalyptus-trees along the shore. Two things stand out from that journey. One – that olives are undoubtedly elves. Gnarled elves that will never grow tired of dancing by the rich brown whorls of the ploughland. If I were an etymologist, I could probably prove that elf and olive are the same word. Two – that the goats in Cana are enormous – the size of New Forest ponies. I'm surprised it wasn't mentioned in the Bible. Clearly those goats have come to Cana since.

Now we are in that ugly gray house and the old American

---

While communication at first could take months, so that Frank joked that there must be someone in the army post office whose brother he had kicked at school, airmail-letter speed gradually improved to mere days. He even received the answer to one cable he sent home that same afternoon, surely via Phantom's 'secret' Cairo-to-Richmond wireless link. In early September Frank was angry at the prospect of being offered sickness-related home leave. Theo had discovered that two of Frank's fellow officers had been sent home, the ailment of his commanding officer being, moreover, eczema. She was 'ringing Generals' like mad, neither for the first nor for the last time, and he wrote sarcastically that he expected at any moment to receive anonymous contributions to the cost of an artificial leg, his fever by now having 'probably grown to the stature of the Black Death'. Besides, he wrote solemnly, one did not take sick leave when the fate of centuries was being fought out in Russia.

Here was a continuing source of irritation, and he tried to laugh

Private Collection

away their fears. Remembering his family's 'insane desire for martial photos' he sent them a 'really tough photo' of himself in a stout leather jerkin, hair cropped like a stormtrooper's and a pipe clenched in his teeth. 'Perhaps you'd like a close-up of me in a gas mask?'

Noting the plentiful guile in his make-up, he concealed from his family that his septicaemia had been serious enough to induce paralysis: for a while he was unable to move his limbs. There was also no occasion for him to disclose to them that, of the twelve out of his OCTU who in March the previous year had volunteered for the Middle East, by late 1941 two had been killed, one had died of typhoid, two had been taken prisoner, two more had been wounded and one disabled. Frank had longed to join them, but was deemed too young. Even the youngest was three years older than he was: had he been accepted, would he now too be under the sand? He naturally also withheld from his parents his despondency at how fast the death-toll of Wykehamists was rising, but did not keep from them that he was going into action, writing to them in November: 'diarising up front is forbidden'.

'Folks on high' had from August taken a renewed interest in Frank's unit, seeing that it had a role to play in the coming liberation of Tobruk from its long siege by General Erwin Rommel and his Afrika Korps. In late October Phantom mobilised at last. The delay caused by his long stay in hospital – 'repair shop for men' – separated him from his unit in the Western Desert and must have been doubly frustrating. It was probably in hospital that he found time and inspiration to write his best-known poem, which, one may surmise, slowly developed out of his musings about the virtuous Job's sufferings and came to stand as both his own epitaph and – as has been noted – that of his entire generation.

> As one who, gazing at a vista
> Of beauty, sees the clouds close in,
> And turns his back in sorrow, hearing
> The thunder-claps begin
>
> So we, whose life was all before us,
> Our hearts with sunlight filled,
> Left in the hills our books and flowers,
> Descended, and were killed.
>
> Write on the stone no words of sadness
> – Only the gladness due,
> That we, who asked the most of living,
> Knew how to give it too.

As with his elegy for Rex, this poem is a single sweep of feeling. Once more, the reader feels intimately addressed by a solitary line of conventional reflection: Frank's best-known poem's wide appeal depends on its traditional values. Iris had commented that his own qualities of 'simplicity tinged with melodrama' could be felt in his poems. His language is indeed simple, but his prophetic rhetoric at last here transmutes melodrama into stoicism.

———

En route from his hospital on 17 November, Frank stopped for two hours at a staging-camp where the wounded were gathering to be sent home, before reaching Shepheard's Hotel, that famous landmark, at midnight. Cairo in November was less nightmarish than in summer and there were more pretty girls about. He had three days before rejoining his unit in the desert. He was knee-deep in mail accumulated during his weeks away sick. The total bag for two months was six parcels, thirty-seven airgraphs,* twenty-four letters, seven postcards and two telegrams. Too excited to sleep, he stayed up till four in the morning, eating olives and sandwiches, reading and re-reading his mail, seized with uncontrollable laughter, and writing a long, long letter home.

He compared his sensation to standing in a roomful of people all talking at once, eight of whom he wanted to embrace, another fifteen grasp by the hand, agree with, riposte or apologise to. What a remarkable, unbelievably lovable family they were and how lucky he accounted himself! And essentially a family of deep thinkers too! From Iris there were both letters and airgraphs: gloomy and, as always when she had not seen him for a long time, full of affection. He had evidently been denied that warmth *in propria persona*, and still had her 'under his skin'. While giving his 'folks' a précis of all his correspondence he paused to commend to his father some 'mysterious lines' from Auden's *Letters from Iceland*:

> The tall unwounded leader
> Of doomed companions, all
> Whose voices in the rock
> Are now perpetual,
> Fighters for no one's sake
> Who died beyond the border.

* An airgraph was a single quarto sheet distributed and collected by post offices, sent to a processing station, censored, given a serial number and microfilmed with 1,700 other messages on 100 feet of film. When in April 1941 the first airgraph dispatch arrived in London from Cairo, 50,000 microfilmed letters were found to weigh just thirteen pounds instead of three-quarters of a ton. On arrival each airgraph was developed, magnified and delivered in a manila envelope. Newspaper correspondents estimated in July 1943 that the maximum number of words on an airgraph was 830.

These were in the direct line of English poetry, good not because by 'poets who moaned' but because they were by poets concerned with the English life around them. (What constituted the 'line' of English poetry was a hot Thompson family topic.)* Like much in Frank's story, this verse unwittingly predicts his own last weeks as the tall leader of doomed companions, fighters who also died beyond the border. This letter-storm had made him homesick for the English countryside and for his own set, 'people with home woven ties and untidy hair whose ideas and emotions are in such a mess, but who know better than anyone how to make a friend and keep one'.

His mother sent a cheque for £10 to help him take sick leave. He declined the cheque and the chance of leave alike. Soldiers were commonly found later in Cairo going without home leave for five years. Frank's schooling in the manly virtues would proceed uninter- rupted. Bledlow itself, with its tension between his father and his fierce and manipulative mother – who every few months beckoned him home – would not see his return.

---

Like many soldiers he suffered sexual frustration: 'any girl who catches me in the first month after I've landed will have me wrapped round her little finger even if she's got a mind like a tuppenny thriller and a face like the back of a lorry'. His closest Winchester friend Tony Forster, also serving in Cairo, recalled his and Frank's visits to the 'murkier side' of the city, though fear stopped them 'sampling the fare'. As this was pre-penicillin such fears were wholly rational. Some 140,000 troops were stationed in wartime Cairo and there were seven separate VD clin- ics helping the unlucky with the consequences of queuing to enter brothels. Frank and Tony made indecent advances to two shoe-shine

---

* Frank debates this 'line' in letter after letter – for example on 24 February 1942: 'Last night we were seven officers in the mess together and someone produced Palgrave's *Golden Treasury*. Each of us had to choose two poems and read them out himself. I chose "Old ship" that any man is bound to love and is about this part of the world; and [Edmund Waller's] "Go Lovely Rose" one of the few poems that is unquestionable like a tib [cat] or a white violet. I wish I could have read some Campion.'

boys, but Tony thought they might be taken seriously and be up before the courts.

Frank, too, mentions visits to brothels where he once made sure no one knew he had French letters with him, evidently feeling divided – since a condom must have lessened the risks of infection – about whether he really wanted this shamefully functional form of release or not. He had also been hiding his condoms in base camp for fear of shocking his batman until young Lorton, hearing it claimed that he did not frequent prostitutes, protested with husky pride that he certainly did. On another occasion Frank spent no money 'as I was stony broke. Chatted with repulsive Rosetta and her girls.'

He sounds somewhat at ease in this scene and would claim two years later to Iris Murdoch to have messed up his sex life by taking physical love far too lightly, condemned to the classic dichotomy of seeing women as whores on the one hand and unattainable Madonnas on the other.* Two things are beyond dispute. He may not have died a virgin, but he did retain a certain puritanism; and, although he liked to flirt, he never experienced a physical affair with a woman whom he loved and admired.

EP was in this regard luckier. Theo that spring told Frank that EP was out of doors, that he was eating enormous meals and – with wholly unconscious ribaldry – that he 'had been offered a mount at any time he wants it by a Mrs Clark (aged 30) who is running a small farm near by – horses & goats!' Wendy Clark was nearly thirty-three and taught her three children the myth that EP, aged nineteen, came in to apologise for the damage he had done her cottage fence with a tank. In fact EP had just reached seventeen and was on a horse and cart when he called from nearby Biddesden Farm and met the remarkable Wendy who, as Theo believed, 'worked on the admiration of young men', her seduction technique including the fiction that she 'suffered from a serious ailment' and so needed physically to be comforted. Their affair helped EP's confidence and he appreciated her hospitable, bohemian

---

* In notes towards a late 1943 Cairo story, he distinguishes the cheapest and most repulsive whores who offer merely outdoor release from the 'flash five quid fillies'.

Wendy Clark with husband Geoffrey and children Francis, Helen and Miles, plus sheepdog, Robin, 1941.

household – 'a kind of alternative society through which all kinds of gifted people flowed', including Leslie Baker, devoted friend to Katherine Mansfield. EP's friends were welcomed too. When Theo in 1943 learned the nature of their relationship – the year EP was stationed abroad in North Africa – she 'went on the war-path' and confronted Mrs Clark, who held her own.

But Frank did not have his brother's luck. He agreed that he must surely be a prude on noticing how much he disliked the 'S and M' in Hemingway's stories: why write about a well-to-do man dying of gangrene only because he failed to take proper precautions ('Snows of Kilimanjaro')? Why depict a woman facing an abortion for the sole reason that she has been careless ('Hills Like White Elephants')? Then he disliked Robert Jordan in *For Whom the Bell Tolls* winning a friendship by telling a story 'obscenely discreditable' to himself. Hemingway's perverse mentality was on display. Or was Frank himself, he wondered, just a little old-fashioned? Yes, he was. Though famously ribald himself, he found *Tristram Shandy* too bawdy and digressive: there was a

distinction between what he allowed himself to say and the dispensa-
tion he permitted others.

He could never stand a love story unless it was an integral part of the
plot, and in his own case a love affair did *not* seem part of the plot. He
bared his soul to Désirée Cumberledge, commending his parents to her
– 'Drop in on Bledlow. If I'm written off, be sure to. You'll find they
know all about you' – and commending her to his parents: 'Girl in a
million, wish you could meet her, if she wasn't a pacifist I'd want to marry
her.' When Désirée announced her engagement in a mere cursory
airgraph her casualness disconcerted him. Yet she had been virtually
engaged before until the poor boy was killed flying over Germany, and he
wished her better luck this time. (She never found it. She died unmarried
aged seventy-two in 1992, an active Anglican and retired schoolmistress.
Among her possessions were many letters from Frank.)

He certainly did not want to marry the jovial daughter of some
hunting squire 'or any woman who wasn't fully as charming as Tolstoi's
Anna or Natasha or Kitty or Princess Mary', a half-joke suggesting that
his habit of idealising women died hard. In his more sober moments he
liked to consider himself a lifelong bachelor. The 'very long and cheerful letter' that he posted to Iris Murdoch that June of 1941 has not
survived: Iris, writing briefly to Theo to share news of his arrival in
Egypt, admired his 'genius for finding all experiences fascinatingly
interesting'. In September she wrote to him to say that she liked the
'sweet verse' he had sent her. She was happy that many friends had
followed him to Egypt, including Leo Pliatzky. He wrote to her again
on 10 and 21 November.

------

In Shepheard's Hotel he carefully packed all he needed into one kitbag,
a slim bedroll and a haversack. He left behind in one suitcase at a 'base
dump' all the letters he had received since arrival and in Cairo itself two
suitcases and a tin trunk containing his diary, poems and short stories.
While it was 'one hundred to one against' these ever reaching his family
without him, if that happened he apologised in advance for how shockingly badly written his diary was – he had simply logged interesting,

amusing sights and lovable and strange characters for future use, perhaps in a novel, with no time to mould each entry into the artistic unity that he thought one of the chief joys of diarising. This is, by the way, overly modest: he secreted fluent prose without apparent effort.

In his best epitaph Frank pictures his generation leaving behind their 'books and flowers'. From his own small library of seventy-five books he carefully selected fourteen to take into the Libyan Desert. Some he slipped into his service dress tunic. You never knew when you might get stuck with nothing to do – as had just happened during his two months with septicaemia. His selection included *Moll Flanders*, Gorki's 1907 novel *Die Mütter* (which he loved despite being unable to find a copy except in German), Hemingway's *For Whom the Bell Tolls*, *Three Men in a Boat* and some books in Arabic and Italian together with dictionaries for those two 'languages of most immediate value': they were after all about to fight Italians as well as Germans.

He caught his train from Cairo at midnight on 21 November 'in one of those inspired scrambles' that featured prominently in the life of the Thompson family. He had not merely lost his travel warrant but forgotten to bring provisions or water bottle. By the time he rejoined his unit, Phantom had undergone adventures. First was the threat by the Eighth Army's Brigadier Jock Campbell, never forewarned of their arrival, to have the whole outfit arrested as spies. Happily one patrol, led by the acutely short-sighted Edgar 'Herbie' Herbert, secured the squadron's first prisoners by shooting at what Herbie took to be gazelle, only for them to put up their hands and surrender – because they were in fact three Germans on a motorcycle combination. Then Carol Mather's patrol was charged with the task of simulating the signal traffic of an armoured division attacking from the south near Jarabub; for four wearisome days they concocted and transmitted bogus messages on the air, to try to dupe Rommel's spies.*

The Allied relief of Tobruk after its 240-day siege on 27 November

---

* While regimental historian Philip Warner optimistically implies some success, Mather, the officer in charge, wrote sceptically, 'I cannot believe it was very effective' (Carol Mather, *When the Grass Stops Growing*, London, 1997, p. 59).

followed nine days of fighting and was first reported to HQ by Phantom. By the 23rd Frank had rejoined his unit, deploying with the 17th Indian Brigade. This was his longest single stretch in any one country – five months from November 1941 to April 1942 'beneath the Libyan dog-star', as he expressed it lyrically to Iris Murdoch. The phrase was not just romanticism: at night in total blackout they navigated using Sirius (the dog-star) and once, as Frank reported, 'steering slightly to the right of the moon'. The experience was hallucinatory, with camel-bushes only at dawn finally losing the shape of ambushing marauders. They drove in close convoy in choking dust; the vehicle in front often stopped when its driver fell asleep at the wheel.

Now at last he saw action and came under fire. On 25 December Benghazi fell, one of its deserted Italian villas soon providing Frank with a flea-ridden billet. His stock of books there had increased to twenty-two, swollen by the occasional volume reaching him from home.* Frank's collection now also featured three captured German novels; and here was one tiny sign that the fortunes of war at last were changing.

---

* For the delivery of mail in the desert, see the following chapter. That December Nikolai Bakhtin's *An Introduction to the Study of Modern Greek* arrived in the middle of nowhere and Frank devoured it 'almost at one gulp'. Leo Pliatzky meanwhile watched a motorcyclist arrive in the dust of the desert with a letter from his old college requiring him to pay his overdue battels (the bill for board and provisions).

# 9

## Under the Libyan Dog-star: 1942

I know that you must die my Comrade
Die gaily as the sunset glows on Hermon . . .
For you and me and the young vine leaves death is the end.
But life goes on for ever.

'Red Gladiolus', April 1942

Christians have a panic confidence that after death their own personality
will be translated to some place in the ether . . . The Buddhist view . . . the
only one that begins to make sense . . . [is the] idea of the individual
personality merging back into the mainstream of consciousness.

Letter, 26 July 1942

While Frank sickened with septicaemia, EJ was welfare officer at the
RAF camp near West Malling in Kent, where red tape, a huge burden
of letter-writing and physical frailty distressed him; after two months of
feeling increasingly useless, ill and 'past it', he left. He felt a failure. On
the Denham Studios set in Buckinghamshire of Powell and Pressburger's
'hands-across-the-sea' movie, *49th Parallel*, he and Theo had shaken
hands with the actor Leslie Howard; they later attended the film's gala
opening. But his film plans came to nothing. Nor would any newspaper advertise his new collection of poems, *New Recessional* (June 1942),
and fears of an establishment conspiracy further depressed him. The
cartoonist David Low – a new friend – introduced him to H. G. Wells,

who talked 'less delirious rot' than EJ had expected. But friendship could not compensate for the absence of official war work. India remained his raison d'être.

Was Britain fighting this war to preserve the imperialist status quo or to create a brighter, more progressive future? India was a test case. Two and a half million Indians fighting on the Allied side were proving crucially important in the Middle East and North Africa alike. EJ's *Enlist India for Freedom* (1940) explains why they had the right to expect their cooperation to be rewarded by independence. One obstacle was India's 650 princely states, and his work-in-progress *The Making of the Indian Princes* (1943) again suggested how to move forward. When he communicated with members of the Government (Stafford Cripps or Clement Attlee), when he wrote for *The Times* or the *New Statesman*, visited the House of Lords, broadcast or appeared in a panel at Kingsway or Conway Halls, India was the topic.

He thought the ineptitude of the British Government and the crassness of Indian nationalist leaders roughly equal. Nehru, who learned of this, wrote to him: 'please do not carry away all this bitterness against my poor unhappy country'. EJ strove to be fair-minded. He did not agree that hatred between the Muslim League and the Hindu Congress Party proved India's unreadiness for self-rule; such strife was simply another result of bad British government. But he also never gave up faith in the British Empire as a potential force for good and accordingly canvassed Dominion status for India, like Canada or New Zealand. This was exactly what Sir Stafford Cripps offered India in his failed March 1942 mission. Gandhi scorned this as 'The post-dated cheque of a failing bank', and promptly launched his last campaign, the Quit India movement, that led directly in 1947 to independence. The morning after Gandhi's speech all major leaders and 100,000 other Indians were arrested, demonstrators fined or flogged and some shot. This final imprisonment of Nehru lasted three years. Then in April 1942, on his way to meet with Cripps, EJ's close friend Geoffrey Garratt – with whom he had co-written *The Rise and Fulfilment of British Rule in India* – was killed by a bomb.

India compelled Frank's and EP's imaginations too. At Corpus Christi College in Cambridge EP, now eighteen, gave a talk on India,

'background, social conditions, history – Congress, Muslim League
&tc'. And Frank, serving with an Indian brigade followed by three
weeks in an Indian Army hospital, sent home enthusiastic reports.
Indians were 'the neatest, cleanest and most dignified soldiers in our
army', first-rate soldiers and good technicians too. When he took four
broken springs to an Indian workshop they had them mended and
back on the vehicles within four hours. He thought India a tragedy, a
half-disgruntled colony dragging at Britain's feet unconsulted when it
could play an important and dignified role. At the end of 1942 Theo
and EJ both feared that EJ's letters to Frank had been stopped after he
had written seditiously about the India Office, and Frank meanwhile
joked that his father, after being used to 'sort the whole shemozzle out'
as 'Man-of-the-hour', might be appointed Lord Coneygar* of Bledlow,
KCBE [sic]. He wrote to Désirée that 'My father is the best-loved
Englishman in India, my mother and grandfather the best-loved foreign
folk in Syria . . . My dearest wish is to carve a similar niche for myself
in Greece, Jugoslavia or Bulgaria – or even the vast territories of old
Muscovy.'

———

Practicalities absorbed Theo. She corresponded with the BBC Overseas
Service about a talk they wanted her to write in Arabic; chaired a WI
meeting where Great War survivors shared their experiences; helped
organise the investment of £2,000 each for her sons from her wealthy
Brooklyn relatives. EJ's handicapped brother Alfred – dropped as a
child, simple and given to fits – moved to lodgings two miles away
where he worked in a corset factory and was a Methodist lay preacher,
visiting Bledlow at weekends. Alfred, whose simplicity was the butt of
many jokes, was good, serious and loyally tended by the Thompsons.
'Uncle Alfred informs me', EP wrote to Frank, that 'Venice is a place
and that St Paul did a lot of missionary work in Troy.' Theo, who grew
vegetables, bought Alfred an orchard with sixty young trees, where he
planted a kitchen garden.

* The Coneygar was a piece of land abutting the Thompson house in Bledlow.

After the USA had entered the war in December 1941, she pondered her own indebtedness to what she called its 'unusual form of society'. One American friend in London was Marchesa Louise de Rosales, who told Theo about being entertained as a child by the King and Queen of Bulgaria in their cliff monastery-palace overhanging the Black Sea, and about her work as a nurse in Italy during the Great War. After Louise's chauffeur left to work in an aircraft factory she patriotically gave away her 'enormous Packard or Buick' to the Red Cross, hiring a car when visiting Theo from the Connaught Hotel where she waited out the war. Her maid, Drummond, took photos of EP kitted out in his uniform as an officer in the 17th/21st Lancers, when he spent a night in Louise's suite in summer 1943. (He was grateful that the army taught him about the insides of a car, electricity, wireless, first aid, as his liberal education had entailed no applied learning.) Theo and EJ, too, sometimes stayed at the Connaught, to take in a show or a film. She found Walt Disney's jokes about stork-babies in his 'tricksy and cute' film *Dumbo* vulgar.

Theo cultivated London-based Phantom officers. Lieutenant John Fitzwilliam, training the next generations of recruits in Richmond, advised during summer 1941 about how to get money and messages to Frank and gave news of sick leave granted to his fellow officers to return home. Captain Sir John Wrightson, Richmond HQ's gloomy intelligence officer, also rang Theo several times with news of Frank. And Wrightson helped her on 14 January 1942 cable fretfully: 'No word from you since November 19. Please signal at once how you are. Love from us all. Mother.' Wrightson, she assured EP, 'chalked it up to Frank's credit that he told us . . . that no news was good news . . . we ought to hear within 3 days'.

Russian sufferings moved her. She raised money for the Russian war effort, joined the Fabians, thought constantly of her two boys, worked on a Puffin picture book and, despite rheumatism, polished the communion rail of the village church, 'at which I, a Non-conformist, will never kneel'.

———

Frank had been in Libya for two months, and would stay a further three. He called the war in North Africa 'a game of shuttlecock': five separate 'swings' went alternately to the Axis or the Allies, each failing when the victors lacked the capacity to follow up or exploit their success, in long exhausting tank battles resembling medieval jousts. Four days after Frank had rejoined his squadron the Eighth Army relieved the long siege of Tobruk, driving 350 miles west to capture Benghazi on Christmas Day itself. This was Operation Crusader, with 118,000 Allied troops taking losses of 17,700, and Axis forces taking even bigger casualties. One month later, on 28 January 1942, Rommel recaptured Benghazi with three months' army rations and one million cigarettes going up in smoke, before retaking Tobruk in May. Shuttlecock offensive and counter-offensive ended only with General Montgomery's decisive victory at El Alamein that November.

In all Frank crossed the Libyan Jebel Desert three times. He first came under fire after the battle of Sidi Rezegh on 30 November 1941 when attached to a raiding column of the South African Armoured Cars trying to cut the coastal road and shoot up enemy transport. After the ritual dusk brew-up, when sausage or bully sizzling in cut-down petrol tins was consumed with the indispensable cup of *chai*, they moved forward jerkily through the night in close formation, Frank and Lorton singing softly together.

Frank, who had a sweet tooth, was drowsily eating the last bar of captured chocolate that the South Africans had given them when the column stopped, under red and white lights indicating streams of bullets and machine-gun fire. When his wireless operator jumped out and dived under the vehicle ahead Frank at last understood that Italian Breda posts were shooting vigorously at them: he had missed his opportunities to experience fear, courage, nonchalance or excitement. On another occasion they got mixed up with some German tanks, but he affords no details. Allied and German tank crews were so battle-fatigued that they often leaguered down for the night in close proximity, and – since each also had vehicles captured from the other side – with confusing and comical results in the morning.

Frank evoked an air raid in a poem – 'the black winged planes like bees in swarm with steady droning . . . wheel overhead and descend: crash after crash resounds, dust fountains the horizon'. The first time he and Lorton were dive-bombed by Stukas – the best and most precise dive-bomber of the Second World War – they were on top of a fuel dump holding a petrol can and did not even run for cover. But they soon learned to shelter in a slit trench, despite Hoppy's pronouncement. Frank experienced during raids a mixture of terror and humiliation that reminded him of 'a schoolboy awaiting a caning', while the courage of the anti-aircraft gunners inspired him. During the December advance to Benghazi his unit sent a raiding party behind enemy lines to report battle progress with Frank busily enciphering. Lorton received a painful bomb splinter wound below the shoulder but, plucky and uncomplaining, was back in action by spring.

War alternates boredom with terror, and Frank once got his men spending two whole days digging his wireless truck in against air attack, then a third digging it out again because it was stuck. When Rommel after a lull rallied in January, Frank's unit was attached to 7th Indian Brigade making a 'brilliant escape' from Benghazi – retreating at 40 mph towards the Egyptian border. Frank spent months on the Gazala Line, where the white houses of Tobruk with its blue harbour featured as their desert metropolis, and won a few days' comfort at Eighth Army HQ.

There was a pervasive dread of getting lost in the featurelessness of the desert, whose place names rarely corresponded to anything recognisable. Chance encounters were the more memorable. He met French NCOs trying to bag a hare, appreciated the unfailing courtesy of his first Poles and watched British cavalry officers passing by in dandified dress. He ran into an unnamed schoolfriend, killed months later, who gave him tea in his dugout at Bir Hacheim.

With access to intelligence about where units were, he sought out Leo Pliatzky in his field army workshop dugout, and arrived singing 'Whitworths are a girl's best friend'. They had not met since the Blitz two years before and Leo, 'the old cynic himself', was delighted. They enjoyed a can of warm beer each while Leo, observing a new physical confidence and coordination in Frank, wondered whether this followed

*From left to right*: *standing*, Jasper Backhouse and Carol Mather;
*seated*, Donald Melvin, 'Lt X', as Frank captions himself, and George Grant.

from his loss of virginity. (That women the following year were still refusing to dance with Frank because of his clumsiness suggests that this 'new coordination' had its limits.)

The extraordinary desert spring blossomed from late January, and Carol Mather saw Frank intoxicated by its beauty, recording twenty-seven different species of flower, in immense drifts of red, yellow and blue. By April Mather noted drily that 'Frank was reading Greek poetry and dreaming of the egalitarian society to come – from the safety of the officers' mess tent!' Frank's attempts to raise the Red Army banner were met with polite amusement.

Fear of a German breakthrough in the Caucasus in pursuit of Iraqi oil caused Phantom's redeployment that April to Palestine and Syria, where it was to report on pro-Vichy French sentiment, and give an account of troubles on the Syrian–Turkish border. Its members left the desert with some sadness: it was a mesmerising place, its very vastness accentuating the intimate camaraderie of small unexpected campfire welcomes, sharing tea laced with rum under the immense canopy of desert stars. The burned-out tanks and planes would soon be picked clean by Senussi tribesmen; meanwhile it was 'not a bad desert', having been enriched, Frank wrote, by 'some of the finest deeds of courage and endurance in Man's history'.

His five months in Libya were harsh, alternately dull and dangerous, confusing and memorable. Frank and H Squadron alike, despite mistakes, found their feet there. However, the Eighth Army while in Libya soon moved away from Phantom to J Service instead, which listened in to forward radio traffic 'chatter', including the Eighth Army's own, for an up-to-date account of the progress of a battle.

Frank chronicled the campaign in a retrospective journal. The remains of Graeco-Roman civilisation in Cyrenaica, erstwhile bread-basket of Rome, stimulated his imagination, the hem of the Hellenic world almost more fascinating than the heart. This theatre of war reminded him of Syria while remaining essentially African. As they proceeded north out of the desert, they were startled by the sudden green hubbub of the delta.

---

Although for weeks or months they had little water to wash with, mail – 'dearest thing next to tea to the heart of a soldier' – somehow happily filtered through, on one occasion arriving during a dull interlude between dive-bombing raids. While censoring his men's letters Frank was shocked by the braggart heroics and exotic lies of one, the repetitions of another, but recognised the opposing needs to soothe or stimulate your relatives back home. He too prettified conditions for home consumption, offending neither decorum nor security. When in March 1942 Theo yet again raised the question of his going home for treatment, he berated her angrily. True, two of his fellow officers had been invalided home, but his commanding officer 'Brian Frank's eczema made him resemble a leper; Gerald Pinckney had every bone in his foot crushed by an armoured car'. His last boil had disappeared in January; he was taking 'vitamin tablets' and drinking 'half a pint of lime-juice each day'; he 'often' ate fresh meat and bread and wore 'comfortable' desert boots.

Carol Mather one month earlier reported such a plague of desert sores that simply putting your unbandaged hand into your pocket removed the skin, leaving a bloody mess: clearly no vitamin tablets or lime juice were then in evidence. When Frank told his parents that his Major had been captured – 'poor old boy' – so that Frank had to take command for five challenging days, he omitted to tell them that Dermot Daly had been so incapacitated by hand sores that he was an easy target for a German snatch raid. Frank naturally also withheld the news that on briefly taking command the previous month, still aged only twenty-one, he had consumed a bottle of whisky the day before.

Those privations that he could turn to lyricism or wit Frank would admit to; others he kept silent about. He acknowledged Benghazi's fleas: 'vast forces of dangerous and determined guerilla fighters' left behind by the Italians. He lyricised the formidable cold 'penetrating, eating through innumerable layers of clothing into the bone itself so that I can't write'. And when fearsome sandstorms blew he admitted huddling like others in the back of the truck demoralising himself, really hating the desert.

On dry nights they slept in the open, so the March rains took him by surprise. He had been prepared for heat – tank metal by afternoon was so searingly hot you could fry an egg on it – as for thirst, flies, weariness and high explosives. 'But when the great father of camels countenances torrential rain he is definitely going beyond the terms of reference.' He came back drenched after a day's work on an old battle-field salvaging parts from smashed vehicles, to find his bedding soaked, while Herbert (the fellow officer so short-sighted he mistook a German patrol for a group of gazelle), unable to spot his tent at 200 yards, wandered most of the night in the rain, sleeping for a few hours wrapped in an old tarpaulin. Herbert was exultant on reappearing at 9.30 a.m. to find that his bed, unlike Frank's, was still dry.

Frank confessed some truths. Water to wash or shave in was so rare that they grew 'bearded like the pard'; a single hot bath in many months at Agedabia constituted an event. Frank's pleasure in *For Whom the Bell Tolls* was diminished by the fact that even Hemingway baulked at admitting how Robert Jordan's feet must have stunk, lest his love scenes lose credibility. When in early February a bottle of beer each and new clothing appeared, the old rags they had been wearing had to be burned on a bonfire. Leo Pliatzky together with his corps were lice-ridden, and Frank's probably were too. ('Our own soldiers get [lice] quite frequently,' he noted.)

Censorship would not have permitted him to share the tally of Phantom H losses by February 1942: two captured, two invalided home, one disciplined for an unnamed misdemeanour, a casualty rate of 10 per cent. But he operated strong internal self-censorship too. Not only was he silent about vitamin deficiency and lice, which concern for his family's peace of mind made him downplay, but he called his work early in 1942 during the lull between campaigns a 'soft' job, 'beer and skittles' compared to the daily routine of Britain's ordinary fighting troops.

He had a sunny disposition, and enjoyed painting little vignettes to charm his audience. So he recorded in a quiet rear area of the desert a soldier who kept six quails under his bed. All lived together in contented domesticity until one day after gas-attack practice the soldier strode back into his tent disguised by his respirator: the birds fled as one quail never to return. He also evoked Biscuit, the spirited kitten thrown in for want of four piastres change when he bought a bottle of chianti in Benghazi; Biscuit travelled curled up in the driver's hat untroubled by mechanised movement, and even got on with Bully, a black and white puppy kidnapped the following week. Frank spent his spare time teaching Biscuit to fight for his country against a piece of paper and some string.

———

To Iris Murdoch too he described Biscuit and also commended the 'warm-heartedness and simplicity' of Maxim Gorki's peasants in *The Mother*. She replied ironically that she and he were scarcely straightforward peasants so much as 'bemused intellectual misfits'. Or at least she was. But she brooded over his phrase 'simple and warm-hearted': it struck her imagination forcibly. Six months later she was writing to another friend in Egypt about Frank as being 'maybe too simple and warmhearted'.

Frank shrewdly thought Virginia Woolf's characters in *Between the Acts*

either absurdly conventional or 'too sensitive to live'. He had a growing
dislike of introspection. He wrote to his folks on 15 February 1942:

> the young Englishman's faculty for introspection lessens to almost noth-
> ing with the end of adolescence. Very rarely now do I find myself
> inspecting the murky mass of incoherence a metaphysician would call
> my soul. My chief intellectual interests are in the earth and the people
> on it, especially 'the characters' and myself as a potential 'character', in
> the figure I cut to the outside world, which probably bears no relation
> to the one I would find in the silences of my own mind.

What of the motto 'Know thyself', drummed into him at school?
Marcus Aurelius and Thomas à Kempis were great in spite of their
introspection, he riposted, not because of it. He ridiculed the 'tracking
down [of your] mental fleas' which made nineteenth-century Russians
wretched and ineffectual. When in 1943 Iris demanded a response to
the news of her having lost her virginity he argued that 'I think Tolstoy
and Chekhov went as far into the minds of our fellow men as it is profitable *or seemly* to go.' He rejected what he called 'continued
psychological kit-inspections'.

Here was a new theme. It was partly his way of evading capture,
refusing criticism, safeguarding privacy and independence. Communists
and bluff professional soldiers alike embraced simplicity, and 'One
forgets unless reminded constantly that one has ever been a civilian or
had any [other] raison d'être.' It is also his surrender to the masculine
culture of the mess.

Warm-hearted simplicity was increasingly Frank's persona. 'The
more I see', he wrote from Libya, 'the less I understand why civilisation
has gone to the bad, when there are so many good people.' The lack of
bitterness in his letters impressed both Iris and Leonie Platt (née
Marsh), whose husband longed to see a German plane crash with no
survivors, but who doubted whether Frank were capable of the same
hatred and who wrote saying she knew his gun would jam because he
had 'real brotherly love in him' and would not wish to kill.

It was possibly due to observing him in his role as the unit's Education

Officer that one of his men told him he was too restless to be a school-master post-war as he wished. He noted ruefully – but probably accurately, had he survived – that he would have to try and hack his way in life as a journalist instead. Frank feared that his impatience meant also that he would never settle down anywhere long enough to marry or have children and that meanwhile soldiering looked like being his first and only profession. So far as a journalistic future went, his letters are effortlessly readable, brilliant reportage and full of wild leaps of imagination – as when, in one, he compares Charles I and General Robert E. Lee as 'reactionaries who went down with great dignity' or Lincoln with Lenin as twin heroes.

His 250,000 or so words written during the war (letters, diaries, poems) bear testimony to his obsessive urge to turn life into narrative, and he wished he had the eyes and ears of Tolstoy. But his surviving stories are – at best – apprentice work. Iris Murdoch none the less accurately saw that he was designed to be a teller of tales and noted his propensity always to 'hit upon the picturesque' in life as in words.

Americans began to appear in the Middle East after the USA entered the war in December 1941. He was moved to see the American flag fly. While knowing that Old Glory was brandished against California Okies and Detroit steelworkers, it still seemed to him to stand for something bigger and more progressive.

He tested out these theories that April during a week's leave in Beirut, staying with his mother's American cousinry, Meg and Leslie Leavitt, with visits to the Dodges, Glocklings, Freidingers. He liked staying in an American household, appreciated American accents and manners, and thought the American University of Beirut a beacon of sanity in a backwater generally badly misgoverned. One Beiruti recalled and praised his great-grandfather Henry Harris Jessup and Frank visited Theo's father's grave. He was proud of being a Jessup. He would like any daughter of his to speak with an American accent; his wife would have to have one too. He noted that The Heights, the Jessup house at Aleih, was now valued at £5,000.

He also rekindled acquaintance with Anglo-Levantines such as Cecil Hourani (at Oxford with him in 1939) and, in Aleppo, Ernest Altounyan (whom the Thompsons had met at Lake Coniston in 1933: his and Dora Collingwood's children were the originals for Arthur Ransome's Walker children in *Swallows and Amazons*). He read Ernest's *Ornament of Honour*, his strange poem addressed to T. E. Lawrence, and in Jerusalem met his attractive daughter Tacqui. Such visits made him reflect that he belonged to a definite class of people with whom he instantly felt at home: Leavitts, Nicholsons and by implication Altounyans – educated, intelligent people who valued good conversation enough not to dilute it by card-playing, cinema-going or allowing their children to dominate.

None the less Phantom, where he was number two, was now his home. He was gazetted captain on 8 September 1942 but told nobody at home; his parents discovered this promotion only five months later. He thought his new commanding officer George Grant one of the kindliest and most rational of men.

*From left to right: standing*, Jo Adams, John Pearson-Gregory, Frank, Graham Bell and Norman Radcliffe; *seated*, Angus McBain, George Grant and Maurice Avril. Frank's caption reads: 'I had the sun dead in my eyes – also a touch of fever. I look like a French bicyclist.'

After a brief refit in Cairo, H Squadron was now sent to Syria, where the previous summer the Allies had defeated pro-Axis forces, and – as in Iraq and Iran – installed a puppet ruler loyal to their interests. Phantom had the job of going into the unoccupied part of Syria to discover a port and airfield prepared by sympathisers for German invasion, and establish which officials were still actively pro-Vichy. It also reported via long-range wireless on the dispute between two Bedouin tribes across British lines of communication with the southern Russian front and explored points of passage for mechanised transport on the Turkish–Syrian border: UK forces might have to cross 'if things deteriorated in Turkey'. All this was accomplished by 13 June and shows Phantom's roving brief. Frank's French and fledgling Arabic surely helped in this work.

Carol Mather left Phantom and returned to the Commandos, and last saw Frank 'getting itchy feet' in Syria, wanting to return to action either in Libya, where the news worsened, or elsewhere. He minded very much being left out of the current fighting, in which first-rate chaps were chucking their lives away 'like cigarette-ends'. In June 1942 George Grant helped him apply to return to the now mechanised Royal Horse Artillery, where he hoped his knowledge of desert warfare, wireless communication and mechanised transport would help him avoid a desk job. He requested Theo neither to send telegrams asking him to change his mind, nor to betray his plans to Phantom HQ in Richmond.

Frank longed to share the dangers of war, and experience a communal sense of purpose. Summer 1942's alarums and excursions at first promised both. When Rommel recaptured Tobruk and the Eighth Army fell back to El Alamein, Phantom was abruptly recalled to the Western Desert, the men trekking nearly 2,000 miles to get there in eight punishing days. Disappointment followed, and indeed their worst month of the war awaited them in Burg-el-Arab on the Egyptian border, passing wireless messages for a tank delivery regiment.

'You'd better not try plotting my moves over the last two months: they're too nonsensical,' Frank wrote home that August, now en route back northwards to Iran. The prospect of cooperating with the Red Army defending the Caucasus was 'a job [he'd] rather have . . . than any other': nearly 1,200 tons of freight went through Iran each day to the USSR by rail and vast quantities also by road. Frank gave up his plans to leave Phantom, now part of the newly formed Paiforce – Persia and Iraq Force. From a base in Hamadan it could help guard Russian supply routes and listen in for any German breakthrough of Russian defences. 'Fielding long-stop to Brother Ivan' was not as suicidal as gunnery, but interesting, important and – he boasted – 'by no means safe either'. Above all it promised the likelihood of meeting Russian soldiers. Perhaps Phantom might still deliver the danger and adventure he sought.

Meanwhile an airgraph from Winifred Carritt stunned him. Brian had died on 1 July, after six weeks of TB.* Like Rex the previous year, Brian was only twenty-one. But this news was far worse: unlike Rex, Brian was neither conventional nor conservative. Their shared Communism made a close and vital bond. From Arborfield army train-ing camp where he taught young women to use predictors on anti-aircraft guns they took him to the Osler Sanatorium in Headington, and finally home, where Brian died on the balcony overlooking the Boars Hill garden that for Frank held so many memories of discussion and play. Winifred ended bravely: 'Don't be too sad but work all the harder to fill up the gap he leaves . . . We spoke often of you . . . Victory in 1942.' Frank replied that Brian had been an integral part of Thompson family life, effectively another brother to him. Theo, eloquent in grief, tried to console Frank that TB made its victims in some way happy or at least optimistic, and yet 'some things are utter loss . . . My heart aches for you night and day.'

Memories gathered. Brian dining and smiling, Brian tossing his blond forelock when they last met, unexpectedly, in Leicester Square in 1941, both hands clasping Frank's before he turned and walked away into the crowd. He tried out different goodbyes, from the American 'So long Fella, been good knowing you' to the quieter British (to Iris) 'I shall always be glad at the thought of him.'

---

* Brian probably had tubercular meningitis, according to Andrew Gardner's surviving brother, a doctor, in 2009.

He proclaimed Brian a 'new can-do type' lacking all Frank's own inhibitions from the past, while in private registering that Brian's letters, despite being emotional and hence un-English, were yet 'half-strangled' too. Frank and Brian fully shared discomfort about emotion.

Fifty years later Brian's elder brother Gabriel (Bill) praised the *sancta simplicitas* Brian and Frank shared. This was partly sentimental, partly true. Frank believed that the way Brian over-simplified life was valuable and instructive. Writing to his Eton tutor of the flashes of comradeship he treasured, Brian added tellingly, 'It's as though one could stretch out a hand when one is happy and feel it clasped by millions of people all over the world.' The potent illusion 1930s Communism offered is here distilled into a phrase: an end to injustice and loneliness, and an escape out of 'half-strangled' English inhibition into simple, communal certainties.

Frank received Brian's Dragon eulogy containing that stirring phrase that November. It inspired 'Aubade', a poem in letter form he sent to Mrs Carritt, starting: 'Hullo Brian! Writing to you from Persia. / Here is a picture that you would have liked . . . / Morning. North, on the snow mountains, / Black thunder-clouds . . .' He communes with a kindred spirit whose courage and strength he celebrates, summoning him to greet a dawning new age. The same month he wrote to his parents quoting Cecil Day Lewis's 'A Time to Dance', declaring that Brian would always be 'my friend who within me laughs', a beloved figure reminding him of happiness.

------

By July 1942 his correspondence with the newly engaged Désirée had faltered, while that with Iris Murdoch flourished. She four times addresses Frank in her letters as 'Brother' while he reciprocated with 'Soul-sister' or 'Tovaritch' (Comrade), stressing their political affinity. His feeling is apparent from his translation of Pushkin's 'Ya Vas Lyubil':

> I loved you once. Who knows but even now
> Love in my soul may not be wholly dead?
> But never let it trouble you. I vow
> I would not hurt you by a thing I did.

I loved you once in silent desperation.
Shyness and envy wracked me numb with pain.
I loved you once. God grant such adoration
So true, so gentle, comes your way again.

Frank manages to convey the stylishness of the twenty-year-old Pushkin's Russian. He also wrote a story about a Gunner Perkins who wished to express passion by letter to his girlfriend Helen, rather than ponderous thoughts about books and politics. 'If only he had had the courage before he left. Now it was too late, you could never break down barriers by letter.' 'Helen' is an interesting *nom de guerre* for Iris: the Greeks died at Troy for another Helen.

Towards the end of 1942 each appealed for greater intimacy. Frank was depressed from jaundice when he reflected on the vagaries of their friendship: 'Three years & a bit since I joined the Army. More than that since you & I first exchanged *Weltanschauungs* [worldviews] in a room at Ruskin. Now I am 22 instead of 18, and you 23, almost a matron. Looks like being another three years straight before we meet again. We shall probably find we have both changed out of all knowing and have nothing any longer in common.' But her letters – 'a golden gift, a winged gift' – meant a lot to him. 'They strike fire immediately. And when one arrives . . . I am impelled forthwith to answer it . . .' He would like to see her post-war. He repeated the appeal in April 1943: 'there are only four people left in . . . England who can speak almost as clearly on paper as with their lips. Three of those are my closest kin and the other one is you.'

On 22 January 1943 Iris reciprocated by evoking her loneliness within the 'miles and miles of frigid protective atmosphere' in the Treasury, where she was now an assistant principal. Her bohemian period in Fitzrovia, where she would collect new admirers, was starting. But she wanted to find 'the patient mind which is prepared to comprehend my own & toss me back the ball of my thought'. Each shared the gift of making the other feel understood.

And Frank increasingly appealed to Iris's imagination. Her 24 November 1942 letter conveys two opposed views of courage in which he features. On the one hand she hopes that he will stay as far from the firing line as ever, wanting him to be a hero but without endangering himself. To her fellow romantic Frank, any charge of timidity would have stung. 'I am quite certain you have all the qualities of a stout fella, without the necessity of a vulgar display,' she reassured him.

But Iris had been rereading T. E. Lawrence's *The Seven Pillars of Wisdom*, and later in the same letter records an indescribable 'reverence for that book – for that man . . . To live such a swift life of action, and yet *not* simplify everything to the point of inhumanity – to let the agonizing complexities of situations twist your heart instead of tying your hands – that is real human greatness.' Lawrence was the man of action most admired by Iris's future philosophic heroines Simone Weil and Simone de Beauvoir. Iris praised him as a 'world-changer who never lost his capacity to doubt'.

T. E. Lawrence, she now tells Frank, is 'the sort of person I would leave anything to follow'. Here was a crude bribe that worked elsewhere. Iris persuaded another Oxford contemporary, the ex-pacifist Paddy O'Regan, into joining SOE where he won an MC and bar: imitate T. E. Lawrence and win love and admiration, including hers.

And Lawrence had haunted Frank's childhood: he had excavated in Carchemish with Rex Campbell Thompson's father, was friend to Robert Graves, Gilbert Murray and Ernest Altounyan, was cousin to EJ's good friend Lord Vansittart, and had once even visited the Thompson family home for tea. Theo and EJ had attended T. E. Lawrence's memorial service in St Paul's in 1935, recording it as 'a bit too domestic and stuffy for anyone as "stark" as TE'. In January 1943 Frank was reading the Marxist Christopher Caudwell, another admirer of Lawrence.

Where Iris's nervous self-consciousness can – to this reader – be arch and irritating, war was making Frank grow up faster. Iris repeatedly contrasted her own romantic dreaminess with Frank's relative realism. Indeed, when she wrote flippantly of the glamour of the East, he by contrast described its misery that killed all joy and hope in him, as it had in his father earlier.

In the summer of 1942 Frank wrote home that he was lucky to be in touch with one or two chaps whose 'views on life are very much the same as mine' – code for CP members – though the affinity did not preclude disagreements. Indeed Frank told Iris he was tired of militant socialists with no historical perspective or ability to make allowances for people's class background.

Frank, not for the first or last time, refused the Party line and held it in contempt. He had read not merely the official Bolshevik historian of Russia Mikhail Pokrovsky but also, as we have seen, critics of Russia like Bernard Pares, as well as Eugene Lyons in his *Assignment in Utopia*, from whom Frank was surprised to learn that 'apparently the Famine [of 1932–3] could have been stopped'. Frank thought the doubts and criticisms of both Pares and Lyons honest, deserving of respect and not to be dismissed with unthinking Party catchwords such as 'Whiteguard, Trotskyite, or Social Democrat', a lazy habit he despised.

EP himself was involved at Cambridge with the Communist journal *Our Time*, by which Frank was not impressed: it showed a tendency to caricature generals as idle if not cowardly. In a long crucial letter he took his brother to task also for jibes about a Harrovian fellow trainee. 'It's a mistake to hate people because of their class,' he wrote, since each class was a victim of its environment – and neither were all the upper class cads, nor all workers Sir Galahads. This is good Marxism, yet rare, and fifty years later in *Beyond the Frontier* EP praised Frank's lack of dogmatism.

EP's reaction at the time, when he was still only eighteen, differed, and in a 1945 letter he criticised Frank, as we have seen, for espousing the 'rather easy cynical philosophy of Winchester at his time together with its lazy all-embracing humanism', by which EP probably meant that Frank's tolerance extended even to Old Harrovians. He thought Frank offered to humanise Communist doctrine 'to the point of glossing over it'. Frank, sensing this, apologised that the New Thinking he had been trying to digest at Oxford had all been vomited and none had entered his bloodstream, which was still all Winchester and Horace and a tinge of Lytton Strachey. And it was now that he declared his mind 'more inclined to love than analyse'.

He made other, more congenial CP friends. Peter Wright, 'a German teacher before the war'* and now in the Intelligence Corps, was also sent to the brown and dusty hills of Persia and feared a German break-through. Wright noted an unusual, slightly mysterious reconnaissance unit called Phantom that moved in armoured cars and whose officers would drop by to study maps or gather information about German advances in the Caucasus. One tall young subaltern who collected such information in a quiet self-effacing way gave an impression of uncommon intelligence and sensitivity. He was very modest about speaking some Russian himself and spoke of Russians as if they were human beings.

Wright did not learn Frank's name and so was doubly impressed when, that Christmas in Baghdad, a rather unkempt Frank not merely invited him to lunch but greeted him by name. On the bookshelves in Paiforce officers' mess were books by E. J. Thompson, whose talks at Larkhill Wright had appreciated two years earlier; and over lunch he was overjoyed to discover that Frank – 'by Jove' – was related to EJ, and then Frank's copy of Christopher Caudwell's *Studies in a Dying Culture* (sent him by EP) alerted him to their shared Communism. Wright, whom Frank thought 'the best bloke I've met since leaving England', promptly borrowed the Caudwell. They saw a lot of one another from then on, and both the following year joined SOE.

---

Though accounting himself second to none in the family in his regard for the Indian people, Frank's enthusiasm wavered that autumn. A clumsy Gurkha mess waiter shoved his fist over the mouth of a beer bottle, letting the beer pour unhygienically over his hand while serving. Frank, sickening with hepatitis, blamed the poor diet of tinned sausages, tinned bacon and tinned salmon with no fruit or veg apart from the odd apple and reassured his anxious parents that the cause was not vodka. (After recovery, his uncertain liver made him moderate his alcohol intake.)

* Wright's SOE personal file makes clear that he knew French and Spanish, not German.

On 18 October 1942 he was bright yellow and so depressed and lacking in energy that he hardly opened a book and struggled to write even one letter a day. The tiny so-called Indian 'hospital' – one medical officer, one cook and three orderlies – dispirited him further. Small sallow Indians squatted around in groups, or dashed up 'saluting about five times' or gabbled away incomprehensibly. They irritated him, and Frank's internationalism faltered. 'Let them live their ways and us ours . . . when I'm ill I'm afraid they give me the creeps.' He felt relief in thus being 'really wicked and insular once in a while'.

Still yellow-eyed in hospital he began a series of Russian-conversation lessons at five shillings an hour from Terterian, an Armenian wine merchant and political refugee who pleased him by calling him in Russian 'little Dove'. Terterian spoke no English so, though his grammar was imperfect, everything was said in Russian. His tales of Stalin's terror made an impression. Frank, writing both to Iris Murdoch and to his parents about the number of people Stalin had personally had poisoned, listed six, then added that he assumed that Stalin's disposal of the Bolshevik Sergei Kirov by other means than poison (he was shot) was to 'break the monotony. Old Bolsheviks never die. They only get bumped off by Stalin.'

Terterian's list of Stalin's victims is partly fanciful: Lenin, Kirov, Ordzhonikidze, Dzerzhinsky, Frunze. Since the lie that Stalin poisoned Lenin was concocted by Trotsky, Frank was right to be sceptical about Terterian's 'trite calumnies'. Yet the list is of course not entirely an invention, and in Rostov around 1920 Terterian knew Sergo Ordzhonikidze very well, saving his life and having his own spared in return. Ordzhonikidze's death in 1937 has never been properly explained.

When Frank left hospital he yet again assured his mother that, though still yellow, he did not intend to take home leave. The following month he adopted a small ginger cat whose ears he cleaned with a turkey feather and linseed oil and which he nicknamed 'Koba' – like Stalin himself. Unlike another cat that left mouse entrails as a present on his camp-bed, the only mouse Koba destroyed was one the sergeants caught and presented to him. Koba, Frank concluded, had 'no traits in common with his namesake'. Even if Frank doubted some of Terterian's instances, he evidently countenanced the idea of Stalin's murderousness.

Persia had Russian civilians, films, restaurants and foodstuffs, and in Teheran a Russian bookshop (where he found lives of various Soviet leaders including Lenin and Stalin, and *Crime and Punishment*, and was soon reading *War and Peace* in Russian, just as the following July on Malta he read it – with greater ease – in Italian). Encounters with Russian soldiers, however, were rare. From 10.30 to 12.30 each night, crouched over a small wireless, he listened in to Radio Moscow, learning new phrases, finding out all he could of how Russians perceived and endured the war. From 11 p.m. onwards Moscow broadcast at slow dictation speed, providing front-page copy for local newspaper editors all over the Union to quote verbatim. He understood nearly every word.

His first Russian soldiers put him in mind of Brian, and then of Iris Murdoch: fellow Communists both. To Iris on 4 September 1942 he excitedly described his first Russian soldier, cap tilted in a jeep, singing lustily all the way down the dusty road in a loud unbroken monotone. On 3 October he hitched a lift on a truck for forty miles with his first native Russian-speaker – a huge, ugly, taciturn Ukrainian from Kharkov who threw up his hands in disgust at Persia and Iraq: rotten countries with nothing to be said for them. Frank by contrast thought Persian poverty a yardstick for the achievements of the USSR.

Soon he evoked for Iris a setpiece – a radiant Persian November day, clear sky with few clouds – and a conversation. Under the gentle winter sun and against snow-white mountains with shifting cloud-shadows stood delicate poplars in a valley rioting with red and yellow leaves. Mammoth dark-green Russian convoy lorries were refuelling at a village petrol pump, their drivers in overalls and great floppy fatigue-hats stretching their legs and checking their vehicles. One Russian driver, a great thug with a mop of yellow tow for hair, stood grinning at Frank.

'H'are ya doing?' I shouted at him in Russian.

His grin broadened as he heard his own tongue. He came slowly towards me, 'How am I doing? Well. Very well.'

He came & leaned on the door of my truck grinning thoughtfully, feeling none of our western obligation to continue conversation.

'Splendid news from Kavkáz [Caucasus]' – I said. We had just heard of the first victories at Ordzhonikidze [a city named after the Bolshevik].

He grinned again. 'You think it is good?'

'Yes. Very good. Don't you?'

He thought & grinned & looked steadily at me for nearly half a minute. 'Yes. It is very good.' Another half minute devoted to thinking & grinning. 'Yes, it is just as Comrade Stalin said. He said. 'There'll be a holiday on our street, too.' (*budet i na nashei ulitse prazdnik*) And so there will! So there will! There'll be a holiday on our street too!'

We both laughed at this. 'Yes!' I said. 'So there will! There'll be a holiday on our street too!'

Though Frank talked in Russian with Polish friends for more than three hours, it is likely that this was the longest Russian conversation with a Russian that he ever had. The traffic cleared and they moved on, but for hours after his heart laughed and sang as it had not for months.

'Who is this handsome man?' reads Frank's caption.

Frank, still recovering from jaundice and somewhat yellow, heard in everything a spirit saying, 'You go to hell! It's worth while being alive, whatever you say!'

———

His conversation with the Russian driver suggested that Stalingrad, albeit with unimaginable casualties on both sides, would resist the Germans. If so, Phantom's useful life in Persia would soon be coming to an end. On 4 December Frank's unit crossed into Iraq to serve with the Tenth Army near Baghdad. One of their fifteen-hundredweight trucks was converted into a coop for a dozen Persian turkeys which escaped and were found, on 22 December, roosting on a nearby lavatory roof and recaptured. For Christmas dinner the men ate roast turkey, sausages and Christmas puddings while their master of ceremonies led toasts of beer to absent friends. Frank loathed Iraq, where he had to command his unit, but it is only here that we glimpse him as a CP activist.

# A Desultory Tale: January–September 1943

Death should not be allowed . . . more of a victory than is its due . . . or allowed to corrupt life with its sterility.

*Letter, 3 May 1943*

When I think I have reconciled myself to the idea of dying, is this merely the death-wish, a defeatist attitude to the complexities of life? Don't think so. Normally I take a healthy pleasure in living . . .

*Diary, June 1943*

A cable from Theo alerted Frank to her Arabic broadcast with the BBC Overseas Service on 4 January 1943. Negotiations had taken months, involving fees for writing and recording (ten guineas) and advice on stage fright. Her talk, beginning 'I am Zahle-born-and-bred', designed to attract Syrians to the Allied cause, mentioned that she had a son serving in the Levant. Theo and EJ, seated at one of Balliol College's super short-wave sets, found she had misremembered the wavelength and so missed her own talk; Frank near Baghdad had better luck. The mess wireless was tuned in, his fellow officers disappointed that Theo didn't end 'H'are ya, Frankie!' Frank, able to follow little, recognised her customary vigour: it was the first time for two years he had heard her voice.

In this fourth year of hostilities Theo and EJ's younger son would also be drafted abroad. Despite Theo's patronising efforts to get him to follow popular Frank and thus inherit his brother's friendships

EP and Sandy, 1943.

ready-made, he left for Algeria. Frank pictured him lugging suitcases to a waiting taxi, nipping into the kitchen for a sandwich and one last glass of milk while EJ scuttled across the croquet lawn in slippers for a book EP simply *had to* read on the voyage while the Great Muvver called out of the bedroom window: 'Aren't you taking your gasmask?' EJ provided his own vignettes of home life, depicting Theo as 'acidly witty' and meek only when she burned a saucepan or was caught simultaneously in two motoring offences. Coming across her typewriter unawares with a letter beginning 'Darling Frank', he inserted the words 'I wish I were a good Muvver.' Simple jokes leavened wartime privations.

'Pre-war' signified happy. When in February the exiled King of Greece joined Oriel high table, EJ enjoyed 'a pre-war dinner'. Next month Theo unlodged a box of pre-war sweets but pronounced them 'bad for his throat'. In May they attended the wedding of a private secretary of Churchill's whose bride wore a pre-war wedding gown – wonderful for Theo to see – costing seven clothing coupons only.

Clementine Churchill was there plus Brendan Bracken with his enormous red wig-like mop of hair obstructing EJ's view. Everyone wanted news of Frank.

After four years of war Theo noted that mothers meeting casually hesitated to ask after each other's menfolk, lest there be bad news, or no news at all. Nancy Nicholson's son David Graves was killed in Burma. Then Frank's Dragon contemporary Andrew Gardner, of the Boars Hill gang, was in August 1943 found dead by his bike in Oxford, aged twenty-one. Theo wondered whether such a non-war-related death might be even worse for the family.*

EJ 'moiled and struggled on alone' that year, campaigning about the famine in Bengal. Around three million died there, in part because the British were exporting Indian rice to the Middle East – a crass and shameful return for Indian loyalty. EJ 'busked an interview', in Theo's expressive phrase, with the new Viceroy, General Wavell, who told him that the India Office denied that the famine was real.

———

Storm Jameson, as we have seen, wrote of the intransigent idealism of both Thompson boys. Idealism can cause priggishness, whose comical effects were on display when Frank rebuked his batman Lorton for not getting excited about seeing Jerusalem. Frank in a poem celebrates two Lorton-like squaddies in conversation: '"Well Bill? Yer glad yer came out East?" / "Ho yuss! I wouldn't have missed this for quids!"', glossing this exchange: 'Oh England! Oh my lovely casual country! / These are your lads, English as blackthorn-flower . . .' The same affectionate Wykehamist paternalism prompts Frank to record Lorton's claim to have had 'an *inkling* of Latin' at school when he meant a 'smattering'.

The errors of the educated get corrected too. Frank fumes against the semi-literate officers who think every Jew a cad best off underground, and every striker deserving to be shot: he was as indignant as if he were a Jew or striker himself. He rants against the ruling-class English

* His brother Dr Michael Gardner said Andrew died of a 'conus' effect – a tumour on the artery at the base of the brain (conversation with author, 3 July 2009).

– finished as world leaders, tired, dishonest, moral cowards without imagination, who had lost all capacity for idealism or adventure, enjoying second-rate pleasures. He raged against his fellow officers. Only Donald Melvin, an ex-solicitor with whom he had sailed out on the *Pasteur*, had never put his mind to sleep, but Melvin was now dead. One fellow officer scorned the idea that the war was being fought to make a better world afterwards: if it were as simple as that why not stage a world war every twenty years to guarantee steady progress? This joke gave Frank pause. Officers displayed a sickening lack of curiosity about the countries they were living and fighting in. With such leaders it was small surprise that their men had no pride in the struggle for human liberty and were apathetic about seeing the beauty or learning the history of the Middle East.

Four dismal and hateful winter months in Iraq in 1942/3 were made worse by Frank's having to take charge for five weeks while Grant retrained. Happily the tide of war was turning in the Allies' favour. Before El Alamein in November 1942, as Churchill later quipped, the Allies enjoyed no victories – and afterwards suffered no defeats. Taken together with the agonising Soviet victory at Stalingrad, it at last seemed probable that Germany might lose the war.

---

An improvement in airmail speed followed these Allied victories: a letter of Frank's dated Tuesday 27 April arrived in Bledlow on Wednesday of the following week. This did not merely make communication much faster – 'almost like peace-time' – but enabled those quarrels that needed recent anger or live resentment to fuel them. Correcting each other's errors of spelling and grammar was a standard Thompson joke. Frank blamed one altercation with his father on his own 'violent childish tangent' about RAF ground staff after he had very nearly been killed by the panic-stricken driving of one a fortnight before. It is notable that he does not dream of holding his father to account for this argument, blaming his own 'childishness' instead. In October 1943 he confessed 'au fond I'm still hopelessly childish and it breaks out now and then'.

If Frank stayed childish, EJ helped keep him so. When in 1942 EJ had a story of Frank's published in *Time & Tide* and another in the *Guardian*, or a selection of his letters in the *New Statesman*, he gave Frank no prior warning of publication – as Frank remarked to Iris. Perhaps he saw Frank's writing as an extension of his own. His attitude helped inspire a crisis Frank underwent in 1943. Its roots in his father's censure, in his relationship with Poles and in Iris's embarkation on a love-life that necessarily excluded him are worth examining.

His father sent him on 5 April 1943 a stinging rebuke. While praising the generally high standard of Frank's 'superb' letters as, at their best, 'natural easy prose, as matter, and as poise and self-carriage', he indicated that his late 1942 Teheran visit had seen a deterioration to, in EJ's damning phrase, the telling of 'a desultory story' entailing 'third-rate ways of amusing yourself and drab companions'. He and Theo would not be altogether sorry if Frank presently got himself into 'a livelier and usefuller life'. For 'desultory' read 'unheroic'.

This conceited letter hurt and dispirited him, but Frank (typically) did not say so. Nor did he remark on the implicit assumptions that his war was being fought for his father's entertainment and that he was a free agent. EJ's early drollery to EP – 'Kill an Italian if you get the chance and I promise to pay the fine' – conveys similar assumptions. For Frank's enormous output of letters home from March 1941 was indeed designed to entertain as well as reassure, a performance-art for domestic consumption. Frank had apologised for one long discursive late-1942 letter as sounding 'pretty stupid but I so rarely give you an hour-by-hour account of my doings, I thought it might amuse you'. EJ was not amused.

He and his father held many assumptions in common, and Frank travelled with the collection of his father's books that had impressed Peter Wright. He met few officers who had heard of his father: EJ's taunts that he never read his books notwithstanding, he studied and referred to them frequently. Frank devoured *Crusader's Coast* for its account of Levantine plant life. He re-read and admired *An Indian Day*, requested and got a copy of *Burmese Silver*, and appealed in his diary in June 1943 under his page-header 'THE DEATH-WISH' to his father's novel *These Men, thy Friends* as a source of wisdom:

When I think myself reconciled to the idea of dying, is this merely the death-wish, a defeatist attitude to the complexities of life? Don't think so. Normally I take a healthy pleasure in living & still have a great many ambitions. One feeling I must fight – 'At least, if I'm killed, then everyone will think well of me.' Despicable this, revealing complete selfishness & inability to imagine the sorrow one's death might cause to one or two people. I seem to remember something very fine in *These Men thy Friends* where Colonel Hart gradually masters his soul in the face of death, must read it again.

———

Frank's admired father had won the MC for bravery in Iraq twenty years before, and as an established writer addressed this experience in *These Men, thy Friends*. Frank elected his father mentor in questions of life and death and the courage required for both. After EJ had tried to write a play about the Buddha, Frank often declared himself sympathetic to Buddhism.

He wrote home warning of the importance of receiving letters for his well-being, mentioning queer moments 'when it's almost impossible to believe that one has kinsmen anywhere'. Theo sensed that he chivalrously hid his dejection for months at a time so as not to demoralise others,* and tried to jolly him into realising that he had three relatives in England who adored him – 'and not to mis-conceive one remark of Dadza (about "desultory living") as intending to deprecate you, Frank'. Thus she identified the precise phrase that had wounded him.

EJ also asked Frank why death removes the fellows he does, leaving alive those who are 'long ago rotten-ripe for cartage to the dust-heap'. He thus proclaimed himself somehow 'finished', living vicariously only through his sons. He was ashamed that his own war was so unheroic and 'desultory'; no doubt he projected this shame on to his sons, together with a wish for them to excel in his place. True, to both sons

———

* Theo wrote, 'You are a brick, Frank . . . You never tell us if you are feeling "down" – not until a year or so later! Sometimes I wish you would burst out and tell us what you feel when things go wrong, as they *must* at times . . .' (14 June 1943, UNC). A recent airmail letter-card from him – by contrast – had improved family morale at once.

during 1941 EJ wrote facetiously, "'Let them as wants their bloody George Crosses 'ave 'em'" as a Princes Risboro sergeant observed.' Yet a countervailing rhetoric also obtained.

Iris, as we have seen, purveyed precisely the same double message, insisting that she should only like Frank to be a hero if this could happen 'without the necessity of a vulgar display', yet praising T. E. Lawrence's swift life of action and, as we have seen, calling him 'the sort of person I would leave anything to follow'.

Both EJ's injunction to Frank to dedicate himself to 'a livelier and usefuller life' and Iris's cheerleading came at an interesting moment. That April Frank first heard about the Special Operations Executive (SOE), another irregular formation, dreamed up in 1940 by Churchill, that invincible romantic,* to coordinate action against the enemy by means of subversion and sabotage, including propaganda. British liaison officers or BLOs were to drop into occupied Europe to help 'set it ablaze', and films such as *Heroes of Telemark* and, more recently, *Charlotte Gray* present a glamorous picture of their work. It is worth noting at the outset that SOE's leading historian (and Frank's friend) M. R. D. Foot doubts that – morale-boosting apart – SOE achieved very much. And yet surely the value of morale itself in wartime is incalculable.

Frank, in any case, was immediately attracted and excited, making the final move that September in order to fight in Greece, which always represented liveliness and usefulness. SOE was the exact opposite of 'desultory'. It added a tincture of dangerous adventure that might satisfy even so stern a task-master as his father. And so he wrote, 'I agree with Da about desultory living – not one of us shed a tear on leaving [Persia].'

---

* Frank probably heard of SOE through Peter Wright that April in Alexandria. He had some immunity to Churchillian rhetoric. Aerogram from M. R. D. Foot (13 Mar. 1943, UNC): 'don't decry the baroque heroics of the PM; those who see straight aren't harmed by them, & they help to keep on the rails those who can hardly see at all'.

Another factor making Frank feel that his war had thus far been desultory and unheroic was friendships with Poles, who he declared in 1942 'had suffered more than any nation in Europe'.

In woods outside Smolensk in April 1943 German soldiers found graves with the bodies of some 14,000 Polish officers* murdered two years before by the Soviets. When Germany broadcast this, Stalin lied that these Poles had been murdered by Nazis in 1941. And Frank believed this Soviet lie. He thought Nazism in its death throes was blackening the Bolsheviks as a bogeyman to frighten the West and win allies, and that the Poles were 'tactlessly' taking the Germans at their word.

Before judging Frank too harshly it is worth recalling that the truth about what we now call the Katyń Massacre was admitted by President Gorbachev only as recently as 1990, when he confessed that the USSR had wanted to destroy or damage Poland as much as did Hitler. Frank's refusal to believe that the Soviets murdered these (and other) Polish officers was shared by many at home who feared that Poland would endanger Allied unity. His father criticised the 'unreality' of Polish ambitions and Poles' 'swelled head' about erstwhile glory and lost territories while Iris in 1945 lost her temper with an anti-Yalta Pole.

Meanwhile, the Polish government-in-exile in London demanded an independent examination of the recently discovered Katyń burial pits, following which Stalin used this threat that his responsibility for the mass murder he had ordained might be revealed to break off diplomatic relations. Idealistic Frank, noting (typically and optimistically) that the Russian writer Pushkin and the Polish poet Mickiewicz had both liked one another and also been bullied by the same Tsar, was flummoxed.

He had first sighted Polish officers in the Western Desert in 1941, and he accounted himself a 'keen supporter' the following spring of the tens of thousands of Poles who had escaped with Colonel Władysław Anders from the USSR,† gathered in camps near Teheran. He started to

---

* Initially 4,400 bodies – the full tally became clear later.
† Anders was released by the Soviets from the Lubyanka prison, where he was tortured,

learn Polish as well as Russian – a feat notoriously vexed by the kinship between the languages; given the large number of Polish troops in the Middle East, he thought it might come in useful. He mock-modestly boasted that his Polish was at first so simple that he could use it 'merely on the telephone, to wage a political debate, or to discuss pre-Raphaelite painting'.

Admiring Polish courtesy, charm, sense of fun and courage, Frank made new Polish friends. Notable was Emilia Krzyprówna, aka Mila, an Auxiliary Territorial Service (ATS) corporal in Paiforce in Iraq, whom he taught English while learning Polish himself. Mila had been an unambitious civil service clerk from a comfortably-off Kraków family when the Russians and Germans invaded in September 1939. Strafing by German planes meant that her evacuation eastwards to Lwów took a nightmare three days instead of the normal three hours. In the USSR she became a road worker. Although in August 1943 Mila discovered after four years a sister called Anna living in Gedera in Palestine, she had reached Persia in 1942 alone and with nothing, unsure whether any family at all had survived. 'Quite fairly pretty,' Frank called her hesitantly, adding chivalrously 'first-class smile' and classifying her as one of the 'little people', backbone of this anti-Fascist war, who gladden his heart. Frank and Mila exchanged photographs and affectionate letters in Polish, and Iris noted his closeness to a Polish girl whom he called by the warm diminutive 'Miluska' and who sounded nice and allowed him to 'thou' her. (Meanwhile EJ warned, 'Don't think too much of Polish girls.')

Then there was the interpreter and writer of Polish children's books Życki, whom he had first known in Persia, who shared Frank's surreal humour and who discovered his own younger brother in Baghdad. He talked to Frank about recent Polish history and embarrassed him by dancing a *krakowjak*, a vast moon-faced man of forty doing a ludicrous

---

with the intention that he should form a Polish army to fight alongside the Red Army in 1941, but continued political friction with the Soviets as well as shortages of weapons, food and clothing led to the eventual exodus of Anders's men from the USSR together with perhaps 75,000 Polish civilians via the Persian corridor into Iran, Iraq and Palestine.

'This cat – for my Dear Teacher, Mila', 14.vi.43.

hornpipe in battledress among the palms, or rushing forward on all fours to show how he had stormed a Bolshevik barricade near Lwów. And then Piotr Adamski, also approaching forty, whose twin brother was a prisoner of war in Germany – where Frank noted that Slavs did not survive long in captivity.

Frank understood Polish fear and hatred of Germany and of Germans very well and joked about it. *English officer*: 'Once the war is over there can be no indiscriminate killing of Germans.' *Polish officer*: 'Certainly not! It must be thoroughly well organised!' Yet he could not 'read' Polish–Russian relations and believed Poles out-and-out liars about Russia. His father commended his simile about Poland having the 'vitality of a hawthorn hedge that has been cut and laid – times beyond counting', but Frank somehow overlooked Russia's role as a leading Polish hedge-trimmer.

The Poles, 'rabid nationalists' spreading 'envenomed' propaganda, had been telling atrocity stories about their internment in the USSR, propaganda that went on twenty-four hours a day and under 1,000 horsepower pressure. Frank protested that the Russians would not have deported and interned 'a few hundred thousand' Poles without reason. Deportees from the landowning and commercial classes had a 'bad record' – that is, were reactionary – and so were unlikely to be willing to help shore up Soviet defences, and 'justice meted out to a class takes precedence over injustice to individuals': a startling, dislikeable and unique instance of his talking like a loyal apparatchik. While it is true that Polish deportees were required to perform menial labour in the USSR, this contrasts favourably with the 'criminal softness', in Frank's view, of the British towards Fascists interned on the Isle of Man. He appears unaware of his own implicit and insulting analogy between Pole and Fascist. While Poles complained of hunger, fatalities and filth in the USSR, photos of Mila in Russia showed her looking fit and well, and while he acknowledged that some Poles did arrive in Persia lice-ridden he pokes fun at Mila's petit-bourgeois indignation when he asked her if *she* had been lousy.

———

This issue of Polish–Russian relations helped split the Iraqi Communist Party, and Frank got involved that winter in attempting to heal the divide. He was shocked by the constitution of Iraq, a British puppet state whose military dictatorship recognised neither political parties nor trades unions; even the right to form an anti-Fascist league had been refused. Underground parties circulated papers, but the printers were liable to arrest, their presses to confiscation. Only one left-wing paper existed legally. The Iraqi Communist Party with its small following of Baghdadi shoemakers organising illegal unions was backward, possessing in Arabic only the *History of the Bolshevik Party*, thumbed through in each crisis for advice.

The Polish forces' 'great anti-Soviet propaganda campaign' was having some effect, and two factions of the Iraqi CP, split over how to elect leaders – as almost certainly over the truth of the Katyń Massacre – attacked each other. Frank tried to help. First of all he wrote that winter about Polish anti-Soviet propaganda anonymously and influentially in two rival underground Iraqi CP papers, analysing and exposing it. While these articles don't survive, their gist is captured in a letter home.

After discussion with other sympathetic people, Frank and Jacobson, his Phantom colleague, arranged a meeting under Frank's chairmanship, his word to be final. Frank and Jacobson told the Iraqis that their squabble was hindering the progressive struggle, and worked out a joint programme. Frank also helped them elude censorship and establish contact with the older Syrian CP, which promised books and advice once unity could be demonstrated. But neither side was willing either to publicise the fact that such an accommodation had been reached or to join forces.

---

This is the only moment when we glimpse Frank's CP activities: consulting with unnamed British CP members, chairing Iraqi CP meetings, helping the membership elude censorship and opening channels of communication between Syrian and Iraqi CPs. Small wonder that EP's detailed 1946 report after meeting Frank Jacobson advises his parents to omit all this from the family's commemorative *There is a Spirit in Europe*: 'Most of this was outside Frank's range of duties(!)' The exclamation mark is EP's: article 451 of the King's Regulations forbade any serviceman from participation in the affairs even of mainstream political parties, let alone the CP.

A new field of speculation opens up, like the one we glimpse on learning that Iris Murdoch as an assistant principal in the Treasury had 'borrowed' and copied state papers which she took to dead-letter drops in a tree in Kensington Gardens. This happened probably during 1943 and 1944. The Party was quite capable later of blackmailing members whom it had thus enticed into betraying official secrets. We sense a darker world, remote from our own.

If Frank had survived the war with his political passions intact – a leading question – he was exactly the sort of exploitable public school product the Communist Party often groomed as agent or spy. His friendship with Mila while repudiating and despising her politics is rare evidence that he might have been capable of active duplicity beyond conventional politeness or diplomacy. Yet this deceit – if it can be so described – had limits. When he was visiting Mila at her ATS hostel for an English–Polish lesson, one girl by mistake switched on the 'Internationale' on the wireless. The ensuing shrieking and slamming of doors by some dozen other Polish girls disturbed in varying stages of undress by this anthem of the detested Soviet enemies who had deported them made him 'laugh until he nearly broke a rib' and Mila had to rebuke him. He took no trouble to disguise the mischievous pleasure he took in their discomfiture.

Frank has few hallmarks of an agent. Not merely did he have no right-wing cover or front – unlike Guy Burgess and Kim Philby, who deliberately joined the Anglo-German Fellowship to disguise their real leanings, or Bill Carritt's beautiful wife Margot Gale – but there is nowhere that Frank did not announce his politics or ensure that these were widely known and understood. EP believed that Frank was not in touch with King Street – the CPGB headquarters. Nor is it likely that he spied for the USSR or had a Soviet controller. During his three years abroad he rarely spent more than five to seven days in any one place before being moved on unpredictably: the nomadism that prevented settled love affairs rendered double-dealing difficult too. His four months in Iraq – like his six weeks in Iran before being hospitalised for jaundice – were very untypical.

His period of busy CP activity overlaps with his five weeks of command in January–February, when the unit idled, George Grant the senior officer was away retraining, and Frank was acting CO, hating – at twenty-two – this 'nightmare of command'. Nor was Frank a loyal cadre. He lacked blind faith and could not quell his habitual independence of mind.

He found it difficult to read Iraqi history, which he thought simply dire, with the 'positiveness' that his Communism demanded. Iraq prompted in Frank aversion and despair. True, his liver was weakened from hepatitis and he drank now only in company, noting his parents' fears that he might become alcoholic: his view was quite literally 'jaundiced'. Acknowledging his being ignorant and 'not quite balanced', he thought the Middle East 'misgoverned and demented in a thousand ways', where men for millennia had been born and died among flies and filth and stench. Iraq was the worst. In summer a furnace withering men's souls and in winter a bottomless damp mud that made one feel one was rotting away – it was impossible to feel fit there. 'This is not a country that men should be expected to live in.' The gulf between locals and the soldiery depressed him too.

A water vendor drinking water scooped from the drain running down the middle of the street filled him with horror, and Islam itself seemed not merely 'bogus', but the death-wish incarnate. He wrote to Iris that, as with his father before him, 'the utter poverty and human degradation is a thing which comes to weigh on the mind incessantly, until one can get joy from nothing . . . The misery of the east is a thing which you cannot imagine.' He had an especial detestation of Muslim funerals and widows with their 'dry hysteria': death should not be allowed to corrupt life with its sterility, or allowed more dominion than was its due.

Iraq made the Western Desert seem by comparison 'like Buckinghamshire', while Baghdad was the devil's residence, without a single street that would not shame Princes Risborough – homesick analogies. The poverty, the worst he had ever seen, nauseated him, dirt and chancres or body-sores reigning everywhere. He took his stand on complete independence for Iraq, adding prophetically, 'don't force any Englishman to go near the place'. Like Iris he adopts at times a note of tragic humanism entirely at odds with 'official' Communist optimism.

———

So, despite mouthing the rhetoric to the Iraqi CP that 'justice meted out to a class takes precedence over injustice to individuals', he refused in practice to treat all Poles simply as reactionary enemies of progress. To his parents and to Iris by contrast he detailed the sufferings of individual Poles instead. Frank and Adamski spent all Sunday afternoon on 7 February 1943 sitting in a café, meditating on the basic sadness of life. Adamski let Frank read a letter from Tosia, his fiancée, still in Poznań in German-occupied Poland where he feared for her safety. The dry ink of this letter seemed to ache with restrained longing and a courage maintained only by the most rigid self-control.

Cut out all sententiousness about strength through suffering. Think of the millions of people to whom this war has brought nothing but utter irredeemable loss. Piotr and his Tosia are both close on forty. If the war leaves them both alive and sane, they will still find little peace in an embittered and factious post-war Europe. For us, who are young, and have the faith that we can recast the world, the struggle that comes after will be bearable.

Frank felt very deeply for the countless peaceable people who could never, because of age, upbringing or environment, wholly join the progressive struggle and 'would never know peace in the one short life allotted to them'. This mature breadth of sympathy is remarkable.

Mila's predicament in exile in a labour camp in the Urals the previous year moved him too. Her country had ceased to exist and her whole family had suffered under German occupation. Yet instead of sympathy in the USSR she met with a new hard life, surrounded by a race of 'rough, straight-forward, mildly inquisitive bears'. He listened for hours to Mila's imitations of the deep-voiced Russian peasants (muzhiks) who yelled at her that she was a wealthy bourgeois who had 'tortured the people'.

Mila could not have tortured people if she'd tried, though he picturesquely adds that her landowning family 'must have done so often'. Frank imagined her slaving blamelessly in an office every weekday, in order to go dancing on a Saturday evening and 'lie in' on a Sunday morning. He pictured her arriving in Sverdlovsk with three trunks and two fur coats, an orphaned white-collar girl whose country had just been bombed and whose life had been smashed to pieces from under her. The Russians, he argued, would have done better to appreciate that a) nobody except the most vicious criminal should be made to feel that the whole world is against them, b) an individual does not always react along with her class and c) 'in a world as filthy as it is today, one should remember how helpless and how lonely the individual is, and that kindliness, especially when it costs so little, is a policy that justifies itself'. Noble sentiments.

He brooded about Mila and the fate of others like her. Twelve weeks after this letter, and long after parting from Mila, he is still complaining to Iris from Egypt about how she was treated in Sverdlovsk. He could still quote verbatim Russian insults shouted at her. 'How stupid class generalisations sound when applied to individuals.' However much we steel ourselves to hate institutions and even bodies of men that are striving for evil ends, there was no point in trying to hate *men*. 'We'd be wasting our time . . . Worse than that – we'd be losing our own virtue,' he admonished. (It was in a similar vein that he had chided his brother that July: 'It's a mistake to hate people because of their class.')

That Frank at twenty-two understood that hatred entails loss of virtue is reason enough to honour and admire him. That he wrote in this style to both Iris and his brother EP, both more loyal CP activists than he was, makes clear how impossible it would have been for him to conform to any dogmatic Party line. He was too much of a rebel to obey the rules.

His new Polish friends taught him another lesson, too. Frank reckoned that, exile abroad and the deaths of friends apart, his war had been easy. The Poles had by contrast suffered greatly. Was it perhaps Frank's moral duty to suffer more?

———

Frank was responsible for administration, supplies and discipline, 'just like Muvver at Bledlow' he quipped, but could not get very excited about wrestling with a soldier's marriage allowance or finding out why the Quarter-Master Sergeant (aka QMS) overdrew rations. His additional role as the Unit Education Officer, however, offered his political passions a creative outlet. The Army Bureau of Current Affairs (ABCA), founded in August 1941, purveyed a new and often radical concept of adult education in the Middle East, especially after Alamein, when it became notorious for spreading socialist ideas, triggering Churchill's hostility for that reason.

He and his fellow Communist Sergeant Jacobson invited lectures from the men: an old India hand gave a talk on snakes. Then Frank staged a quiz when, as Brains Trust question master, he was startled to find only 'trick-questions' or riddles submitted, designed to catch others out. He patiently explained that the purpose of discussion was the quest for truth. He was pleased at the turn-out despite the men's suspicions that he was serving them 'propaganda'.

That Frank's politics were well known is clear from a Poetry Prize competition he organised. A fellow officer submitted a very promising poem as if from one of the men, waiting for Frank to talk excitedly about the genuine reserve of poetry latent in the masses before revealing the practical joke. Frank had the previous year mounted a so-called Wall Newspaper about the USA, made up out of newspaper and magazine cuttings and his own captions, entitled 'Salute the Yanks', which explained that although the USA, as could be seen from John Steinbeck's *The Grapes of Wrath*, had poverty and unemployment like England's, it none the less had also a healthier spirit of democracy than England's, and an impressive history of struggle against oppression.

Now Frank and Jacobson's Wall Newspaper entitled 'Life in the USSR', using cuttings from the special 29 March 1943 issue of *Life* magazine that Theo sent out to him, with its soft cover photo of Stalin, can have left little doubt about his political sympathies. While his QMS made snide innuendos to the effect that he suspected Frank of being 'Red', Frank in his turn guessed that a new Phantom officer named MacIver had Communist sympathies because he was reading Tom Wintringham's *English Captain*. Wintringham, once in the CP and now promoting the new Common Wealth Party, had visited his parents at Bledlow and Frank noted that his 1939 novel about Spain was mainly still read by those sympathetic to the CP.

Frank gave talks too. On 12 January 1943 he spoke on occupied Europe, a topic on which British newspapers said little, but as a self-taught expert he was frequently quizzed. He made terrifyingly clear what was at stake. His marathon covered some fifteen countries in (roughly) the order that they fell: Germany itself, Austria, Spain, Czechoslovakia, Poland, Denmark, Norway, Holland, France, Hungary, Romania, Belgium, Bulgaria, Yugoslavia, Greece, Italy, Finland – instancing collaboration and resistance in each. He detailed the murder by the Nazis of 54,000 Jews at Babi Yar near Kiev, followed by the killing elsewhere of one million Jewish men, women and children by machine gun, torture, hunger and what Frank quaintly calls 'lethal chamber'. We now know that by October 1942 more than two million Polish Jews had been murdered, but the Wannsee conference decreeing the Final Solution had happened only one year before, so Frank's talk, based on the *Daily Worker*, the newspaper *Soviet War News* and listening in to Moscow Radio, was comparatively well informed. Being in an intelligence unit doubtless helped.

This talk was a tour de force. Intended to be one hour long, it lasted for two but nobody yawned. Frank's passion for explaining exactly what a Nazi victory could mean for his listeners' families – slave labour, starvation, torture and mass murder – compelled his audience. He left them in no doubt that the future of humanity itself was at stake in the coming struggle, his picture of course the simplified one favoured by Hollywood – a fight between Light and Dark, ignoring Allied disunity and Soviet brutality towards the Poles (and Finns) in particular.

The following day he staged a debate on the motion that 'Germany should for world security cease to exist after the war'. It was defeated by fourteen votes to four, a common-sense outcome that pleased him. He was never what was called a 'Vansittartist', one who believed that the complicity of all Germans in aggression must be punished by violent and total defeat. Eighteen was also a large turn-out for an entertainment devised by an officer. He understood the resentment felt towards officers and – while he never bought into Marxist cant about 'the inevitability of class-struggle' – thought such resentment natural. He also gave a talk on the make-up of the modern German Army, whose professionalism and tradition of conscription he admired and thought the UK could emulate, albeit not the German tradition of expecting blind obedience from troops kept ignorant of war aims and strategies.

The Beveridge Report had been circulated in December 1942, with its blueprint for a post-war National Health system. Frank naturally approved, despite fearing that it did not go far enough. Its assumption that a pool of unemployed would continue, guaranteeing cheap labour, Frank found offensive. He preferred G. D. H. Cole's harder-hitting *Great Britain in the Post-War World*, which charged capitalist states with criminally sanctioning mass unemployment, international aggression and the rise of Fascism. Cole encouraged in him the belief that only force could dethrone capitalism and create a free internationalist post-war Europe where the means of production would be reorganised – the only time Frank appears to back the use of force in peacetime politics.

Beveridge none the less endorsed the hope that peace would inaugurate a new social order and provided a rallying point. Frank chaired a discussion on the report in April 1943 which he judged very lively and successful, confining an ex-Tory MP to only five minutes, making a pro-Beveridge speech himself and startling a bewildered Indian major who was amazed to learn that the British wartime Cabinet had in principle already accepted Beveridge.

His political isolation lessened after early April when his unit returned to Egypt. Here, to the alarm of the authorities, was a ground-swell of radicalism. It was in Cairo that autumn, 1943, that the six monthly idealistic Forces Parliaments started.* In Alexandria Frank got 'very successful' discussion groups set up in a number of the soldiers' clubs, and invited speakers of various nationalities to talk about their own countries, sometimes speaking himself both on Beveridge and on 'Who lives in the Balkans? And why is it so bloody?'

He observed the upsurge of discussions about post-war reconstruction, encouraged by their socialist tendency while deploring the prevalence of mouth-shooters. These activities generally cheered him up and made him more optimistic. He was touched that March to find that one officer had compiled a forty-page form-book for the local races plus an impeccable index, as also to discover two others huddled over the lamp long after midnight, checking and rechecking the evening's poker scores. Perhaps he had underestimated the 'tremendous reserves of energy' such officers possessed after all?

---

In mid-April Frank's unit, its vehicles undergoing repair near Alexandria after their epic journeyings, was shaken out of boredom by learning that a Special Assault Detachment was on its way out to help them get fighting fit by 1 August for the invasion of Rhodes and/or Turkey:

* See Chapter 11.

Operation Accolade. Ten unfortunates were to learn Turkish, which did not faze Frank, who also arranged for an equal number to learn modern Greek, applying himself to both languages.

By June these plans were overturned and replaced by the Sicilian landings instead. The Special Assault Detachment under Captain Alastair Sedgwick, who had recently distinguished himself during the disastrous Dieppe raid, arrived in Suez. The only thing wrong with Sedgwick, it was jested, was that he was still breathing. Unpopular though Sedgwick was, Frank decided that he liked him so long as he 'didn't have to work with him'.

Before they set out, a cynical clean-up was staged to impress the inspecting Secretary of State for War, Sir Percy Grigg. Phantom H was now attached to the Durham Brigade of the 50th (Northumbrian) Division, the Eighth Army's sheet anchor, despite enduring a typhus epidemic for weeks. Yet only Grigg's visit procured them baths. The desert camp-floor was swept and prettified, unusually good food was served, and a wireless appeared in the men's mess, still in its case so it could be packed and sent away again immediately after. The atmosphere of blatant hypocrisy depressed them all.

Montgomery gave a tired and uninspiring pep talk in a vast barn-like cinema on 24 June and Frank found him more likeable and less arrogant than he had expected, but felt his exhortations lacked warmth. He wanted Monty to congratulate them for what they had already achieved and to tell them he knew he could count on them in the coming battle. What they got was lacklustre.

They sailed on the *Winchester Castle* on 4 July, on board which, one day out, the men were finally told where they were going and handed copies of *A Soldier's Guide to Sicily*. Frank's own pep talk on the 9th to his five men, three of whom had never been under fire, went 'I don't think it's going to be a bad party but there's bound to be quite a lot flying about and you're bound to feel frightened . . . The Brigadier will be frightened too . . . and personally I'm always scared stiff . . . but as the Major said "You've gotta overcome it."' This seemed to amuse them.

He could not drink himself silly even had he wished to: his

jaundice-damaged liver protested and he distracted himself instead reading fruity passages from sixpenny novels. He encouraged himself with the belief that gentle people made the best soldiers, watched the officers make asses of themselves, and was greatly struck when the Durham soldiers sang 'Keep yer Feet Still Geordie Hinny': 'Let's be happy through the neet / For we may not be sae happy through the day. / Oh give us that bit comfort, keep your feet still Geordie lad / And divn't drive me bonny dreams away.' A working man forced to share his lodging-house bed berates his undesirable partner for waking him up just when he was dreaming of gaining the elusive object of his affections, Mary Clarke. The pathos of this comedy of frustration, and the men's singing alike, moved Frank to tears.

Frank brooded about the coming casualties, as yet mercifully hidden from view; he imagined fearful Italians awaiting invasion exactly as he had done in Suffolk in 1940, and made himself unpopular going round telling and retelling his poor joke that the 9 July storms were caused by 'four million Italians with the wind up'.

They landed in Sicily in the early morning of 10 July near Avola in the south-east, Etna's cone clearly visible behind. He knew his perspective was unique. While his men feared Sicily as a barren, waterless, disease- and sirocco-scourged hell peopled with imbeciles and murderers, for him, by contrast, this was the island Theocritus, the Emperor Frederick and Matthew Arnold had all hymned, 'an eclogue' itself, where Pindar had eulogised the tyrants of Syracuse, and where Aeschylus lay buried at Gela. The interest of Frank's notes on Sicily (later worked up into a 10,000-word diary) lies in how he sets moment-by-moment detail within this much larger picture, relating classical Greece to the coming defeat of Fascism.

On the belated night-time approach Frank encouraged his unit, dished out the rum ration, lit up his pipe.* An overpowering smell of citrus and wild mint greeted them, followed by two accurate mortar shells fifteen paces behind, killing the crew of the landing-craft, setting

---

* Saying to himself a German phrase that he liked: *Es gibt immer Zeit eine Pfeife anzuzünden* (There's always time to light up a pipe).

the stern ablaze. Frank observed one AMLO* officer drop to his knees, ashen-faced with terrified eyes. A tall lance-corporal striding a few paces in front fell groaning, his trousers suddenly turning bright red as if by magic when shrapnel hit him. Another in front limped and fell, an arm and leg pretty well torn off.

Frank, too busy to feel terror, helped his badly shaken men lug a cumbersome barrow through shell-induced twig-and-pebble showers and then, to calm them, into a safe wadi reeking of thyme, mint and lemon, encouraging them to start blackberrying. Looking at him a little oddly, they joined in. His description of the scene as 'placid and unreal' reads truthfully, as does his account of the healing mechanism that led him to fantasise a honeymoon return to Avola post-war, to show off the scene to his wondering bride.

Despite the navy having landed his brigade many miles off course, and some American parachutists suffering 'friendly fire' as a result, the English, 'whom Europe understands so little and needs so much' – a reciprocal state of affairs, he noted – 'had returned to her after two years of absence'. A memorable day: on to the Sicilian coast of an enslaved continent, the promise of freedom itself had just landed. Frank settled to writing messages and to eating their excellent forty-eight-hour ration: one tin of bully, biscuits, dripping, raisin chocolate, boiled sweets, 'tea-sugar-and-milk-powder' brewed on a small aluminium Tommy cooker fired by petroleum gel.

He disapproved of one British patrol looting 'records, gold rings, god-knows-what'. Though thinking himself an 'Old Soldier' he hoped he never became as hardened as that. Indeed he spent hours tramping out of his way because a boy of sixteen had had his tuppeny-ha'penny watch stolen by a British soldier and he hoped to find the guilty party. He meditated mordantly that when the Germans conquered an Eastern European town, they, by contrast, shot 50,000 inhabitants and sent the best-looking girls to military brothels.

The Sicilians he met were hungry, and he forecast (accurately) that food-ships would relieve them soon. Meanwhile he and his men enjoyed local

* Assistant Military Landing Officer.

'"Self" between "Spud" and "Sam", my two wireless operators on the Sicilian landing. Two of the gentlest creatures who were ever made NCOs even in our civilian army, and, as is the way with such people, quite fearless.'

tomatoes and wine and marvelled at the speed with which Italian soldiers, having practised gangster-killing by shooting men in the back, threw down their arms and made a grand opera of surrendering, sometimes bursting into tears.* There were Stuka attacks, and also Stukas shot down, and further Bofors shells especially on the port, and ferocious midges at night, but Frank often slept well before his departure on 15 July for Malta, too lazy on occasion to dig himself into a slit trench, though requiring his men to. Sicily fell by 17 August and Italy surrendered on 8 September.

This was Phantom's last makeshift campaign. One historian paints a chaotic picture of bad communications on their voyage out, during their five-day stay, and again on leaving Sicily, when H Squadron split into three parts, with Frank, five other officers and fifteen other ranks

* Compare Keith Douglas's detestation of the Italian soldiery, whom he graphically depicts combining cruelty with servility and cowardice (*Alamein to Zem Zem*, London, 1946, reprinted 1996, p. 54).

marooned for a week on Malta, maddened by a stream of orders and counter-orders directing them first to return to Sicily, then to fly to Sousse in Tunisia, next to go to Alexandria and finally to 'stay in Malta' at all costs. It took until mid-August for the squadron to reassemble in Egypt, after three weeks in Tripoli.

Frank's first aeroplane flight – Malta to Tripoli – alarmed him considerably. He marvelled at the uneasy sensation of flying as at the lack of identity checks and feared that any German agent could fly on British planes without being questioned once, from Senegal to Teheran. He thought flight a bad augury for the planet's future. It was too fast and too precarious. It made him feel old-fashioned.

———

On 14 June Theo had written, 'I think we have the right to hope that we may see you [next year], Peace or no Peace. The only danger . . . is that the sight of you walking in the gate might give us heart failure from sheer joy. Such strong joy after such long waiting would surely do *something* to us . . .' It seemed to Theo and EJ that both their sons haunted not only their daylight hours but even their dreams during the night, in equal measure.

Theo's phrase 'strong joy' inspired him on Malta to scribble another rapid poem, surely one of the best verses on the great wartime theme of homecoming. Here he renders the pain of exile and longing for peace and restitution of normal family life intensely personal, before universalising them once again as aspects of a Europe-wide condition. His poem represents the best of Frank, his twin abilities to make the reader feel intimately addressed, and then also suddenly make himself vanish in the final two lines, turning into an oracle for his generation:

> Will it be like that? Will the train pull into the halt
> Below the Barleycorn, wait while I dump my kit,
> Then chug away to Chinnor? Will all of you be there?
> Can you fix it like that? Gods of the Chiltern Woods!
> Will it ever be like that? I doubt it.

Shall we climb the hill together, the four of us,
Between the hawthorn-hedges, not breathing a word of war
Or dreary desert, discussing important things,
A name for our new cat, the apple-crop,
Bee-orchids growing on the Coneygar?
Will it really be like that? God Wotan grant it!

Tea with lemon by the lavender bed,
To be at peace, not trying to be a soldier!
The cornfield rippling in the evening light.
Among known walks, not feeling myself a stranger!
In that cool haven of my yearning
To rest with eyes half-closed and savour,
Along with millions Europe over,
The still strong joy of our returning!

His inclusion of place names stopped Frank on grounds of security from sending this wonderful poem home. His parents for the first time read it – among the last he wrote – after his death.* They would have loved the twin irony and constraint of 'important things, / A name for our new cat'. How vividly he conveys the pathos of yearning to be allowed to stop 'trying to be a soldier' and everywhere 'feeling a stranger', the pleas of so many conscripted men. But he had one year more of both to endure.

During his three weeks in Tripoli Frank found himself one day queuing for lunch next to his first cousin Trevor Vivian, an 'exceptionally nice, modest lad' wounded at El Alamein, after which he had blown himself up experimenting with a mine detonator. Trevor talked with nightmarish insincerity about the 'good fun of fighting', asking 'what fun Frank had had'.

Frank confessed to feeling very frightened, on occasion nearly sick;

---

* It is also unaccountably missing from his *Selected Poems* (2003), but can be found in Theodosia Jessup Thompson and E. P. Thompson, *There is a Spirit in Europe: A Memoir of Frank Thompson*, London, 2nd edn, 1948, p. 135.

he would be happy never to hear of another man killed or family bereaved. War could only be enjoyed, he reflected, at the expense of one's humanity. He visited fellow officers in hospital, some grievously wounded in Sicily, and reflected on the dishonesty of most war reporting with its references to laughing, eager Tommies, and proffered his own Sassoon-like parodic *rapportage* of the Sicilian landings, in which the bullets lamming into one man's head rip it open like a shell of ripe peas: not much *fun* there.

As for poor Trevor, he would the following month win the MC for knocking out four German tanks during the Salerno landings and, in a flying accident in March 1946, be killed.

———

Frank reported to his parents that Iris had become an assistant principal in the Treasury after she won a First, and that war had saved him from the indignity of gaining a degree inferior to hers. Admirers of Murdoch like myself are inclined to make much of Frank's and Iris's 'star-friendship' – Nietzsche's phrase for affinity complicated by distance, a life-habit of hers – appropriating Frank's fascination to her cause. When I wrote her *Life* and learned that Frank in Egypt started studying Turkish concurrently with Iris in London I assumed that this was Frank's way of serenading her at long distance. I now know that Phantom HQ's April 1943 directive required H Squadron to learn Turkish in preparation for the possible invasion of the Dodecanese Islands.

Turkish apart, much linked them. Both were brilliant would-be writers of omnivorous curiosity, lovers of Shakespeare and Communists marked by the 'heroic struggle' for Spain. Both were romantics. Iris Murdoch in March 1943 wondered what the future held for them all: 'Shall we ever make out of the dreamy idealistic stuff of our lives any hard & real thing? You will perhaps. Your inconsequent romanticism has the requisite streak of realism to it – I think I am just a dreamer.' In 1939 Iris had been Frank's chief muse and inspiration. Increasingly in 1943 he was hers. His soldier's life abroad made him grow up faster than her. She acknowledged an 'understanding' between them: 'I feel in a peculiar sort of way that I mustn't let you down – yet don't quite know how to set about it.'

One aspect of 'letting Frank down' was taking lovers. She soon confessed that there had been two men, neither of whom she loved, and that she was happy at having set aside her burdensome virginity. She wrote with the confidence of one who has hitherto enjoyed the emotional upper hand but who now fears that her news – albeit itself a token of trust and esteem – might 'anger' him. He replied on 26 April that only jealousy or righteous indignation could be a cause for anger and that he had no right to either, not having thought of her as a body for four years, and having messed up his own love-life too: dividing women into distant princesses to be idealised and 'tarts' to be used.

The chilly, virginal Iris he had known two years before had given way to the promiscuous Iris of the dozen years leading up to her marriage in 1956, when sex seemed to her an aspect of friendship and often led to confusion. He claimed to feel 'joy' on her behalf that she had been rescued from her icy virginity, but issued warnings. She should beware of the contempt and hatred of men, especially those to whom she gave herself. On the whole Frank thought:

> that it is better to abstain altogether until one falls head over heels in love. Men who had never slept with anyone before their wife, tell me that the first weeks of their honeymoon were an ecstasy they have never known before or since – an ecstasy which those who have already partaken of the fruit will never know.

For all his bohemianism and Communism, Frank was a conventional product of his class and time. When that December Frank inveighed against wartime adultery, divorce and people making 'a mess of their lives' a Miss Papadimitrou* commented more in sorrow than in anger that Frank was 'very old-fashioned'. He did not

---

* Miss Papadimitrou was doubtless one of the three Greek girls in Alexandria who he would boast (see Chapter 11) were wearing his badge.

disagree. His standards of marital fidelity were, he confessed, '1860 Baptist chapel'.

His leisure occupations in summer 1943 – visiting the races, a concert of classical music, playing tennis, joining the Anglo-Hellene club, eating quantities of cake – are unremarkable and, apart from visits to the Greek theatre, conservative. If he was secretly active in the CP in these months, no record of this survives. He disapproved of air travel, of the infantilism of Hollywood and the Andrews Sisters, and censured Americans for keeping their (superior) Forces clubs closed to their allies when British ones were open. Such views could all have been voiced by his father, then bemoaning the lonely, girl-hungry GIs lounging all afternoon outside the Clarendon Hotel in Oxford.

He ended his letter by inviting Iris to continue sharing confidences: 'I talk a lot of nonsense when I answer them, but maybe I understand more than I let on.' He saw that Iris feared that her new bohemianism might cause her to forfeit his friendship, and that she placed a value on his good opinion.

Iris's news unquestionably disturbed him none the less. A 'bigoted' atheist, he went to a service in the Greek Orthodox cathedral in Alexandria to think things through before answering. He soon asked his parents to tear up his will, which mentioned Iris, and an accompanying letter, which may also have done. M. R. D. Foot, to whom, alone of his correspondents, he was willing to sound vulnerable, received from him, dated mid-May, a 'wildly melancholiac letter' which so disturbed him that it prompted two letters in reply, urging him not to despair, of the world or himself, until Frank angrily persuaded him that his worst fears about the risk of his self-harming were 'baseless'. The most likely trigger for Frank's desolation is this news that Iris was taking lovers. Not merely did the war mean that 'real life' was passing Frank by, but he stood in danger of losing the woman he still claimed after four long years of war as his *princesse lointaine*.

Michael Foot's worries about Frank cannot have been eased when Iris, after lengthy pursuit, agreed on 9 July to be his first lover, though Michael understandably did not tell Frank, who only learned this unwelcome news in his last weeks in occupied Serbia in 1944. It may have played a part in his reckless decision to enter Bulgaria.

Michael meanwhile was bothered by Iris's growing fascination with Frank. On 16 September she wrote Frank (but did not send) the love poem 'For WFT', mentioned earlier, whose conceit is that when they were physically close in Oxford, she measured their distance; now they are separated he is close to her heart:

> Not far from the green garden, folded in
> Your room, your story & your arms, I guaged [*sic*]
> With a heart quietly beating the long
> Long gulf between us. Summer hung
> Its colours on the window, & a song
> Swept over us from the gramophone.
> Now, in a sad September, gilt with leaves,
> I am without you, & as many miles
> Of sea and mountain part us, as my thoughts
> Could then imagine of our separateness.
> [Yet you speak simply & your human voice
> Gentle as ever: *deleted*]
> – Yet, listening at last, I have caught
> That human echo in your tone that might
> Call me to love. Nearer, far nearer to my heart
> You lie now, distantly in your grief's desert than
> When all your candid years did homage then.

Small wonder if Michael during the months of his unhappy liaison with Iris sometimes felt himself a stand-in for Frank.

Not that they were her only suitors. On 21 July Frank wrote home from Tripoli that he had run into Hal Lidderdale, a 'small, dark-eyed humanist' working in an anti-aircraft ops room. They caught up with each other's news, Frank charging himself with 'shooting a line' by dint of things implied. Frank and Hal shared a progressive politics, deploring their respective officers' messes, with their endless card-playing and drinking, anti-Semitism, complacent prayers for a long war of attrition in the USSR, philistine lack of curiosity about the countries where they were stationed and indignation that every old palace in Rome had not yet been obliterated. Frank claimed to find the other ranks more open, inquisitive and sympathetic.

Frank also shared with Hal a love of Iris and his claim 'not to have thought of her as a body for four years' was in part clearly chivalrous bluff to diminish her guilt about her love-life. Indeed he wrote that 'Hal and I are really rivals for Iris, but the fair object of our rivalry is so remote in time and space that that only serves to cement our friendship. At the moment I think Hal's leading quite comfortably [as] Iris goes to stay with his mother.'

Probably the reason Iris did not visit Bledlow was because Theo did not approve of her bohemianism. Nor did Frank, who criticised Oxford friends then marrying in order to enjoy sexual love rather than for procreation: 'If I ever marry, I shall have plenty of children,' Frank announced a trifle priggishly. And though Iris's news, even so, did not put her out of commission, another girl soon distracted Frank.

# PART THREE

# Beyond the Frontier
## 1943–7

# Recasting the World: September 1943–January 1944

For every [democrat] that is killed or mutilated by the Gestapo [and their allies] two more are made by that example . . .

Letter, 25 December 1943

But a democrat has a great advantage over the people whom he is fighting. Even his death is, in a sense, creative. When a democrat dies – that is, a man who has shown . . . by word and action that he cares more than anything for democratic freedom – then one, ten or a hundred new ones are created by his example . . . When a fascist dies the effect on his confederates is the reverse.

Letter, 18 January 1944

The ex-schoolmaster and fellow CP sympathiser he befriended in Baghdad, Peter Wright – 'best bloke I've met since leaving England' – had joined SOE from the Intelligence Corps on 19 April 1943. Since Frank at once started scheming to join SOE himself, Wright probably told Frank about the organisation then. It took him five months. On 10 September he finally said goodbye to Phantom, newly excited about the future, yet much moved by this leave-taking from men he had sailed out with in March 1941. His father praised Frank's description of this tearful farewell as 'almost worthy of Tolstoi'.

He spent that weekend in Shepheard's Hotel, exactly like two years earlier before another momentous change – going to fight in the

Western Desert – taking stock once more in a letter home. As in November 1941, he sorted out his kit, putting surplus possessions into store. He contrived for Tony Forster to inherit his Phantom job the same day he left, and Forster – driven by his batman Lorton whom Forster also inherited – took three bags of Frank's books, papers and letters to Aunt Meg Leavitt in Beirut on 23 September. Evidently Frank from the start eschewed a desk job and wished to travel light. Specifically, he hoped to be dropped into Greece.

He had many motives for moving. That July Frank again read *War and Peace* (in Italian), which had 'passages almost as real as if I had lived them', struck like many by how its brilliant characters dwindle finally into commonplace middle-aged dullness. Rupert Brooke had avoided that unheroic fate in the previous war, after being famously hymned by Frances Cornford: 'A young Apollo, golden-haired, / Stands dreaming on the verge of strife, / Magnificently unprepared / For the long little-ness of life.' Might SOE help Frank avoid the 'long littleness of life' and thus stay inspired and venturesome?

He feared he was vegetating in a ration-consuming unit stuck in transit camps without much possibility of training. Phantom's relative failure in the Middle East one of its officers attributed to the hostility of the military establishment towards a private army getting informa-tion for the high command. Phantom's fortunes changed around the time Frank left and during the final two years of war it gained credibil-ity: in every Allied campaign henceforward it operated with forward units and played an important role.

Leaving Phantom also resolved the paradox of his youth. On exiting his tent on 23 May 1943 and observing a group of men not putting their heart into PT, he yelled 'Come on! Let's see a bit more life in that!' He soon realised with a mix of delight and embarrassment that the trainees were senior naval officers, not a man below lieutenant-commander – a ranking equivalent to major. Frank had spent three years impersonat-ing a grown-up. Maybe he could afford to stop.

Although Frank when they first met was twenty-two, Peter Wright like others took him for twenty-seven or twenty-eight. Frank had to hold his own with people ten years older, giving orders to seven officers with an average age of thirty, and adopting their mannerisms as protective camouflage. Addressing another twenty-three-year-old officer as 'Young man' and pipe-smoking were further pieces of theatre. Meeting twenty-year-old Rifle Brigade officers made Frank feel old, and he observed, optimistically, that Englishmen of his class altered more between twenty and twenty-three than at any other period. Yet inside he still felt hopelessly childish and it broke out when he devoured sweet buns or Russian children's books, or found himself weeping on bidding farewell to his Phantom unit where he was known as 'the Gaffer'. He celebrated childishness thus: 'Without going all James Barrie . . . the real, the enduring people are those who have kept something of the child within them.'

His squadron earned a good chit for their cheerfulness and efficiency in Sicily, but their saluting was never very smart. Frank himself, long-haired and bohemian, was certainly not the disciplinarian a second-in-command was supposed to be. Finally, he accounted himself very frightened of generals. And now a prospect of escape from all these pitfalls offered itself, rebutting his father's charge that his life had become a mere 'desultory tale': in Greece.

---

The type of patrician Englishman who viewed Greece through a romantic mist distilled from Byron, Keats and the tragedies of Aeschylus and Sophocles was affectionately parodied in Louis de Bernières's *Captain Corelli's Mandolin* as 'Lt Bunny Warren' who parachutes into Kephalonia in 1942 talking Homeric Greek. Bunny spoofs a type exemplified by Frank. On 23 May he had written to Iris Murdoch from Alexandria:

> Today I want to talk to you about Greeks because they are staunch anti-fascists, because they are simply among the best people I have met, because they are very much the same as the Greeks who fought at Scamander and Marathon, drove their chariots by the weeping firs on the Hill of Kronos or packed the slopes of the Acropolis to hear the *Agamemnon*.

The idea of a direct continuity between the old Hellas and the new was shared by other Wykehamists. In August 1943 in a Tripoli restaurant he ran into his schoolfellow Christopher Seton-Watson, driving trucks from Cairo to Algiers, who had won an MC during the 1941 retreat from Greece and still romanticised that country. Frank admired his 'gentle sane bravery'.

On 13 September Frank reported to SOE Cairo, housed in Rustum Buildings – a well-appointed block of flats known to every Cairene taxi-driver as 'Secret Building' – where he met Seton-Watson's brother Hugh 'mumbling into his beard' in a basement and noted that Monty Woodhouse, for whom Frank had 'fagged' for one unhappy term at Winchester, was also employed there. Frank found that he was to keep the rank of captain and worked with Peter Wright 'to get the hang of things', taking afternoon siestas in Peter's flat near by.

Like the Seton-Watsons – and John Pendlebury, who had been killed in 1941 – Monty Woodhouse was yet another philhellene Wykehamist. On 26 November 1942 he had helped blow up the Gorgopotamos viaduct, severing the Thessaloniki–Athens railway line and thus cutting what was wrongly thought to be the main supply route to Rommel's Afrika Korps – one of the most spectacular wartime acts of resistance in occupied Europe. Although called 'Major' by Frank, Woodhouse in fact – at twenty-seven – had just been gazetted colonel, heading the Allied Military Mission to Greece, where he took the Italian surrender, his gingerish hair and eyebrows dyed black to make him look Greek. His co-saboteur Eddie Myers was now visiting Cairo.

By autumn 1943 SOE Cairo was running eighty such missions in the Balkans. Operation Animals had recently scored another success by blowing up the Asopos railway bridge, persuading the Germans to divert two divisions to Greece away from Sicily during the invasion Frank had participated in.

Frank lied to his parents that his was 'a safe job. You know me well enough – I wouldn't volunteer for anything dangerous . . .' He told them truthfully that his new job was 'hush-hush' but contrived a way to communicate about it. His closest friend from 1940 in Richmond,

Rupert Raw, was also in SOE: he advised his folks to drop in, in North Oxford, on Rupert's wife Joan.

Theo soon lunched with Joan Raw and that October in a letter to Frank praised the Greek Partisans, while EJ wrote to his sons that 'If either of you gets into the Balkans, may you find the place where Apollo rose as apple king' – the theory about Apollo's origins long attractive to Frank.* On 1 November, EJ wrote of a possible landing in the Balkans: 'We are not as crass as we appear . . . hints dropped in the press tell us more than we let on . . . we know what perils you both have to face . . . those Greek and Jugoslav patriots must be the world's ace heroes.' EP, too, started learning modern Greek and continued that autumn in Algeria.

Frank had joined Phantom in 1940 in the hope of getting to Greece but, while he was sailing, Greece had fallen. Now he joined SOE for the chance of playing a part in Greece's liberation. He had been studying and practising modern Greek in the intervening three years and must have looked an excellent recruit. And SOE was famously hospitable to Winchester men.

On Frank's letter-headings SOE Cairo appears as 'GHQ Liaison', 'MO4' and 'Force 133'; during its four years of active existence it changed its name seven times, each new name corresponding to a change of structure. During the same period it had eight heads: three civilians who mistrusted soldiers and five senior officers who mistrusted politicians and diplomats. SOE was responsible to the Ministry of Economic Warfare through its HQ in London, to the Foreign Office through the diplomatic representatives of the latter, and to the commanders-in-chief for its operational activities. This triple responsibility was a source of confusion and reflected uncertainty about its role. It was in perpetual flux, lacking internal cohesion: four months after the first party of British parachutists were dropped into Greece, SOE Cairo – scandalously – had lost all record of their names.

---

* See p. 147.

His Phantom colleague and fellow CP member Frank Jacobson wrote that Frank was known and loved 'not simply by a few intimate friends but by a large section of the progressive forces from Alexandria to Baghdad and beyond'. An invisible history is implicit here: Communist sub-culture in Egypt revolved around the Rond Point bookshop near the Cairo Opera, selling the biggest selection of magazines, newspapers and political pamphlets in the Middle East, including *KD: The Middle East Forces Anti-Fascist Monthly*, printed clandestinely in Haifa, then smuggled into Cairo by train. *KD*'s editorial adviser was Major James Klugmann, second-in-command of the Yugoslav section in SOE, who almost certainly recruited Frank that September, seeing that Communist BLOs had a special usefulness among Balkan Partisans because of common aims and sympathies. According to one source, Frank and Klugmann talked for long periods, probably in Shepheard's Hotel, about their shared 'blind faith' in the Partisans, East European literature, Christopher Caudwell's *Studies in a Dying Culture*, their Communist ideals and Klugmann's passionate belief that CP members again needed to join up with socialists within an alliance recalling the Popular Front in a war for 'national liberation, peoples' liberation, colonial liberation'.

Above all, there was the smart converted cinema off Suliman Pasha Street, once called La Potinière and now renamed Music-for-All, with cheap but good food, a place hospitable to many different cultural events including those staged by ABCA and ENSA* – among them a Music Appreciation Society that had since 1942 been meeting weekly in a quiet back room, convenient cover for a Marxist Study Group. Within the central space in Music-for-All the six famous Forces Parliaments convened, with up to 500 men attending, starting in September 1943. During the 1 December Parliament a motion to nationalise the distributive trades was passed with an overwhelming majority, as was an Inheritance Restriction Bill on 1 January 1944. Press interest was keen, and war correspondents and photographers were invited. After German propaganda broadcast news of the 'mutinous radicalism' of the British

---

* The Entertainments National Service Association or ENSA provided entertainment for British armed forces personnel.

forces in Egypt, the mock-Parliaments were stopped, their leading members posted to the Far East and the future Labour MP Leo Abse held in prison for participating in a debate to nationalise the Bank of England.

These Forces Parliaments are famous for many reasons. First they show the doublethink that made the British fight for democratic freedoms denied to their own fighting men. Then the Parliaments portend the July 1945 election when Churchill was unceremoniously kicked out of office and the clear message conveyed that the country would never again return to the vastly unequal and unjust days of the 1930s, to depression and unemployment. For ten days in Cairo that July other ranks refused to salute officers.

Lastly in Music-for-All socialist and CP voted on a single joint Labour ticket. This was consonant with Labour and CP uniting some years before to create the University Labour Federation, reflecting consensual politics that we remember as the Popular Front, a consensus that – whether Frank attended any of the first four Forces Parliaments before being dropped abroad or not, which we do not know – he found sympathetic.

Everything about Frank belongs to this one particular historical moment, when Hitler had to be beaten and a new, better world created.* His final letter to young Edward in April 1944, stressing the need for 'a new communal ethic', was utterly of its time. Indeed M. R. D. Foot wrote to Frank in August 1943 about the 'Need to build up some . . . communal feeling in Europe so that we don't win the war only to lose the peace.' Here was that optimistic consensus between a far leftist like Frank and the more cautious Michael which was famously charted in Paul Addison's 1975 work *The Road to 1945* and which Frank's brother later termed the 'radical populist euphoria of 1944'.

Frank was a typical 1930s intellectual, fashioned during the years of the Popular Front, that genuine alliance of left-radical opinion which

---

* A spirit famously satirised in a song by A. P. Herbert: 'Oh, won't it be wonderful after the war / There won't be no rich, and there won't be no poor . . . Why didn't we have this old War before?'

simplified the world by dividing it into two opposing camps, Fascist versus anti-Fascist, free man versus slave, and hence white versus black. Young Edward, forty years later, elegised this as 'that half-democratic, half anti-Fascist time, when the chances of life were shared, the young gave priority to the injured, the sick, the children and the old, and the pursuit of private privilege was deemed contemptible'. Edward called the period 1936–46, in a stirring phrase, 'the decade of heroes' – of which Frank was notably one.

The Popular Front came into being in 1935 during the Seventh World Congress of the Communist International uniting all parties that opposed Fascism. They were to stop Fascism for good, and Frank was soon to pay its pieties tribute in his most famous letter, which gave the title for his posthumous memorial volume *There is a Spirit in Europe*. This winning spirit, he divined, was 'broader and more generous than any dogma'. In other words it recalled the Popular Front. (Iris Murdoch in 1940 had noted Frank's 'simplicity tinged with melodrama': the hero fitted his period perfectly, simplicity and melodrama belonging to the moment of the Popular Front itself.)

One commentator wrote, 'Spain was the first and last crusade of the British left-wing intellectual. Never again was such enthusiasm mobilized . . . Disillusion had not yet sapped the idealism of the young.' Frank was so deeply marked by the Spanish Civil War that Mussolini's fall in July 1943 appeared to him 'the work of John Cornford, Ralph Fox and the Carritts', all of whom fought, and some died, in Spain. Frank remembered those men who, 'in the Sierras and on the banks of the Ebro, bore the heat of the day alone, fighting against hopeless odds'. Their efforts had paid off and the Italian surrender was 'the final victory of the Asturian miners and Barcelona working men who proved the idea that freedom and Fascism can't live in the same world, and the free man will always win'.

This is very striking. We who come after know that freedom and dictatorship can not merely cohabit, but have done so promiscuously for sixty-odd post-war years, and will probably continue to make uneasy bedfellows. Frank's certainties belonged to a period of political idealism as remote from us as the Romantic Revival two centuries earlier, of which his heroic age was the last flowering.

The hope, however admirable, that freedom would finally defeat Fascism in some apocalyptic showdown was never likely to be justified by results, if only because freedom and servitude cohabited within the Alliance itself: the USSR, for all Frank's and Edward's illusions about it, was scarcely a free society, but in its own way would prove in time to be a corrupt tyranny as brutal and terrifying as Nazism.

To this Frank was not entirely blind and deaf. If he wrote at this time to Catherine Dalton (née Nicholson) to the effect that 'When the Communists come to power after the war, as they surely will, I will be the first to be hung as a heretic,' then he knew he was exactly the kind of independent-minded sympathiser who would soonest be purged in post-war Eastern Europe. He had the self-abnegating commitment to a secular faith shown by many CP members but lacked their fear of independent thinking or their masochistic attraction and submission to authority.* Such criticism as we have from him of the USSR is mild. For example he was sceptical about whether the Battle of Britain had been adequately reported in the Russian press at the time – or reported at all. (German bombers were in 1940 said to be fuelled with Russian oil, the two dictatorships then in monstrous collusion.)

Yet there is still much that is starry-eyed in his feeling for Russians and Slavs in general. It starts with the Russian language itself, 'a sad, powerful language [that] flows gently off the tongue like molten gold', compared to which – he wrote from parachute school that October of 1943 – 'Polish and Czech seem nervous and restless, Bulgarian poor and untutored, Serbo-Croat – probably the next most satisfactory, just a little barbarous, a fine language for guerillas and men who drink slivovitz in the mountains . . .'†

---

* Compare Frank writing sceptically to Iris (14 Aug. 1943, UNC) of Aragon's collection of poems on Dunkirk, *Le Crève-Coeur* (Heartbreak), which both loved and which was then enjoying cult success: 'How strange that the only decent poet in this war should be a communist! I can't understand that, can you?'

† He was translating an article by Ilya Ehrenburg, who argued that the post-war world would be 'built by people who have lived through much, who have been enriched by defeats and victories, who have opened up in themselves seams of feeling they never knew they had . . . [and] a morale born in sacrifice, blood and fire'. Frank heartily

There was much discussion among the Allied leaders at the Cairo
and Teheran conferences of the role of Balkan guerrillas, to the gratifi-
cation of Frank's SOE colleagues in Cairo – a matter to whose political
complexities we return. Indeed a high-level deputation of Greek
Partisans, aka Andartes, which had arrived in August was still in Cairo
for the first week Frank spent at SOE; its members were at first roughly
mishandled, leading to Lord Glenconner's resignation, and left only on
17 September.* Frank probably met them, as he also met Yugoslav
Partisans that December.

Meanwhile the death-throes of Fascism did not lessen its vileness,
the egoism of one man – Hitler – causing a bloodbath in Europe. Had
even the reign of Attila the Hun been as bad as the Nazi Terror? Frank
doubted it. The Russian newspaper *Ogynek* carried pictures of murdered
women, of gibbets and of 'the whole of proud Kharkov desolate'. The
ordeals of Warsaw and Belgrade over three years were intensifying and
the Germans had just set fire to Frushka Gora – the so-called 'Jewel of
Serbia' with its ancient monasteries, an important centre of Partisan
resistance – thereby igniting thirteen centuries of Serb pride. Frank
refers weekly to new horrors, and the 'deluge of black anger' they inspire
in him. He quoted Ilya Ehrenburg: 'You could not call [the Germans]
beasts: the bears would be offended.' He agreed with his brother that
this 'Devilry' needed to be driven out of Europe: his rhetoric dwelt on
the Last Days, Judgement and the Redemption of history.

———————

He had managed in 1940 to stomach the Soviet Union's aggression
against the Finns and even countenance its savagery against the Poles.
The more vexed the politics of the war became, the simpler and more

———————

endorsed Ehrenburg's sentiments, adding *in propria persona*: 'It's a grand world we will
be building, and the business of building will be far more interesting and exciting than
any of the so-called adventures that war brings.'
* They travelled to Cairo with assurances of safe passage from SOE Cairo, only to find
themselves in danger of arrest on arrival. Lord Glenconner, SOE Cairo's head, felt his
integrity impugned by this breach of good faith: see his unpublished memoir in the
Imperial War Museum.

streamlined his language. Frank understood the living power of rhetoric, which his father the previous April called both 'matter' and 'poise
and self-carriage'. That month, too, he praised *Antony and Cleopatra* to
Iris, a play both admired: 'There is something uncanny about the way
in which these slightly sordid middle-aged lovers, who have talked very
little else but drivel for the first three acts, suddenly rise in the last two
to the very pinnacles of poetry, and blaze their trail across the mind of
humanity for all time.'

Trail-blazing was on his mind. On Boxing Day he wrote her a letter
that quoted from his translation of Mayakovsky's 'The Secret of Youth'*
about casting the world anew:

> With the passing of the year I seem to have come to a watershed in my
> life . . . I think I shall soon have a change in my way of living which will
> give me a real chance. Nothing else matters. We must crush the Nazis and
> build our whole life anew. 'If we should meet again, why then we'll smile.'†
> If not, why then those that follow us will be able to smile far more happily
> and honestly in the world that we all helped to make.

While Michael Foot wrote to Frank angrily on 25 May 1943 warning
him against taking suicidal risks in his longing to finish either Fascism
or himself – 'Neither a true choice nor a true opposition' – Frank and
Iris by contrast shared a do-or-die, all-or-nothing romanticism. And
the apocalyptic note in these last months of his life runs through all his
letters in a vein of heroic simplicity. He repeatedly prophesies – and
invokes – a final unifying of Europe to defeat Fascism.

> My Christmas message to you is one of Greater Hope than I have ever
> had in my life before. There is a spirit abroad in Europe which is finer
> and braver than anything that tired continent has known for centuries,

---

* 'The Secret of Youth': 'The young ones / those are they / Who, when the fighters' ranks
are thinning / In the name of all young folk / say / "We shall recast the whole of living."'
† Brutus: 'If we do meet again, why, we shall smile; / If not, why then, this parting was
well made' (Shakespeare, *Julius Caesar*, Act V, scene 1). In his last letter Frank quotes a
later scene from the same play.

and cannot be withstood. You can, if you like, think of it in terms of politics, but it is broader and more generous than any dogma. It is the confident will of whole peoples, who have known the utmost humiliation and suffering and have triumphed over it, to build their own life once and for all . . .

This letter continues: 'For every one that is killed or mutilated by the Gestapo [and their allies], two more are made by that example . . .'

This piety that even a democrat's death is in a sense creative he repeated on 18 January 1944. For, by showing that the democrat cares more for freedom than for life itself, 'one, or ten or a hundred new ones are created by his example'. The death of a Fascist had the opposite result.

This directly recalls the early Christian author Tertullian (AD c. 160–220), for whom Christian martyrs' blood was seed, so that 'the more you mow us down, the more numerous we grow'. Thus Tertullian encouraged those in prison about to be fed to the lions, opposing a Christian death to the false ideals that comfort pagans. Christians are soldiers of the living God, and no one becomes a soldier without painful training. Prison and martyrdom are that training ground. Frank always liked best of Christ's sayings 'the one about losing one's life and gaining it'.

This millenarial sub-text now lends his prose its intense and heady excitement, taking force from a Marxist version of the End of Days: that the death of Fascism entailed the inevitable birth of something new and better, a faith essentially religious. It underlies his pious hope that the terror bombing of German cities that was making the London Blitz look 'like a nuisance raid . . . may outlaw war for ever'.

The family felt this quasi-religious charge first. It is appropriate that one year later, on 27 November 1944, Theo wrote to young Edward, then fighting in Italy, asking him to choose one of two given moments on Christmas Day to read Frank's 'Christmas message' when she and old Edward also planned reading it in England. They hoped against hope that Frank might have been taken prisoner and be alive and thus the family would keep faith with Frank's spirit.

Frank needed training for the coming battle. A running series of nick-names points to his lack of coordination – at school 'Caliban' and in his OCTU 'Tarzan'. In SOE Frank was 'Ham' for ham-fisted. That – by contrast – he was soon observed during a single morning prosecuting to successful conclusions conversations in Polish, Arabic, German, French and Italian evoked (he noted) silent awe.

He went to commando school, where they taught skills that included sabotage and the use of small firearms; boxing lessons improved his fitness and coordination. He insisted he had at last caught up with his own strength and 'had the makings of a powerful thug'; photos show how remarkably handsome he had also grown. Commando school was followed by parachute school at nearby Ramath David in northern Palestine, starting on 22 October 1943 with one week's preparation for five drops, of increasing difficulty, over three days. A Pole with a wooden leg called Andrew Kennedy (aka Andrzej Koverski) accompanied parties emplaning for their first jump, always first out of the aircraft. The theory went that if a Pole with a wooden leg could jump, so could you: 'It worked with outstanding success.'

The main discussion points of these ten days were fear and courage. During the preparatory week, he dreamed roughly three nightmare descents per night, tangled and struggling in the rigging lines. He was being tested: it recalled working late at school for an exam. He noted in his diary, 'so, you see, it's really rather good fun', yet he also pointed out that even when instructors with fifty jumps behind them did demonstration jumps, some after hitting the ground were still tense and shaking for minutes. A flush of courage was needed just to get you out of the door. An officer from the preceding intake who bragged that half an hour's heavy bombardment was a far more searching test of courage none the less admitted to Frank being 'shit-scared' for his first three jumps, adding: 'if you've known that fear and overcome it, I don't think anything is going to scare you'. Such was the theory.

This officer had volunteered to become a parachutist on vague rebound from a girl for whom he did not much care. Frank considered how arbitrary were many significant life-choices, how randomly everybody was shaped and blown. He admired the camaraderie, courage and resourcefulness of his fellows, their hatred of having life cut and dried. He used the metaphor of 'jumping' for the inbuilt uncertainty of life itself, wondering where he would 'land' in civilian life, as a journalist, general, actor or teacher.

And he played with other futures: writing a DLitt on the Decembrist rebellion of 1825 and becoming a Workers Education Association (WEA) lecturer in Slavonic Studies, or researching a whole raft of disparate Slavic topics.* Then he might be a *Daily Worker* correspondent in Shanghai (living in China was a persistent 1943 fantasy), a painter in Samoa, a biographer of Trotsky or a London University historian. Bulgaria, as well as China, recurred.

---

* These Slavic interests included Stenka Razin (Cossack rebel, 1630–71), Pugachev (Cossack rebel, 1774–5), Lomonosov (Russian), Stambolisky (Bulgarian), Vuk Karadžić (Serbian) and Niemcewicz (Polish).

Perhaps he would lecture with the British Council on Oscar Wilde to Sofia University students, or – another favourite daydream – even manage a one-man rose farm in Bulgaria. As often, 'Bulgaria' meant escape. Theo wrote promising to buy him a motorbike to offset his restlessness.

Meanwhile the ordeal of parachuting loomed, and the drugs others used to lessen terror were feeble jesting, drink and benzedrine. Frank refused alcohol until his final night, when he bought some wine. He had a temperature – either flu or sandfly fever – causing him to sweat through two pairs of pyjamas in one night and accepted aspirin and quinine to deal with night-sweats.

The first and easiest drop was from a Hudson – a door-jump at 1,000 feet. Frank dived clean into space and ideal air conditions and, after the slipstream had shaken him like a terrier with a rat, was wafted away without ever coming to the correct position of attention. He experienced neither bliss nor terror as his chute opened and he drifted awkwardly down to a landing that recalled a hard rugby tackle. Fever dulled fear and feeling alike.

But soon after he landed, the last parachute of the 'stick' came down at more than double normal speed – not as they hoped a container, but a man roman-candling, his chute failing to open and his screams clearly audible as he plummeted to earth. He broke one leg but sustained terrible internal injuries from which he soon died.

It was an ill beginning. A brisk pep talk from a flight-lieutenant advised a hearty breakfast, assuring them that this happened only once in 10,000 drops and that 'you're just as likely to get killed riding a bicycle'. This failed to lift their spirits. Frank observed his own difficulty experiencing pity for someone he did not know and a self-centred annoyance that the anxiety of future jumps would now be intensified. The second was from a Vickers Wellington (aka a Wimpy): a narrow-aperture jump with the extra fear of hitting your head. He watched the sweating faces and bulging eyes of his stick-mates straining upwards in prayerful farewell before joining them, whacking his head on landing and endangering his ankles.

The night before the third jump Frank dreamed of twenty descents.

This was a traditional time for some to pull out of the training (like Peter Wright, who had first told Frank about SOE). But although this jump had the added scare-factor of being from only 600 feet, so your parachute had less time to open, he landed swiftly with a very gentle side collapse. The man ahead of him on the fourth – at only 500 feet – froze, and had to be pushed out of the plane, while the next chap refused point-blank; but Frank flopped out like a sleepwalker, hitting his pack on the doorway, spinning and burning his hand in the rigging line before gently landing.

The fifth and last was the night jump and in prospect the most eerie and terrifying. He drifted towards a flaming beacon but managed to land, with only a moderate thump, to one side. He had now graduated, and celebrated with a bottle of red wine during a rowdy party.

Frank took stock afterwards in a hotel in Alexandria. He had first felt tested during five months in the Libyan Desert in 1942, next in his five days in Sicily that July. Parachuting was his third 'blooding'. He was moderately pleased to have gained his 'wings'. While his senses had often been numbed by the terror of jumping, and he never felt master of himself until several seconds after hitting the ground, he had learned that he need not be paralysed by terror. His conclusion was both heroic and sententious, that 'Every man is a weapon in this fight, which will only end when we achieve some mythical perfection. My tempering has only just begun. I mean the process to be thorough.'

———

One week after gaining his wings Frank was publicly rebuked by a Greek girl. In May, immediately after he had received news of Iris's deflowering, he and two other officers and seven NCOs were deputed to learn modern Greek for three mornings a week with a view to a possible Phantom landing in the Dodecanese Islands. Young, comely Maroula Thalis came out from the Berlitz School to Sidi Bishr camp outside Alexandria with black lively hair, fierce restless eyes and a figure that 'gave one all the wrong ideas when she started rubbing the

'Love (Eros) and the Cat. A Love Story'.

blackboard'. She liked people and had humanity and an attractive way of collapsing with laughter during class. Frank sent her cat-stories for homework. He listed her virtues, ending with integrity, being religious in just the right way and 'less of a tart than any girl I've met', suggesting the fear of female sexuality that he had confessed to Iris.

Maroula crops up in his letters and diaries over the following six months, moved by the flowers he sends when the unit discontinued Greek lessons (preparing now for the Sicilian landings instead). Their attraction was mutual: she enjoins him always to be 'serious', teaches him to tango, takes him to watch her play basketball and frets over his thinness.

She was no doubt again useful for practising modern Greek when, from September onwards, he hoped once more to be dropped into her country. Maroula was one of three Greek girls in Alexandria wearing his badge. Women have taken keepsakes from fighting men for centuries, and you could buy badges for a few shillings at a Naafi store-counter.

Neither the RA nor SOE was among the few regiments so proud as to discourage the custom.

She once lunched with him unchaperoned in public – the 'height of immorality' among stuffier Alexandrian Greeks – and pinched his arm twice when dancing with him. Frank, who we know 'could flirt only in a foreign language', sounds in all this a thoroughgoing spinster. He took fright when he found himself the only non-family at her nephew's baptism: this was 'a bit final'.

Old Edward warned him against 'sirens' and implied – possibly accurately – that the tale of the rich older man Maroula's father wanted her to marry was a ploy to entrap him. He also reminded Frank that a young English officer now was an enormous catch. 'There are absolutely first rate girls [elsewhere],' EJ exhorted, pretending that he was president of a permanent Selection Committee for Vetting Prospective Cats and Wives, the latter more serious – 'for a Tib if not up to standard can be drowned'. Both his sons had 'atrocious taste in girls' – no doubt a reference to EP's love for Wendy and Frank's for Iris.

Theo's contribution was to 'terrorise suitable damsels' into writing to Frank. One was Tony Forster's sister Fifi, whom Theo called 'cocksure of herself, a good hearted little piece'. The education given clever English girls appalled Theo: never letting them discuss even the wartime news, let alone its political implications, sent out into the world 'well-bred little pale white mice, silly and unable to do up a parcel properly or look up their own trains, giggling and trembling at the sight of a telephone or a railway guide . . .' Theo noted a second category of girls who should be trained merely to be charming dance partners, 'dizzy, completely foolish, ravishingly pretty and well-turned out . . . glamour girls'. Neither category enticed Frank who, judging these views 'extremely just and neatly phrased', agreed that he would be hard to please. (Theo probably doubted that any girl was good enough for her son and quite possibly hoped at some level that his heart belonged to Mother.)

On 6 November, when in the half-light of Ramleh Square in Alexandria he met up with Maroula fresh from a Berlitz class, she noticed

Frank wearing his 'wings', November 1943.

the parachute badge newly sewn on to his arm. She stamped her foot and gave him a 'rocket', no doubt fearing his being dropped into occupied territory. 'How *stupid* you are! Weren't you happy with [Phantom]?' she demanded in Greek. Frank bowed his head until the storm passed and then suggested dinner the following night. From his diary: 'with a really nice girl one doesn't want to talk about significant things . . . I've never met anyone so lively, so full of laughter, so little evil. It would take very little to make me fall in love with her.' Maroula and Frank called each other 'thou' in Greek, implying intimacy; she called in on him each day.

Frank longed for mutual sexual love and believed marriage its proper context. On Malta that July he had been 'sick with envy' at all the courting couples, and cheered up his furious, downhearted men after they saw newspaper pictures of Canadian soldiers marrying British girls: would there be anyone left to marry when they got back? Old Edward pretended that Canadians were marrying only girls who were 'good riddance', so that a 'helluva pick' of beautiful ones would await his return: he understood Frank's fears. Indeed Frank's story 'Lofty Fades Away' concerns a nihilist who, seeing life as futile, wishes before death to father a child. Frank's gay friend Roger Keyes* offered to help find him a wife.

Considering all this his rejection of Maroula – in love with him and able to bear his children – requires explanation. Frank's invention of contradictory excuses for not marrying Maroula suggests confusion. He claimed first that he would not marry till he was forty-five – and then to Maroula's daughter – and followed that by pretending to be not only an atheist but also an anarchist. After that he further insulted her by inventing a fiancée at home. Frank aptly called Maroula 'my Nausicaa', after the princess whose love for Odysseus exiled by war was never expressed but who mothered him instead: Homer knew the painful chastity that war imposes.

Frank tried to explain to his parents, writing: 'You ask for an explanation of my cable NOT MARRIED YET. We could have fallen in love but – for all that I seem weak-willed and impulsive – I have a very definite plan for living . . . my wife would have to have far fewer illusions than Maroula, or the same as mine, craziest of all – *that the whole of life can be cast anew* [emphasis added],' the phrase from his Mayakovsky translation implying that he would marry if not a Communist, then at least an idealist.

The same phrase crops up in his Boxing Day letter to Iris: 'We must crush the Nazis and build our whole life anew.' Iris, whose first novel would carry the epigraph "'Tis well an old age is out, / And time to begin a new,' was his true soul-sister. And Frank seemed to recognise his own dreamy romanticism when in his diary he admired Don Quixote as the 'lofty visionary who had no regard for material and practical interests'. His old loyalty to Iris was arguably as quixotic as his new dedication to the Bulgarian Partisans.

---

* Herbert Morgan Roger Keyes (1913–2007) was the Balliol don who had overseen the OULC play *It Can Happen Here* in March 1939 and whom Frank met again in Cairo, now a captain in the service of the Royal Sussex Regiment and the Intelligence Corps.

Indeed there is an echo between Frank choosing unattainable, distant, complicated Iris over comely, accessible Maroula and his choosing the Bulgarian over the Greek Partisans. In both he opted for some ideal impossibility, and for an heroically difficult goal. A hint of this tendency haunts his praise to Iris of *Antony and Cleopatra* that April, a play that promised 'us lesser folks . . . that we might . . . provided we still have the grace to be dissatisfied, know a moment like Antony's, – at any rate that we are not *doomed* to be Octavians . . .' 'The grace of dissatisfaction' is a striking phrase, one he associated both with politics and with love for Iris. 'One must never forget one's *princesse lointaine*, otherwise one is in danger of becoming satisfied and that would be the end of all living,' he wrote on 1 November. Thus he finally jilted Maroula for Iris – or for his idea of her.

Iris uses the word 'romantic' of Frank four times in nine months. Under his enviable guise of apparent practicality she well understood Frank's dogged otherworldliness.

———

The simplicities of the Popular Front were by late 1943 making way for a much more complex world, and Russian military successes were creating new anxieties. The Thompson family, as always, were shrewd observers. Theo around Bledlow village for two years propagandised Aid to Russia. In this fourth winter of the war, she wrote:

| We have in England | In Russia |
|---|---|
| Fuel (though restricted) | Millions of men, women & children bravely face cold, starvation . . . and death fighting our common enemy |
| Food (though rationed) | They need food, clothing, medical supplies |
| Our own homes | |
| And quiet Nights | |

A collector will call at your door between Nov 7th and 14th. If £90 is raised, Mr Wooster has promised to add £10. Watch the thermometer opposite the Post Office. Proceeds of the Whist drive on Nov 17th will also be added.

She raised £109 for Russia week in 1942 and £107 in 1943. Not bad, she thought, for a hamlet of 150 houses. On hearing over breakfast the grand swinging chorus of 'Soviet Fatherland' on the wireless Theo wept into her porridge. EJ, stirred too, agreed that 'one lives for the Russian news'.

Frank noticed how 'smugly pleased' everyone was by Soviet victories, for people hoped that Germany might as a result move twenty or thirty divisions to the USSR, which would – he feared – in turn delay the liberation of Warsaw and other cities. Russian victories brought other dangers too. Old Edward feared – accurately – that, if the Russians demanded a post-war corridor to the Aegean, nobody would have the moral right to refuse them, and Balkan nations would thus be condemned to subservience to the USSR. Young Edward also observed from Algeria how some feared the Russians might get to Berlin first, before the Americans and Brits, and thus bring Bolshevism into the very heart of Europe.

Frank, EP and like-minded people had long agitated for a Second Front, to gain the Soviet Army some relief. EP now feared that this might be hastened for bad reasons: Russian victories might stimulate those in the UK losing interest in total war to 'fight politically against the Russians' – competing with them for control of liberated territories. The Americans were amassing food supplies as a weapon against 'anarchy' among the liberated peoples; food could be useful as a bribe to keep them sweet and biddable for capitalism too; in a starving continent only governments that Americans deemed 'safe' would be given control of food.

Nowhere was the embryonic Cold War clearer in 1943 than in Greece and Yugoslavia. In both countries the Partisans divided into two opposing camps engaged in mutual strife over which would control the country post-war, one Communist, the other (in Greece) Republican or (in Serbia) Royalist. In Greece a bloody civil war, which would not end until 1949, was just beginning.

Which factions was SOE Cairo to back? The Greek case was complicated by Churchill's gratitude to King George II of the Hellenes, the British Empire's last remaining ally during the dark days at the end of 1940. He wanted Greece post-war to be a monarchy and a democracy, and, in the infamous 'percentages agreement' between Churchill and Stalin determining – in effect – which countries post-war would be on which side of the Iron Curtain, the USSR would not demur. SOE tried vainly in Greece to bind both sides together into a single movement under British command. By November Churchill had been persuaded by the Foreign Office to 'liquidate' the Communist-led EAM and ELAS* who 'must be starved and struck at by every means in our power', a proposal vexed by the fact that there were eighty British personnel serving with ELAS units. The Yugoslav case was opposite: Churchill was persuaded during 1943 unequivocally to support Tito's efficient and well-disciplined Partisans and to abandon support for Mihailović's Chetniks, who were secretly assisting the Germans. Klugmann may have prepared the way by doctoring relevant statistics; and Fitzroy Maclean, leader of the British military mission to Tito, met with Churchill in Cairo at the beginning of December. This clinched Allied support for Tito by the Big Three just agreed at Teheran, and played a role in Frank's decision to ditch Greece for Yugoslavia/Bulgaria.

---

Frank encountered these tensions head-on, as Peter Wright, also working in SOE Greek section, witnessed. They attended daily briefings that they termed 'Prayers', perhaps because enshrining false pieties. They were led by a Captain Dan Norton, Greek-speaking and with an MC won on Crete, who induced in Frank furious indignation by exaggerating the successes of the Republican Partisans under General Napoleon

* EAM was the political branch of the CP and ELAS the military. EDES was Zervas's Republican Partisan Movement.

Zervas. Norton simultaneously minimised the role of the CP Partisans, by whom Frank was tremendously impressed, as they were already the more disciplined and by far the bigger group. The internal politics of Greece reproduced in miniature the international rivalry of the USSR, USA and Great Britain.

Norton made clear that SOE's help would be given generously to Zervas and only grudgingly to the CP Partisans. Frank believed – wrongly – that the Gorgopotamos had been blown up only by the latter, and that the British, in attributing this action to both groups, were lying. They were not: that act of sabotage represented the only British success ever in getting the two sides to collaborate. Since then the two groups had been rehearsing the first stages of ferocious civil war. Its repercussions reached Cairo when Greek troops in the Near East mutinied and the British imprisoned them.

Frank and Peter Wright had what Frank termed daily 'commination services' during which they denounced the British establishment and the 'Bankers and Brewers' governing SOE and agreed how much better the world would be after the defeat of Fascism. Frank struggled for weeks to control his anger and then for a further spell to have his assignment changed.

By 1 December he had disentangled himself from his promise to be dropped into Greece and was working at a desk job once again. He put a brave face on his disappointment by writing gloomily to Iris that he supposed now that it might not be a tragedy if he survived the war. In a tone of resignation, he now proclaimed his enjoyment of sedentary pleasures: 'more and more of my delight in living comes from isolated moments of perception . . . The Nile at sunrise, a tortoise-shell cat . . . a small girl in a grey frock, with long black cavalier curls . . . picking white chrysanthema, and the last white roses before the frost'.* For

---

* 'I have been stripped of my few remaining illusions in the last year – (I speak solely of political illusions) – and harbour now a great deal of malice towards some. I have lost altogether the pseudo-heroic mood I had three months ago, when I first volunteered for parachute duties. I still press for more active work because it seems to suit my temperament better than sitting in an office, but I don't worry overmuch. If they choose to keep me at a base now my training's over, they may. I feel it won't

three sad weeks he tried out this new role of disenchanted, desk-bound seer.

But he was pressing for a fighting role elsewhere in the Balkans and accomplished this on 24 December: he was now to drop into Serbia to liaise with Bulgarian Partisans. It was safer for them in Serbia than in Bulgaria proper. His Slavophilism, his knowledge of Russian and his politics must all have recommended him for the job. He also knew a little Serbo-Croat and now turned to Bulgarian – one of those languages, he boasted, that like Italian were handed you on a plate: 'simply Russian as a Turk would talk it'. He had in 1941 noted that 'even the old peasant Bulgars will turn [against Fascism] in the end – just you see'.

Peter remembered Frank just before he set out as 'a fine dreamer, a versatile scholar and a true internationalist'. He was cheerful and confident, keenly aware that he was going not just on an adventure, but to liberate Europe from Fascism. 'How wonderful it would be to call Europe one's fatherland, and think of Krakow, Munich, Rome, Arles, Madrid as one's own cities,' he had rhapsodised earlier. Now he added: 'My eyes fill very quickly with tears when I think of what a splendid Europe we shall build.'

––––––––

In Bulgaria a kindergarten, a station and a biscuit factory have all been named after Frank Thompson, the country's second most famous Englishman (Gladstone being the first). From the perspective of Sofia it is tempting to read Frank's story – on the analogy of Thomas Hardy's poem 'The Convergence of the Twain' – as if his and Bulgaria's rendez-vous were forewritten in the stars. And indeed his longstanding fascination with that country is mysterious and uncanny.

––––––––

be a tragedy if I survive the war. I can see so many evil men and so many myriads of petty men surviving well entrenched, and I don't think that I, for all my manifest vices, am either of these. I believe that every man of goodwill is going to be badly needed in the years that lie ahead. But for all that, I would rather be now on the Sangro River – I know that for certain and don't say it to reassure you nor even myself' (10 Dec. 1943, UNC).

Yet Frank was on Bulgarian territory proper* for exactly one fort-night before his capture and execution, and he opted to fight with the Bulgarian Partisans as a way of resolving various types of confusion, only four weeks before his departure. At parachute school he had pondered the capricious smallness of men's lives and fates. When he was dropped into Serbia on the night of 25 January 1944 Thompson family politics affected his decision to go there.

His parents unwitttingly provided him with an urgent motive. Letters from them had waited in the wrong pigeon-hole in the post office for weeks, until after he had learned by 18 December from a mutual friend that they were plotting to get out to the Middle East themselves. EJ secured leave of absence from Oriel College and cabled Theo's cousin Bayard Dodge, President of the American University of Beirut, and wrote also to several others about a job in the Levant or Egypt, telling Frank partly disingenuously, 'It would not be fair to have your parents on your doorstep.' Frank, mulling over whether or not to be dropped to work with the Bulgarian Partisans, saw that they might well come to Cairo and sent a very long, vehement and muddled reply, bristling with caveats.

He warned his parents that Cairo's literary/social scene was second rate and would hardly replace their existing circle of friends in Oxford and London. Cairo was now a forgotten backwater. He resented their supposition that he might not want them so close. Now grown up, he boasted, he was 'beyond being embarrassed' by their proximity. It was not as if he were concealing 'three Turkish mistresses'. He implied that he had recently extricated himself 'by graft and lying' from a stooge job (referring to Greece). While he cautioned them on 18 December that he was, however, 'not one of the fixtures of Cairo' and that if he were still there when they came out he would be 'extremely bad-tempered', what he actually feared was his parents finding him still trapped in a mere desk job.

On 24 December he agreed, after days of uncertainty, to be dropped

---

* 'Bulgarian territory proper' refers to the country's pre- and post-war boundaries: not to Macedonia or those parts of east Serbia and Thrace claimed by Bulgaria from 1941.

Private Collection

into Serbia to liaise with the Bulgarian Partisans, a far more dangerous undertaking than Greece. Meeting some Yugoslav Partisans visiting Cairo had just made a positive impression. But the prospect of his parents' arrival in Cairo in 1944 – such powerful personalities that, love them though he did, he *had* to be away from them – played another part in his reckless decision: he never showed himself less emancipated from parental influence than by this gesture. They never knew about this synchronicity.

Frank wrote, '1944 is going to be a good year though a terrible one,' greeting the prospect of his Via Dolorosa with exaltation. Soon he wrote to EP and his parents of an old Chinese proverb: 'Of two sons, only one should be permitted to make a fool of himself and as the elder I claim this as of right.' He, Frank, would soon put his life at risk: EP, who had the makings of an exceptional leader and would be needed after the war, was to take better care of his chances, and – he repeatedly admonished – avoid putting their parents through the possible loss of both their children. And when the war ends, whether Frank was there to introduce them or not, EP should meet up with Iris Murdoch, a 'Compleat Humanist', and they could work out his scheme of Dialectical Idealism together. Thus Frank prepared for his own sacrifice.

# With the Partisans: January–June 1944

I did, in the beginning, make the mistake of regarding this war as an interlude, but not now . . . [It] is an integral part of one's life, perhaps its consummation.

Letter, June 1943

Frank parachuted from a Halifax flying together with three other planes from Brindisi over Dobro Polje in Serbia on the night of 25 January 1944. They had attempted a run one week earlier, when cloud cover had prevented a drop and they had returned to base. That is what the pilot noted; Major Mostyn Llewellyn Davies, who heard the planes, observed clear skies and put down their failure to a signals muddle instead. Confusion marked this enterprise early.

Frank, wearing a knee-length leather coat, landed together with Gunner/Signalman R. G. Watts and fifty-six containers with a total net weight of 4,235 pounds, including 108 grenades, 840 pounds of explosive, two W/T sets,* a generator, twenty-six machine guns with 11,000 rounds of ammunition, and rations, dry food, boots, socks and clothing. It was bitterly cold. His revolver cocked, Frank gave the parole 'Bulgarian Partisans?' and was answered in English 'Yes.' One appealing story tells of Frank – much taller than most Partisans and pleased to be safely grounded – picking up a short informant

---

* W/T = Wireless/Telegraphy

The National Archives

Major Mostyn Davies, *c.* 1942.

and swinging him around as you might a child. He and Davies now met.

Davies was a brave, determined and resourceful ex-civil servant who, together with his new wife Brenda, née Woodbridge, was recruited into SOE in 1942, a man of exceptional charm, talent and potential. He worked at first in west Africa, later in South America; his present assignment was to make contact with the Bulgarian Partisans, about whom SOE knew very little and wanted to learn more. In pursuit of this aim he had been dropped the previous September in Albania and travelled through many hazards across former Yugoslavia towards the Bulgarian border, supported by Sergeant John Walker (an explosives expert), Sergeant Nick Munroe, aka Muvrin (a Canadian-Croat interpreter), and Corporal James Shannon (a wireless transmitter operator). Davies's numerous adventures included losing a horse and a mule over a precipice, eating mule, living and sleeping rough, using sulphonamide drugs successfully on a frostbitten Partisan, and trying to assuage fierce fighting between Serb Partisans and what Davies – with interesting carelessness – terms Albanian 'Chetniks', after which he travelled with a party made up of both these murderously hostile elements, whom he successfully exhorted to cooperate against their common enemy, the Germans – a proceeding demonstrating his remarkable mettle.

British liaison officers or BLOs were instructed to obtain as much information as possible on the political situation and maintain contact with Partisans without entering into 'heavy commitments'. In return the BLO was expected to solicit from SOE drops or sorties consisting of arms, clothing, medicines, food and (sometimes) mail from home. Without such supplies, in hostile territory, the Partisans could not always survive, let alone fight. Davies's greatest headache was an absence of sorties, and hence of food and arms, so Frank's arrival together with such supplies was doubly welcome. But thereafter there were few drops. A mission without sorties was a liability to all Partisans, imposing on them an obligation of protection in a dangerous area, while the three pack-horses necessary for carrying the BLOs' heavy radio, accumulators and charging engine slowed them down, restricting their mobility. So the Partisans accused Davies of eliciting sensitive political information while providing little in return.* And absence of sorties meant that the Partisans went hungry, were poorly armed and were increasingly vulnerable as they awaited drops at pinpoints until late at night, one day after another, shivering in the snow while exposed to the growing risk of enemy action. Mistrust abounded and tempers frayed.

Flying sorties was scarcely an exact science. The commonest reason for the failure of a plane to get through was lack of gaps in the cloud-cover: the pilots' shorthand for this condition on their so-called manifests (reports) was 'Met' for 'meteorological'. Other reasons included engine failure, the reception party unable to light, even when using petrol, the agreed brush flares – including dummy flares to mislead the enemy – or the pilot dropping loads off-course and losing them. On the night of 7 and 8 April Fascist Bulgars lit flares when planes approached, in order to divert them, and gained thirty-two

---

* John Tregidga, a BLO in Serbia from 3/4 June 1944 working with Serb and some Bulgarian Partisans, noted the tendency to regard a British mission purely as an instrument for obtaining supplies, while 'intelligence of any sort was something Partisans passed to the British, if at all, only after repeated requests'. Moreover this often turned out to be unreliable 'and not infrequently completely false'. National Archives HS 9/1481/8.

chutes' worth of supplies for their cunning; another time a sum equivalent to 100,000 US dollars was dropped to the wrong side. Some
pinpoints were lost because the mission was attacked by Fascists and its
members had to flee in order to save their skins. Frantic memos show
how well Cairo understood Davies's and Frank's frustration when, as
often happened, weather prevented Cairo offering more support – and
how much was at stake.

Neither the numerous and relatively more experienced Serbian
Partisans nor the far fewer Bulgarians understood this. Flying was
a new technology, in which the simple-minded had excessive faith;
Frank himself had flown for the first time only the previous August.
They observed that the Allies could bomb Sofia when they did not
make drops in Serbia, and so blamed failure of sorties not on
rational causes but on capitalist conspiracy or sabotage.* Every
Bulgarian account details the increase in drops after Frank's arrival
– when the weather changed – and ascribes this to Frank himself,
while Mostyn Davies is described as prevaricating or slandered as
welcoming parachute drops only because they brought his favourite foods. One ludicrous account claimed that most of the cargo
(generally in excess of two tons) was delivered for the personal
needs of the British.

Such theories remind us that Balkan Communists (Bulgarian or
Serb) and BLOs were not natural allies. Serb Partisans commonly
refused the sovereigns carried by BLOs in case gold was seen as
buying their loyalty; forty-two gold sovereigns were found on Frank
when he was captured. When Davies praised one Partisan called Ivan
(who was killed crossing the frontier) as exceptional for 'never once
[trying] to lead me up the garden path', an implication of mutual
mistrust is clear. Bulgarian Partisans did not inform Frank that they
had their own radio with links to Moscow, which might have been

---

* However, the SOE agent Basil Davidson, himself at one time briefly in charge of
Yugoslav operations in Cairo, assured the Partisan General Slavchko Trūnski that the
British fear of Bulgaria going Communist post-war did indeed impede drops (Slavko
Trūnski, *Grateful Bulgaria*, Sofia, 1979, p. 51), a view he also voiced elsewhere.

used to contact Cairo.* Even Frank learned to treat Partisan promises 'with reserve'.

Bulgarian Partisans themselves warned SOE against dropping agents into Bulgaria itself since its Partisans 'lead a very mobile and insecure existence and the language difficulty would be very great'. Frank's mission, called Claridges, was accordingly to remain behind on the Serbian frontier as a rear base while only Mulligatawny, Mostyn Davies's mission, which Frank came to reinforce, moved into Bulgaria itself. Until that time the two missions were to move and act as one. But the Yugoslav section of SOE was moving to Bari in Italy, while the Bulgarian section stayed in Cairo. Claridges was at first liaising with Cairo via Bari, where the officer in charge of sorties

R.F. THOMPSON

---

* This radio was operated by Ivan Peychev and Pavel Tsarvulanov. Yanev, citing Tsola Dragoycheva, *The Victory* (1979), recounts its moving from the 2nd to the 1st Brigade (*The Man from the Legend*, ch. 5). See also Trŭnski, *Grateful Bulgaria*, p. 37. This is surely the second transmitter that Kenneth Scott was so puzzled by during his interrogation (see p. 324).

signalled that pressure of work and under-staffing were delaying transmission of signals: 'No transport. No clerk. No office equipment. No secretary. No hope.' Meanwhile Frank's photos in his SOE personal file give him the initials 'RF' instead of his correct initials 'WF': a tiny omen of the part human carelessness would play in what followed.

During the January that Frank landed, a new repressive organisation, the Bulgarian State Gendarmerie, motorised and with heavy weapons, was created expressly and for the sole purpose of killing Partisans – a token that their nuisance value was real. By 1 July 1944 there would be no living British personnel in Bulgaria not in captivity, and the few BLOs arriving after that date would be ejected by the Russians that September. For both Mulligatawny and Claridges, the scene was set for disaster.

———

Frank had hesitated for at least forty-eight hours between 22 and 24 December before agreeing to work with the Bulgarian Partisans. SOE's plans for that country were unclear and might generously be said to represent a gamble. On 24 December – the same day Frank agreed to be dropped – the head of SOE London's Balkans section Lieutenant-Colonel David Talbot Rice was writing a memo expressing his doubts that it would ever be possible under present circumstances to infiltrate large-scale missions into Bulgaria and predicting accurately that a *coup d'état* would happen there only after the Russians arrived.

SOE had individual experts for Greece, Yugoslavia and even Albania, but the Bulgarian brief was a mere sub-set of the Yugoslav. In Cairo Frank's schoolfellow Hugh Seton-Watson – eldest child of the doyen of scholars of Central Europe and co-founder of London University's School of Slavonic and East European Studies, R. W. Seton-Watson – was best known for his expertise on Yugoslavia, where he had lived. Hugh was strongly anti-Mihailović, and pro-Tito – like the Communist agent James Klugmann, who was second-in-command in Yugoslavia. There was no SOE expert on Bulgaria.

Both Klugmann and the then leftish Seton-Watson probably

imagined Bulgarian Partisans as having the same qualities and fighting capacity as Yugoslav Partisans, whose mystical effect on Britons Evelyn Waugh observed at first hand in July 1944 and satirised in his *Sword of Honour* trilogy. Waugh's Communist character Major Cattermole, perhaps loosely based on Klugmann, reported women Partisans sleeping chastely with the men, undergoing surgery without anaesthetics and on ideological grounds renouncing menstruation. *Time* magazine articles show that Waugh only slightly exaggerated: they indeed sang Partisan songs during amputations without anaesthetics, sexual morality was puritanical, and they made a tightly disciplined and hotly idealistic force. Those Frank met in Cairo in December galvanised him too:

> In the past few days I have had some profoundly moving experiences. I have had the honour to meet and talk to some of the best people in the world . . . people whom, when the truth is known, Europe will recognise as among the finest and toughest she has ever borne. Meeting them has made me utterly disgusted with some aspects of my present life, reminding me forcibly that all my waking hours should be dedicated to one purpose only . . . no men are more disarming in their gaiety than these . . . who have known more suffering than we can easily imagine.

The case for supporting SOE activity in Yugoslavia (as in Greece) was clear. Tito's Partisans numbered over 250,000 and were good at killing Germans, while there were between 50,000 and 100,000 ELAS Partisans in Greece – movements so successful that they were, as we have seen, publicly endorsed at the late 1943 Teheran conference, where a Second Front in the Balkans was discussed and rejected. By contrast nobody in SOE London was greatly interested in Bulgaria. So the views of Hugh, expert on Yugoslavia, were questioned by Lieutenant-Colonel Stanley Casson, a London archaeologist brought into SOE in autumn 1943 as an unbiased adviser writing 'most interesting papers' on Greece.

Cairo outlined two scenarios. The first ran: undermined by SOE sabotage, the Bulgarian Government surrenders, leaving all its occupied territories and ordering the immediate withdrawal of German troops. But Germany, exactly as it occupied Italy after its surrender in September

1943, and as it would do in Hungary in March 1944, would then invade
Bulgaria, vital for German interests and with plenty of quislings.
Better, Cairo argued, implement option two: Bulgaria should delay
surrendering until Allied troops were close enough to win it over to
their side.*

Casson mocked: 'This document lacks all realism.' No Balkan state
had ever contrived 'a delayed surrender', which could only empower
the diehards controlling state machinery. Against the Bulgarian
Partisans stood the best-organised police service in the Balkans and an
officer corps of experience, size and determination, both of which
would be liquidated should the Partisans seize power.

Moreover Bulgaria was united mainly in self-preservation. While
Yugoslavia and Greece were both occupied by the Germans, and (on
the whole) longed to get rid of them, Bulgaria, like the Nazi puppet
states of Croatia and Slovakia, was an obedient German ally.

It will be noted that Casson can scarcely be accounted fair or unbiased. Bulgaria was in fact the only country within the Hitler bloc that
declined to fight Russia, and was the only one where there was a real
Partisan movement. Further, like Denmark, it saved most of its Jews:
while non-Bulgarian Jews from the territories it had annexed from
Yugoslavia and Greece were rounded up and sent to Poland, the majority of those in Bulgaria proper survived the war. Finally, Casson ignores
Serbian aggression against Bulgaria, not least at the battle of Slivnitsa in
1885.

For forty years, Casson accordingly felt, Bulgaria had the single
foreign-policy goal of becoming the most powerful Balkan state and
dominating its neighbours. That was its motivation both in the disastrous Second Balkan War of 1913, in secretly allying with Germany in
1915 and in refusing to join the Balkan Entente of 1938. The prize was

* Hugh's optimism may have been influenced by his being – though later Tory – then anti-
Mihailović and pro-Communist, and accounted during these years a Soviet sympathiser by
SOE's Cairo chief of staff, Brigadier C. M. Keble: see William Mackenzie, *The Secret History
of SOE*, London, 2000, p. 132; and Nigel West, *Secret War*, London, 1992, p. 83. Also see his
*Oxford Dictionary of National Biography* entry: 'His early sympathy with the Soviet Union
was justified by his generation on the grounds that Stalin was Hitler's only opponent.'

always aggrandisement – seizure from Yugoslavia in 1941 of Macedonia as 'ethnically Bulgar', and of Thrace from the Turkish frontier to the River Struma from Greece. Both occupations were notably brutal: 'most murders were accompanied by torture, most rapes . . . ended with murder'. Germans accounted Bulgarians a simple and only half-civilised ally.

Casson saw no sign of disintegration in a people who could scarcely be war-weary as their 800,000 soldiers had as yet experienced no fighting. Bulgaria's refusal to make war on its old ally Russia meant that the Soviet Legation stayed open in Sofia throughout. Casson doubted, furthermore, that the Bulgarian Partisans were an organised body imbued with any coherent idea of liberation. He questioned both the efficiency of their organisation and their strength: 'I think we are staking a lot on a body of rebels about whom we know almost nothing. All we know of them is what they said about themselves to Mostyn Davies.' He got the impression that – 'in the usual Balkan way – the Bulgarian Partisans had blown their trumpet long and loud in the ear of the simple Briton'.

The 'simple Briton' had his first person-to-person contact with Partisans of the Fatherland Front (or, from its Bulgarian initials, the OF) on 4 January 1944; until then, there was only courier contact. Two men from Sofia, Delcho Simov, a wireless expert (cover-named Gorsho), and Vlado Trichkov (cover-named Ivan), arrived in East Serbia. The latter was a forty-six-year-old metalworker, a Spanish Civil War veteran, and – as he would only much later reveal – political C-in-C of the whole Bulgarian Partisan movement. Although Frank thought Trichkov had a 'very good brain and a broad European outlook' it is ominous to learn that he was also famous for 'bombastic oratory'.

After conferring with these two, Davies signalled Cairo that there were 12,000 Bulgarian Partisans. These had attacked town halls, burning records that might incriminate rebels; had destroyed the machinery in a gold mine in Tran; had attacked a sawmill and a munitions dump elsewhere; and – lacking explosives – had destroyed trains by the simple expedient of removing the tracks. Bulgars had to be, if that were possible, even braver than Serbs; their dissidents in 1923 had been thrown

The National Museum of History, Sofia

Yordanka Chankova leading an attack to liberate a frontier village, *c.* 1943.

alive into furnaces. But their Partisans were inexperienced and far less numerous.

Some of this sounded encouraging, but Casson was right to think that Davies dangerously overestimated their strength. While he acknowledged that his judgements might need recanting when he got to Cairo that month,* he feared that 'we are wasting sorties on them at the moment'. He advocated instead a diplomatic drive, and delaying infiltrating BLOs and missions until the Russians advanced south-west from Romania (which happened only in late August) plus 'constant bombing' for six weeks. The differences between Yugoslavia and Bulgaria are clear in their reactions to such Allied bombing: Yugoslavs, while scarcely welcoming the bombing of their towns, understood the point of it in the war of attrition against the Germans; Frank's captors

---

* Casson hoped to take command of SOE's section working into Greece, but never got to Cairo: the aircraft taking him there crashed just after take-off from Cornwall, in circumstances never fully explained.

by contrast took their furious resentment over the bombing of Sofia out on him from the day of his capture.

Calling Davies 'the simple Briton' does not seem unjust. Exaggeration of Partisan power by a factor of ten was normal throughout occupied Europe, and Cairo soon gave the probable total number of Bulgarian Partisans as a paltry 2,000 – eleven detachments, each of around twenty men. Even in August 1944, its moment of greatest activity, when there were 'almost daily attacks upon government offices . . . and upon requisitioned stock', one source claims that membership of OF reached only 3,600, and the Agrarians who dominated it resented Partisan activity since its major consequence was to bring reprisals on villagers who were often Agrarian sympathisers. The OF, a coalition of democratic opposition forces, excluded right-wing Agrarians or Democrats, since both disapproved of sabotage. So Davies also overestimated their unity of purpose. By March 1944 SOE was wondering whether the fate of Bulgaria was even relevant to the war effort 'as events were moving so fast'.

The most optimistic guess of 18,000 Fatherland Front sympathisers and/or Partisans coincides with the Russian approach in August. And after Soviets had invaded on 8 September and at once started to impose their own system, executing over 2,000 adherents of the old regime and imprisoning more, the number swelled retrospectively. In this Bulgaria did not differ from every other country suffering enforced regime change, France included.* One SOE source argued that September 1944 was not even a Partisan revolution, 'for it is well-established that many of the Partisans first heard of [the Bulgarian *coup d'état*] from a broadcast the morning after'.

Meanwhile in London the Treasury on 2 March, Casson's doubts notwithstanding, voted £50,000 towards SOE support for Bulgarian Partisans who, it was gambled, might have 'a certain nuisance value' holding down enemy forces. SOE Cairo's intention had been to have twenty missions in Bulgaria by the end of 1943. There were, apart from Mulligatawny and Claridges, only three other missions, none of which

---

* Rana Dasgupta's fine novel *Solo* (2009) shows Bulgaria bullied by each neighbour in turn – Turkey until 1878, Germany after 1941, and finally the USSR from 1944.

could even enter the country proper: Missions Jampuff, Mizzen and Triatic were stuck in Thrace, and Mostyn Davies was to die in Serbia. Four miles from the border in mid-December, Davies gazed out across Bulgaria's snow-covered mountains and signalled to Cairo that he found them mysterious.

———

An SOE narrative put together from Mostyn Davies's signals covers the first two months of Frank's time in Serbia. Davies hoped that Frank would help him with his 'enormous task' of building a Bulgar Partisan force. 'Superhuman' might be more apt.

Shortly after reaching Serbia Davies recorded that 'The Bulgars had shot seven villagers' to discourage aid to Partisans. Yet – despite such terror, and despite ambushes and skirmishes – Davies generally sounds upbeat. On the January day that Frank dropped, evidence of the low morale of the Bulgarian Gendarmerie had encouraged Davies: a Gendarmerie detachment asked the Partisans not to attack them, sending welcome cigarettes as a peace offering. One company of Partisans already by 30 December consisted almost entirely of Bulgarian deserters who 'proved first-rate chaps'. Twenty more deserters arrived on 14 March, with a further forty expected shortly.

That such army deserters might switch sides again if disappointed in the hope of an easier life, Davies overlooks. And about the sufferings he and his men endured towards March – frostbite, hunger, exhaustion, diarrhoea and battle-wounds – his narrative is also silent. As it is also about the mistrust between the British and Partisans.

The Bulgarian Partisans' dependence on widescale mobilisation causing desertions to their ranks is one factor in making them sound an incoherent and unpredictable force. When Davies proposed that two Bulgarian companies (that is, between 140 and 500 men in all) hold one pinpoint to ensure a drop, Trichkov told him this was impossible without help from Serb Partisans. And when Davies mentions Partisan exploits – for example, the theft of over thirty kilometres of telephone wire to be reused as a Partisan phone line – it is generally Serbs who are praised, not Bulgarians.

Although Serbs and Bulgarians were historical enemies, Communism made both sets of Partisans at least in principle internationalist, and Serbs accordingly assisted the British attempt to arm and develop a Bulgar Partisan force. Frank was impressed by their effort to find common ground vis-à-vis the post-war status of Macedonia, to which both laid claim. On the night of 4 February two planes successfully dropped loads, the explosives being divided into two, one to be cached in Serbia, the other for use in Sofia. Six days were spent organising this, in deep snow, the Partisans succeeding in getting village labour to clear the necessary tracks. Delcho Simov went back to Sofia to arrange transit of some of the contents of the fifty-six containers there; Vlado Trichkov stayed with the mission.

On 10 February they moved five miles south to a new pinpoint (called Clara), and waited. But by 26 February Cairo had regretfully to inform them of the impossibility of flying any more of the sorties allotted them: of the thirty Davies requested that month scarcely any had arrived.

Delcho Simov returned from Sofia on 17 February accompanied by Kamenov, commander of the Sofia zone of the OF, and three days later harassment by Bulgarian Gendarmerie forced them to move. None the less on 4 March Trichkov brought back from Sofia another OF representative, a forty-two-year-old lawyer, Gocho Gopin (code-named Dragan). His journey had taken fifteen days and he was suffering badly from frostbite. Davies explained to him the position vis-à-vis flights. He was to act as liaison person between the Partisans and the mission.

By 8 March, there were still no sorties and relations with Partisans were distinctly strained. Davies was once again accused of extracting information while giving nothing in return. One battalion of Serb Partisans and another of Bulgars were immobilised at pinpoints awaiting drops that never arrived, while the snows now melted fast and the Gendarmerie rallied for a big attack.

During the second week of March, however, their luck seemed to change. Despite shortage of both arms and food they won a battle at Bistrica, where a number of Gendarmerie were killed – possibly eight; and though two Partisans were badly wounded, none died. They were further encouraged by a BBC broadcast on 10 March that took a less anti-Bulgarian tone than before. This may have been in response to Frank's and Davies's signalled objections to an earlier hostile broadcast. London now appeared willing to distinguish between the Fascist Bulgarian Government and a population by no means necessarily of the same political complexion. Moreover the same day news reached them of the discovery of a German petrol cache plus the route of seventy trains each of thirty carriages carrying fuel.

By 13 March Kamenov had decided he could ill afford to wait any longer and left for Bulgaria with a detachment of Partisans with whom he hoped to liberate territory around Tran, leaving Dragan to liaise with Davies and Frank. The prospect of having liberated territory within Bulgaria itself was an inviting one. Furthermore, on the night of 14 March, after a wait of around six weeks, two planes at last flew sorties and the following day all supplies were across the frontier. On the 17th another successful sortie increased everyone's high spirits.

But this run of good luck changed abruptly. On 18 March the missions signalled Cairo that they were surrounded by an enemy force of at least 25,000 – soon thought to be even larger – and would be many days on the run. This was the last message Mostyn Davies sent.

What followed was reported by Frank later, almost certainly over the wireless transmitter set belonging to a third mission. They abandoned their horses, buried their stores and equipment except for one W/T set which was to be carried by a Partisan, and fled by nightfall. On 19 March they reached Ruplje, a party of 200 men hiding in the woods till noon when they were encircled by a mixed force of Chetniks and Bulgars whom they fought off until dusk, Mostyn Davies observing the battle from a nearby hill. The Partisans then waited in intense cold for three hours after which, thinking the enemy gone, they tried to slip away, only to fall into a second ambush. The column scattered in complete disorder, Davies's haversack being dropped by a fleeing Partisan: the explosives expert Sergeant Walker, though heavily loaded, saved the gold sovereigns with which all BLOs were provided and some maps. Frank requested Cairo more than once for promotion for Walker, whose expert mechanical skill keeping the W/T going the previous year when it badly needed repair had also impressed Davies. Wireless operator Corporal Shannon was never seen again: Frank asked later for his grave, if found, to be marked with the single word 'SHANNON'.

By dawn the party, now about eighty strong, rested up. They resumed their march on the evening of 21 March when they immediately ran into yet another ambush and, after an exchange of machine-gun fire, scattered into the woods. They decided to split into two groups, Sergeants Walker (the demolitions expert) and Munroe (the interpreter) going off in one direction (they rejoined Frank three days later), Frank, Davies and Signalman Watts in another. They thought it hopeless to try to cross the Morava river without a guide, and turned back on the 22nd to proceed towards Crna Trava, lying low in a village for one day.

Mostyn Davies was by this point exhausted, his feet in dreadful

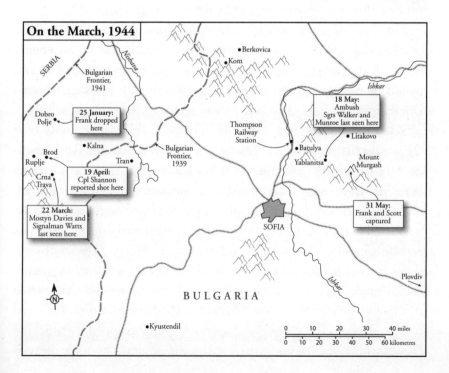

condition; Watts was suffering acute diarrhoea. Around dusk Davies pointed out to Frank that the house in which they were resting was being surrounded by armed men who had crept up unobserved in the gathering gloom. The only possibility of escape lay through a rear window which faced woods across open space some 200 to 300 yards away. Frank left in this way and, though fired on, reached the woods, where he heard further gunfire, what sounded like the forcing of the door and the explosion of a grenade followed by silence. Neither Davies nor Watts was seen again. After watching for five minutes, Frank made his way through the woods and hid for a day or two in the snow until rescued by a kindly peasant, who showed a small Partisan unit how to reach him.

———

Frank, having tasted the power and malice of the enemy, met up on 24 March with Walker and Munroe at the village of Bistrica eight miles away. Partisan commander Dencho Znepolski believed that Frank had sheltered within a six-foot snowdrift together with Gocho Gopin for two days and nights. He wrote: 'We found Gopin and Thompson looking weak and exhausted, yet still safe and sound, and in high spirits. Just like little children, they rejoiced at seeing the squad come back from the march with some 230 fighters still alive . . .' Rumours about Davies's fate – probably first robbed before being tortured and killed – continued for months.[*]

Claridges had lost not just Davies but also its radio, and Frank and Gopin now walked thirty miles to meet up with an SOE mission called Entanglement to re-establish communication with Cairo, at Radovnica,

---

[*] Frank's Bulgarian biographer Kiril Yanev recounts that Davies met his death somewhere in the Ostrozub area. Army soldiers captured him during one of the raids and immediately knew that they had an important figure 'and he was an Englishman at that. They searched him thoroughly and found some pounds and a massive gold ring (a lucky charm Davies had brought all the way from Britain). They tortured and beat the Major, and eventually shot him. According to Dencho Znepolski, Davies's execution was necessitated by the fact that he had been robbed of his possessions, and there was a need to cover that robbery . . .' (Yanev, *The Man from the Legend*, ch. 4).

which they reached by 12 April and where they stayed three weeks, developing contacts with the Partisans and their General Staff. Frank was now head of both Claridges and Mulligatawny missions and his having survived up to this point saved what remained of both missions. He was, it is worth remembering, twenty-three.

Awaiting them was Claridges' new signalman Sergeant Kenneth Scott, son of an engineer, born in Forest Hill and educated at Dulwich College, who had dropped there solo on 7 April, in military uniform with rucksack, pistol and brandy flask but without gloves and, above all, without a code-book, which had been dropped separately and in the wrong place. The ensuing drama about the missing code-book and subsequent attempts to get new codes to Frank and Scott absorbed much time and energy. Frank at one point asked Cairo whether they, like him, had a copy of *Death Before Honour* (a 1939 thriller by J. V. Turner, aka 'David Hume'), whose opening paragraphs could in that case be used to generate a code for purposes of encryption.

In 2002 Scott remembered Frank as an intellectual who in the evenings would read poetry, in which Scott took little interest, and who otherwise had more sympathetic allegiance to the Partisans than to him, spending time with them improving his Bulgarian. They rarely slept in buildings and one night, camping in the rough with few or no blankets, huddled together in a group to keep warm. Snow was unusual at that time of year but it was still very cold. As Scott was the sole survivor (he died in 2008), his first-hand 1944 narrative is the basis for what follows.

Reports of Bulgar troops approaching from the west caused them to retreat between 1 and 10 May to the Kalna area, where there was a stronger Partisan presence, despite Frank's wish to stay with the 2nd Bulgar Brigade near Crna Trava, a wish he felt accorded better with his brief. Two days later, on 12 May, Trichkov informed Frank that his Partisans were leaving immediately, via a town called Kom, for central Bulgaria. This sparked off intense discussions lasting for days. Among the most urgent questions was whether Frank and Scott should follow.

Before that, on 21 April, a group of Anglo-American journalists associated with *Time* magazine happened by on horseback.* The Partisans
eyed enviously these sleek, well-fed men, full of themselves, travelling
with saddles and ample baggage, and announcing insouciantly that
they were on their way back to Italy via Albania by submarine. But they
also offered the missions a chance to write letters home. RAF drops had
brought Frank letters dated up to 1 March. One cable from Frank
congratulating his parents on their silver wedding arrived on 12 March
and another on his mother's birthday (17 March); he had probably,
with his usual care, organised these in advance before leaving from
Cairo. A third, praising Bledlow's success in the Salute the Soldier
campaign, he evidently sent via the American journalists that April
from Serbia.

Now he was also able to pen his last three surviving letters, which
convey a self-contained wisdom unusual in a twenty-three-year-old. To
his parents he recalled the Old Testament: '"A certain man drew a bow
at a venture, missed the venture, but hit the King of Israel." In the same
way this letter is rather a long shot, since mail in this area isn't very
regular. Let's hope it reaches you.'

These letters, which took months to arrive, are self-effacing, other-
centred. This owed, his family shrewdly saw, as much to self-censorship
as to military exigency. He responds with his customary careful gallantry
to each item of domestic news, to descriptions of wildlife and of Bledlow
at war, and to reminiscence of London during the Blitz. He tries to reassure his parents that he would not compete with his cousin Trevor's MC
– despite his own good record in Sicily, to which he alludes. 'You needn't
fear . . . I've got a remarkably clean pair of heels, and now hold the record
for the twenty yards sprint for three major battle areas.'

---

* *Time* magazine 22 May and 26 June 1944 details some adventures of four Allied
journalists dropped into Yugoslavia that spring: *Time*'s Stoyan Pribichevich, Reuters'
John Talbot, Fowler – an American photographer – and Slade, a British photographer.
They posted Frank's letter home, though it was dated 21 April, only on 24 June: getting
out of occupied Serbia was not always easy or fast. John Talbot was taken prisoner when
the Germans staged their air attack on Tito's HQ at Drvar, Bosnia, in May 1944 and
spent the rest of the war in a prison camp.

Yet his acquiescence in the idea of the bombing of Rome suggests a new battle-hardened intransigence. 'How can there be any question when a certain number of old buildings are to be balanced against the whole future of humanity, against man's chance of ordering his life with dignity or becoming a helot [slave] for ever? . . . what is most precious now is free men' – that is, not ancient buildings.

Before asking his parents to give his love to friends and relations 'to whom I should be writing if I weren't so darned lazy', he hints at his state of mind. He had been working hard, he hoped to some purpose, 'keeping brave company – some of the best in the world'. He was enjoying his first European spring for years: violets, cowslips, plum blossom, the shocking loveliness of breaking beech-buds. But England, he reassured them, was the country where 'they really knew how to organise spring' and, homesick, he longed to see 'dog's tooth violets and red-winged blackbirds again before I go over the hill'. He hopes the food parcels he has arranged from South Africa are OK and is amazed to hear that some lemons had finally arrived: 'You carefully avoid saying what they were like and no wonder!' The contrast between these treats and the potatoes and meal-flour soup the Partisans often ate is striking.

Frank's letter to EP – engaged in the bloody five-month assault on Monte Cassino – anticipates post-war pleasures: co-writing a political book on what the far Left has to offer professionals such as doctors, scientists, engineers, on whose ethics chapter EP is to help; a long walking tour with EP, stopping at many pubs and discussing everything – 'So keep safe.' Frank relishes the post-war choice for himself between writing a play, going in for journalism, and returning to Oxford to read History: Slavonic languages interest him less since he 'already speaks a number'. That might be a hint as to his whereabouts. 'Keep yourself safe,' he repeats, adding with rehearsed casualness the second time, 'it's important that you should.' He evidently intuited the risks he and his 'excellent companions' might soon take.

These letters, written fifty days before Frank's death, provide first-hand clues to his morale, and help address his friends' fears that his subsequent heroism was suicidal. Leo Pliatzky wrote the previous December, 'I think the sooner you get out of these *Ashenden*-esque outfits and into some nice steady, stay-at-home job, the better it will be.' *Ashenden: or the British Agent* was Somerset Maugham's 1928 novel about First World War intelligence: Leo feared that Frank at the end of his life was play-acting and so took foolhardy risks. Yet Frank's concluding remark to EP – 'Daddy tells me you have been making an ass of yourself about a yellow flower "Some kind of vetch": don't do it again!' – at least suggests their old tone of relaxed family teasing and badinage.

----

Much of this belongs to the routine anti-heroic rhetoric of that war. His letter to Iris Murdoch written that 21 April, by contrast, is the only one in which he jousts uncomfortably with real intimacy, before fending it off. Since he superscribes this letter 'Captain WF Thompson' he evidently never learned that he had been gazetted major.

Irushka!

Sorry I haven't written for so long. Old Brotoloig* seems to have been monopolising my attention. I know forgiveness is one of your chief virtues.

Three airmail letter-cards from you, bringing me up to the end of JAN. A great deal of talk about weariness of soul, even among your good friends. You know quite well there's no danger of your succumbing to it. You have springs within you that will never fail. I want to hear no more of this [illegible] nonsense.

I can't say precisely what your role in life will be, but I should say it will definitely be a literary-humanistic one. You should continue fooling about. [Illegible] shall be able to compare notes. I shall write a preface to your translation of Levski's poems & you will bestow the same honour on my life of Vuk Karadzic. We might organise quite a neat little racket. I think we should let Lidderdale in on it with a special brief to deal with Slovenian folk poetry & Pliatzky will be allowed to write Steinbeckian stories about Greek harbour-towns

----

* Homeric epithet for Ares, god of war, meaning plague-like or baneful.

which we shall approve from our Olympian heights as 'bearing the authentic smell of the Levant'. Foot shall be our chief authority on Turkey. Does this restore your faith in yourself & your 'mission'? It certainly should.

I can't think why you are so interested in MORALS. Chiefly a question of the liver & digestive organs I assure you. On one occasion when I had to go without sugar for a month, I felt by the end of it as though I could have won a continence contest against Hippolytus.

αμματων δ'εν αχηνιασ
ερρει παο 'Αφροδιτα*

My own list of priorities is as follows:

1. People and everything to do with people, their habits, their loves and hates, their arts, their languages. Everything of importance revolves around people.

2. Animals and flowers. These bring me a constant undercurrent of joy. Just now I'm revelling in plum blossom and young lambs and the first leaves on the briar roses. One doesn't need any more than these. I couldn't wish for better company.

These are enough for a hundred lifetimes. And yet I must confess to being very fond of food and drink also.

I envy you and Michael in one way. All this time you are doing important things like falling in and out of love – things which broaden and deepen and strengthen the character more surely than anything else. I can honestly say I've never been in love. When I pined for you I was too young to know what I was doing – no offence meant. Since then I haven't lost an hour's sleep over any of Eve's daughters. This

---

* From Aeschylus' *Agamemnon*, lines 418–19, a Chorus concerning Menelaus going to war when Paris abducted his wife Helen, and meaning 'because they lack real eyes, all their love (Aphrodita) goes for nothing'. See Peter J. Conradi, *Iris Murdoch: A Life*, London, 2001, chs 5 and 7, for Frank's and Iris's passionate admiration for *Agamemnon*.

means I'm growing up lop-sided, an overgrown boy. Ah well, – I shall find time, Cassius, I shall find time.

All the same, I don't think you should fall for 'emotional fascists' – Try to avoid that.

No news about myself. I'm very fit & couldn't wish for better company.

Lots of love

from Frank

How much should we read into this? By praising the Serbian writer Vuk Karadžić (1787–1864) and the Bulgarian revolutionary Vasil Levski (1837–73) he implies his position, in defiance of military censorship, on the Serbian–Bulgarian border.

Iris Murdoch's three airmail letter-cards do not survive but evidently they chronicle the progress of her disaster-prone love-life. She found adult sexual passion – one theme of her future novels – bewildering and ungovernable and was therefore seen by some as a bitch or wrecker. She confessed that she had taken Frank's schoolfriend and rival M. R. D. Foot as a lover the previous summer, before hurting him by bedding and falling obsessively in love with the economist Tommy Balogh – the 'emotional fascist' whom she stole from her new flatmate Philippa Bosanquet. Her careless cruelty caused nearly everyone involved (herself, Philippa and Michael) grief about which she is evidently – while starting to think hard about morality – affecting 'world-weariness', a stage on the journey to remorse. A whimsical list of literary tasks Frank allotted post-war to Lidderdale, Pliatzky, Foot and himself is also – quite inadvertently – a list of four of her suitors.

Frank's injunction to Iris to avoid falling for 'emotional fascists' like Balogh is telling. Balogh was the first of a series of unresponsive bullies to whom Murdoch found herself masochistically drawn. Balogh preceded David Hicks, then in Cairo, to whom she was briefly engaged in 1945; the writer Elias Canetti followed in 1952–6. If this phrase ('emotional fascist') was Murdoch's own coinage, Frank advises a char-acteristically wise restraint.

In response to Iris Murdoch's renewed fear that she was causing

Frank pain, he reassures her that he had never loved her, had been too young even to understand the meaning of the word when he had been supplicant and she held the power. Now their roles are reversed.

But to say he had never loved her is partly disingenuous. Precisely one year earlier, the previous April, he had reassured her about her loss of virginity, disclaiming jealousy ('nearly four years since I thought of you as a body') and anger ('no cause'), cautioning her about male misogyny, and sharing his sadness that he had 'messed up my sex-life . . . by taking physical love far too lightly' and so missed experiencing mutual sexual love. The element of chivalrous bluff noted in this insistence on his own nonchalance recurs now. His avowal 'I can honestly say I've never been in love' is partly self-protection and partly an attempt to lessen her guilt.*

Theo in 1948 would comment, 'I wish Frank had married – had, at least, had some home of his own for his spirit on earth. Iris was not enough.' Why was Iris Murdoch not enough to make Frank wish to survive? Frank's 1944 letter suggests one answer.

He refers to two plays. Euripides' *Hippolytus* concerns a man who dies after his stepmother tests his chastity: Murdoch in 1946 made her own translation of it. When Frank says he could win a continence contest with Hippolytus, he boasts that he is beyond sexual desire, while acknowledging as a result growing up lop-sided, an overgrown boy. That Hippolytus is vindictively destroyed by the gods for this boast he must have been uncomfortably aware. One important reason Iris Murdoch was 'not enough' for Frank's spirit on earth was that she was, as well as far away, otherwise engaged emotionally and sexually.

He simplifies himself as the down-to-earth soldier-poet whose touching list of earthly joys once more recalls Brooke's poem 'The Great Lover'. (Major John Henniker-Major, who met Frank in Serbia at this time, remembered his possessing 'a childlike intelligence, the innocence

* Frank's close friend Tony Forster believed that Frank and Iris might well have married happily had he survived, and that Frank would not have countenanced infidelity: letter to author, 1998.

of Rupert Brooke, but he was not a baby'.) His list also matches the pared-down pleasures of Partisan life, often on the run, sleeping rough and happy simply to find oneself alive for one more day.

Shakespeare's *Julius Caesar* Act V had provided the leitmotiv of his December letter, with Brutus' 'If we should meet again, why then we'll smile.' He now quotes Brutus from a later scene about finding time, later, to grieve for the death of Cassius, after the battle of Philippi. 'Friends I owe more tears / To this dead man than you shall see me pay.' The ironies of 'I shall find time, Cassius, I shall find time' are poignant. Time was now in short supply.

If a code is observable here, it is one that suggests undisclosed emotions: *Julius Caesar* is much concerned with betrayals of friendship, of which Iris too had arguably been guilty by taking Michael as a lover in place of Frank himself. Frank's praise for Iris and Michael for doing 'important things like falling in and out of love', which, he argues, broaden and deepen and strengthen the character, is generous to a fault and probably sincere,* though by the time his letter together with rumours of his death arrived, such lines must have packed a retrospective sting.

If these developments in London felt to Frank remote, that emotional distance was one that had to be achieved and was not a simple given. One Partisan called Kiril Plashev years later remembered Frank standing stock-still by a village wall, reading a letter from home, utterly absorbed and lost in his own private thoughts.

———

Some have compared Frank's entry into Bulgaria to T. E. Lawrence's exploits, implying that he disobeyed Cairo's orders, or showed suicidal recklessness – in one account even threatening Kenneth Scott with a pistol to get him to cross the border. But this move, however foolhardy, was deliberated over some weeks. As early as late January Mostyn

---

* Compare, for example, his lines about 'important things' from his untitled 1943 poem about homecoming: 'discussing important things, / A name for our new cat, the apple-crop, / Bee-orchids growing on the Coneygar?' See p. 255.

Davies signalled that he had refused a request for Frank's assistance to Partisans elsewhere in Serbia since 'events in Bulgaria' might necessitate his presence there. And Cairo agreed.

On 22 April Frank radioed that Serb and Bulgarian Partisans were discussing a joint offensive within a fortnight to create liberated territory within Bulgaria around Kyustendil. There was no free territory anywhere inside Bulgaria, but Frank believed the population in areas such as Sredna Gora and Tran – which Kamenov had set out five weeks earlier to help free – to be 'pro-Partisan'. Although the OF had promised that Frank 'would be inside Bulgaria within three weeks', he had 'now learnt to treat with reserve all such messages'. While he had learned to measure the distance between bombast and accuracy, a development whereby he might enter Bulgaria was clearly being discussed.

Frank was as yet unconvinced of its wisdom. On 29 April he warned that Bulgarians were so demoralised after twenty years of Fascism that '1) No repeat No large scale revolt by Army and People against Germans can be expected. General collapse on Italian lines most to be hoped for, with harassing actions by OF supporters. Workers' revolts in Varna, Sofia, Plovdiv also possible. And 2) The Bulgarian Partisan movement though it has wide popular support is too badly armed and scattered to be made into serious nation wide force before Big Day.'* Frank advised the continuing bombing of military targets, and the reinforcement with arms of Partisan units, to the south and west of Sofia and near Plovdiv and Botevgrad. And he requested from Cairo 'general direction soonest'. There is no evidence that he received an answer.

Yet, after the first week of May, a change of heart is apparent. A Major Saunders from Entanglement reported 'Met Thompson on gallop. He going Bulgaria.' Frank was 'galloping' for fifteen days to evade capture: 40,000 Bulgarian troops with some German

---

* 'Big Day' probably refers to the putative rebellion in Bulgarian towns advocated by the CP in early May rather than Operation Zeppelin, the deception plan to keep the Germans occupied in the Balkans with a perceived Allied offensive, reducing the number free to engage the Allies landing in France during the Normandy invasion.

detachments and an HQ in central Serbia, supported by aircraft and artillery, had recently been dedicated to the single task of hunting down Partisans, with rewards for each one caught dead or alive, and for each house burned down. With flippant good humour Frank signalled on 3 May, 'We are being chased by Bulgars . . . pinpoint closed. Cheerio.' And then Frank and Major Dugmore in Entanglement sent a joint signal on 5 May: 'imperative have arms and food soonest for this joint force' – they were travelling with 1,000 hungry and unarmed men. Dugmore was a gentle, sage, courageous South African, with judgement and generosity of spirit, who had been in contact with the Bulgarians before Davies.

Dugmore, however, had suffered so badly from the winter that Major Henniker-Major was flown out to replace him. The latter wrote that Frank was desperately tired and dispirited both by Davies's death and by lack of encouragement or direction from Cairo. Henniker-Major, who liked Bulgarians and thought they made reliable soldiers, none the less judged these Partisans an inexperienced and low-level mix of individual deserters and Communist civilians from the towns with the 'unreal and slightly horror-comic air of a brigand army, boastful, mercurial and with an inexperienced yen to go it alone'.

The Hristo Botev Partisan brigade, 1944, at Sredna Gora.

Frank had constantly to fight both to avoid being taken over by the well-organised Yugoslav Partisans and also to avoid being led off on a lunatic expedition by the Bulgars, who insisted they were now going to Bulgaria where they could persuade the people to rise and set up resistance areas.

Frank was so exhausted that on one march he fell over a cliff into a river; and all of Henniker-Major's party fell asleep. The wireless, too, received a dousing, from which it did not recover. Henniker-Major none the less reported Frank full of hope. On the nights of 10 and 11 May twenty successful sorties were flown, and the air was full of containers, divided half to the Serbian and half to the Bulgarian Partisans. Frank signalled, 'This is the biggest encouragement Bulgarians have had since Mostyn arrived . . . after last night and a few more like it, stream [of recruits] may become torrent.' Yet Frank continued to argue against the dropping of further British agents: 'We have eight Englishmen here now, which is thought maximum handicap for any Partisan unit entering spring gallop.'

A two-day council of war followed, probably near Kalna, where a well-known Montenegrin Partisan judged the organisation of Bulgarian Partisans incredibly bad and strongly advised Frank to stay in Yugoslavia.* Dugmore too thought the Bulgarians so reckless and unreliable that he went so far as to ask Henniker to disavow the OF to SOE Cairo. But theirs was not the only counsel.

Georgi Dimitrov, leader of the Bulgarian CP waiting in exile in the USSR, from Moscow was urging the Bulgarians to enter their own country to stimulate revolt in the cities. This was both doctrinaire and crazy: the Serb Partisans' success stemmed from their operating brilliant hit-and-run guerrilla raids from the hills, and carefully avoiding towns. But around 10 May the Bulgarian Politburo – also in Moscow – ordered the 2nd Brigade to leave at once for the second largest city, Plovdiv, to help stimulate national revolt there. And Cairo in its last surviving directive – 25 April – had instructed that 'Thompson should

* The revolutionary General Tempo, aka Svetozar Vukmanović: see his *Struggle for the Balkans*, London, 1990, *passim*.

remain longest possible with OF delegates . . .'* This instruction to remain with the Bulgarian Partisans helped shape Frank's fate.

He was none the less doubtful. Scott felt that Frank did not want to go into Bulgaria, but the Bulgarians insisted they knew their own country and were going anyway and at once. Frank had no time to secure Cairo's confirmation and his 'impatience of delays' may have played its part in what followed. Henniker observed that Frank, fearing it might appear that the British were afraid to share the risks their friends took, reluctantly and with misgivings thought that it was his duty to go. He felt disillusioned with the failure of support from Cairo, and the Partisans pressed him to accompany them. While fully realising the folly of going into Bulgaria, and the negligible chances of survival there, Frank decided to take the gamble.

The expectations of receiving further large shipments of British weapons by air were so exaggerated in certain people's minds that they assumed unrealistic proportions. And Frank similarly hypothesised that, if the mission went across, this might trigger a new atmosphere in which 'a mass-uprising would take place'. Exactly such a new atmosphere, after all, had that April come about within southern Serbia itself. On 16 May Claridges requested blind drops for five pinpoints to supply five different detachments or *odredi* within Bulgaria, whither they were setting out the next day. It was the final signal from them that Cairo received.

The following day, Wednesday 17 May, Frank and Scott, accompanied by around 180 Partisans, entered Bulgaria. Their mission included Gocho Gopin, liaison delegate between Claridges and the Bulgar Partisans, Vlado Trichkov (political leader) and Dencho Znepolski (military leader). Trichkov, waving a tommy gun, made a grandiloquent speech declaring himself Partisan C-in-C and they crossed into Bulgaria 'as if it were a Sunday school outing'. They hoped to join up

---

* The instruction continued: 'and failing this with Tran Odred' (E. P. Thompson, *Beyond the Frontier: The Politics of a Failed Mission, Bulgaria 1944*, London, 1997, p. 34). The Tran *odred* or detachment did not penetrate far into Bulgaria, so staying with them might have saved the lives of Frank and his brigade.

with remnants of the Chavdar Brigade, which had been effectively wiped out a fortnight before, but the guides sent to tell them had all been killed too. They had some English boots and uniforms which had 'gone to their heads', some arms, no compasses, and for maps only Frank's and Scott's silken map of the Balkans. They crossed in a state of euphoria in full daylight, under vigilant enemy air reconnaissance, without guides and off-course.

Second Sofia brigade on their 'long march', May 1944. Frank third from right.

Scott's narrative describes the first ambush soon after crossing, by twenty Bulgarian Gendarmerie armed with knives. One Partisan was killed, Dencho received three stab wounds, and a policeman was taken prisoner who, in order to gain lenient treatment, claimed to be a married recent conscript with children. When his papers showed that he was both single and a member of the regular forces, his head was smashed in with a rifle butt.

Despite constant police patrols they crossed the Iskar river in daylight and captured an ardent Fascist whom they forced, hands bound, to guide them for two days; probably the Partisans shot him later during a skirmish. Wrongly believing that they were in Partisan territory, they stopped in Lakatnik to rest for some days and buy food for the march. But after less than an hour reports arrived of an approaching Gendarmerie patrol by whom they were harassed until dusk; and they were soon further beleaguered by Bulgarian troops approaching with mortars whom, forewarned by scouts, they managed to bypass. Their march was quickly turning into little more than a succession of disorderly routs.

They were now travelling short of food, in unfamiliar and hostile territory, where – it was becoming apparent – they constantly risked betrayal to the Gendarmerie or army. Keeping to the mountain heights offered some security, though the army was also establishing hilltop posts throughout the area: such garrisons fired a single shot to signal the sighting of Partisans, which acted as a useful warning to the Partisans themselves. A much-needed rest in a wood on 18 May was interrupted by machine-gun fire at noon; encircled, they scattered, splitting into two groups. Frank fled with Scott, around twelve Partisan officers and five or six other ranks including three women. Although Frank was struck in the back by a bullet while making a getaway, this fortunately lodged – scholar-soldier that he was – in the dictionary he carried in his haversack, saving his life.

From the safety of the far river bank Frank and Scott were dismayed to see a Bulgarian Gendarmerie party leading their mules away still loaded with supplies. They were squatting on an unstable gravel slope, the sound of which when one Partisan slipped alerted a Bulgar policeman: well-aimed machine-gun fire soon followed. Search for a new hide-out was delayed by Trichkov having been shot in the ankle, by a new party of Bulgar troops proceeding northwards, and by their own exhaustion and hunger. They slept the night in thickets on a hilltop; their only food had been a small quantity of cheese captured not long after entering Bulgaria when they destroyed a factory that villagers told them provided cheese for Germans.

After buying provisions they resumed their march eastwards around

25 May, redistributing their few remaining weapons and intending to join up with the Murgash Partisans.

But Frank and Scott (by this stage with a compass, and near a village called Batulya) decided they had travelled too far south and discussed returning to the Yugoslav border, a route they now knew. Trichkov's ankle wound was not healing and slowed them down to three miles a day over rough country. They had been ambushed each day and the Partisans had had no military leader of their own since 18 May. They claimed they had no wireless communication. Frank had lost confidence in the remaining Partisans with whom they were travelling.

Frank and Scott therefore agreed, when opportunity presented during the next skirmish, to split from their group and hide in the forest. After lying low until it was safe, they would continue at greater speed towards Sredna Gora, where they hoped to join up with another Partisan group headed for Sofia/Plovdiv and re-establish contact with Cairo. This decision makes sense of Frank's half-jokey remark reported by Scott that September: 'These Partisans are no good: maybe we should find some better ones.'

Three Partisans were soon detected at the skyline trying to run away; one was detained and brought back to the main body. A meeting was called at which orders originating with Trichkov were read out by his deputy, to the effect that deserters would be shot, as would those discovered eating clandestine supplies.

On 30 May the Partisans debated their plight while in an orchard eating cherries so unripe they had no stones; Frank and Scott attempted to eat leaves with salt and then divided a live wood-snail, Scott eating the tail, Frank the head. After this, for two hours, they fell silent. They now had lice – enemy number two, they joked. So desperate were they that three Partisans were detailed to acquire food in the local village, despite its being occupied by an army unit. They returned with fresh bread which was divided between everyone with great care, Frank and Scott using their hats to avoid losing any crumbs. Then, exhausted, they slept in the orchard and surrounding woods.

After a Gendarmerie patrol was spotted at dawn 300 yards away, they decided not to move further. But at 14.00 a patrol of twenty men approached from the village where their presence had evidently been betrayed – possibly by a deserting sentry promised amnesty or by guides offered bribes* – and two hours later fired the first bullets into the wood. Frank and Scott, as they had planned, split from the group, moving uphill while the Partisans were fleeing down and hid between four trees in ground cover of dead leaves and branches.

They could hear small-arms and mortar fire, and the excited shouts of Anna, one of three women Partisans who had stayed with the group and who, despite her painful shrapnel wounds, killed several Bulgar troops with grenades. The copse in which they were hiding was approached from both north and east by troops who, from ten feet away, spotted Frank and Scott, shot at them and then captured them.

Four soldiers dragged and brutally kicked them while those soldiers who could get close enough, the escort of four included, struck them with fists, pistols and rifle butts until an NCO arrived. Both had their hands tied behind their backs, Frank with a belt, Scott, whose hand was poisoned and swollen, with a rope, the bonds stopping circulation, cutting almost to the bone. In the village where the bread had been bought peasants turned out to swear, spit and strike them with fists and any heavy articles they could seize. The recent bombing of Sofia, which Frank had encouraged, played its part – they realised – in this hostility: some accounts report Sofia 25 per cent destroyed, with thousands killed. Frank, extremely weak from lack of food, the march and ill-treatment, lost his balance and collapsed.

———

After preliminary questioning to ascertain that they were the British fighting with the Partisans, they were taken to a cellar where a well-dressed civilian beat them with a thirty-inch truncheon with a hard core, while soldiers, policemen and other civilians crowded in the doorway to watch. Orthodox interrogation by a commanding officer who

---

* Yanev names two brothers whom the Partisans had appointed as their guides, who betrayed them for money: Dimitar and Alexander Hadzhiyski (*The Man from the Legend*, ch. 5).

had extracted information about the mission and its history from a captured Partisan followed; he promised them that, as uniformed members of HM Forces, they would – as Frank requested – be treated as prisoners of war. Frank was shocked that his captors seemed to know every fact about his activities and movements. His and Scott's possessions were set out on a table, and a Bulgarian lance-corporal who knew some English eked out Frank's 'scanty' knowledge of Bulgarian.

They were soon taken to a school at Litakovo near Sofia where they shared a room with the two Partisans who had deserted on 30 May, the three villagers who had sold them bread, and another Partisan, all handcuffed. At each stage there were further beatings, spitting and kicking in front of an audience of soldiers, Gendarmerie and citizenry, a stream of sightseers rendering sleep impossible. The screams of two women Partisans who had been captured too, Anna and probably Yordanka, continued through the night, accompanied by sounds of heavy furniture being thrown around: they were never seen again. Some of the men were decapitated. Frank was taken for three hours of interrogation at around three in the morning and returned haggard, scarcely

The National Museum of History, Sofia

able to stand; Scott followed. Then there was a more military and clear-cut interrogation, in front of two W/T sets, only one of them recognisable to Scott: he wondered – accurately – whether the second set had been taken into Bulgaria unknown to them. Many questions concerned the SOE signals school in the Middle East, the exact station to which Scott had signalled, and the whereabouts of other British missions in the Balkans. These questioners were formidably well informed.

On 1 June Scott's request for medical attention to his injured hand was granted, the doctor especially interested in discovering where Frank had learned Bulgarian; it is one of many horrible ironies that his meagre knowledge of the language probably helped to incriminate him as a 'spy'. During the following twenty-four hours sightseers (and Scott's poisoned arm) rendered sleep impossible; and on 2 June Scott was taken off into individual imprisonment in Sofia. He was needed to operate his wireless set in an attempt to acquire information from Cairo's replies useful to his captors.

He never saw Frank again and was told around 11 June that Frank had been shot. 'C'est la guerre,' his messenger shrugged, when asked why. He was also told that Frank had died bravely. No details were vouchsafed; and an authoritative account of Frank's death was not published until 2001, in Kiril Yanev's *The Man from the Legend*, a narrative to which we return in Chapter 14.

On 9 September, after fourteen weeks' captivity, Scott was released and made his slow way back, via Istanbul and Cairo, to London.

# Conversing with the Dead: 1944–7

'Who killed Cock Robin?'
'I,' said the Sparrow,
'With my bow and arrow,
'I killed Cock Robin.'

'Who saw him die?'
'I,' said the Fly,
'With my little eye,
'I saw him die.'

Traditional

The month Frank died EP pondered the cruelties of war. Serving with
the smart 17th/21st Lancers (motto: 'Death or Glory') he had taken part
in the prolonged battle for Monte Cassino, which fell on 18 May 1944,
followed on 4 June by Rome. The Allied advance up Italy unwisely
advocated by Churchill (via Europe's falsely named 'soft underbelly')
was vexed by mountainous terrain, by Allied supply lines stretching
ever longer, by the withdrawal of troops to fight in Normandy, and by
ferocious German resistance. Each day incessant shelling and mines
caused new casualties. In the week that Frank died, EP was engaged in
the battle for Perugia, and his squadron of fifteen tanks had been
depleted to a mere five, of which he commanded two. EP survived a
shell splinter denting his tin helmet and instructed his sergeant in a

Sherman tank to lead the advance into the city while knowing the risks attendant on being in the lead tank, which was often knocked out by enemy shells. Indeed the driver, co-driver and wireless operator were all killed.

To make sure, a German soldier threw a hand grenade into the turret, looked inside and poured petrol in before setting the tank on fire. EP next day found a pile of ashes in the driver's seat, moulding the shape of the lower half of a man. Conceivably on the grounds that this had made identification of the bodies harder, the army elected to send each next-of-kin Missing Believed Killed messages, in this way extending a false hope of possible survival. As each new hope is disallowed, grief is revivified – a cruel protraction, EP recorded, of the anguish of bereavement. Though this is EP writing forty years later, even in 1944 the cruelty of this message was clear to him. And, at just twenty years of age, it was he who had to answer the piteous, self-effacing letters of relatives:

> My brother was all I had in the world . . . and I would like to know a few more details, if the spot where he was buried is marked or did the explosion make this impossible . . . Please did one of his friends pick some wild flowers and place on his grave?

> If you really could get me a photo of his grave it would set his wife's mind at rest as she is greatly grieved . . .

EP's own reaction to stress was, since childhood, a bout of impetigo. He did what he could to offer comfort and abbreviate the grief of enquirers by giving the deaths a definite term; he of course did not tell them that, in the causal sequence of command, it was he who had directed them towards these deaths.

The news that Frank had similarly been declared Missing Believed Killed reached him in October, and sixty-five years later his commanding officer Val ffrench-Blake, who thought EP highly intelligent and sensitive, and enjoyed listening with him to his 78s of Bach's Double

Violin Concerto on the mess's wind-up gramophone, recalled how 'cut up' he had been. EP sailed for home, probably from Venice and on compassionate leave, entrusted with ffrench-Blake's diary, on 26 May 1945. He spent the sixteen-day voyage co-writing a play about Balkan Partisans, and later that year published his first prose, the story 'Drava Bridge' about Partisans in Yugoslavia. Modern warfare was the ultimate negation of individual agency; only the low-technology warfare of Partisans, he believed, could still be termed 'heroic'. As for his parents, they were about to suffer exactly the hideously protracted bereavement that EP decried.

On 14 June Theo wrote pleasantly to Frank, 'Does Stalin do his washing-up?': she would welcome his ideas on this aspect of 'post-war living'. A wind from the future was blowing strongly now that the Second Front had opened, and she described D-Day in Oxford to Frank. Over the eight o'clock news they had first heard of German forces clashing with landing craft, but only the sight of vast flocks of troop carriers flying north-east home over Wain Hill and past Risborough caused them to understand. In the Cadena coffee shop a Lady Richards confirmed to Theo that 'It had started'.

Troops awaiting D-Day had been 'sealed off' to avoid rumour spreading and maximise surprise to the Germans, thus also increasing surprise at home. Lunching on Banbury Road with Barbara Campbell Thompson, the news started to filter through: 4,000 ships and 12,000 planes had been involved. Theo observed the 'huge and most unusual' queues she had ever seen, irregular and restless: donnish men, North Oxford women, charladies, young cigarette-smoking men who might have been Communists or reporters. She wondered whether they were queuing to see some great politician until she understood that all they wanted was newspapers, which were getting snapped up at inflated prices between leaving the van and landing on the pavement. Two round-helmeted American doughboys each with an *Evening News* offered to get Theo a newspaper. She began to measure the momentousness of the day's events.

Theo communed with Frank about the courage asked of men: 'One can hardly bear to think how brave they have been and are being . . . the world will never know all the courage that has been built into the success of this venture.' Frank, unbeknown to them, had played his small part in the creation of a Balkan distraction, thus tying down troops far away from the Normandy landings.

———

At fortnightly intervals through the summer of 1944 EJ and Theo received cables signed with Frank's name: 'Am safe and well, letter received, parcel received'. On 28 June Theo wrote asking 'What parcel? We sent nothing but a few *Lifes*.' One cable from Frank on 7 July reading 'Letters received many thanks', and ending 'Well and fit' did EJ 'immeasurable good'. Although throughout August Theo's letters to Frank were returned 'Addressee is reported missing', the uncanny illusion of his post-mortem existence was unhappily sustained by Frank's having pre-paid Stuttaford's in Cape Town to send Bledlow regular foodstuffs: as late as 16 September Theo was thanking Frank for his welcome gifts of crystallised and baked fruit and tinned tongue – 'the greatest luxury, even in peace-time'.* A fortnight earlier the slapdash wording of a final cable on 3 September aroused suspicion: 'Fondest love and kisses', signed 'Thompson'. These bogus telegrams caused distress: Theo and EJ wondered whether Frank had been captured and the cables maliciously sent by the Germans.

In fact these messages were a form of well-meaning subterfuge, sent by hard-pressed cipherines in Bari instructed to keep up the morale of British missions and their families.† BLOs dropped into hostile territory, cut off from normal communication, often had time on their

---

* Stuttaford's wrote to Frank on 8 March that his credit of £2 11s was enough for only five more parcels.
† As SOE Albanian section's spring 1945 Report shows, stress on welfare – 'one of the most important aspects of the Section's work' – was a key element. Letters and parcels from HQ, duly censored, were prepared for dropping to the various missions. Books and periodicals, sought and bought locally in Bari or Cairo, were dispatched in the same way. Current literature was extremely hard to obtain but even 'old favourites' were welcomed by men with a great deal of reading time. I owe this point to Rod Bailey.

hands to worry about personal affairs. To mitigate the difficulties of letter-writing, fortnightly telegrams purporting to come from the man himself were sent from Italy to relatives at home. These EFM or Expeditionary Force Messages used numbers denoting a phrase of which at any one time three might be combined: a statement of health, acknowledgement of receipt of letters, and a greeting. SOE recommended that these cables 'should never be sent after wireless touch with the mission concerned has been interrupted'. This was a lesson learned the hard way, and by December 1944 Thompson family agitation brought the 'appalling practice' to a halt.

Meanwhile Theo and EJ were also grappling with the fact that EJ had stomach cancer – sometimes referred to by Theo as his 'ulcer'. Theo tried to conceal the true facts of his illness from her sons, until 19 August when the doctors gave EJ up as inoperable and incurable and she petitioned for compassionate leave for both boys. Her cable to Frank's commanding officer received no reply: 'we feel that Force 133 is rather indifferent to families of its men', she commented. Theo then approached a friendly brigadier who advised that unfortunately Frank was 'in an area where it was very difficult to communicate with him'. By then EJ had started responding to X-ray treatment and on 7 September they cabled again, suggesting that Frank after all postpone taking leave since 'If Frank *were* in the Balkans, say Jugoslavia, as we imagined him to be, he would (with the Russians sweeping through as they seemed likely to . . .) hate to be snatched out of it.' Despite the absence of proper letters, they still hoped that he would turn up 'when that part of the war ends'.

Theo accordingly had Frank's room cleaned and his piano reconditioned at considerable expense and gave detailed thought to Frank's post-war life: 'Daddy says you must use your first ½ year writing your book. Then, in October, New College.' When EJ's condition worsened she cabled a third time, which accelerated the arrival of Frank's Missing Believed Killed telegram on 21 September. To compound their sufferings, this was according to one source soon followed by a macabre, unnerving cable thanking Theo for her letter and sending his love.

Bureaucratic ineptitude apart, the reasons for this delayed notification were not sinister. Scott in captivity in June attempted to alert Cairo by inserting girls' names into his messages – Cecily, Anne, Phyllis and so on – to spell 'captured'. After the Gestapo stopped this, his messages arrived full of other deliberate errors which – as one of SOE's best signals operators – could not be accidental. Cairo accurately concluded that he and Frank had been captured and Scott was operating under duress; they hoped Frank might have escaped and be making his way towards a neighbouring mission.

Cairo knew that it was a matter of life and death that they give no hint to the Gestapo, or Scott would quickly have been murdered: he was safe only so long as the Germans were convinced that Cairo was fooled. A tense game of double bluff ensued, Scott repeatedly requesting sorties so that his captors could score easy successes by shooting down Allied planes. SOE Cairo had to think up every possible plausible excuse for not sending sorties, to delay the Gestapo's suspecting anything amiss. Everyone concerned passed three anxious months.

For analogous reasons Frank, even after rumours of his fate began to circulate, could not be declared Missing Believed Killed until after the Bulgarian collapse on 9 September when Scott suddenly found himself released into Sofia: the Germans scrutinised every such notification, which once again would have endangered Scott. Moreover it was Scott alone who might be able to provide the circumstantial evidence on which the case for Frank's probable demise could be based, and which therefore had to await his debrief in Cairo.

This was how SOE saw it. To EJ and Theo it seemed that the authorities obstructed all their attempts to uncover the truth. Lieutenant-Colonel David Talbot Rice, Head of SOE for the Balkans and Middle East, nevertheless set up an interview with his deputy Major E. C. Last, who 'looks after the country in which your son was operating'. This took place on the afternoon of 1 November 1944. Room 238 in the Hotel Victoria on Northumberland Avenue was, as in good spy fiction, secretly dedicated to SOE use. Major Last found the interview 'rather difficult' and its aftermath worse. Neither Thompson had at this point ever heard of SOE and did not understand that what they were told was 'in confidence'. They wondered whether SOE stood for Subversive Activity in Occupied Enemy Territory.

EJ organised the flurry of Bledlow initiatives that immediately followed. He placed on 4 November in *The Times* a Missing notice, requesting that any information should be sent to the parents; the *News Chronicle* on 15 November carried a half-page article, 'BRITISH OFFICER LED BULGARIAN PARTISANS: NAZIS MURDER MAN ON SPECIAL MISSION', describing Frank's leading 'one of the most hopeless and dangerous enterprises of the war'. Then, after an *Evening News* journalist had been shown Frank's room in Bledlow, the paper brought out on 20 November an article mentioning EJ and Theo's wish to publish a memorial volume. Finally a short notice in the *Daily Telegraph* on 28 November announced that EJ sought news of his son.

Major Last was affronted and disturbed that details compassionately vouchsafed should so quickly enter the public domain, offering comfort and intelligence to the enemy and 'endangering other BLOs in the field'. EJ, who knew Bulgaria had been 'liberated' – it had indeed no more Germans (or for that matter SOE agents) active anywhere – was unimpressed by Last's complaints, and continued campaigning. So Theo told EP's friend Arnold Rattenbury, 'I'll look after Bobby Vansittart and the Foreign Office; you look after Harry Pollitt [of the CPGB] and the Comintern.' And EJ duly wrote to his friend Lord Vansittart, then out of office, requesting an investigation into the circumstances of Frank's death and on 10 November to Churchill requesting prosecution of the Bulgarian war criminals. Both letters were forwarded to the War Office. Theo also got her sister Marie-Jo in the USA to request information on Frank's death, via the State Department, from the British Embassy in Washington DC.

In response SOE planned to send personnel to Sofia to help the Allied Control Commission (ACC) investigate Frank's murder. When the Foreign Office at first refused permission, Major Last feared a 'violent reaction' from the Thompsons, who failed to see that, since the ACC was now the official ruler of Bulgaria, its negotiation of the terms of the Armistice took priority. They also understandably exaggerated

Frank's importance – one only out of seventeen missing Britons in Bulgaria, ten of them pilots – and also ignored the fact that every SOE officer about to be dropped into enemy territory knew that his chances of trouble if captured were very high. 'It was part of one's routine training.'

While Theo was admirably level-headed, EJ had a tendency to 'fly off the handle', ungovernable and impenitent. He boasted to SOE of having consulted five different newspaper editors, and threatened that he could also have 'Questions asked in the House'. One year later he did so. EJ feared the dominance of those for whom secrecy – taking cover under so-called 'security considerations' – was becoming a mania, one he rudely labelled crypto-Fascist and thought far worse during the present war than during its predecessor. An efficient Thompson family campaign against the British establishment was picking up speed, outlasting EJ's death in April 1946 and continuing, under EP, a further half-century.

———

The Thompson family were not alone in their uncertainty about whether Frank was alive or dead. On Sunday 3 December 1944 Rachel Annand Taylor wrote, in a weirdly curlicued hand, from her Bloomsbury flat the first fan letter of her long life. 'Dear Mr Frank Thompson, Please pardon my intrusion . . . if I do not inscribe my note instantly I shall lose courage and forbear,' she began, affecting a note of shy girlish distress. A seventy-year-old Scottish poet admired by D. H. Lawrence and by the severe Richard Aldington, her discovery of Frank in the *Observer* that dreary Sunday afternoon suddenly kindled into delight. Frank's poem 'Soliloquy in a Greek Cloister' evoked a Greek Orthodox priest from St Catherine's Monastery in Sinai: 'Lover of Cypresses, a friend of death, / With fierce black beard, weak mouth, a drunkard's eyes'. It caused her to inhale far-off Byzantium 'like a whiff of perfume' and to discover Music, Vision and Strange Imaginative Vibration. What more could one ask? 'If you have a moment's leave, will you tell me if you have published a volume? Perhaps I should know. I do try to follow new poetry . . .'

EJ, still piecing together Frank's story, replied that the true sequence of events was as yet very unclear. After June they had received no letters and the family had – like Rachel Taylor – been writing to a phantom, and receiving cables from the dead Frank in reply. Frank's younger brother fighting with his regiment in Italy joked quite unintentionally, 'Do write soon: you are becoming quite a ghost-voice.' It was EJ himself who had submitted Frank's poem for publication in the *Observer*.

Rachel Taylor replied to EJ with a sentimental fluency. 'So the poet who suddenly seized my attention was indeed "of the golden race" as the Greeks described those who died young in battle; and his life and death were greater poetry than even his verse.' A photograph EJ had sent her, she felt, conveyed the expression on Frank's vanishing face with unusual perfection, 'intellectual force & sweetness of temper & the radiance of the idealist . . . alas, we are in desperate need of such as he . . .' Yet perhaps it was good, she added, that Frank had been spared the bitter disillusionment of the coming post-war world.

Private Collection

Frank sent Iris a copy of this photograph on which, together with the second half of line 2 of Alcman, Fragment 26, he wrote, 'To Irushka, whom I miss these long years.'

Rachel Taylor advised his parents to collect fifty poems of quality for publication. Of Frank's verse his father accurately wrote that 'His style was more traditional than I fancy he wanted to think, but what does that matter?' Neither Taylor nor Frank despised lyricism. A selection of Frank's verse soon went out to editors and fellow poets. Oxford University's Clarendon Press had just published Edward's *100 Poems*: might they wish to publish his elder son's as well? The Press took the advice of Gilbert Murray, who cherished a photograph of Frank in his Boars Hill library, and who – by coincidence – was Rachel Taylor's mentor too.

Murray wrote to OUP that everything about Frank's gallant and brilliant mind and the real beauty of his character gave special interest to all he wrote; some of this feeling would get through to the general public who did not know him, but not much. 'As to the poems themselves, they are above the ordinary level of such recent poetry as I know, and some are really beautiful . . . but there is more promise than achievement.' Frank, had he lived, would have written more and rejected some of these. OUP accordingly wrote to Theo that, although they had, exceptionally, published Edward's volume, poetry was not really 'in our Oxford province at all'. The Thompson family should try Faber's instead.

Others agreed about the provisional and unfinished nature of Frank's work. One small publisher thought many poems too private, some too academic, and the bulk too young or too near their subject. A commemorative volume might be published, to include some prose pieces and letters. *Penguin New Writing* editor John Lehmann, noting how interested the Russians were in Frank's heroic reputation as a martyr in the Partisan cause, wrote from the Hogarth Press to say 'the poems by themselves don't make sufficient impression, but they would do, bolstered by letters and prose'.*

Other consoling replies followed. John Arlott, remembered today

---

* On 18 January 1946 Lehmann, then helping to make gramophone records of poems by soldiers killed in the war, wrote again wanting to include some by Frank 'in whom the Russians are very interested'.

for thirty-four years of *Test Match Special* cricket commentaries in his Hampshire burr, but then a policeman-poet and novice broadcaster, had been writing fan letters to Edward about his poetry since 1941. He liked Frank's immensely too: 'a poet and a man to my taste'.* The poet Patric Dickinson, also working for the BBC, agreed. Both admired Frank's 'Damascus Road', duly broadcast the following spring.

Rachel Annand Taylor in a new letter to EJ conveyed well the strange quality of Frank's life story and verse alike: 'I have not really said what I feel. It is difficult. You have communicated to me a spiritual experience – of pain illuminated by a kind of elation, the elation that can be caught only from contact with great beauty. And I am profoundly grateful.' Pain illuminated by elation: grief somehow shot through with joy. Such is the stuff of tragedy. Frank's story, and his best few poems, shine out with both emotions, as also with his humour.

Soon a hundred more letters of condolence arrived. Few were as stylish as Taylor's, and style mattered to the Thompsons. An official letter, condemned as 'Conventional verbiage, sub-adolescent', read: 'you will be glad to know that your son was one of those extraordinarily gallant men who volunteered to be parachuted into enemy-occupied territory to attempt to contact the guerillas'.

A feeble yet 'sweet' letter from Frank's first cousin Graham Vivian foolishly suggested that 'It may console you to know that he was a Major.' This too was ridiculed: as if mere rank could atone for Frank's loss. Cousin Graham's story illuminates Frank's: a Bailey Bridge expert fighting in Italy, he trod on a mine two weeks later and was killed, four Sikhs bringing his body back through heavy fire. When his brother Trevor visited his regiment, two Sikh soldiers wept and kept a three-day fast in Graham's memory. Trevor too was killed months later in a flying

---

* Arlott wrote two letters from Southampton, dated 5 and 29 March 1945, requesting Frank's dates of birth and death and his rank, and declaring that he 'would v much like to come & visit'. EJ had sent a number of poems which Arlott liked and hoped with luck to use in 'the magazine [*sic*]'.

accident and Graham's afflicted parents sought solace for this loss of both their sons in séances. One medium impressed them by telling them that Graham had been a secret poet, and on searching his effects they were astonished to find poems in both English and *Scots Gaelic* – Graham having a Highlands fetish. What the Balkans were to Frank, Scotland was to his first cousin Graham, a focus for passionate romantic aspiration.

'How mysterious', Edward mused, 'even those closest to us are.' He might countenance his sister Molly's claim to have spoken during séances both to her nephew Frank and to her own dead sons 'if those in the afterlife were not always doing such incredibly boring things'. A second fan letter (from another writer living in a Richmond hotel) echoed this macabre theme: '. . . I thought I was addressing the author of that fine poem directly – Perhaps I was! Who knows. You will have the happiness of reunion, if not here, then on the other side.'

Theo did not consult mediums, despite being encouraged to do so by Gilbert and Lady Mary Murray, but reached out in other ways. She wrote, 'One understands nothing about these things, one can only believe that there IS life after death.' On Remembrance Sunday, 11 November, she recounted in a letter to EP, her heart felt unaccountably light and free – 'as if Frank were happy that we had done something. I told Daddy – and I wondered what it was.' They had sent his poems to be typed at last and had met delegates from Bulgaria. Perhaps, she wondered, on Armistice Day 'when people's spirits go out in such a wave of remembrance and love to the spirits of those who have died, it is easier for them to be in contact with us. Certainly nothing would so lift a burden from life as to know that Frank knew of our love for him.'

Graham Vivian might not yet have developed the gift for saying the right thing. EP, a tank commander in Italy, differed. When EJ wrote to him on 29 September, 'This is a sad letter to write to you Palmer old chap,' reporting Frank's disappearance after 31 May, EP swore in reply that he and his brother had both had the happiest of childhoods. Edward replied, 'No words meant so much to us as your saying that,' and even Theo, writing independently, admitted that this comforted them 'a bit'.

Though she and Edward tried to keep alive a faint hope that Frank might miraculously reappear post-war as a POW, Theo despaired. Her favourite son had died. She feared that her two boys had been conscious of strain in the home; she feared that they thought of the family house as a 'stark, bleak' place; she feared that her and Edward's letters had been trivial and inadequate. She wished she had been the kind of mother who finds it easy to tell her sons how much she loves them, but knew her own stiffness and inhibition. 'I hope you know, Palmer dear, how very much loved you are. Do you think Frank knew? Or was I too "fierce" – the old family joke?' She could not express how trivial and vulgar their life seemed besides that of Frank. 'That he, so greatly needed, should go. That we, so useless and second-rate, should be left to carry on. More than ever we pray for your safety & so longed for return.'

Edward echoed her. If EP did not survive the war, 'there is literally nothing now for which we should want to live'. At least Frank had died without being troubled by the knowledge that EJ was fighting stomach cancer.

EJ told Theo she was wrong to blame herself as inadequate; it was nonsense for her to imagine that Frank did not know how deeply and purely he was loved. For his own part it never worried him if his own poems and many books – so much concerned with India – had made little appeal to Frank. EJ, born in 1886, conceived himself a late Victorian, his writing clogged with false and sentimental ways of thought. His consolation had been to hope that his two idealistic sons might help put the post-war world 'grandly right' while he, in honourable retirement, applauded. His letters had until this point abounded in facetious family in-jokes, and he had played the clown through three long years of separation. But intense grief can cut to the bone, through masks and poses, depriving us of the use of voices not absolutely true. Now, at last, he became serious, even solemn, enjoining EP: 'It is now more than ever essential that you shall survive [this war] for it is by you that [Frank] will live on.'

The injunction to survive was the easier of two charges. The burden of memorialising and then of somehow representing Frank – 'by you . . . Frank will live on' – was a tougher assignment. Both EP's first and his last published books – *There is a Spirit in Europe* (1947) and

*Beyond the Frontier* (1997) – commemorate his adored elder brother. He was not a man to take responsibilities lightly.

---

The most exclusive unofficial club in 1945, Frank's first cousin Barbara recalls, was that of bereaved mothers. Theo, to her credit, was too proud to make parade of grief or request sympathy on such terms. She wrote that 'it seems sometimes unbearable that someone we all loved so passionately should have taken his resolve & gone his way so separate from us all – that we should have had no knowledge of this testing of his strong courage, no message of this victory, at the time . . .' Her child had entered Calvary without her: the parallel is implicit in her decision to call Frank's murder his 'victory'. The family agreed. 'He took his own way & made his own high choice.'

Theo blamed Frank's 'self-censorship' for keeping the family from him so completely. Frank wrote 'lovely, witty, darling letters. It is like having Frank in the room with you,' she accurately noted. And yet he was far more discreet than other officers: 'his letters could have been published with full military approval the day they reached us. He never mentioned operations, localities, units, *anything*.' Theo understood that the needs of wartime censorship were somehow augmented beyond the call of duty by Frank's private code of chivalry, a topic for the next chapter. The family had to deduce changes of unit by scrutinising his shifting addresses and guess even at changes in his rank. Putting together an accurate picture of his war was going to be difficult.

On 25 November Edward wrote to EP that he and Theo had 'practically given up all hope of Frank . . . I am afraid the loss is not one we shall soon get over: you know how inexpressibly dear Frank was' – the exact phrase used by his sister on the death of their brother (another Frank) in January 1917. As for EP, he noted a recurrent desire to find the precise point in the chain of causation at which the catastrophe began, as if the fateful story could then magically be retold differently, with a happier outcome.

---

On 29 November, fearful that EJ would probably pass it all on to *The Times*, SOE sent Bledlow the report of a Major Strachey. Snaffle Mission, which had dropped into Bulgaria, discovered that everyone there was speaking of Frank's courage and endurance with the greatest respect: 'He spoke our language and learnt our songs, he endured the danger and hardships with us during a time of ruthless repression . . . his name will not be forgotten.' This, EJ wrote, was 'the first comfort we have received'. Scott when captive had also been assured that Frank died bravely.

Further comfort was on its way. To a World Trade Union Conference at County Hall, London from 6 to 17 February 1945 came 204 representatives from sixty-three countries. Among two from Bulgaria was a schoolteacher named Raina Sharova, who had met Frank during his imprisonment and agreed to see Theo and talk about her son's last days. Her account has been hugely influential in constructing Frank's reputation as martyr-hero and she claimed, falsely, to have witnessed his execution.

'The Story of a Great Englishman' was published in the *News Chronicle* on 8 March: Sharova was its main source, Sofia radio and newspapers were others. Four officers died with Frank – one American, one Serb, two Bulgarians – and eight other prisoners. Fifty-seven of Frank's companions had already been executed. Frank and the American were tortured – we do not know how, but some Bulgarians had their eyes gouged out.

Much of the article constituted a highly coloured account of Frank's 'show-trial', with Frank answering bullying questions 'in fluent Bulgarian'* while calmly smoking his pipe: 'I am ready to die for freedom. And I am proud to die with Bulgarian patriots as companions.' At this a passionately weeping old woman stands up and announces that the audience sides with the brave Partisans. As she is struck to the floor, Frank and his Partisans are marched off to the castle where Frank raises the clenched fist of freedom, all the audience joining

---

* Yanev says Frank mixed up Serbian and Bulgarian words (*The Man from the Legend*, ch. 6); General Slavcho Trŭnski when I met him in 1998 agreed.

in, and he and his men die with raised fists too, in one version singing Botev's 'Anthem to Freedom'. The sobbing spectators declared this one of the most moving scenes in all Bulgarian history, and Frank now stood towards Bulgaria as Byron did to Greece.

This story was invention, propaganda by Communists seeking a legitimising heroic ancestry for the new regime.[*] They *decided* – as Bickham Sweet-Escott, advisor to SOE's Force 133, wryly observed – to turn Frank into a hero and Sharova was their stooge. She left an equally vivid account of meeting EP and Theo in London in February 1945 when EP was still in Italy. (Not all of this was fake. Theo's eyes filled with tears when Sharova recounted telling the captured Frank not to despair as the Russians were approaching; Frank had replied: 'I don't despair. But time flies very fast.' Theo gave her dried flowers to place on Frank's grave.)[†]

EJ charged the War Office with not doing all in its power to uncover evidence such as this. Memos make very clear official embarrassment that the Thompsons by mid-1945 now knew far more – had many more details at their disposal – than the War Office itself.[‡] In the hostile stand-off between the Thompsons and officialdom, however, officials could not admit this.[§]

When the War Office sought hard evidence of Frank's death in May 1945, EJ suggested it contact Raina Sharova. Under oath she swore on 14 November that though she had briefly visited Frank in prison 'she

---

[*] When Philippa Foot and I visited Bulgaria in 1999 we found nobody at all – neither General Trŭnski, nor the Litakovo headmistress Todorka Kosteva, official guide to the monument and the events of 1944, nor anyone else – who believed that Frank had been put on trial. The tale of the trial is also discounted by Frank's Bulgarian biographer Kiril Yanev.

[†] EJ was too ill to attend. The account of meeting EP as well as Theo is in Yanev (*The Man from the Legend*, ch. 9). Presumably Sharova in later life conflated the 1945 meeting with Theo alone in London, which both *News Chronicle* and Trŭnski, *Grateful Bulgaria*, p. 66, alike make clear did happen, with the 1947 visit of EP and his mother to Bulgaria.

[‡] By December 1944 EP's file for *Beyond the Frontier* suggests that his parents had already had the chance to interview, among others, Peter Wright, Hugh Seton-Watson (who recorded that he confided in them 'more frankly than he should') and Major Strachey.

[§] An attempt to mediate with limited results was made by George Mackeson, a mutual friend of Talbot Rice and EJ, who had painted EJ's portrait.

did not, rpt *not* witness execution'. She would none the less prepare a statement about all facts known to her; the ACC, making other enquiries in the meantime, was suffering from the 'habitual dilatoriness' of Bulgarian bureaucracy. Sharova's version of the execution scene was accordingly disavowed by EP in the second, 1948 edition of *There is a Spirit in Europe: A Memoir of Frank Thompson*. Yet it was – regrettably – resurrected in EP's posthumously edited and published *Beyond the Frontier* (1997)* and thus made its way into Frank's current (2004) *Oxford Dictionary of National Biography* entry.

EJ now had a reputation for being willing to 'burst into print on the slightest provocation'. A 4 October 1945 SOE cable concerning the cancellation of a Bulgarian War Crimes Mission has 'The Thompson Case!' written on it, the exclamation mark suggesting that the whole anguished drama was being treated with a weary or cynical knowingness. On 6 November 1945 the newly elected MP Francis Noel-Baker asked the Secretary of State for War to make a full statement about the circumstances of Major Frank Thompson's death.

Friends rallied. Gilbert Murray, expert on Greek tragedy, wrote: 'You and Theo have gone very near the limit of human suffering this last year, and we think of you both constantly.' Psychological torment apart, EJ was now in non-stop physical pain.

---

Probably because of their war with officialdom, the Thompsons never learned of Soviet culpability. The ACC in Sofia was dominated by the Russians both numerically and through their systematic humiliation of the British and (even more) Americans by means of petty and Kafkaesque restrictions on their numbers, movements and mail. Thus SOE had arranged in November 1944 for two of its officers, Colonel S. W. Bailey and Major Norman Davis, to proceed to Sofia to investigate Frank's death. Davis had lived in Bulgaria, spoke the language (plus Russian) and was familiar with SOE's work there from its earliest

---

* 'Witnesses reported that they died with clenched fists and the partisan slogan "Death to Fascism" on their lips' (EP, *Beyond the Frontier*, p. 86).

days; Bailey also spoke Bulgarian. For six months they waited patiently while the Russians prevaricated until SOE gave up. SOE's subsequent attempt to bring in two further investigators, Major Macpherson and Sergeant Scott, fared no better. They were 'kept on ice for months', before being told to disband in October 1945. SOE noted that it was now absolutely unimaginable that the Russians would allow any Britons to roam the country asking questions. Was it best to tell EJ this in strictest confidence? They decided not to.

The family had been promised the first of Frank's effects in April 1945 – two Bibles, one in Greek, one in English, plus a diary containing manuscript notes – but waited in vain for their arrival. In July a contrite letter from a Miss Lovibond at the War Office explained that she had learned that a soldier had to be Presumed Dead before his effects could be released. Frank was now so classified, his kit and belongings finally sent off on 10 July 1945, but by October the Thompsons had still received nothing. Without certification there could be neither probate, implementation of Frank's will nor closure for his parents. Every single new enquiry necessitated fresh form-filling. War Office memos regretted 'so many muddles, difficulties and delays'.

———

The journalist Ilya Ehrenburg – whom Frank idolised – broadcast from Moscow on 8 October 1945 that the British appeared not to know that those who had tortured and murdered Frank Thompson had been tried and executed. EJ wrote promptly to *The Times*, citing Ehrenburg and bitterly complaining of the many honours Frank had received in Bulgaria, comparing this with the shameful silence about his martyrdom at home.

Relief was at hand. On 4 March 1946 a Colonel K. Savill, investigating war crimes from 20 Eaton Square, was notified that the Bulgarians had after thirteen months' delay written to the ACC providing the names of Frank's murderers and their sentences. The Soviets were now increasingly in charge in Bulgaria and 2,000 convenient scapegoats had been found to indict and execute for some of the crimes of Fascism. Frank's murder, which had contravened the Geneva Convention, was certainly one such crime.

In front of the Deputy Prosecutor, an Orthodox priest, the Secretary to the Court and a Dr Spirov, according to the letter to the ACC, the following five were found guilty of having shot and murdered seven Partisans in late May: Stoyan Lazarov (aged twenty-four), Angel Tsanishev (twenty-nine), Boris Vassilev (twenty-nine), Ilya Tupankov (twenty-four), Gorcho Mladenov (twenty-five), and the last-named was found guilty of having also killed and 'persecuted' eighteen people in battle. Most denied that they had fired at Frank – or claimed to have fired over his head. They were none the less executed at ten in the evening on 7 February 1945. Their families were also fined 100,000 lev each and one-third of their property was confiscated. By no means all details are accurate or clear,* and nor was any explanation as to why this news had taken one year to reach the ACC in Sofia forthcoming.

Savill was welcome to pass all or some of this on to EJ 'in case you deem it fitting', a qualification suggesting the arrogant secretiveness that the Thompsons rightly resented, and a settled mutual hostility.

News came late for comfort. In constant pain for months and furious

* This letter was sent on 23 January 1946 from the Bulgarian Minister of Foreign Affairs Petko Staynov to Colonel-General Biryusov, the ACC's Vice-President: that Biryusov was Russian may finally have expedited disclosure. Frank is inaccurately said to have been killed in early July: he died in June, probably on the 10th.

One Boris Likanov Stoyanov, who was found in possession of Frank's shoes, is said alone to have admitted guilt. A further group, charged together with the original five with 'atrocities', claimed to have fired over the Partisans' heads: Ilya Dushanski and Boris Lukanov (sic, with a 'u') Stoyanov, who admitted that he had killed three out of six or seven Partisans. Georgi Tzelov admitted that he had tied up two of the group before firing. Stoyan Gergov refused to admit that he fired. Tupankov fired 'with his machine gun'.

Elsewhere in another archive yet another list of culprits is named. Here six 'subordinates' (sic) are said to have been tried by the Novoselski and Botevgradski People's Courts, sentenced to death and executed: for their role in the interrogation Georgi Manov, Dicho Dichev and Boris Tomov (none of these is mentioned in the 23 January 1946 letter); for their role in the execution Stoian Lazarov, Angel Stanchev and Ilia Tupankov (who correspond, albeit with differences in transliteration). Only Tupankov admitted his guilt. He and Manov both claimed that Stoyanov had confessed that he himself shot Thompson (Veliko Tarnovo letter N-4454/19–20.12.1945). The name of Dimiter Avgardski, whom we know independently to have been present at the execution, is unmentioned in either of these sources.

at his inactivity, EJ was at home in Bledlow, attended by Theo, EP and his nurses, approaching his sixtieth birthday and dying with hideous slowness. When EP asked whether he should tell Nehru, much involved with the run-up to Indian independence, EJ told him to mind his own business: Nehru had more important matters to worry about. No less a personage than the Viceroy Lord Wavell had brought Nehru in prison the news of Frank's death; and Nehru, who wrote at length to his sister about Frank's courage and his idealism,* had also written movingly to EJ from prison about how much such friendships as his had meant to him over the long years of struggle.

EP disregarded his father, sent Nehru an air-letter and got a reply post-haste. One evening when his mind was clear from drugs, EJ sat up in bed reading Nehru's letter thanking him for his life's work on India's behalf, before letting it drop upon the sheets. He died a few days later, on 28 April.

---

* 'Poor Edward is dying of cancer. Frank's death has been a terrible blow to him, but, at the same time, he is very proud of him' (*Before Freedom: Nehru's Letters to his Sister 1909–1947*, ed. N. Sahgal, London, 2004, p. 461).

14

# Afterlife

How can I live among this gentle
obsolescent breed of heroes, and not weep?
Keith Douglas, 'Aristocrats'

The family thought that the BBC had an unofficial ban on mentioning
the Bulgarian Partisans, that the British Government moreover refused
permission for Frank's two Bulgarian medals to be awarded – the Order
of the People's Liberty (First Class) and the Military Medal – and that
Frank's desk officer Hugh Seton-Watson, who met them and talked
very frankly in 1944, had been reprimanded for getting Frank such aid
and sorties as he had contrived. Family grievance was not assuaged
when Kenneth Scott – whom they met in Room 238 in the Hotel
Victoria on 3 January 1945 – received the DCM (Distinguished Conduct
Medal). Why had Frank received no British decoration? They ignored
the fact that posthumous decorations were then almost never awarded,
and indeed Mostyn Davies's DSO (Distinguished Service Order) had
come on 1 June, which, though after his death, just preceded his being
officially declared Missing Believed Killed.

It was Mostyn Davies's mission that Frank had been dropped into
Serbia to support, and the difference in the way each man was treated
after his death is remarkable. Davies's widow Brenda, like the
Thompsons, sought proof of her husband's end. She had also served in
SOE and had not, under promise of secrecy, told Mostyn's parents

about their son's demise. Lacking the Thompsons' contacts and savoir-faire, she sent SOE the March 1945 *News Chronicle* article that purported to reveal the truth about Frank's death, in order to try to accelerate disclosure about her husband's. In vain.

Neither her suffering nor her ignorance ended in the 1940s. In the late 1950s she communed with her dead husband at what she understood to be his only memorial, in the Phaleron war cemetery in Athens, and later believed from Stowers Johnson's 1975 book about Frank called *Agents Extraordinary* that Mostyn was buried in Gerdelicka near Ruplje in Serbia. She was accordingly agitated and distressed in 1990 to discover from the spring Special Forces Club magazine that his grave *in Belgrade* had just been blessed, a venue nobody over nearly fifty years had troubled themselves to mention to her. An ex-SOE officer named Captain Edgar Chavasse, working for Graves Registrations from 1946 to 1988, had exhumed what was left of Mostyn Davies's remains: his notes make for the grimmest reading.

Comparison with Frank is salutary. Davies was as brave as Frank and gave his life for the identical cause: each man spent the final six months of his life working towards the liberation of Bulgaria, and SOE justly recorded Davies's leadership after his death as both 'heroic and inspiring'.[*] Yet Davies is to this day devalued in Bulgarian accounts as cold, arrogant and condescending when not defamed as delaying sorties or – as we have seen – organising them exclusively to deliver his favourite foods. EP brilliantly showed in *Beyond the Frontier* how Mostyn Davies was encoded as the 'bad' or imperialist BLO, while Frank was gilded as the 'good', democratic BLO.[†]

Frank, together with thirteen Partisans, was given a ceremonial reburial at Litakovo on 12 November 1944, with a weeping crowd of

---

[*] Davies's courage, charm and resourcefulness were, independently, admired by his good friend, SOE's Bickham Sweet-Escott; see his *Baker Street Irregular*, London, 1965, *passim*.

[†] In a 1977 Bulgarian TV film about Frank, General Trŭnski heavily implied that Davies might have been betraying Partisan positions to the enemy: see *Major Frank Thompson* in the British Film Institute. In *Beyond the Frontier*, ch. 1, EP reported Trŭnski as accusing Cairo of doing precisely the same.

Frank's ceremonial reburial at Litakovo.

50,000 in attendance. The contrast with Mostyn Davies, a forgotten name on casualty lists, is stark. Nineteen-forty-five saw a second ceremony on the anniversary of the first, the Consul's wife Mrs Boyd-Tollington taking out rosemary and thyme from Theo's garden together with some English earth and the Orthodox priest placing on the graves a libation of wine and fresh apples. Frank, long intrigued by the possible connection between Apollo and apples, would surely have approved. A third ceremony on 15 July 1947, which Theo and EP got permission to fly out via Prague to attend, featured a solemn observance in the National Theatre in Sofia, a retracing of the march with Partisan survivors up to the scene of the final battle and a reconsecration of his grave. Asked where Frank's remains should find their final resting-place, they decreed that they should stay with his comrades in Litakovo. On the unveiling there of a memorial to Frank, the crowd knelt as if at religious observance. Some moving film footage survives of a black-clad Theo, austere and dignified at the graveside, consoling bereaved mothers

Theo and EP with Bulgaria's President Dimitrov, July 1947.

of Partisans. On return she became Hon. Secretary to the Anglo-Bulgarian Friendship Society.*

In public officialdom was blamed for Frank's loss. In private his parents feared their own complicity. Perhaps it had all started long before the war? A neurotic perfectionist with a love of control, Theo wrote in 1935 that she feared that the way she and EJ had brought him up had nearly 'broken Frank's spirit': he was too patient and philosophical for his age, and they had praised him insufficiently.

Frank, EJ added, was almost without flaw: his only weakness was thinking himself older than he was. 'When fourteen he thought himself eighteen and so on . . .' At twenty-three he had deemed himself fit for a hero's death; EJ judged this precocious. Moreover Frank was 'too

---

* EP proceeded directly from Sofia to help build the legendary Šamac–Sarajevo railway in Yugoslavia with his future wife Dorothy Sale: see E. P. Thompson (ed.), *The Railway: An Adventure in Construction*, London, 1948. A Major Frank Thompson Brigade comprising Britons went to Bulgaria in 1947 for a brief sightseeing tour, reorganised and returned as a working brigade to Bulgaria the following year.

restless to stay out his time at Winchester, and in his one year at Oxford, utterly restless'. Frank's inbred wanderlust also played a part in the choices that led directly to his loss.

Theo at least was aware of dangers. She strongly argued against the BBC in 1947 making a radio play about Frank out of the family's well-received commemorative *There is a Spirit in Europe*, in which they collected some of Frank's poetry, letters and journals. A second edition was to come out the following year, but a radio play was a step too far.* Theo feared unsympathetic portrayal of the Partisans, heartbreak for EP and herself, and the contempt of those who might think they were pushing Frank's story for publicity's sake, making Frank unpopular with his friends. Even her good friend Nancy Nicholson – the recent death of whose son David had been unaccompanied by any fanfare – had said to Theo, 'You *do* get yourselves into the papers, don't you!'

---

Pain from terminal cancer and having to deal with officials infuriated EJ equally. Believing the legend that Frank had avowed himself Communist† and thus needlessly risked his life upset him greatly too. But disquiet at his own complicity may also have disturbed him. Frank's schooling at Winchester certainly inculcated the classical ideal of 'the good death, the public death', but his father had groomed him for the role of tragic English hero too. One schoolfellow maintained that

---

* Roger Woddis, playing in *The Russian Question* five nights a week at the Unity Theatre in London, had in November 1947 interested the BBC in a possible radio programme on Frank and *There is a Spirit in Europe*.

† A letter from Colonel Jack Collins to EJ dated 24 February 1945 suggests that Sharova's untruth that Frank died giving the clenched-fist salute might have been one source of EJ's dismay which caused him to baulk at a clause in Frank's will bequeathing a sum to the CP (Bodl. 5285 fol. 33). Final settlement of Frank's estate seems to have been accomplished in 1947. EP twice asserts that Frank declared himself Communist (*Beyond the Frontier*, p. 85). No Bulgarian source agrees – see, for example, Yanev, *The Man from the Legend*, ch. 4: 'he never disclosed his political affiliation'; Trŭnski (according to Yanev's account) typically recorded that, when asked what he thought of Communists, Frank said that he respected them, but was always careful to distance himself from any imputation about his own political beliefs. Once again Sharova's CP propaganda created mischief.

Frank's parents had a major responsibility for his end: he had never outgrown his upbringing. Not for nothing had he written in 1942, 'My father is the best-loved Englishman in India, my mother and grandfather the best-loved foreign folk in Syria . . . My dearest wish is to carve a similar niche for myself in Greece, Jugoslavia or Bulgaria.' He had moreover obsessively contemplated mortality, as his poems demonstrate, and prepared himself for immolation. Few poets have essayed so many epitaphs for themselves.

If Theo worried during the 1930s that they had 'almost broken Frank's spirit' (through refusal to offer him praise), EJ had infected Frank with his own alarmingly high-minded chivalry. EJ, believing in the heroic virtue of going to the edge, had as we have seen expressed in October 1940 the bloodthirsty sentiment that to become a man entailed necessary ordeals. He wrote that it should 'cost . . . everything a man has, to face the breaking of body and mind'. And Frank was also trying to redeem himself from his father's taunt in April 1943 – the month he started scheming to join SOE – that his life risked turning into 'a desultory tale'.

Moreover EJ had been writing a play about the recurrent type of Wandering Englishman in Balkan history. This was a character who – in EJ's view, like Byron – symbolically sacrifices himself to redeem Britain's historical guilt and bad faith by a 'gesture'. Frank, who deplored the influence of Byronism on Pushkin and Lermontov and had reasonable doubts about the 'mischievous doctrine' of atonement too,* none the less took an interest. In December 1943, when Frank opted to be dropped into Yugoslavia, EJ's 1924 play *Atonement* was restaged. Frank acted out his father's symbolic message himself, a sacrificial English lamb in the Balkans.

This accords with the most accurate† Bulgarian biography, Kiril Yanev's *The Man from the Legend* (2001), which starts by claiming that historically Great Britain has always been against Bulgaria, supporting the Ottoman Empire, and then at the Berlin Congress causing Bulgaria's

---

* Frank agreed with Rebecca West in *Black Lamb, Grey Falcon* (1941) that it was an amazing affront to suggest that God should exact and others tolerate a vicarious atonement, that is via Jesus Christ. He declared himself by contrast more and more drawn to Buddhism.

† Except that Yanev sometimes uses the unreliable Stowers Johnson as a source.

'ill-fated historical development'. Indeed Churchill himself called Bulgarians a 'peccant' or guilty people, deserving the 'sharp lesson' of having their cities bombed. Frank's sacrifice is thus to Yanev '[a] sort of atonement for the sins of the British leaders towards Bulgaria', and Frank is loved by Yanev's fellow Bulgarians for the same reason.

Frank's father was not prejudiced in favour of Bulgaria either. In a bitter letter to Major Last on 1 December 1944 EJ says he wishes Frank had stayed in Yugoslavia, whose villages were pro-Partisan and whose guerrillas were of proven quality. But two main reasons, EJ surmises, made Frank decide to join the march into Bulgaria, a country which EJ rightly saw to have been weighing the advantages of abandoning its support for Germany while waiting for the USSR to get close before surrendering. First, Frank's one clear directive was to stay with the Bulgarians. Secondly, Frank refused to allow them to think – after all they had been through – that he would let them face new dangers without him. EJ saw Frank as exhibiting a suicidal 'chivalry', in context a significant word.*

The word 'chivalry' merits reflection. We know that Frank, just before leaving for the Balkans, was for weeks in Cairo prevented from writing by a broken finger, acquired when trying to get some drunken soldiers off a tram only to have them put him through the window instead. 'One can't really blame them.' Not to blame Christmas drunks for causing you grievous bodily harm is indeed quixotic. But it was in character: the man who interpreted for him for three hours after his capture reported that Frank, so weak he lost consciousness, on being given a glass of water offered this first to Scott. That too has the ring of truth about it, as well as reprising the warrior-poet Sir Philip Sidney's famous end. When a cupful of water was brought to Sir Philip, mortally wounded at Zutphen in 1586, he handed it to another wounded comrade, saying chivalrously, 'Soldier: your need is greater than mine!'

Chivalry, too, arguably made Frank a lesser poet than Keith Douglas,

---

* Major Dugmore reported that 'few men would have taken such a stern view of their duty; he could have chosen a safer alternative, but at the last moment, he refused it, and marched off; I didn't see him again' (letter to EP from Kenneth Matthews, citing Dugmore's SOE report, 1945).

with whom he otherwise has much in common. Douglas died in the same week, at the same age (in Normandy), and also lived in awe of an heroic father and failed to experience happy sexual love. Both poets fought in North Africa where both wrote of the cruelty and cowardice of Italian soldiers, and both described looting. But Frank is more chivalrous to Italians and more shocked by the looting, and it is hard not to think that – for all his bohemian and Communist sympathies – he is ultimately a less original poet than Douglas, who might have had Frank in mind in his marvellously moving poem 'Aristocrats', which celebrates the chivalric hero's last stand:

> The noble horse with courage in his eye,
> clean in the bone, looks up at a shellburst:
> away fly the images of the shires but he puts the pipe back in his mouth.

> Peter was unfortunately killed by an 88;
> it took his leg away, he died in the ambulance.
> I saw him crawling on the sand, he said
> It's most unfair, they've shot my foot off.

> How can I live among this gentle
> obsolescent breed of heroes, and not weep?
> Unicorns, almost,
> for they are fading into two legends
> in which their stupidity and chivalry
> are celebrated. Each, fool and hero, will be an immortal.

> These plains were their cricket pitch
> and in the mountains the tremendous drop fences
> brought down some of the runners. Here then
> under the stones and earth they dispose themselves,
> I think with their famous unconcern.
> It is not gunfire I hear, but a hunting horn.

> Tunisia 1943

Frank was also far less sure of his vocation than Keith Douglas, who entrusted most of the poems he wrote in the desert to Terence Tiller and Lawrence Durrell. Frank considered both 'minor poets' and channelled his literary aspirations, if at all, through contacts back in London, or left them to his father to look after. Encouraged by a foreword in the second volume of *Penguin New Writing* soliciting contributions from serving soldiers, he in November 1941 sent two untitled stories to John Lehmann, together with a chivalrous stamped-and-addressed envelope, and waited one anxious calendar year before these were returned unread, with an official stamp indicating that damage had rendered the package undeliverable. He made no further attempt. His father's friend General Jack Collins published Frank's fine account of the Libyan campaign, 'Desert Memories', in the spring 1943 *Army Quarterly.*\* He did not submit his poems for publication: his father did so on his behalf.

Unlike Keith Douglas, Frank was unsure whether poetry would be his métier, and made no attempt to ingratiate himself with Cairo literati. 'The British Council people aren't awfully thrilling . . . Dancing attendance on . . . Roger Keyes and Prof Bryn Davies . . . is a galaxy of minor poets. Bernard Shaw, Terence Tiller, Lawrence Durrell,' he warned his parents on 18 December 1943. Frank knew Bryn Davies well enough to leave some of his effects with him when he was dropped into Serbia, while calling him 'a second-rate brain'.†

He frequented the elegant café Groppi's, enjoying their famous cakes cooked in clarified butter, but there is no evidence of his cultivating the doyenne of the Cairo literary and social scene Amy Smart or frequenting the Anglo-Egyptian Union at 179 Shria Fuad al Awali, haven of Cairo's English-speaking literary life, or contacting such Cairo literary magazines as *Parade*, *Personal Landscape* or *Salamander*. If he had had the time or inclination to network in literary Cairo, he would most

---

\* Frank sent this off in January 1943 (Bodl. 5285 fol. 30). 'Desert Memories' was in 1947 deservedly republished *in toto* in *There is a Spirit in Europe*.
† Frank was introduced to Bryn Davies by Hal Lidderdale and Roger Keyes (who was Davies's Assistant Professor) and, while it is possible that Davies failed to encourage Frank's literary aspirations, it is more likely that Frank never 'sold' himself.

likely have met Murdoch's future fiancé David Hicks, editing *Citadel* magazine from July 1942.

The fact is that Frank wondered whether writing poetry might be a youthful habit he would one day outgrow. Had he known that – like the mythical songster and greatest of poet-muses Orpheus – he was to die terribly and in Thrace, such foreknowledge would surely have elicited a wry smile.

In 1978 young Edward accepted an invitation to deliver the three Camp Lectures at Stanford University, choosing to return to the question of how Frank's sacrifice had been received on both sides of the Iron Curtain. The following summer he and Dorothy revisited Bulgaria where they were 'kidnapped' by officialdom and fed the legend that SOE Cairo had daily betrayed Claridges' positions to the Royalists. At exactly this time EP was equally disturbed and distressed by rumours circulated by a schoolfellow of Frank's to the effect that Frank had

EP and Theo at the graveside, July 1947.

entered Bulgaria only by threatening his Signals Sergeant with a pistol
– denied by Scott; that Frank was betrayed to the Fascists for a large
sum – possible; and that his end was 'unpleasant'. The strange symme-
try between these two opposing sets of legend helped inspire and drive
his narrative.

By 1981, when he gave the lectures, the arrival of Cruise missiles in
Britain had supervened. Edward, revered leader of the renewed movement for disarmament, was necessarily distracted by attacking the
opposing ideologies of the Cold War. He apologised that his three lectures
were consequently ill prepared. Their full title was 'Journey across the
Frontier: Tracking the Cold War to a Source: The Balkans, 1944'.

The Peace Movement informs *Beyond the Frontier*, the slim, elegant
book put together by Edward's widow and published four years after
his death, for Frank is here the Cold War's first martyr, wickedly
betrayed by both West and East, a thesis deserving scrutiny. Edward
thus ponders whether Dimitrov wished to destroy the Bulgarian
Communists of the 2nd Partisan Brigade with his murderous and
lunatic diktat that they proceed to Plovdiv. 'The Soviet state disliked
the self-activating revolutionary democracy of the Partisans only a little
less than did the western allies', for such Partisans – unlike Dimitrov
himself – had not learned to toe the Moscow line.

But *Beyond the Frontier* also indicts Strategic Air Command for
abandoning Frank and then Churchill for wanting him dead. To this
observer Frank's end already seems fated without such theories; the
culpability of SOE was not in abandoning Frank but in sending him
on an ill-thought-out mission in the first place, his doom made even
more probable by Dimitrov's intervention. But before considering EP's
new claims it is necessary to remember that 87 per cent of SOE files
were destroyed after 1945 and what remains today is a fraction of once
available evidence. Edward thought this destruction a malign attempt
to bury guilty secrets, which is one possibility. What is certain is that
much of the weeding was random and pointless, and establishment
conspiracy, if it existed, was less monolithic than Edward believed.

Yet Frank's loss aroused in EP many fears and suspicions. Visiting
Bulgaria in 1947 Edward – like Theo in a highly charged emotional

state – heartily disliked Frank's Winchester schoolfellow Robert Conquest, now ACC Press Officer, whom he thought a 'very hostile' establishment agent, actively obstructing all honours due to Frank. In reality Conquest, though now famous as Stalinism's scourge, had been in 1937–8 a CP member, and accounts himself in 1947 still sympathetic to the USSR. It was Conquest himself who approached Vladimir Topencharov, Bulgaria's Deputy Foreign Minister and Press Director, with the suggestion that honouring Frank would bring credit equally to the Bulgarian CP and to Britain. It was thanks to Conquest that the Bulgars renamed Prokopnik station after Frank, placed a bas-relief of him there, and staged the ceremonies attended by his mother and EP. Of the seven British soldiers who died in Bulgaria with Claridges and Mulligatawny, Frank alone was singled out for beatification.

Edward further believed that Frank's Partisans were deliberately starved of sorties.* He could find only twenty-four sorties flown between February and May 1944, a time when urgent Cairo memos bemoan the bad weather that delays sorties and emphasise the desperate need for them, to avoid repetition of the disaster that befell Mostyn Davies. Yet if such a reduction had coincided with Frank's odyssey across Bulgaria, Cairo by EP's own admission received no messages from Frank after 11 May, so no sorties could in any case have reached Claridges, on the move non-stop and thus unable to establish pinpoints for drops.

In fact Sweet-Escott claims that, after a reduction due to the claims of Yugoslavia, sorties to Bulgaria actually increased, while Dencho Znepolski remembered that in March, April and May Partisans were 'better armed than the regular [that is, Bulgarian] army – every Partisan group of eight had one machine-gun, four sub-machine-guns and loads of bombs and ammunition at their disposal'. Znepolski details air deliveries for which he signed inventoried receipts, sometimes driving more than 200 ox-drawn sleighs to a mountain top to collect muni-tions that required many horse-drawn carts to take the supplies away

---

* EP claims that on 21 April 1943 all Balkan operations were put on hold while elsewhere writing of the sky on 10 and 11 May thundering with containers from around thirty sorties (*Beyond the Frontier*, pp. 32 and 93).

after they had been brought down from the mountains. He specifies 5,000 rifles, between 300 and 400 machine guns, between 700 and 800 sub-machine guns, much ammunition, sanitary materials, high-quality warm British Army clothes, waterproof and snow-resistant leather shoes, woollen socks, fine woollen underwear, the whole khaki-clad squad and 2nd Partisan Brigade starting to look like English troops.

British sorties aside, they also acquired such large quantities of Italian and German guns that they hid some in dug-outs and ammunition dumps. They even tried to return guns borrowed from Yugoslav Partisans: the English reproached them for disposing of items specifically dropped for Bulgarian use.

---

EP also believed that Frank's murder on 10 June had the tacit approval of Churchill, who certainly hated Communists and spoke of getting rid of them. On 13 April in a minute: 'We are purging all our secret establishments of Communists because we know they owe no allegiance to us or our cause and will always betray secrets to the Soviet, even while we are working together.' By 'purging', Churchill surely meant sacking rather than liquidating Communists, but a sleight-of-hand on EP's part blurs the difference.

EP further maintained that the Bulgarians made it a condition that, if the UK stopped stimulating Partisan/Communist activity, Bulgaria would agree to turn democratic. Two facts trouble this hypothesis. In early June – during the precise week of Frank's imprisonment – Churchill formally proposed that Bulgaria post-war should be in the Soviet area of concern. The UK faced major problems in Greece and Yugoslavia, so in a tit-for-tat policy of benign neglect, it agreed to ignore Soviet interference in Bulgaria in return for Soviet tolerance of British interference in Greece. Churchill had no post-war game plan for Bulgaria for which Frank could be sacrificed. Moreover within twenty-four hours of Frank's capture, on 1 June, Dobri Bozhilov's pro-German government resigned in response to Soviet pressure, and Ivan Bagrianov's pro-Western Cabinet did not formally take office until the day of Frank's execution. With whom was this supposed British deal entailing Frank's murder to be brokered?

This fast-changing politics might not encompass the whole story. It is always possible that intentions sown earlier that year by Churchill saw a belated harvest. What remains certain is that Frank was killed by Fascists. If his destruction had also been plotted by both Churchill in London and Dimitrov in Moscow that would have turned him into a proto-hero of the New Left – a forerunner of EP in 1980, then fighting capitalism and Stalinism simultaneously.

———

'He was the kind of boy who became the butt of bullies and I, too little to protect him, would intervene with flailing fists and tears.' This is EP's seminal recollection of their time together at the Dragon School, when EP was six or seven and Frank eleven. Its relevance is clear: Frank was once again in 1944 the butt of bullies when EP's tears could stop neither his torture nor his murder. EP in 1978 recalled Frank's genera-tion as 'too bloody innocent by half . . . too open to the world, and too loyal to each other to live.'

Survivor guilt – as well as the nuisance of being his mother's less favoured child – travelled with him. 'It is by you that he [Frank] will live on,' EJ in 1944 had enjoined, and Frank's influence on Edward cannot be exaggerated. Contrary to popular misconception EP played no part in the famous Communist Party Historians' Group, but was heavily involved in the Party's organisation for writers whose company he preferred, and throughout the 1950s taught as much literature as history to his WEA students in Yorkshire. Edward, like Frank (and their father), at first thought himself foremost a poet.

One day in the 1960s Theo was unnerved to learn from a fellow train passenger reading her younger son's *The Making of the English Working Class* that this major work of research and synthesis pioneered the then entirely new 'history from below', that he was widely regarded as the leading historian of his generation, and that he was acclaimed by some a genius.

Family piety absorbed him. It is not just that his first and final books commemorate Frank; he spent part of one New England summer researching his and Frank's Jessup ancestry; and among his last books is a homage to his father, *Alien Homage: Edward Thompson and Rabindranath Tagore*.

Part of Edward's life work would be what he called 'liberating the intentions of the dead', among whom Frank was foremost. When, in 1956, he and his wife Dorothy faced the trauma of leaving the CP, Edward was affronted by Bill Carritt's reproach that Frank would have stayed. Furious, he wrote a very sharp – even for him – letter to Bill. He doubted that Frank would have stayed even as long as 1956, and this doubt seems just. Frank was the least doctrinaire of Communists – in Robert Conquest's felicitous phrase, more 'contrarian' than apparatchik. Tony Forster never took Frank, either, for a dogmatic Communist.

Edward was inspired throughout each phase of his writing by what he memorably called 'the Decade of Heroes' from 1936 to 1946, when Marxism was still in his view authentically liberal and individualistic; and chief among those heroes was Frank. Edward revered his beloved elder brother as a touchstone, an emotional and moral reference point in all his writing and political thinking. His belief in the 'total mendacity' of modern nation-states owed something to his reading of Frank's last months too.

EP died in 1993 and his daughter, the writer Kate Thompson, provided two moving footnotes. She thought it strange – and perhaps just as well – that her father should have died without ever learning the exact details of Frank's death. Not that it made any difference to the story. Frank's power for her resided far more in the voice that still comes through his poetry and his letters than in the archetype of the hero. In some ways his death puts him where he would have wanted to be: 'pulls him into the present even more firmly, into a common stream of humanity where people are still being shot in ditches every day . . .'

Among the things in her father's study was a package of soil with Theo's handwriting, which she had taken from Frank's grave in 1947. Kate had no idea what to do with it. 'Nothing was as difficult to deal with as that packet. I can still see the room now, with nothing left in it except the furniture and that little corner of a foreign field left on a desk beneath the window . . .' In the end she took the packet outside to the magnolia tree beneath which her father had died. And under this Kate scattered the soil. Kate's poem, 'Lily-White Boys', written around this time, contemplates the grief of all families who lose a child in war:

> In this full rolling flood of years
> There is somehow time,
> And somehow plenty,
> For remembrance.
> Of how each evening brought
> Returning heroes,
> The climber, the window breaker,
> The bearer of the bleeding nose,
> As they raced against it,
> The wind sprang dog-rose blossoms on their cheeks.
>
> If we had known our sons were born as extras,
> How then would we have built their boyish courage?
> Look here for this is how it is.
> This image is your destiny.
> For they were laid out, even as
> In funereal green
> They fell.
> On their faces the final bloom
> Lily-white.

---

Theo in 1948 (as we have seen) wished Frank had married – 'had, at least, had some home of his own for his spirit on earth. Iris was not enough.' Did love of Iris cause Frank to risk his life? An angry letter from Michael Foot in 1943, when Frank was disturbed by her loss of virginity, warned him, as we have also seen, against taking suicidal risks in his longing to finish either Fascism or himself: 'Neither a true choice nor a true opposition.' His decision to enter Bulgaria came soon after he learned of her affair with Michael: was his reckless disregard for his survival a peevish reprisal for her troubled love life? Iris never said so.

She protested that she could not regard him 'as a suicide, however noble-minded ... he ... so much knew how to enjoy living', while acknowledging to EP:

> all the feelings of sickness about not having loved him enough – which was true at the start, though not later. And the sheer sickness of loss. You have a difficult job [commemorating him]. Then his opinions, his splendid positive uncompromising faith in the world's people. Oneself, one goes on changing, and can't argue out with him one's shifts of opinion on the USSR, one's compromises with life. It's not easy to write about him, even a few paragraphs of a letter, he was pure gold.

Iris sent in November 1945 a selection of Frank's letters to Theo to use in *There is a Spirit in Europe*. Theo explained to EP that Frank had 'in several instances said things more clearly to her than to any of us', and she is the only non-Thompson in the memorial volume thus honoured. On her return from Bulgaria in August 1947 full of the moving scenes she had witnessed, Theo invited Iris to stay at Bledlow

Iris Murdoch on Oxford Street, winter 1946–7.

for two nights, and probably gave her Frank's edition of Catullus, found on him after he was shot.

Frank came increasingly to haunt Iris. He first appears in an abandoned wartime novel as Mark, who wishes to write a book on Frank's favourite Greek poet Pindar. Mark is acutely focused as having the rare combination of 'great intelligence with great warmth'.* 'Voi che sapete', which Iris had heard in Frank's rooms in New College in spring 1939, makes an appearance. Mark 'wants to act, he wants to commit himself', and feels consumed by a flame of love enabling him to rise above 'the mud of ambiguity' and indecision in which the others are embroiled. He is to be offered – but may reject – an Oxford Fellowship. A lengthy analysis of the last free Spanish elections in February 1936 reflects Frank's view of the Second World War as a continuation by other means of the Spanish struggle. Mark identifies more with Lenin than with Christ, since Lenin is 'less concerned with the value of his individual righteousness' and thus the more completely self-effacing of the two.

In 1975 a retired schoolmaster called Stowers Johnson published his bad book about Frank entitled *Agents Extraordinary*. Murdoch wrote angrily to *The Times* about its portrayal of Frank as a grim and fanatical megalomaniac trying to be Lawrence of Bulgaria, rashly and romantically leading his men towards the false dawn of a liberated Bulgaria. Her Frank 'had a horror of violence' and never dreamed of himself as a hero but was 'delicate, scrupulous and tender . . . never the victim of dreams of violence or illusions of grandeur'.

She captured her own sense of grief and mysterious causality best in the long poem she dedicated in 1977 to his memory, 'The Agamemnon Class, 1939', ingeniously conflating the death of Frank with that of that earlier hero, Achilles, on Troy's 'windy plain'.

> What was it for? Guides tell a garbled tale.
> The hero's tomb is a disputed mound.

* Philippa Foot observed in 1999 that in John Bayley Iris at last found someone who resembled Frank in being both brilliant and warm-hearted, combining – like Iris Murdoch herself – head and heart.

What really happened on the windy plain?
The young are bored by stories of war.
And you, the other young, who stayed there
In the land of the past, are courteous and pale,
Aloof, holding your fates.
We have to tell you that it was not in vain.
Even grief dates, and even Niobe
At last was fed, and you
Are all pain, and yet without pain,
As is the way of the dead.

In January 1979 at the Bulgarian Embassy she recorded a TV programme about Frank which she found moving and upsetting. At the end the director gave her a Roman coin sent him with an anonymous letter from someone present at Frank's death – presumably a collaborator. The letter writer said that Frank when captured had in his pocket a volume of Catullus and that coin. Having heard of the documentary film being made about Frank, he asked that the coin be given to 'the most suitable person' in England.*

She wrote to General Trǔnski, who was involved with the film and writing his own book on Frank, that he:

> was a very various person . . . gentle, quiet, very reticent and modest and also eccentric in a very English way. He didn't seem in the least framed to be a soldier. In fact he was very like . . . a sort of English hero who is very, very quiet and is interested in flowers and birds . . . One wouldn't have imagined him as a soldier, but he was, when it came to it, a very good and brave soldier . . . he was a very absolute man . . . This absoluteness, courage, this feeling of being willing to make sacrifices was part of his character. One wasn't surprised when he became the kind of hero he was. We who loved Frank waited most anxiously to see him again, but when it was not to be, one felt that it was as he would have wished it. He died

---

* The volume of Catullus authenticated the coin. She, Tony Forster and EP contemplated writing a book together about Frank; nothing came of this.

for a cause that he believed in . . . I think he was someone who was very
happy . . . and died in a way he would have understood or approved, if
one can say that about somebody's death when they die so young.

And she wrote to EP around 1980 that 'In a sense of course it wasn't
worth it, nothing in the subsequent state of the world seems worth it in
relation to such destruction, because of the complex nature of causality
and because of the shabbiness of the outcome. And yet of course –'.
The sentence is left deliberately unfinished.

The night of 26 July 1980 she had a significant dream that she had
married both John Bayley and Frank, and was nervous of how this
*ménage à trois* would work out. But they all got along splendidly, and
were happy together. Frank appeared at the top of a steep slope, dressed
as a soldier, wearing a black cap that foreshadowed his murder.

In 1988 Iris announced to the *Mail on Sunday* that she and Frank,
though not engaged, had 'hoped to be married'; friends who had known
both Frank and Iris well, such as M. R. D. Foot and Leo Pliatzky, were
bemused by this rewriting of history. Since she set store by the truth,
what prompted it? It has been argued that his assumption of the role of
tragic hero required his recasting in this larger role as her fiancé – 'each
need[ing] to be nearer the centre of the other's story to give the drama of
his execution its due weight'. But if so, why did she wait over forty years?
In any case, just as she came to call herself Anglo-Irish, and to imply a
grander ancestry than was the case, so with a novelist's fabulating imagination she unquestionably believed this invention too. She told close
friends that her love-life had frequently been unhappy and out of balance:
either she or her beloved cared too much for the other. Frank thus became
the first significant possible husband who had eluded her, in a series that
notably included the refugee poet Franz Steiner, whom she very probably
would indeed have married, but who died in 1952.

Certainly Frank's life inspired her and he became one of her noteworthy
muses. Thus Frank's death could serve new purposes. He influenced her
depiction of ascetic warriors: Felix in *An Unofficial Rose* (1962) and the
Buddhist General James Arrowby in *The Sea, The Sea* (1978). She is remarkable among liberal novelists in thus treating the military profession

sympathetically, emphasising its propensity for self-sacrifice rather than for violence; Frank Thompson was a big reason for this. Not that her picture of Frank was ever entirely tame, and when Philippa Foot intuited that the opposition between the wild Pat Dumay in *The Red and the Green* (1965) and the more hidebound Andrew Chase-White reflected the rivalry between Frank and Michael Foot, Iris concurred. Her Frank was rebellious too, and not simply otherworldly. When, at the end of *The Red and the Green*, Frances thinks of the 'inconceivably brave' Irish dead of Easter 1916, 'made young and perfect for ever', Iris is surely thinking of Frank. EP too compared Frank's death with the 'symbolic confrontation' of Easter 1916.

In *The Black Prince* (1973) Iris's alter ego says that she reveres no one except great artists and 'those who say No to tyrants'; it was Frank who had died defying tyranny. Then *The Book and the Brotherhood* (1987) envisages a confrontation with a zealous figure who, like the dead Frank, has stayed ideologically pure while the world around him has compromised its ideals.

One of Iris's final diary entries, in November 1995, invokes his memory. And thus, too, in her last and unpublished book of philosophy Iris wrote of those who resisted Nazism and Stalinism as 'reflections of pure goodness, a proof of [Good's] connexion with us as a reality, as a real possibility'. She surely had Frank in mind.[*] Iris's friend Philippa Foot, who brought Iris the news of Frank's death, shared this view of him, and it fed her interest in the book entitled *Dying We Live* – prison letters from Germans executed for defying the Nazis, who wished their own symbolic sacrifice of life itself to witness the depravity and cruelty of Nazism. Frank's value, as it were, for both Philippa Foot and Iris consisted in his living proof of such connections during the most terrible of centuries.[†] For Iris Murdoch Frank grew to combine the roles of heroic martyr, potential husband and lost soulmate.

---

[*] The first chapter of this book, which concerns Heidegger and Wittgenstein, has now been published in Justin Broackes (ed.), *Iris Murdoch: Philosopher*, Oxford, 2011.

[†] Iris's friendship with EP proved durable. She wrote in 1958–9 at his request a review of Pasternak's *Dr Zhivago* for his journal the *New Reasoner*, borrowed his second name when in *A Severed Head* (1961) creating her American demon Palmer Anderson, and flew out with him to New Delhi to commemorate Indira Gandhi in 1987.

Today, with benefit of hindsight, Frank's mission reads as if doomed from the start. In 1944, by contrast, no one could have foretold exactly when the unstable Bulgarian government would collapse, when the Russians would arrive to trigger regime change, or when the long-awaited popular uprising might begin. Wars are not won if people do not take what seem to be desperate chances, and Frank's mission was one such.

Frank had managed to equip some 500 Partisans after Mostyn Davies's death and to maintain contact with his base. He had won the trust of a 'vital, unruly people', with good reason to be suspicious of all foreigners. During the terrible march he was once so exhausted he fell into a river, asleep. Yet he never complained, and always declined the offer of a horse, saying that he was young – still only twenty-three – and that the horse concerned should carry a woman or a wounded Partisan. Of all the SOE officers who died in Eastern Europe, he alone is thought of kindly by the country in which he fell. Generations of Bulgarians will always associate England with the martyr of Bulgarian liberation.

A Russian joke runs: Communism purveyed a certain future, while rendering the past totally unpredictable. So Frank and the other BLOs were first seen in Bulgaria as heroic allies in the fight against Fascism, a mystique sensationally enhanced by CPGB Secretary Harry Pollitt's reference in December 1948 to Frank as 'one of our party members'.* The Kostov trials a few months later suddenly reversed this: BLOs were now imperialist agents infiltrating on behalf of the Western Allies, and two prominent Partisan comrades – Znepolski and Trŭnski – were brutally interrogated for months in jail, branded spies for having associated with Frank and other BLOs, as also with Titoism.† Rehabilitation

---

* At the Fifth Congress of the Bulgarian Communist Party.
† On 31 March 1949 Kostov was dismissed from his post as acting President of the Council of Ministers and in June indicted for spreading anti-Soviet propaganda. Dismissed also from the Central Committee, expelled from the Party and deprived of his seat in the National Assembly, he was tried that December along with ten others. Among grounds given for his execution was the charge that he had acted under orders from the British, American and Yugoslav intelligence services and had contact with

in the 1970s – when Trŭnski, now Deputy Minister of Defence, commemorated Frank in *Grateful Bulgaria* – was followed after 1989 by BLOs now turning into Soviet agents intent on establishing Soviet hegemony. As if to illustrate this Kafkaesque trajectory Prokopnik station, renamed 'Thompson' after Frank in 1947, was then threatened with denaming after the Berlin Wall came down.

Around 1994 Frank's memory was kept alive by the British Defence Attaché in Sofia, Colonel Robert Pearson, who greatly admired Frank. His picture hung in the Embassy and Pearson arranged a fiftieth anniversary service near the Litakovo monument to Frank and his comrades. Pearson took Frank's sister-in-law Dorothy Thompson and her eldest son Ben along the trail the Partisans had followed during their long march into Bulgaria – a walk that he had previously videoed.

A man who had led a Partisan column agreed to meet Pearson to share his memories, but was visited first by the secret police who claimed he had been a British agent supplied with British weapons. This was 1994, post-Communism, and yet he changed his mind about speaking to Pearson. Truth-telling in a small country with bullying neighbours will always be tough; outlandish conspiracy theories abound. But a recent book suggests how Frank's reputation may settle. Kiril Yanev, a Fatherland Front journalist, fell under Frank's spell when doing his military service after September 1944, spent decades collecting stories about him and published *The Man from the Legend* in 2001. What follows is culled mainly from Yanev.

Relations between Bulgarian Partisans and British liaison officers were strictly formal; use of titles emphasised distance and minimised risk of false promises. Both Davies and Frank were reticent, and Frank admitted only that he was a Labour supporter, a democrat and a staunch anti-Fascist. But Mostyn Davies's reserve was experienced as arrogant and supercilious and he was personally blamed for the non-appearance of sorties; while Frank's was warm-hearted and sympathetic to the Partisan

---

members of the 'British Intelligence Service'. In the war between Muscovite and home-grown Communists, of which Kostov was the best-known victim, contact with BLOs such as Frank was now presented as proof of 'treason'.

cause, and when rebuked for the non-appearance of sorties, he evinced a sense of personal shame that by contrast won him credit.

Frank could express a lot quietly and simply. When on 19 May a village meeting was called, at which Vlado Trichkov, Gocho Gopin and Frank spoke, his speech was vivid, emotional and full of sense; one survivor recalled that 'Frank was a true poet . . .' He enjoyed humour, joking that not all Britons were conquering imperialists – possibly an attempt to smooth feathers ruffled by Davies. If Frank elicited sensitive information about the structure of the Fatherland Front and Partisan movement, he did so, unlike Davies, without forfeiting liking or trust. While BLOs were supposed to stay above the fray politically and support no single faction, it no doubt helped that, while denying that he was himself Communist, Frank admitted that he 'respected' Communists.

Davies managed two phrases in Bulgarian that point to the terrible realities of their long march, Partisans often falling asleep in a standing position: 'Marching not good' and 'There *will* be arms supplies.' Frank, who sometimes muddled Bulgarian with Serbo-Croat, learned Bulgarian songs and poetry. He was a very intelligent man of high culture with an expressive face: tall, young, slim and handsome. He spoke slowly, seriously with a concentration somehow unbecoming to his age. Sometimes he burned some note or lay on the ground, his eyes fixed on the sky as if in deep thought. He had the foresight to insist that the wireless set and horse to carry it be kept away from any fighting, together with some strong men to carry the set if anything happened to the horse.

There are other touching vignettes. Frank in prison, requesting through the open door with gestures a cigarette from a middle-aged lady. The next day she shows up again, when food is served, managing to slip him a packet of cheap cigarettes. He feels in his pockets for something to repay her kindness but everything has been taken from him. A kind smile lighting up his tired and pain-stricken face, he rips the right epaulette off his shoulder saying, 'I have nothing else I can give as a token of appreciation: take this as a keepsake.' That has the authentic Frankish ring about it.

On capture he bravely insisted he be granted POW status. He requested medicines, bread and spring onions, which he got, his first food for fifteen days, and yoghurt, which Stoyanov jested he would get plenty of in Kingdom Come. He complained once when lunch was late.

Kocho Stoyanov was notorious for making Litakovo, where he committed many atrocities, a Golgotha for Partisans. Yordanka was horribly tortured; Frank, too, was physically broken by savage beatings and probable torture,* yet police records show that he never gave anything away. When villagers asked why one gendarme beat Frank so hard, he replied: 'Because he keeps his head high.'

Stoyanov's aide-de-camp, Dimiter Avgardski, who helped execute Frank but whose own life was spared, recorded his memories for both Trŭnski (1979) and Yanev (2001). Frank smoked a pipe, he never lost heart, his guards respected him. His boots were stolen and he said nothing when Stoyanov, to humiliate him, stepped on his naked feet. He conducted himself with poise and dignity and did not look frightened or alarmed. The manner of his death gave his captors 'a strong shock'.†

They walked outside under the evening sky on Saturday 10 June, along a country path, their steps heading uphill to Turskoto Kale,‡ the guards swearing. They stopped by some barely discernible, crumbling walls, Avgardski's torch lighting up the prisoners' faces to identify them. Frank was tied to Hristo Vasilev Gurbov and Lazar Stoyanov Atanasov.

Captain Yanko Stoyanov§ said: 'Major Thompson, we are going to

* Bulgarian Partisans were subjected to electric shocks. Dorothy Thompson (letter to author, 15 Feb. 1999) recalled the film-maker Tony Simmons at an unspecified later date uncovering some of Frank's clothing, whose condition strongly suggested torture.
† This 'shock' was surely the realisation that what Frank represented politically would supplant Fascism. Avgardski is testifying, probably in the 1970s, at a time long before it seemed feasible that Communism in its turn would fall and be supplanted: the possibility that Avgardski needed to propitiate the powers-that-be may place a limit on his veracity. So his version of Frank's end with speeches from both parties is probably prettified to give the event gravitas. Naku Staminov's account (see Prologue above) seems more probable, with Frank yelling in angry protest.
‡ The Turkish Citadel.
§ Captain Yanko Stoyanov, who executed Frank, was no relation to the General Kocho

execute you by shooting.' Thompson replied: 'Remember that my government has sent me here and will be looking for me. And you, captain, will
be held responsible.' A gendarme called Pacho went up to the three men
tied together, tripping Frank's feet so that he fell face down, dragging the
other two as he did so: the preferred position for executing prisoners.

Before Frank can be shot – according to Yanev's and Avgardski's
narrative – green sparkles start to swarm in front of his eyes, causing
him wonderment. Fireflies, imitating the myriad stars above, twinkle,
flicker and fill him with joy.

———————

These fireflies function in Yanev's narrative as outward signs of Frank's
apotheosis – they are Bulgaria's parting gift to a man sacrificing himself
to safeguard the nation's future, and making 'history itself bow before
the stubborness of his conscience'. And yet Frank would have hated
special treatment, being cast in this way as a hero when so many –
including Mostyn Davies, Nick Munroe, James Shannon, Watts,
Walker, Trichkov, Gocho Gopin and Yordanka and countless others –
all died and are forgotten, and his Bulgarian comrades suffered so
abominably, their severed and sometimes eyeless heads piked in the
village square before his own murder.

But then, perhaps exactly because he would so genuinely have hated
being invidiously singled out in this manner, his good name in Bulgaria
is assured. Frank's raid provoked the Germans and the Royalist Bulgarians
into reprisals so atrocious that these helped prepare the ground for their
own overthrow: in this way even the Partisans' defeat helped them achieve
their aims. He stands for internationalist comradeship, self-sacrifice and
that brief moment of the Popular Front so long ago. A time when hatred
of Fascism lent sense and purpose to life and death alike.

———————

Stoyanov who interrogated and (probably) tortured him, and who blew his brains out
in Pancherevo, a suburb of Sofia, in early September 1944 before the Partisan patrols
could find him. Moreover, neither apparently corresponds to any 'Stoyanov' in the letter
sent to the ACC detailing the punishment of Frank's murderers.

An English-speaking acquaintance of Yanev's was assigned an unexpected task. A bulky, worn and muddy haversack of strong green
canvas, with many compartments and pockets, zips and fasteners, was
carried into his office. It belonged to some English officer who had
been taken prisoner after the battle of Batulya and he was ordered to go
through it and provide a detailed description thereof.

There were no guns, cartridges, maps or compasses: these had all gone to
those interrogating the Englishman. The translator had to deal only with
many papers needed for someone traversing long distances through valleys,
mountains and rivers, until being caught and taken prisoner. The clerk
found English–Slav dictionaries in one of which a bullet had stuck, hollow-
ing it out and saving the life of its owner. He also found diaries and notes:
observations on the Bulgarian national character, episodes of Bulgarian
history, descriptions of different Partisans and associates, portraits of people
met on the road and landscapes. In one notebook the translator found
something unusual: an 'English to Tran dictionary'* with colourful words,
phrases and anecdotes from the Tran region. But what moved him most
was an English translation of a short story by the good writer Yordan
Yovkov (1880–1937), 'Along the Wire'. Years later Yanev learned that Frank
had worked on this translation together with Gocho Gopin in their few
spare minutes. 'So maybe that was their secret occupation,' joked one of
the Partisan commanders who was told this story.

The clerk reported that the haversack was the mobile office of an
exceptionally gifted, original, highly intelligent personality who, despite
all the hardships of the battles and the marches, despite all the risks and
dangers which he had faced at every turn, had kept thinking rationally,
gathering observations and material for his future work – a man who
remained deep down in his soul a poet.[†]

---

* Tran is a Bulgarian dialect spoken in the areas north of Sofia, named after the Tran
region near the border with Serbia. Hence the surname Transki/Trŭnski.

† Frank's haversack may have been destroyed by ignorant police officers or stolen, or
taken to Moscow by the NKVD, the Soviet secret police, something that happened to
the belongings of other BLOs in the Communist bloc. No leads in Moscow's direction
have at the time of writing yielded results.

———

Ten years after the war Dorothy Thompson was out walking with Uncle Alfred and one of her and EP's very small boys near Halifax in the West Riding. Family jokes abounded about Alfred – simple but not confused or unpleasant – whom Theo and EJ took under their wing. (When asked for his favourite record, Alfred replied, 'I like to hear the Bishop of Croydon speak occasionally on a Sunday morning.') A Yorkshire neighbour greeted Dorothy and Alfred and admired the baby, saying idly: 'Ah he's a little soldier!'

Alfred flew into a rage and replied that he would certainly *not* be a soldier. 'I had a brother and a nephew who were both soldiers and were killed in the two world wars, and thank you very much but *my* great-nephew is not going to go out to any war.' It was not hysterical or loud and Dorothy Thompson thought it very moving.

# Appendix

# ADVICE TO THE RELATIVE OF A MAN WHO IS MISSING

In view of the official notification that your relative is missing, you will naturally wish to hear what is being done to trace him.

The Service Departments make every endeavour to discover the fate of missing men, and draw upon all likely sources of information about them.

A man who is missing after an engagement may possibly be a prisoner of war. Continuous efforts are made to speed up the machinery whereby the names and camp addresses of prisoners of war can reach this country. The official means is by lists of names prepared by the enemy Government. These lists take some time to compile, especially if there is a long journey from the place of capture to a prisoners of war camp. Consequently " capture cards " filled in by the prisoners themselves soon after capture and sent home to their relatives are often the first news received in this country that a man is a prisoner of war. That is why you are asked in the accompanying letter to forward at once any card or letter you may receive, if it is the first news you have had.

Even if no news is received that a missing man is a prisoner of war, endeavours to trace him do not cease. Enquiries are pursued not only among those who were serving with him, but also through diplomatic channels and the International Red Cross Committee at Geneva.

Further, foreign broadcasts which include names of prisoners of war are listened to by official listeners working continuously day and night.

The moment reliable news is obtained from any of these sources it is sent to the Service Department concerned. They will pass the news on to you at once, if they are satisfied that it is reliable.

There is, therefore, a complete official service designed to secure for you and to tell you all discoverable news about your relative. This official service is also a very human service, which well understands the anxiety of relatives and will spare no effort to relieve it.

2/44.   F.4092.   P.5194.   40,000.   6/44.   Gp.8   F. & C. Ltd.

# Notes

## Abbreviations

*BF* = E. P. Thompson, *Beyond the Frontier: The Politics of a Failed Mission, Bulgaria 1944*, London, 1997

Bodl. = Bodleian Library, E. J. Thompson papers

CN = Catherine Nicholson

CWA = conversation with author

DT = Dorothy Thompson

EJ = E. J. Thompson

EP = E. P. Thompson

FT = Frank Thompson

IM = (Dame) Iris Murdoch

KUA = Kingston University Archive

Lago = Mary Lago, *India's Prisoner: A Biography of Edward John Thompson, 1886–1946*, Columbia, MO, 2001

LTA = letter or email to author

MRDF = Michael R. D. Foot

SK = Simon Kusseff

*Spirit* = *There is a Spirit in Europe: A Memoir of Frank Thompson*, London, 1947; 2nd edn, 1948 (unless otherwise stated, references are to the 1947 edn)

UNC = uncatalogued papers from the E. P. Thompson collection in the Bodleian, identified by date

*WAW* = *Iris Murdoch, A Writer at War: Letters and Diaries 1938–1946*, ed. Peter J. Conradi, London, 2010

## Prologue: 'The Story of a Great Englishman'

1 'a mock trial': this trial legend recurs in Freeman Dyson, *Disturbing the Universe* (1979), Fred Inglis, *The Cruel Peace* (1991) and EP, *Beyond the Frontier* (1997).

3 'nursery rhymes': the lyrics are by Assen Bossev, famous writer of children's poetry; music by Krassimir Kyurkchiiski.

6 'Five other British writers': Rod Bailey, Alan Ogden, Simon Kusseff, a newspaper columnist interested in Frank and Iris Murdoch, and Kenneth Sinclair-Loutit (1913–2003) who entertained various colourful hypotheses about Frank, such as that he might have been, as well as an expendable probe and an honourable soldier, an agent of Churchill, a Soviet agent or a Titoist.

6 'a bulky three-part "Chronology"': this now lives in the Iris Murdoch archive in Kingston University: AS6/1/59.

6 'conducted with Frank's friends': while I remain very grateful for this help, unacknowledged interpolations in Kusseff's work created so much confusion that I had to return to original sources in the Bodleian Library and elsewhere.

7 'Lord of Appeal [mark: *ten*]': Robin Maugham, *Escape from the Shadows*, London, 1972, p. 118. Maugham started a progressive magazine called *Convoy* in which he interested EP.

8 'our own virtue': FT to EP, 5 June 1943, UNC.

9 'highly inaccurate': Basil Davidson to EP, undated, 1980, UNC.

11 'framed to be a soldier': Slavcho Trūnski, *Grateful Bulgaria*, Sofia, 1979, p. 15.

# Chapter 1: The Missionary Position

16 'the serenely beautiful child': Storm Jameson, *Journey from the North*, London, 1969, p. 237.

16 'lose a sovereign': DT, CWA.

16 'a graceful upper-class blonde': as evoked in his *Burmese Silver*, London, 1937, and his poem 'South Oxfordshire', in *100 Poems*, London, 1994, p. 88. DT recalled EJ's admiration for Lady Vansittart as for someone from this 'stable'.

16 'self-righteous men': Bodl. 5356 fol. 27.

17 'closed down so suddenly': Bodl. d. 2702 fol. 62.

17 'Boutros al-Boustani': Bistani, as Jessup spells him, founded the National School in Beirut, was editor of the first modern Arabic encyclopedia and the first two Arabic newspapers. He spoke French, Italian and English, read Syriac, Hebrew, Aramaic, Latin and Greek and translated the Bible into Arabic.

20 'Nominal Christians': it is worth recalling the antiquity of these Nominal Christians. The distinguished Hourani family, whom Dr Daniel Bliss converted to Jessup's form of Presbyterianism, accounted themselves Christian by the seventh century, before Islam reached Syria: see Cecil Hourani, *An Unfinished Odyssey*, London, 1984, p. 33.

20 'a bitter feeling of . . . party spirit': H. H. Jessup, *The Women of the Arabs*, New York, 1873, p. 46.

20 'light and liberty': H. H. Jessup, *Fifty-three Years in Syria*, New York, 1910, p. 113.

20 'acted out in Life': ibid., p. 91.

20 'Statistics were massaged': A. Tibawi, *American Interests in Syria 1800–1901*, Oxford, 1966, pp. 186 and 280.

20  'Cathartic or Emetic': Jessup, *Fifty-three Years*, ch. 7.
21  'amanuensis and drudge': Faith Jessup Kahrl, *Memoirs*, privately printed, 1989, p. 17.
22  'outdid them': Tibawi, *American Interests*, p. 119.
22  'throw stones': Theo to FT, Apr. 1943, UNC.
23  'conformity expected': Tibawi, *American Interests*, p. 276.
23  'lice and bedbugs': Jessup, *The Women of the Arabs*, 'A Chapter for Children'.
23  'language of instruction' George Antonius, *The Arab Awakening*, London, 1938, p. 94: this changed to English from 1880.
23  'literature to politics': ibid.
24  'Armenian': Tibawi, *American Interests*, p. 133 n. 2.
24  'held by Jessup': ibid., p. 281.
24  'natives': ibid., p. 237.
24  '$200 a month': ibid., p. 211.
24  'luxury': ibid., p. 210 n. 3.
26  'rectitudes': Kahrl, *Memoirs*, p. 149.
27  'seventeenth century': Theo writing her Vassar Alumnae record.
27  '$27 million': *Time*, 26 Feb. 1965.
27  'behave obligingly': Kahrl, *Memoirs*, p. 203. Wealthy Uncle Stanley Jadwin – 'he just fell into a tub of butter' – lost his son Stockwell in a motor accident in 1928 shortly after his graduation. As Stanley now had no surviving namesake Faith named her son born in 1931 Stanley. When her sister Beth in competition named a daughter Ida Stanley, Faith's complaints about this affronted bachelor Uncle Paul who cut Faith out of his will and left more to Theo: DT, CWA.
27  'good works': Hourani, *An Unfinished Odyssey*, pp. 33, 4.
27  'all around': Kahrl, *Memoirs*, p. 258.
29  'absurd': Lago, p. 22.
29  'our happiness to you': ibid., pp. 64 and 122. Theo's notes on EJ's life (Bodl. e. 2930-1 d fols 189–213) emphasise his sacrifice 'as eldest boy' and make no mention of Frank's. EJ praised and perhaps patronised Frank to his mother: his 'modest & unselfish simplicity of life' and also his religious feeling made Frank 'worth fifty of him'. See also Bodl. c. 5368 fols 189–213.
30  'wrestling Jacob': Jacob's struggle with an angel is recounted in Genesis 32 and is emblematic of spiritual conflict, especially to a Methodist familiar with Wesley's hymn 'Come, O Thou Traveller Unknown'.
31  'personal nature': Lago, p. 32.
32  'greatest living poet': ibid., p. 87.
32  'more at home': E. P. Thompson and Rabindranath Tagore, *Alien Homage*, Delhi, 1993, pp. 13 and 102.
33  'India's prisoner': E. J. Thompson, *A Letter from India*, London, 1932, p. 32, à propos EJ's novel *A Farewell to India* (1931).
33  'livery of neither': EP and Tagore, *Alien Homage*, p. 10.

34 *'Leicestershires'* reprinted as *Tigers along the Tigris: The Leicestershire Regiment in Mesopotamia in the First World War* (2007). EJ also retold the story of his war in *Crusader's Coast* (1929) and in his novel *These Men, thy Friends* (1927).

35 'beloved': EJ's laboured elegy to his brother fronts *The Leicestershires*:

> Our soldier youth thrice-loved, whose laughing face
> In battle's front can danger meet with eyes
> No fear could e'er surprise;
> Nor stain of self in their gay love leave trace,
> His nature like his name,
> Frank, and his eager spirit pure as flame.

Tagore plus the Elizabethans were his models: neither made for lively verses, or helped him evoke his grief.

36 'dissenting Christian tradition': EP and Tagore, *Alien Homage*, p. 40.

38 'idealists': Jameson, *Journey from the North*, p. 237.


# Chapter 2: 'Stay Away from Boars Hill'

41 'servants and meals': Lago, pp. 140–9.

41 'on the globe': ibid., p. 151.

41 'the soul's eternal safety': ibid., p. 262. The chief evidence is in EJ's *Introducing the Arnisons* (1935); but EJ edited in 1932 *O World Invisible: An Anthology of Religious Poetry*. He was not willing to break entirely with Christianity.

41 'it isn't true': Lago, p. 65.

42 'comical, drawling': ibid., p. 184. This was in 1919 on the way out to India.

42 'traveller's Guide': Bodl. 2695 fol. 228.

43 '£160': soon going up to £241; Lago, p. 193.

43 'provocation': Virginia Woolf, *Diary*, ed. A. O. Bell and A. McNeillie, London, 1977–84, vol. 3, p. 13.

44 'continuing aggravation': EJ took up editing Benn's sixpennies again in 1943–4, now selling for ninepence.

44 'no trouble': Bodl. 5290 fol. 155.

44 'to take it up': S. Deborah Baker, *In Extremis: The Life of Laura Riding*, London, 1993, p. 154.

45 'protective colouring': Dilys Powell, *Villa Ariadne*, London, 1973, p. 44.

46 'a kind of Quaker': Bodl. 5359 fol. 141/2, 25 Nov. 1928.

47 'a suitable answer': Bodl. 5304 fol. 90, 29 Nov 1934.

47 'Methodist prime ministers': Thatcher having converted to Anglicanism in 1951.

48 'silly old man': Bodl. 5359 fol. 141/2, 25 Nov. 1928. This luncheon was conceivably the occasion – never forgotten by Bridges – when he unjustly charged EJ with sharp practice while playing cards: this might account for EJ's asperity. See E. J. Thompson, *Robert Bridges*, London, 1944, *passim*.

49 'every minute': Lago, p. 230.

51 'young women': Manchester People's History Museum, unpublished interview with Gabriel/Bill Carritt, May 1983.

51 'leg of lamb': Gabriel Carritt endorses this memory of inadequate creature comforts, as did his first wife Margot Gale, later Kettle, to DT.

53 'cultural excellence': Michael Carritt, *A Mole in the Crown*, privately printed, 1985, p. 5.

53 'dotty': John Mortimer, *Clinging to the Wreckage: A Part of Life*, London, 1982, *passim*.

54 'dimwit': *BF*, p. 50: 'It was recognized on all sides and most of all by myself, that I was the family duffer.'

56 'high problems': Lago, p. 227.

57 'one other play': *The Last Voyage* (1934) concerned Raleigh. Similarly, *Three Eastern Plays* (with a terminal essay on Suttee) by Edward and Theodosia Thompson (1927). In addition *Skikanta (A Tale. Part I)* by Sarachchandra Chattohyaya was translated by K. C. Son and Theodosia Thompson with an introduction by E. J. Thompson in 1922.

61 'for a house': Theo cited Doit Garratt as another moneyed English wife with a less well-off husband (Geoffrey): source DT.

61 'about money': SK's interview with Barbara and Peter Sloman c. 1998: 'in the 1920s Edward was very worried about the way Theo spent money'.

## Chapter 3: A Class Apart

64 'some of the happiest days': *WAW*, p. 135.

65 'Bible Revision teacher': Walter Oakeshott is named as the stammering master by John Hasted, *Alternative Memoirs*, privately printed, 1992, p. 20. Seymour Schlesinger emailed me (Nov. 2009), 'Oakeshott was perfectly fluent. But his predecessor as headmaster, of whom I was very fond, was Spencer Leeson, later Bishop of Peterborough, who had a marked stammer.'

65 'suitable occasions': another practical joke against fellow Wykehamist Baron von Blumenthal, great-grandson of the Prussian Crown Prince's chief of staff, involved motorcars and a hundred spectators. Though its details are now lost, its aftermath needed the mediation of a third Winchester man, who rebuked Frank for 'still finding the whole thing rather funny'. Blumenthal's letter of reconciliation is dated 18 Sept. 1935.

67 'later changed his name': FT to Tony Forster, Jan. 1939, UNC. 'Poor devil he has changed his name, his nationality, his wace and his weligion, his home and the school he is reading at Oxford; and now he can't think of anything else to change.'

67 'My very dear friend': letter to his family, Nov. 1938. Bodl. d. 2700 fol. 57.

68 'don't you remember?': 4 Nov. 1935, Lago, p. 273.

69 'changed my address': EP to FT, 2 Apr. 1944, UNC. It is very unlikely FT could ever have received this, which also has 'swop' for 'swap', 'serjeant' for 'sergeant' and so on.

70  'larded and furrowed': Bodl. d. 2701.

72  '£115': in the 'Headmaster's Report to the Administrative Governors of Kingswood School, May 28th 1937' it states that the sons of itinerant Methodist ministers paid £38 a year for their education instead of £115. Since a June 1938 letter from FT says EJ was 'preaching' at Kingswood it is conceivable that he got the discount due to a minister. EP's Kingswood file has disappeared so we have no record of what his exhibition was worth. In the 'Headmaster's Report to the Administrative Governors of Kingswood School, February 28th 1941' it states that E. P. Thompson gained an open scholarship, £60, in Modern History, at Corpus Christi College, Cambridge.

72  'joining the sixth form': EP ascribed his success to high Dragon standards.

73  'peers in the other school': G. M. Best, *Continuity and Change: A History of Kingswood School 1748–1998*, Bath, 1998, p. 183. And DT: 'Edward and Arnold [Rattenbury] didn't seem to have had any friends from the Uppingham days.'

74  'Archangel Michael': in Dorothy Sayers's 'lousy' (Theo) play *The Zeal of thy House*, concerning William of Sens.

74  'condescension of posterity': E. P. Thompson, *The Making of the English Working Class*, London, 1963, p. 13. 'Condescension' haunts his writing: in 'The Nehru Tradition' in *Writing by Candlelight*, London, 1980, he is rescuing India from 'the condescension of the West'. In *Persons and Polemics*, London, 1994, pp. 2–9, he rescues Mary Wollstonecraft who now 'needs no one's condescension'.

74  'a bit of a prig': EJ to EP, 13 Oct. 1942, UNC.

74  'certain puritan strains': letter to Wendy Clark, 1945, UNC.

75  'non-conformist conscience': 3 Feb. 1938, UNC. FT led the motion 'that this house would welcome state prohibition of gambling', Frank arguing that gambling was 'not a vice, but a folly'. He lost the motion.

76  'humanism': letter to Wendy Clark, 1945, UNC.

77  'signs of genius': 19 Nov. 1941, UNC.

77  'kept everyone amused': Tony Forster, LTA; Seymour Schlesinger, CWA. Freeman Dyson, LTA: 'I'm sure ribaldry was part of his character.'

78  'break his reserve': Bill Carritt interview with SK, 1990 KUA S6/2/56/30.

78  'become a Catholic': *Spirit*, p. 91. 'Seven years ago I was determined to join the Church of Rome.'

80  'a Communist after a few years': Lago, p. 274.

80  'a libertarian Bolshevik': M. R. D. Foot, *Memoirs of an SOE Historian*, Barnsley, 2008, p. 34.

81  'red ties': Hasted, *Alternative Memoirs*, p. 26. Stowers Johnson, *Agents Extraordinary*, London, 1975, p. 21, implies that Frank at school wore red articles of clothing as acts of rebellion.

82  'psychological problems': Manchester People's History Museum, unpublished interview, May 1983.

83  'runs on without them': 20 Sept. 1936, UNC.

83  'a tag from Lucretius': 'Suave mari magno, turbantibus aequora ventis, E terra

magnum alterius spectare laborem.' This poem was not included in his *Selected Poems* but survives in the Iris Murdoch archive at Kingston University.

83 'to perish, even to kill':
> Watching the armies of the world march past
> In perfect step, eyes sparkling, heads erect,
> Knit with the slowing consciousness of brotherhood,
> Exultant in their glorious ideals.
> What shall we say, my darling: you and I
> Apart on our hillock of mutual sympathy,
> Too tir'd, too sad to join?

83 'he might marry': Catherine Dalton, *Robert Graves against the Gannon Cult*, Eden, NSW, 1998, pp. 5–7. Since after March 1939 Frank was in love with Iris, a love-passage with Catherine probably preceded that date.

84 'probably try and stop me': Colin Carritt's unpublished 2006 memoir, 'The Oxford Carritts'. Noel's wife Liesel (a German Jewess née Mottek) preceded him by six weeks.

84 'must be dead': he died in hospital in Madrid on 13 July 1937. His mother wrote into her copy of Auden's pamphlet-poem and call-to-arms *Spain* that year, 'For Anthony . . . he wanted to offer his life, and if it was taken, merged into the aggregate of all those lives given for Spain, it was his unanswerable contribution to a cause much greater than any single life. All those did not die for nothing . . . For provinces and nations can be signed away, but youth and honour never.'

## Chapter 4: Laughter in the Dark

93 'killed in a war': journal, 20 Sept. 1936, UNC.

94 'Presided at my birth': in the copy FT gave IM this is called 'Farewell to Fame' and is dated spring 1937; in *Selected Poems*, it appears as 'Resignation' and with the alternative first line for stanza 4 'Bruis'd but at rest, in deep green clover'.

96 'more influence': invited to the Athenaeum by his Bledlow neighbour Clement Oswald Skilbeck (1865–1954) on 25 Feb. 1943, EJ saw five people he knew, including Gilbert Murray and Sir John Squire; this prompted his meditation on exclusion.

97 'India's prisoner': EJ, *A Letter from India*, p. 32. EJ does not say when or where this exchange took place; Boars Hill is as likely a venue as anywhere else.

97 'when Gandhi visited': Lago, p. 245; and see EP, *Writing by Candlelight*, pp. 135–49.

97 'passion than reason': Lago, p. 250.

98 'scarcely top-drawer': Frank's niece Kate Thompson writes (LTA, 10 Oct. 2011), 'I think you are overly hard on him regarding the comment he made about Nehru, especially given the setting. Weighed against the overall strength of their friendship and mutual respect, it carries little significance. (Also, a very small point regarding Nehru, he wrote to EJ from prison as well as between spells in prison, on at least one occasion.)'

99 'Pompous, long winded': Ben Macintyre, *Operation Mincemeat*, London, 2010, p. 67; 'distinguished': Woolf, *Diary*, vol. 2, 20 Apr. 1920, p. 32.

99   'domestic politics': the Thompsons read the *Manchester Guardian*, whose leader-writer S. K. Ratcliff was a good friend to EJ and visited.

100  'girl in Brooklyn': DT, CWA.

101  'Alexander Korda': despite Theo's disdain for Korda's *The Private Life of Henry VIII* (1933) in which Catherine Howard sports an *Amurkan* accent. FT to EJ, May 1938, UNC: 'Dadza had better be careful or Korda will be grooming him as Britain's next "Public heartbeat no 1".'

101  'a lot to run': EJ to FT, Nov. 1938, UNC.

102  'as closely as his shadow': Norman Reddaway to EJ and Theo, late 1944, UNC.

105  'the whole boat': FT to EP, 11 May 1938, UNC.

105  'light verse': Imogen Grundon found among Pendlebury's papers Frank's facetious excoriation of the 'Ballade of Damnation' by George E. Gilleron *fils*; FT wrote some witty doggerel of thanks also, UNC.

105  'the writer on India': Imogen Grundon, *The Rash Adventurer: A Life of John Pendlebury*, London, 2007, p. 219.

107  'cricket match the following day': in Winchester rather than at Lord's, therefore not *the* Eton and Harrow match.

## Chapter 5: Oxford in the Age of Heroes

109  'in his cups': the friend was Seymour Schlesinger; Frank's joke was a private one involving someone on screen sharing the name of a mutual friend.

110  'Stop apologising': Leo Pliatzky, CWA, 25 Nov. 1997.

111  'up at Oxford with him': Peter Sloman, Seton-Watson, de Wesselow, MRDF, Cheslyn Jones, Ensor, Wright, Willett, von Blumenthal (aka Charles Arnold-Baker), Seymour Schlesinger, Tony Forster.

112  'wildly, beautifully': *WAW*, p. 107.

114  'rough on the Pekinese': FT, 'Snapshots of Oxford', UNC.

118  'observed in each': Carol Stewart saw in Iris 'simplicity, naiveté, power, and space'. Peter J. Conradi, *Iris Murdoch: A Life*, London, 2001, p. 83.

120  'fullness of your breast': compare Keats's 'Bright Star': 'Pillowed upon my fair love's ripening breast'.

121  'as a counter-charm': FT's version in 'Snapshots of Oxford', UNC, makes the digging-up of the irises his mother's idea, presumably as therapy, and omits mention of the Doug Lowe 'trigger', recalled independently by Leo Pliatzky who did not believe that IM and Doug Lowe were lovers.

121  'political ones . . . exuberantly': IM to EP, *c.* Dec. 1945, UNC.

121  'supplies': Philippa Foot, CWA.

121  'attentiveness': John Willett, CWA, 1998.

122  'easy game': Denis Healey, *The Time of my Life*, London, 1989, *passim*.

122  'permitted fusion': *Spectator*, 12 Jan. 1940.

122  'Monday Club': Robert Conquest, LTA, Apr. 1998.

124  'Greek and Socialism': FT to John Lehmann, Nov. 1941, UNC.

129 'putting [Frank] to bed': FT, 'Snapshots of Oxford', UNC. MRDF (LTA, 30 Aug. 2010): 'I do remember once having to put Frank to bed, drunk, but have no recollection of being ordered to do so; I also remember, more vividly, the march from behind the BM to Belgrave Square; holding one pole of a banner – Frank held the other – marked "Arms for Spain".'

130 'I liked the poem': *WAW*, p. 95. IM doesn't identify this poem, which could also possibly be his later 'To Irushka'.

130 'Frank had joined up': Lago claims Frank was called up in error on 9 Sept., then refused not to obey the summons. No evidence has come to light to support this contention; but Lago's claim that Theo won the battle after which Frank stayed on in Oxford one further year is definitely untrue.

## Chapter 6: Lessons in Gunnery

136 'a devouring flame': EJ to EP, 28 May 1940, UNC. 'That is why some Dutch are "quisling-ing".'

136 'talk about it': Oct. [?1942], 'The last morning was given up to two Indians, who were simply terrible. One – supposed to talk for the Moslem League – turned out to be a Congressman, dull and useless. The other was a Parsee, a ghastly chump with sultry manner . . .' EJ assured Gilbert Murray none the less that some Indian leaders are really great men 'by any standard of any age or land' (UNC).

140 'keen and intelligent': FT's Army Record (held at the Army Personnel Centre, Kentigern House, 65 Brown Street, Glasgow, G2 8EX), p. 3.

144 'access in the army': Trŭnski, *Grateful Bulgaria*, p. 15. Bill Carritt remembers Frank visiting around once every month; Christopher Seton-Watson believed that Frank sought the Party line from the Carritts.

144 'never made an officer': Bill Carritt obituary, *Guardian*, 24 May 1999. Like Frank, Bill Carritt joined the Royal Artillery.

146 'Michael . . . forfeited his pension': Colin Carritt, *The Oxford Carritts*. Though the documents were removed, no one was ever charged; prosecution might have caused the Foreign Office some embarrassment.

147 'In the public domain': Jane Harrison, *Myths of Greece and Rome*, London, 1928.

148 'waste of energy': 18 May 1940, UNC.

150 'exactly popular': Mar. 1939, UNC.

150 'fascination for me': to Désirée Cumberledge, 1 Apr. 1940, UNC.

151 'he was ineligible': two grave figures appeared at Saunders Close on 3 Sept., half an hour after Chamberlain's broadcast, at 11.15, asking EJ to act as air raid warden. On 14 May 1940, the Government made an urgent appeal to all men aged under sixty-five not already serving to become part-time soldiers; by the end of July over a million had done so. Mrs Folley, the Bledlow neighbour who informed EJ that he was ineligible for the Home Guard, was wife of the warden with whom he worked.

152 'separation and anxiety': it seems they returned to Bledlow at the end of July 1941.

## Chapter 7: An Officer and a Gentleman

155 'working in Military Intelligence': Bodl. 5285. fol. 1. EJ wanted Frank's name put forward in the event of war, which he then expected, for a job in Military Intelligence. General Jack Collins responded with advice on how to do this.

159 'Dear Muvverkins': 10 July 1940, UNC.

160 'Virgin Mary': IM's journal entry on 4 June 1945 concerning her visit to Westminster Cathedral ('The candles flicker before the saints & I recall how Frank once lit a candle to the Virgin Mary. I am glad he was here with me') is also open to the more oblique interpretation that Frank's candle-lighting happened elsewhere while her remembering him in that place was as if she 'materialised' him in person.

163 'the breaking of body and mind': Lago, p. 294 (EJ to EP, 11 June 1940).

163 'niggers at once': FT to EP, undated but probably Jan. 1941, UNC.

163 'half-witted boy': Frank gave this copy to Leo Pliatzky.

164 '*Sporting Times*': EJ to FT, 1 Jan. 1942, UNC.

164 'America every day': to EP, Jan. 1940, UNC.

165 'fifty-two different places': FT to his family, 23 Jan. 1941, UNC.

166 'home life': FT to EP, probably Mar. 1940, UNC.

167 'insider dealing': Tony Forster to FT, Sept. 1943: 'Do you think you cd recommend me for your show if there looks like being a vacancy? . . . Lay it on pretty thick?' FT to his family: 'I managed to fix it . . . for Tony' (UNC).

168 'criminality': Peter Baker, *Confessions of Faith*, London, 1946, p. 33.

168 'wildly unorthodox': Graham Lord, *The Authorised Biography of David Niven*, London, 2003, p. 143.

171 '*History of the Balkans*': probably *The Eastern Question: An Historical Study in European Diplomacy* by J. A. R. Marriott (aka Arthur Ransome), London, 1917.

171 'Madonna of the Green Eyes': this will dates from before July 1940, when IM received the poem mentioned. The poem to CN doesn't survive.


## Chapter 8: Cairo Frustrations

179 'Three other officers': Donald Melvin, Edgar Herbert and Graham Bell. They thus had little knowledge of Phantom and also no experience of active service.

183 'started on Arabic': with the help of Edgar Herbert who had worked five years in Egypt and Sudan with the Eastern Telegraph Company.

184 'Dartmoor in fog': Rex, serving with the RAF Volunteer Reserve, died on 4 Apr.

192 'seeing Jerusalem': their first trip on 12 Sept. 1941.

195 'interested him': Forshall left the unit because unable to get on with his successor. Daly is much mentioned in Waugh's *Diaries* (London, 1976), e.g. pp. 487, 494, 511, 515, 546.

195 'an excellent officer': Carol Mather, *When the Grass Stops Growing*, London, 1997, p. 58.

199 'Knew how to give it too.': in *spirit* EP and Theo date Frank's best-known poem to February 1940. No other evidence supports this dating; and against it is the fact that this poem does not appear in the ring-bound collection of his poetry that Frank typed out to give to IM on the occassion of her twenty-first birthday in July 1940.

202 'with a tank': Wendy lived then in Shaw Cottage but moved in 1943/4 to a grander house near by, Clanville.

202 'admiration of young men': Faith Kahrl to Theo, undated, probably 1946, UNC.

203 'gifted people': EP on Wendy Clark's death to her daughter Helen Henry, 20 June 1986, UNC.

204 'letters from Frank': note from Désirée's brother Peter Cumberledge, 1996, UNC. Désirée was born 26 Sept. 1919 in Bengal, where her father was a banker. She won an exhibition to Girton, but elected to go to St Hugh's instead, where she won a scholarship to read English 1937–40, taking a second-class degree. She wanted as a girl to be a missionary; she felt Frank's death deeply and would speak of him in later years in the family.

204 'fascinatingly interesting': IM to Theo, 29 Aug. 1941, UNC.

## Chapter 9: Under the Libyan Dog-star

207 '(June 1942)': Inscribed 'To Theo please God but I shall love thee better after death', Aug. 1942.

208 'who learned of this': when in February 1942, Krishna Menon, secretary in London of the India League, invited EJ to speak at a big Kingsway Hall meeting, EJ replied that if Nehru persisted in requesting independence at once, he might refuse.

210 'unusual form of society': Theo to EP, summer 1943, apropos Margaret Mead's *And Keep your Powder Dry: An Anthropologist Looks at America* (1942), Bodl. d. 2701.

210 'Louise de Rosales': née Louise Bagg.

210 'gloomy Intelligence officer': this was Sir John Garmondsway Wrightson, third Baronet. Philip Warner, *Phantom*, London, 1982, pp. 14–15, makes it clear that it was Wrightson who was given the tasks of exploring Asdic on the sewage pipes, and was later custodian of the pigeon loft.

211 'bigger casualties': 24,500 out of 119,000, with another 13,800 becoming POWs.

211 'enemy transport': no diarising was permitted at the front, but Frank's letters supply a fragmentary record; fellow officers left other accounts, and in April 1942 he compiled a retrospective Libyan diary.

212 'best friend': thus Leo Pliatzky in 1997, though 'Diamonds are a Girl's Best Friend' was written for the 1949 musical of *Gentlemen Prefer Blondes*. The Armstrong Whitworth Whitley was a night bomber introduced 1937, retired 1945.

213 'yellow and blue': *Spirit*, pp. 51–2; and Mather, *When the Grass Stops Growing*, p. 72.

214 'in Man's history': *Spirit*, p. 55.

215 'then in evidence': that lime juice was sometimes to be found is clear from FT to IM, 27 July 1942: 'Beyond the Libyan border the price of whiskey drops by 5/- a bottle. The teetotaller however receives no such stimulus, the price of lime-juice remaining virtually the same' (*WAW*, p. 112).

215 'poor old boy': *Spirit*, p. 50. Daly's poor fluffy Norwegian barge dog they finally sent back to the Delta to avoid the summer heat.

215 'the day before': diary notes, 20–21 Dec. 1941: 'A Visit to Tobruk. I drink a bottle of whisky. 22nd: I take over Force.' To CN, 21 Dec. [1941], he claimed still to make sense despite this intake. UNC.

216 'quite frequently': *Spirit*, p. 88.

216 'warmhearted': IM to David Hicks, Apr. 1942; see *WAW*, p. 195.

217 'would not wish to kill': Leonie Platt to FT, 13 Apr. 1942, UNC.

219 'most rational of men': Carol Mather also calls Grant 'sane and level-headed, the very antithesis of Dermot [Daly]' (*When the Grass Stops Growing*, p. 72).

220 'eight punishing days': the recapture of Tobruk took place on 21 June 1942. The distance travelled was 1,800 miles – see Warner, *Phantom*, p. 52, and R. J. Hills, *Phantom was There*, London, 1951, p. 77.

221 'Brother Ivan': phrase used both to IM, 4 Sept. 1942 (*WAW*, p. 114) and to his parents, 6 Oct. 1942 (UNC) when he adds, 'I am confident we shall never have any balls to stop in this area.'

221 'conventional nor conservative': in 1943 Nicholas Rostov at the end of *War and Peace* reminded Frank 'strikingly' of Rex, 'a rather stupid, hasty-tempered country squire', UNC.

222 'all over the world': Brian's Dragon School eulogy.

222 'within me laughs': C. Day Lewis, 'A Time to Dance': 'My friend who within me laughs / bids you dance and sing.'

223 'the other one is you': *WAW*, pp. 116 and 133.

224 'capacity to doubt': ibid., pp. 123–4.

225 'class background': ibid., pp. 111 *et seq*. This may refer to his fellow education officer Sergeant Frank Jacobson, who wrote to Frank's family claiming Frank never moved from the CP and wished, in event of death, his family to know that his political convictions were unchanged. Since Jacobson and Frank separated in early September 1943 when Frank joined SOE, after which they were stationed in different countries, Jacobson is voicing his own sense of certainty as much as Frank's. Jacobson also told EP in 1946 that there would be no references to him in Frank's diaries or letters because of their shared CP affiliation. How could Jacobson know this? Frank referred freely to fellow CP member Peter Wright in his letters. It is possible that Jacobson was the irritating 'militant' socialist FT referred to in his 1942 letter to IM.

225 'Sir Galahads': 19 July 1942, UNC.

225 'humanism': letter to Wendy Clark, 1945, UNC.

225 'glossing over it': *BF*, p. 61.

## Chapter 10: A Desultory Tale

232 'motoring offences': 5 Apr. 1943, UNC.

232 'privations': 17 May 1943, UNC.

233 'idealism': Jameson, *Journey from the North*, p. 237.

233  'English as blackthorn-flower': 'Tent-pitchers', June 1943, in Frank Thompson, *Selected Poems*, ed. Dorothy and Kate Thompson, Nottingham, 2003, p. 37. When in late 1943 Frank contemplated writing a story about two squaddies on leave in Cairo, he commented that he did not think he knew enough of the background.

234  'almost like peace-time': FT to his family, 2 Oct. 1944, UNC. Both EJ and Theo independently judged the record by May 1943 to be eight days.

235  'remarked to Iris': *WAW*, pp. 136–7. 'Do I write? I've written only three poems & no prose in the last year. Just before that, I wrote quite a little prose. My father got one short story published for me in the *Manchester Guardian* and a selection of my letters *without warning me* in the *New Statesman*.'

235  'similar assumptions': EJ to EP, undated, probably 1939, UNC.

236  'must read it again': EJ's taunt when sending FT *These Men, thy Friends* – 'Anyway you never read them' – seems false.

236  'kinsmen anywhere': 16 Apr. 1943, UNC.

237  'morale-boosting apart': see his entry on SOE in *The Oxford Companion to World War II*, ed. Ian Dear and M. R. D. Foot, London, 2001, pp. 793–6.

238  'Polish ambitions': EJ to FT, 27 Mar. 1943, UNC, and see *WAW*, p. 223: although Britain and France went to war to protect Poland's sovereignty, no forces were sent in its defence, Poland was betrayed into the Soviet zone at Yalta and Churchill forbade Poles from marching in the 1945 Victory parades in London.

238–9  'to learn Polish': his first teacher was a Mme Bonnietska who had spent one year in Siberia.

241  'Iraqi CP papers': we know about these articles from Sergeant Frank Jacobson; see *Spirit*, p. 89, where EP believes the gist of this letter (7 Mar. 1943) and that of the articles to be the same.

242  'Kensington Gardens': John Jones, 'She laughed and sang', *Times Literary Supplement*, 5 Oct. 2001, p. 40.

243  'hallmarks of an agent': Christopher Seton-Watson, who reconnected with Frank in Tripoli in July 1943, while he thought Communists 'used' Frank, believed that it was 'unlikely' Frank was a CP mole or spy: interview with SK, 20 Jan. 1995.

243  'Margot Gale': 'The CP had a number of underground members who were active in Labour and other non-CP organisations. Margot Kettle, for instance, was the national secretary of the NUS when we were students. She was very beautiful and very efficient and was not publicly known to have been a CP member (at that time she was still known as Margot Gale and was married to Bill Carritt). There were a number of others – I was myself asked by the student organiser before I went up to Cambridge to agree to do a job that would have meant keeping my CP membership secret. I said that since I was publicly known in South London as secretary of one of the biggest branches of the YCL I couldn't keep my association with the CP secret.' DT, LTA, Mar. 2009.

243  'nightmare of command': 23 Feb. 1943, UNC.

246  'he admonished': *WAW*, pp. 147–8.

248 'Vansittartist': after Lord Vansittart, a friend of EJ's from 1938 on, through Alexander Korda.

249 'soldiers' clubs': FT to EP, 21 Apr. 1944, UNC.

249 'Why is it so bloody?': see *Spirit*, p. 136, where the Balkans and Beveridge are FT's two pet subjects.

254 'stay in Malta': Hills, *Phantom was There*, ch. 9.

257 'class and time': as he himself noted to IM, Apr. 1943, 'I have a conventional mind formed along Wykehamical lines' (*WAW*, p. 137).

258 'may also have done': the letter requesting that his will be destroyed has not come to light. Source is SK.

## Chapter 11: Recasting the World

264 'A young Apollo': Frances Cornford, 'Youth'.

264 'high command': Norman Reddaway to SK, 7 Aug. 1991.

264 'lieutenant-commander': *Spirit*, p. 99.

265 'the child within them': 18 Dec. 1943, UNC: the context is Frank's admiration for Soviet children's books.

266 'still romanticised': 'Everybody romanticised Greece – I did to Frank when talking about it' (Christopher Seton-Watson to SK, 30 Jan. 1995).

266 'co-saboteur': Myers like Frank was hurt and offended by the pro-Greek Royalist bias he met in SOE Cairo. In August 1943, with a representative guerrilla delegation, Myers left Greece for Cairo. There the delegates demanded, among other things, that the Greek King, George II, should not return to Greece until a plebiscite had been held. This was not what the King or the British authorities wished to hear. The delegation was sent back to Greece and Myers made a scapegoat by the Foreign Office, which unjustly accused him of being too 'pro-ELAS' and having dreamed up the plebiscite idea. Myers was forbidden to return to Greece, though not before he had visited London and nearly persuaded Churchill to tone down his support for the Greek monarchy. A sensitive, loyal man, who in Greece had remained tightly focused on carrying out his brief, Myers was hurt and disappointed not to be going back. Instead, he watched from the sidelines as Greece slipped further into the civil conflict he had predicted. His sister married Bickham Sweet-Escott.

267 'hospitable to Winchester men': partly due to the influence of Sweet-Escott who was in Cairo in 1941 and again there as adviser to SOE's Force 133 for a year from December 1943. In a letter to Frank's parents, 28 Oct. 1944, he says he had never met Frank yet 'many of us feel we have lost a friend & that all of us are certain we have lost a very gallant officer. He was a very brave man and we are all of us proud to have served with him.'

267 'about its role': Monty Woodhouse, *Apple of Discord*, London, 1948, p. 45.

267 'all record': Denys Hamson, *We Fell among Greeks*, London, 1946, p. 149.

268 'Baghdad and beyond': *Spirit*, p. 16.

268 'According to one source': James Klugmann's biographer Geoff Andrews in a work-in-progress cites Stowers Johnson, *Agents Extraordinary*, pp. 64 *et seq*. Nigel West, *Secret War*, London, 1992, p. 196, also claims that Klugmann recruited Frank to SOE. Although West's *Secret War* is not always considered reliable, and although BLOs had to swear to being neither Communists nor Fascists, in practice there were a good number of CP BLOs, especially in Yugoslavia. See also Basil Davidson, *Special Operations Europe*, London, 1980, pp. 86 and 100, for SOE importing thirty revolutionary ex-Yugoslav Canadians as BLOs. Kenneth Syers, who met Frank in Yugoslavia, is another case in point, as is Peter Wright, a military attaché in Belgrade before 1947. Questions asked in Parliament in March and April 1950 concerned the CP activities in Yugoslavia of Kenneth Syers, Peter Wright, Betty Wallace and James Klugmann (see http://hansard.millbanksystems.com/lords/1950/mar/29/communists-in-the-public-service).

268 'colonial liberations': Basil Davidson, *Special Operations Europe*, London, 1980, p. 100.

268 'those staged by ABCA': see Richard Kisch, *The Days of the Good Soldiers: Communists in the Armed Forces WWII*, London, 1985, pp. 9 *et seq.*, for the Army Bureau of Current Affairs, founded August 1941, purveying a new and often radical concept of adult education in the Middle East, especially after Alamein.

269 'he found sympathetic': see Davidson, *Special Operations Europe*, pp. 154–7. Frank could in principle have attended the first three. It was at the fourth, in February, that half the 500 present cast their votes in a mock general election during which Labour 'romped home with 119 votes, Common Wealth (close to Labour) got 55, Liberals 38 and Conservatives came last with 17'. In the March session a Labour 'government' duly took office, complete with King's Speech, while the April 1944 session, which debated the nationalisation of banks, was the last. German radio had mischievously broadcast that British troops in Egypt had taken over and set up Councils of Soldiers and Airmen; and the GOC Brigadier Chrystal arrived with the military police to try (unsuccessfully) to suppress the Forces Parliaments. Many of its leaders were quickly posted to distant places, and Leo Abse imprisoned on an island in the Gulf before being shipped home.

269 'radical populist euphoria': E. P. Thompson, 'Edgell Rickword', *Persons and Polemics*, pp. 238–9.

270 'deemed contemptible': E. P. Thompson, Diary, *London Review of Books*, 7 May 1987, pp. 20–1.

270 'the decade of heroes': EP wrote that 'Marxism, in the decisive emergencies of Fascist insurgence and of the Second World War, began to acquire the accents of voluntarism. Its vocabulary took on . . . more of the active verbs of agency, choice, individual initiative, resistance, heroism, and sacrifice . . . It seemed, as the partisan detachment blew up the crucial railway bridge, that they were "making history" . . . It was a decade of heroes, and there were Guevaras in every street and in every wood. The vocabulary of Marxism became infiltrated in a new direction: that of authentic liberalism (the choices of the autonomous individual) and perhaps also of Romanticism (the rebellion of spirit

against the rules of act). Poetry, rather than natural science or sociology, was welcomed as a cousin . . . Voluntarism crashed against the wall of the Cold War. No account can convey the sickening jerk of deceleration between 1945 and 1948 . . . "History", so pliant to the heroic will in 1943 and 1944, seemed to congeal in an instant into two monstrous antagonistic structures': E. P. Thompson, *The Poverty of Theory and Other Essays*, London, 1978, pp. 264–6. Cf. also Arnold Rattenbury's 1997 view that 'after the war Frank became for many of us an emblem of anti-fascist heroism – a glorious simplicity where much was soon to become murky': 'Convenient Death of a Hero', *London Review of Books*, 8 May 1997, pp. 12–13.

270 'the idealism of the young': Neal Wood, *Communism and British Intellectuals*, London, 1959, p. 57.

271 'hung as a heretic': FT to CN, as recalled by SK. No copy of this letter has come to light.

272 'Cairo and Teheran conferences': Bickham Sweet-Escott, *Baker Street Irregular*, London, 1965, p. 188 (1st Cairo conference, 23–26 Nov.; Teheran conference, 28 Nov.–1 Dec.; 2nd Cairo conference, 4–6 Dec.).

274 'outlaw war for ever': 29 July 1943, UNC.

274 'reading it in England': Christmas was always spent with the Pilkington-Rogers family; in 1944 they stayed one week. The letter was to be read both at 8 a.m. UK time on Christmas Day and at 9 p.m.

275 'Tarzan': EP was also now nicknamed 'Tarzan'. The brothers had grown similar not just in weight but in looks and were now indeed occasionally mistaken one for the other.

275 'ham-fisted': 'my CLUMSINESS and absent-mindedness seem to become more catastrophic with each passing year' (Sept. 1943, UNC).

275 'commando school': probably on Mount Carmel, Military Establishment 102, which boasted a Pole called Stanisław Lazariewicz, among the greatest experts on European firearms: see Sweet-Escott, *Baker Street Irregular*, p. 171. Or possibly on the Red Sea, which SK seems to indicate.

276 'outstanding success': Sweet-Escott, *Baker Street Irregular*, p. 171. Kennedy was the principal lover of Christine Granville (see *Oxford Dictionary of National Biography*).

278 'like Peter Wright': Wright told DT post-war that he flunked parachuting and opted for a desk job instead.

282 'at least an idealist': 18 Dec. 1943, UNC.

282 'And time to begin a new': these lines from Dryden's *The Secular Masque* provide the epigraph to IM's *Under the Net* (1954).

283 'romantic': his letters have 'the genuine romantic Thompson stamp' (19 Oct. 1942); he is 'a romantic too' (17 Feb. 1943) and 'far too much of a Romantic & a Damned Individualist ever to embrace a philosophy essentially so serene [as Epicureanism]' (5 July 1943). Most notably she wrote on 20 Mar. 1943, 'Shall we ever make out of the dreamy idealistic stuff of our lives any hard & real thing? You will perhaps. Your inconsequent romanticism has the requisite streak of realism to it – I think I am just a dreamer. Shout in my ear, please.' see *WAW, passim*.

284  'will also be added': airgraph from Theo, 14 Nov. [no year], UNC.

284  'observed from Algeria': on 7 Nov. 1943, after being rebuked by Frank for being a poor correspondent (justly, he conceded).

285  'with ELAS units': National Archives, *SOE, Operations in the Balkans: A Guide to the Newly Released Records in the PRO*, London, n.d., p. 22.

286  'reproduced in miniature': Woodhouse, *Apple of Discord*, p. 111.

286  'Bankers and Brewers': such as 'Harcourt, McMullen, Tamplin, Glenconner'. Sweet-Escott, another banker, arrived in Cairo only in December.

286  'survived the war': *WAW*, p. 160, 1 Dec. 1943. To EP he wrote on 22 Dec., 'I'm bitterly ruing the day I ever learnt [modern Greek]. It's landed me in a stooge job which I'm finding it difficult to shake off, although I have had offers of more useful work elsewhere' (UNC).

287  'just you see': Nov. 1941, UNC.

287  'what a splendid Europe': FT to EP, 11 Jan. 1944, UNC.

288  'On your doorstep': the British Council had approached EJ and Theo about running a hostel for Iraqis in Beirut, or going to Ankara or Cairo – though EJ feared that being on Frank's doorstep might 'cramp his style'. In October Theo 'in town' visited a friend working in the State Department to enquire about using her Arabic and wrote to FT, 'We may do something more interesting this year than posts of sub warden for air-raids and senior member of the first aid post' (UNC).

## Chapter 12: With the Partisans

291  'perhaps its consummation': *Spirit*, p. 17.

291  'One appealing story': told to DT in 1994. Kiril Markov, aka Zlatan, also recalled Briton and Bulgarian hugging one another with joy; see Kiril Yanev, *The Man from the Legend: A Life of Frank Thompson*, Sofia, 2001, ch. 4.

292  'Albanian Chetniks': aka Balli Kombëtar. 'Chetniks' is Davies's appellation. John Earle, dropped into Serbia in 1944, comments (LTA, 15 Jan. 2012): 'Balli Kombëtar were nationalist and anti-Communist guerrillas, but anti-Serbian and not Chetniks. I think B.K. were Muslim, while Chetniks were of course Serbian Orthodox Christians. Chetniks are deeply rooted in the Serbian folk memory. The word comes from "četa", a company or band of armed men, and chetniks historically fought against the Turks in times gone by and then against the Austrians in World War One.'

294  'One ludicrous account': Robert Conquest, LTA, 22 Apr. 2008. 'Shortly after the war Slavcho Trŭnski, head of one of the few Bulgarian bands that survived – because near the Yugoslav border – wrote a piece in the army paper, perhaps *Narodnaya Voiska*, slandering Davies on these grounds. Conquest was sent to the Bulgarian Foreign Ministry bearing the British complaint. Georgi Dimitrov, by now Prime Minister, had for some time also taken on the role of Foreign Minister. Conquest gave him the letter and explained the position. There were just the two of them in his office. Dimitrov said he would handle this legitimate complaint – and an apology was printed in the next day's press.' But when I met General

Trǔnski in October 1999, two weeks before his death, he was still depreciating Mostyn Davies vis-à-vis drops.

294  'when he was captured': the source for this is Stefan Vimitroff, who had been required to translate Frank's first, three-hour interrogation, and later wrote consolingly to Frank's parents about his remarkable demeanour (FT's Personnel File, National Archives HS 9/1463).

295  'the Bulgarian section': and Albanian and Romanian.

296  'No hope': *BF*, pp. 30, 32. Kenneth Sinclair-Loutit, among others, wondered whether James Klugmann might from Bari have delayed and/or in other ways sabotaged communications between Frank and SOE Cairo. While this is possible, it is hard to see what motive Klugmann could have had in doing so, and Klugmann stayed friends with EP and Dorothy Thompson post-war, until 1956. See Geoff Andrews's forthcoming biography of James Klugmann.

296  'of killing Partisans': Hugh Seton-Watson, *The East European Revolution*, London, 1952, p. 95.

296  'SOE London's Balkans section': and Near East also.

296  'where he had lived': Sweet-Escott in *Baker Street Irregular* claims that Hugh spoke Bulgarian; however on meeting Stoycho Moshanov in Cairo in late August or early September 1944 Hugh spoke to him in French (Yanev, *The Man from the Legend*, ch. 9). Hugh had by 1943 finished writing *Eastern Europe between the Wars, 1918–1941* (1945).

296  'and pro-Tito': Michael Lees, *The Rape of Serbia*, London, 1990, p. 54, points out that Hugh campaigned for Tito in a *Spectator* article as early as January 1943.

296  'no SOE expert on Bulgaria': in London in 1943 Major E. C. Last, working on both Bulgaria and Yugoslavia together, was joined by a Rodney Searight: see Nigel West, *Secret War*, p. 338. Rod Bailey wrote to me in 2010, 'Boxshall . . . was on the Romanian desk and may [possibly] have had some responsibility for watching Bulg ops from London. Possibly Dayrell Oakley Hill in London had an interest in Bulg. Or possibly Jerry Faure-Field. See *Wildest Province* for details of all three. At any event, none were Bulgarian experts. Keep in mind that London could only watch ops in the Balkans from a great distance, temporally and physically. Cairo/Bari had a closer eye on what was going on. Whether Cairo/Bari had a Bulgarian "expert" in the sense that the Albanian Section had Margaret Hasluck, I don't know. But I don't think so.' Rod Bailey's *The Wildest Province: SOE in the Land of the Eagle* was published in London in 2008.

297  'and satirised': see Michael Lees's unreliable *The Rape of Serbia*, *passim*; but also Hugh Seton-Watson in *The East European Revolution*, p. 95, and Elisabeth Barker, *British Policy in South-East Europe in the Second World War*, London, 1976, pp. 93, 95. Evelyn Waugh, *Unconditional Surrender*, London, 1961, p. 165.

297  'renouncing menstruation': John Earle comments (LTA, 15 Jan. 2012): 'Quite true. No drunkenness either, in contrast to the Chetniks. There was a very puritanical spirit. Besides that, though, there was little choice. If there was shelter for the night, men and women would doss down together fully clothed. Women, like

men, had to undergo surgery without anaesthetics because there were none. Women probably "renounced" menstruation because their bodies were too worn out to conceive. This was a question that fascinated Evelyn Waugh.'

297 'hotly idealistic force': 'The sexual morality of the Partisans is almost 100% . . . a few lax individuals have been executed by firing squads'; 'Tito has welded his guerillas into [a fighting force] . . . its spirit is amazing and exhilarating . . . '; 'Churchill had said that Tito's force of 250,000 men was pinning down 14 German divisions': see *Time*, 18 Oct. 1943, 1 May, 8 May and 12 June 1944. Moreover John Henniker-Major, who disliked Waugh, none the less fully endorsed the accuracy of his account: *Independent*, obituary 3 May 2004. See also http://www.cdsee.org/pdf/workbook4_eng_ed2.pdf for the fury of the Serbs when the British dropped condoms to them.

297 'interested in Bulgaria': Sweet-Escott, *Baker Street Irregular*, p. 215.

297 'the views of Hugh': ibid., pp. 84 (Hugh Seton-Watson ran the Yugoslav section in Istanbul) and 219. Hugh took over as second-in-command to Bickham Sweet-Escott for Hungary, Romania and Bulgaria: ibid., p. 203. See also William Mackenzie, *The Secret History of SOE*, London, 2000, p. 132.

298 'the Balkan Entente': comprising Turkey, Yugoslavia, Greece and Romania.

299 'ended with murder': *BF*, p. 23.

299 'bombastic oratory': ibid., pp. 17, 26 and 82.

300 'overestimated their strength': see also Barker, *British Policy in South-East Europe*, p. 189.

300 'the war of attrition': letter from Henniker, National Archives HS 5/192.

301 'around twenty men': p. 2 of 'Information gained by the [Mulligatawny] mission on the O.F.' within National Archives HS 5/193.

301 'upon requisitioned stock': National Archives HS 7/103.

301 'membership of OF': Bulgarian sources put the number higher. 'The number of approximately 10,000 partizans and in additional 27–30,000 supporters (yatazi) is considered as the most reliable : Дочев, Донко, Партизаните – мит и реалност; Социологическо изследване, [Dochev, Donko, *Partizans: Myth and Reality* (Sociological Survey)], Plovdiv, 2004, pp. 9–10; Даскалов, Румен; От Стамболов до Живков; Големите спорове за новата българска история, [Daskalov, Rumen, *From Strambolov to Jivkov: The Big Disputes Concerning New Bulgarian History*], 2009. There was a rapid growth of their number in 1943 at the end of the summer and the beginning of the autumn due to the turn in the course of the war and Tsar Boris's death': Professor Kalinova via Maria Stoicheva, Apr. 2011. Most British sources ascribe the rapid growth of Partisan numbers to the period when Soviet troops were approaching Bulgaria during the summer of 1944: see e.g. R. Crampton, *A Short History of Modern Bulgaria*, Cambridge, 1987, p. 130.

301 'their unity of purpose': Barker, *British Policy in South-East Europe*, p. 189.

301 'The most optimistic guess': *The Oxford Companion to World War II*, p. 134.

301 'One SOE source': this is Norman Davis, writing on 4 March 1946 in SOE HISTORY 68, Review of SOE Activities in Bulgaria, 1939–45, National Archives HS 7/103. This file contains three papers, of which the unsigned third takes a more sanguine view than Davis's.

301 'a certain nuisance value': Sweet-Escott, *Baker Street Irregular*, p. 206.

308 'his last three surviving letters': in 2002 Kenneth Scott, by contrast, remembered that they had time to pen only short impersonal notes (SK).

309 'The contrast between these treats': thus Znepolsky in *Spirit*, 2nd edn, pp. 213–17.

310 'the better it will be': Leo Pliatzky to FT, 13 Dec. 1943, UNC.

313 'Iris was not enough': Theo writing to EP (undated, but late 1948, UNC) – 'I want you to marry' rebutting EP's fear that she was against his marriage. He and Dorothy married that December and their son Ben was born one week afterwards.

314 'his own private thoughts': Yanev, *The Man from the Legend*, ch. 4.

314 'to cross the border': see e.g. Johnson, *Agents Extraordinary*, *passim*; and *BF*, pp. 15–16.

315 'events in Bulgaria': the word 'there' in context could mean either East Serbia or Bulgaria; but Bulgaria is not excluded.

315 'A Major Saunders from Entanglement reported': on 12 May. *BF*, p. 79.

316 'each house burned down': Svetozar Vukmanović-Tempo, *Struggle for the Balkans*, London, 1990, p. 314.

316 'hungry and unarmed men': *BF*, p. 30.

316 'in contact with the Bulgarians': letter from Henniker to EP, 1979, UNC.

316 'to go it alone': *BF*, p. 80.

317 'twenty successful sorties': EP in *BF*, p. 32, says thirty sorties; but records suggest fewer. National Archives HS 5/192 on 11 May cites drops on three dates: three on the 9th, seven on the 10th, and ten expected that night, the 11th, which would have made a total of twenty.

317 'entering spring gallop': *BF*, p. 31. A letter from Henniker to EP (15 Mar. 1979, UNC) says, 'I dropped to Dugmore (at Entanglement) in April. I brought 5 new British Military Missions. Saunders for Crna Trava, Lambie for Macedonia, myself and Syers for the Radan plus Slim Parish an American.' Elisabeth Barker to EP (undated, UNC): 'According to Phyllis Auty (the historian) Kenneth Syers [who was with MI6 rather than with SOE and who did not use the W/T set belonging to SOE mission Demagogue but had his own communications, and whose mission was in any case to liaise with the Serbs rather than to enter Bulgaria] told her Frank suggested that Syers go with him to Bulgaria, but that he replied he was afraid and declined.'

318 'accompany them': interview with SK, 22 Jan. 1999.

318 'assumed unrealistic proportions': Yanev, *The Man from the Legend*, ch. 5.

318 'a mass-uprising': *BF*, p. 81; the former commander of the Crna Trava (Serbian) Partisans, Djura Zlatković, reported as much.

318 'southern Serbia itself': Mackenzie, *Secret History of SOE*, p. 441, on which page Major Dugmore's contribution is also outlined.

318 'Sunday school outing': *BF*, p. 82.

319 'wiped out a fortnight before': by 3 May. See Yanev, *The Man from the Legend*, ch. 5: 'crushed and dissolved . . . defeated'.

319 'in a state of euphoria': According to Yanev: 'We were followed from the very onset

of the operation in Kalna. It is said that planes were taking photos of our march and that the intelligence was analysing the aerial photographs. The secret police agents were alerted . . . What is more, we were moving undisguised, engaging in fights with the enemy along the way and organising meetings in the villages. It must not have been hard to follow our march. We had not organised in advance the connections, the meetings, the secret meeting places with the Fatherland Front committees, with the party organisations and the associates from the Ferdinand, Berkovitsa, Sofia, Pleven and Plovdiv regions. The route had not been preliminarily studied and investigated. We lacked guides to help us move from place to place. We were not informed on time that the Chavdar Brigade had also suffered a heavy defeat, and that, therefore, joining it was impossible' (*The Man from the Legend*, ch. 5).

319    'the first ambush': Scott's narrative puts the crossing earlier (12/13 May) and places the incident near Kom in Bulgaria.

321    'some better ones': reported by Robert Conquest, LTA. Scott told Robert Conquest, in Sofia with the Allied Control Commision that, realising they were on the brink of ruin, they decided to break off.

## Chapter 13: Conversing with the Dead

326    'towards these deaths': see E. P. Thompson, *The Heavy Dancers*, London, 1985, ch. 4, 'The Liberation of Perugia'.

327    'EP sailed for home': Lieutenant-Colonel R. L. V. ffrench-Blake's adjutant Richard Main reported EP's distress to him. His Italian war-diaries, which mention EP, are in the Imperial War Museum. Ffrench-Blake never knew that EP was in the CP and discovered what a 'tremendous left-wing guru' he was only from EP's obituaries in 1993. These made him wonder what EP had felt about the regiment's 'blue-bloods': his own daughter married a son of the Duke of Grafton. CWA, 11 Aug. 2009.

327    'a play about Balkan Partisans': co-written with ex-Draconian Richard Tolson, this is in a booklet in the Imperial War Museum.

327    'published his first prose': *Our Time*, Dec. 1945.

328    'sent by the Germans': *Evening News*, 20 Nov. 1944.

329    'communicate with him': this letter arrived 4 Sept. 1944.

329    'a macabre, unnerving cable': See M. R. D. Foot, *SOE in France*, London, 1966, p. 43. This is uncorroborated by Frank's SOE files at Kew or in the Bodleian Library.

330    'a neighbouring mission': Sweet-Escott on Scott's capture, *Baker Street Irregular*, p. 212.

330    'Room 238': MI9, concerned with escape, with which SOE was on good terms, was also located on Northumberland Avenue, in Room 424 of the Metropole Hotel.

331    'and the Comintern': Arnold Rattenbury, 'Convenient Death of a Hero', *London Review of Books*, 8 May 1997, pp. 12–13.

331 'at first refused permission': on 18 November 1944 – an episode alluded to by Sweet-Escott, *Baker Street Irregular*, p. 215.

332 'one's routine training': MRDF, LTA, 2 Feb. 1999. 'Of about a hundred SAS men taken prisoner in 1944, only six (of whom by a blind stroke of fortune I was one) ever returned.'

332 'A seventy-year-old Scottish poet': 1876–1960 – see her *Oxford Dictionary of National Biography* entry.

334 'what does that matter?': EJ to EP, 11 Nov. 1944, UNC. Frank agreed. A letter written home on 29 Apr. 1942: 'My poems get prosier and more old-fashioned every day. It is a terrible thing to have read nothing but the classics during one's most impressionable years. Now any newer elements have been subtracted and I find myself incapable of thinking in terms of anything but the classics and classical symbols.'

334 'Oxford province at all': 23 Jan. 1946, UNC.

334 'One small publisher': this was Lindsay Drummond – recommended by Lehmann – who on 15 Oct. 1945 suggested Theo try Allen Lane at the Bodley Head, especially as they were just about to publish the poetry of Gervase Stewart, another fine young poet killed in the war.

334 'wrote from the Hogarth Press': on 19 July 1945.

335 'a policeman-poet': Arlott (1914–91) published *Of Period and Place* (poetry) with Jonathan Cape in 1944.

335 'Patric Dickinson': 1914–94.

335 'Damascus Road': broadcast 2 Apr. 1945, BBC Home Service *New Poems* programme: fee of 2 guineas.

335 'two weeks later': 24 Oct. 1944.

336 'incredibly boring things': DT: CWA, 14 Aug. 2009.

336 'Richmond hotel': Mrs Crawford, at Ivy Hall Hotel, Petersham Road, Richmond Surrey, 3 Dec. 1944.

336 'IS life after death': Theo to EP, 20 Oct. 1944, UNC.

337 'should want to live': Lago, p. 314.

338 'his own high choice': 24 Nov. 1944, UNC.

338 'self-censorship': Theo to EP, 25 Oct. 1944, UNC.

338 'the exact phrase': see also the final page of EJ's *These Men, thy Friends*.

339 'the first comfort': writing to David Talbot-Rice.

340 'to turn Frank into a hero': Sweet-Escott, *Baker Street Irregular*, p. 213.

341 'Frank's current (2004) *Oxford Dictionary of National Biography* entry': Rod Bailey has undertaken to revise this.

341 'you both constantly': Bodl. 5304 fol. 124, 22 Oct. 1945. Moreover ten months earlier Murray wrote that the thought of EJ's suffering, bodily and mental, 'really haunts me': 5304 fol. 123, 12 Jan. 1945.

341 'numbers, movements and mail': see Michael Boll, *Cold War in the Balkans: American Foreign Policy and the Emergence of Communist Bulgaria, 1943–1947*, Lexington, KY, 1984, *passim*.

341 'its earliest days': Davis was being held over for job of Press Attaché (that is, Conquest's position), where he 'might not be needed for some time'.

## Chapter 14: Afterlife

345 'the Bulgarian Partisans': *Spirit*, 2nd edn, p. 203.

345 'refused permission': see ibid., foreword: 'The permission of the King – without which no Briton is allowed to accept a medal – is never given to posthumous decorations by a foreign Power.' For names of the medals given, see Trŭnski, *Grateful Bulgaria*, p. 9.

345 'received the DCM': on 10 Dec. 1946: *Spirit*, p. 182.

346 'the grimmest reading': Imperial War Museum, Chavasse papers (Captain E. F. J. Chavasse, ref. 06/23/1) and Mostyn Davies papers (Major M. L. Davies DSO, ref. 03/24/1).

347 'his comrades in Litakovo': see *Spirit*, foreword, pp. 205 and 219.

348 'praised him insufficiently': Lago, p. 273.

350 'body and mind': writing to EP, 11 June 1940 (Lago, p. 294).

350 'writing a play': though SK maintains that EJ sent Frank these lines in a letter, no evidence to support this has come to light.

350 '*Atonement* was restaged': around December 1943, by Ruth Spalding who founded the Oxford Pilgrim Players, a cooperative and itinerant company of actors.

351 'really blame them': FT to EP, 13 Jan. 1944, UNC.

351 'glass of water': letter from Stefan Vimitroff to Theo, 16 Aug. 1946, FT's Personnel File, National Archives HS 9/1463.

352 'both described looting': see Keith Douglas, *Alamein to Zem Zem*, London, 1946, reprinted 1996.

353 'in literary Cairo': see Artemis Cooper, *Cairo in the War 1939–45*, London, 1989, ch. entitled 'The Writers'.

355 'toe the Moscow line': *BF*, p. 96.

355 'rumours circulated by a school-fellow': M. R. D. Foot. Although Professor Foot denied having any recall of this in 2011, a Manchester ex-colleague, with a great deal of circumstantial detail, attested otherwise.

355 'SOE files were destroyed': see Duncan Stuart, '"Of Historical Interest Only": The Origins and Vicissitudes of the SOE Archive', *Intelligence and National Security*, vol. 20, issue 1, 2005, pp. 14–26. Neither I nor Jane Jantet could find in Frank's files at Kew about half his signals quoted by EP in *Beyond the Frontier*. By temperament I'm more inclined to ascribe this to cock-up than to conspiracy, and it is thought that copies of some of Frank's signals survive in Washington DC.

355 'establishment conspiracy': EP maintained that 'the papers of SOE seem to be a kind of private archive to which only selected friends and relatives of the archivist are given access' (*BF*, p. 108). The archivist with whom EP duelled between March 1974 and March 1979 was Lieutenant-Colonel Eddie Boxshall (SOE archives custodian 1959–82), born in Bucharest, speaking accented English and counting in German. Boxshall had before 1940 visited England for a few months only and sometimes coped with outsiderdom by hostility to disclosure. For tales of Boxshall's intransigence see MRDF, *Memoirs of an SOE Historian*, pp. 134–7. Bickham Sweet-Escott to EP, Mar. 1979, UNC: 'I shouldn't worry about Boxshall . . . you [already] have all that is available.'

356 'obstructing all honours': the charge was that the UK had both failed to award him posthumous British honours and enforced the refusal by the Crown for them to take his Bulgarian honours home.

356 'Vladimir Topencharov': he was also brother-in-law of Traicho Kostov – see *Time*, 23 Feb. 1948. Such links were used in evidence by the prosecution during the Kostov trial.

356 'thanks to Conquest': animus was reciprocal. Conquest commented (LTA, Sept. 2008), 'one of the Mission told me that [Theo] was not taken in by the regime, but that [Frank's] brother was!' He added: 'I know, or knew, many British soldiers with fine records who had no awards . . . How does one track such a procedure, and where, if such a procedure exists, do you find the documents, or evidence of my "supporting" non-recognition? Plainly this is one of those legends handed down in families, that one hears of. Meanwhile I am slandered on non-existent grounds!' DT observed (LTA, Mar. 2009): 'I don't think Edward was a good judge of character though I don't mean that he was always wrong. He made immediate judgements on rather superficial things [two examples follow] . . . He let us in for some iffy appointments when we were running the peace movement again by making snap first judgements.'

356 'after 11 May': *BF*, p. 33. In fact a cable from Claridges survives from 16 May 1944.

356 'sorties to Bulgaria': Sweet-Escott, *Baker Street Irregular*, pp. 213–14.

356 'at their disposal': even Slavchko Trŭnski, who can scarcely be accounted reliable, and who says sorties were disappointing and stopped in April (which we know to be untrue), inhibited by a British Government order 'early in May' (*Grateful Bulgaria*, p. 52), agreed that the Partisans were better equipped than the Royalist Bulgarians, though he appears to be crediting Russian drops for those (ibid., p. 37). By April 1944 Trŭnski claims that they were sufficiently well equipped to plan to send a consignment to Sofia (ibid., p. 41).

357 'dropped for Bulgarian use': Yanev, *The Man from the Legend*, ch. 4. Unfortunately the pilots' manifests inventorying each drop measure many items by weight, not number, thus making some details hard to verify.

357 'working together': on 6 Apr. 1944 Churchill also wrote to the British Ambassador in Algiers: 'I suppose you realise we are weeding out remorselessly every single known Communist from all our secret organisations?' (*BF*, p. 95).

357 'Soviet area of concern': Boll, *Cold War in the Balkans*, p. 37. This was a view rejected by the US only on 10 June.

357 'to be brokered?': EP mistakes the date of Bagrianov's accession to power as 1 June, rather than 10 June (*BF*, p. 97). For these dates see Boll, *Cold War in the Balkans*, *passim*.

358 'If his destruction': EP was alerted to the possibility of British collusion in Frank's murder in 1950, when the topic of British involvement in Bulgarian affairs was intensely topical. Traicho Kostov, leading figure of the Bulgarian CP, had just been executed for, *inter alia*, spying for the British intelligence services. Peter Tempest, a fellow Communist married to the London correspondent of *Rabotnichesko Delo*

(the leading Bulgarian newspaper in the Communist era), Brigitta Yossifova, and lecturing in Sofia, wrote to EP maintaining that Nikola Geshev, Head of Department A of the state security service, and charged with defeating the Communists in Bulgaria, was in the pay of the British and had interrogated Frank – a claim unconfirmed by any other sources – before conniving at his destruction. And 'Geshev would never have dared to put [Frank] to death if he had thought that the British authorities valued his life.' (Peter Tempest to EP, 30 June 1950, UNC.)

Frank was certainly astonished by how much his interrogators knew about him and his mission, and it is likely that Geshev had an informer planted among Frank's Partisans, and it is just conceivable that Geshev had been told that Frank was a Communist. Yanev speculates about the informer (*The Man from the Legend*, ch. 4); Stowers Johnson (as always giving no sources) wonders about Geshev discovering Frank's politics (*Agents Extraordinary*, pp. 180–1) and further speculates that the police chief was the English-speaking Bulgarian who visited Kenneth Scott in prison shortly before his release. Geshev was likely to have been severely alarmed by the approach of the Soviets and powerful enough – so the argument goes – to risk taking drastic steps to oppose their takeover. (Geshev was probably shot and killed escaping the Soviets by crossing the border to Turkey around 9 September 1944.) Thus, while captured English and American airmen were sent to the relatively comfortable POW camp in Shumen, those considered to be agents and spies were arrested and treated the same way as their Partisan associates. It is a terrible irony that Frank's fledgling Bulgarian itself probably provoked the suspicions of his captors.

That Geshev was obliged to be pro-German while supposedly in the pay of the British has never deterred advocates of this theory. The ex-Phantom Peregrine Worsthorne endorsed EP's suspicions: 'In executing Major Thompson, the Bulgarian authorities were doing the British government's dirty work' ('Cold Injustice', *New Statesman*, 21 Feb. 1997, pp. 45–6). But nothing about this conspiracy theory today is persuasive. No reputable historian in either country now believes that Geshev was paid by the British. Elisabeth Barker, an authority on South-Eastern Europe during the Second World War, gave a paper at an Anglo-Bulgarian conference at St Antony's College, Oxford, in 1977 arguing that it was 'nonsense that the British had any contact with Kostov or with the war-time Bulgarian Police Chief' (letter to EP, 10 Dec. 1978). Further, Kiril Yanev is also adamant that there was no contact between Nikola Geshev and Frank. There were two separate departments tasked with fighting disruptive activities against the state. While Geshev was head of Department A of the political police, dealing exclusively with the activities of the then-illegal Communist Party, the foreign 'infiltrators' were the subject of the Reconnaissance Division of the army, its Division I dealing with espionage and Division II with counter-espionage. The person heading Division II was General Sava Kutsarov, and Frank was interrogated by Captain Nacho Yolov, from the same unit, focusing primarily on British and American POWs in Bulgaria, in Litakovo; while the decision for his execution came from General Kocho Stoyanov, Commander of the First Sofia Army, a different institution, who decided to pass a sentence in line with what other illegals got.

Yanev insists that there were no points of contact between the police headed by Geshev and Military Reconnaissance headed by Kutsarov (LTA, 18 Oct. 2011).

358 'fists and tears': *BF*, p. 51.

358 'too bloody innocent': EP, *Writing by Candlelight*, pp. 132–3.

358 'foremost a poet': see Scott Hamilton's excellent *The Crisis of Theory: E. P. Thompson, the New Left and Postwar British Politics*, Manchester, 2011. Hamilton has accurately blogged that 'It is hard to believe now, but EP Thompson never intended to become a historian, and didn't even consider himself a historian until at least halfway through his remarkable life. As a young Communist in the years after World War Two, [he] joined the party's literary organisation, not the legendary group of historians that included Eric Hobsbawm, Christopher Hill, Rodney Hilton, and John Saville. Until the late 1950s, at least, [he] considered his main vocation to be poetry. [He] came to history accidentally, as a result of his research into the great English painter, poet, and designer William Morris.'

359 'intentions of the dead': see Bryan D. Palmer, 'Homage to E. P. Thompson', pt 2, *Labour/Travail*, vol. 33, 1994, p. 68.

359 'chief among those heroes': Hamilton, *The Crisis of Theory, passim*.

359 'as a touchstone': as W. L. Webb noted in his moving obituary, *Guardian*, 30 Aug. 1993.

359 'total mendacity': *BF*, p. 98.

360 'scattered the soil': LTA, 31 Jan. 2002.

360 'Iris was not enough': undated, but late 1948, UNC.

361 'how to enjoy living': IM to Leo Pliatzky, 16 May 1945, private papers.

362 'Frank's edition of Catullus': IM's journal, 19 Feb. 1966: 'Venisti, o mihi muneris beati. (With acknowledgements to Catullus 9.5). I have just noticed that the Catullus out of which I copied these words belonged to Frank.'

362 'Lawrence of Bulgaria': *The Times*, 27 Aug. 1975.

362 'horror of violence': Sue Summers, 'The Lost Loves of Iris Murdoch', *Mail on Sunday*, 5 June 1988, p. 17.

362 'illusions of grandeur': *The Times*, 27 Aug. 1975.

364 'hoped to be married': Summers, 'The Lost Loves of Iris Murdoch', *Mail on Sunday*, 5 June 1988, p. 17. In 1996 Iris Murdoch claimed to the present writer that she and Frank were to be married.

364 'wait over forty years?': Rosemary Hill, *London Review of Books*, 22 Apr. 2010, 'I Will Tell You Everything'.

365 'symbolic confrontation': *BF*, p. 42.

366 'contact with his base': Mackenzie, *Secret History of SOE*, p. 495.

367 '*Grateful Bulgaria*': this chapter owes something to that book, as well as much to Yanev, *The Man from the Legend*.

367 'a fiftieth anniversary service': Robert Pearson and the Ambassador spoke and laid wreaths, as did the Bulgarian commander of the First Army. English and Bulgarian versions of two poems – Christo Botev's 'Sharing' and Frank's 'Epitaph for my Friends' – were read and the 'Last Post' sounded.

367 'Pearson took Frank's sister-in-law': together with Stuart Leasor, adviser to the Bulgarian Ministry of Finance in 1994. Unfortunately the video has corrupted and is unwatchable. Stuart Leasor: 'I was working in Bulgaria, in 1993, running a public awareness campaign to inform the public and businesses about the introduction of VAT. However I was living with Colonel Robert Pearson, the UK defence attaché and his family, since I had known them for years, having served together in the 17th/21st Lancers. So I was a sort of quasi-military, in that I used to go the British Embassy a lot, and attended various military do's with the Pearsons. It was outside the defence section in the embassy that I first saw a photograph of Frank Thompson, and this photo led to Robert and my going on his trail.'

367 'he changed his mind': although Bulgaria was no longer Communist, 1994 was before it had any realistic chance of joining the European Union or NATO. Many then in power had transferred straight from a CP whose influence was still extensive, and the secret police probably had divided loyalties. Fears about what stories and untruths might come out from the Communist period preoccupied many. When in 1994 Eastern Orthodox Easter fell on 1 May, some marched so that they could later claim allegiance to either Christianity or Communism, whichever seemed more politic.

367 'outlandish conspiracy theories': one Bulgarian 'expert' on British intelligence work in his country told me in 2010 that the Germans were organised enough and technically able to know exactly when and where aircraft bound for the Balkans were going to drop, intercepted Frank's requests, adding their own wish-list of armaments, and promptly purloined them.

368 'he "respected" Communists': Trŭnski, *Grateful Bulgaria*, p. 52.

370 'stubbornness of his conscience': the phrase is Isaiah Berlin's to describe Anna Akhmatova, see Michael Ignatieff, *Isaiah Berlin: A Life*, London, 1998, *passim*.

370 'reprisals so atrocious': an unnamed SOE observer in 1946 recorded his belief that excessive cruelty shown to Partisans helped turn Bulgarians against the regime and expedited its downfall. See National Archives HS 7/103.

371 'a detailed description thereof': Cf. *BF*, p. 97: 'Thompson's notebooks were seized and a translator was interrogated about their contents before the Regency council.'

372 'Family jokes abounded': for Alfred, see p. 209.

# Select Bibliography

**General**

Conradi, Peter J.: *Iris Murdoch: A Life*, London, 2001.

—— (ed.): *Iris Murdoch: A Writer at War: Letters and Diaries 1938–1946*, London, 2010.

Foot, M. R. D.: *Memoirs of an SOE Historian*, Barnsley, 2008.

Inglis, Fred: *The Cruel Peace*, New York, 1991.

Kingston University: the Iris Murdoch Archive.

Kusseff, Simon: 'Frank Thompson, a Chronology in Three Parts', Archive/Conradi, Kingston University AS6/1/59.

Lago, Mary: *India's Prisoner: A Biography of Edward John Thompson, 1886–1946*, Columbia, MO, 2001.

*The Oxford Companion to World War II*, ed. Ian Dear and M. R. D. Foot, Oxford, 2001.

Passerini, Luisa: *Europe in Love; Love in Europe*, London, 1999.

Thompson, E. P.: *Beyond the Frontier: The Politics of a Failed Mission, Bulgaria 1944*, London, 1997.

——: *The Making of the English Working Class*, London, 1963.

——: 'The Nehru Tradition', in *Writing by Candlelight*, London, 1980.

——: *Persons and Polemics*, London, 1994.

——: *The Poverty of Theory and Other Essays*, London, 1978.

—— and Tagore, Rabindranath: *Alien Homage*, Delhi, 1993.

Thompson, Frank: *Selected Poems*, ed. Dorothy and Kate Thompson, Nottingham, 2003.

Thompson, Theodosia Jessup and E. P.: *There is a Spirit in Europe: A Memoir of Frank Thompson*, London, 1947; 2nd edn, 1948.

## Part One: Between Two Wars, 1919–39

Aldiss, Margaret: *A Boars Hill Anthology*, Faringdon, 1998.

Antonius, George: *The Arab Awakening*, London, 1938.

Baker, S. Deborah: *In Extremis: The Life of Laura Riding*, London, 1993.

Baxell, Richard: *British Volunteers in the Spanish Civil War: The British Battalion in the International Brigades 1936–1939*, London, 2004.

Best, G. M.: *Continuity and Change: A History of Kingswood School 1748–1998*, Bath, 1998.

Carritt, Bill: obituary, *Guardian*, 24 May 1999.

Carritt, Colin: *The Oxford Carritts*, privately printed, 2006.

Carritt, Michael: *A Mole in the Crown*, privately printed, 1985.

Conquest, Robert: *Reflections on a Ravaged Century*, London, 1999.

Croft, Andy: obituary for Arnold Rattenbury, *Independent*, 3 May 2007.

Dalton, Catherine: *Robert Graves against the Gannon Cult*, Eden, NSW, 1998.

——: *Without Hardware*, Towamba, NSW, 1970; 3rd edn, 1980.

Dyson, Freeman: *Disturbing the Universe*, New York, 1979.

Graves, Richard: *Robert Graves: The Assault Heroic 1895–1926*, London, 1986.

Grundon, Imogen: *The Rash Adventurer: A Life of John Pendlebury*, London, 2007.

Hamilton, Scott: *Last Muggletonian Marxist: Studies in E. P. Thompson and the Poverty of Theory*, Auckland, 2008.

Hasted, John: *Alternative Memoirs*, privately printed, 1992.

Healey, Denis: *The Time of my Life*, London, 1989.

Hopkins, J.: *Into the Heart of the Fire: The British in the Spanish Civil War*, Stanford, 1998.

Hourani, Cecil: *An Unfinished Odyssey*, London, 1984.

Jameson, Storm: *Journey from the North*, London, 1969.

Jenkins, Roy: *A Life at the Centre*, London, 1991.

Jessup, Henry Harris: *Fifty-three Years in Syria*, New York, 1910.

——: *The Mohammedan Missionary Problem*, Philadelphia, 1879.

——: *The Setting of the Crescent and the Rising of the Cross*, Philadelphia, 1899.

——: *The Women of the Arabs*, New York, 1873.

Kahrl, Faith Jessup: *Memoirs*, privately printed, 1989.

Lloyd-Jones, Hugh: *Blood for the Ghosts*, London, 1982.

MacGillivray, J. A.: *Minotaur: Sir Arthur Evans and the Archaeology of the Minoan Myth*, London, 2000.

Macintyre, Ben: *Operation Mincemeat*, London, 2010.

Manchester People's History Museum: unpublished interview with Bill Carritt, May 1983.

Maugham, Robin: *Escape from the Shadows*, London, 1972.

Mortimer, John: *Clinging to the Wreckage: A Part of Life*, London, 1982.

Mortimer, John: *In Character*, London, 1983, pp. 99–104 (interview with EP, 'The Guru and the Radioactive Frog').

*The Nicholsons: A Story of Four People and their Designs*, York, 1988.

Powell, Dilys: *Villa Ariadne*, London, 1973.

Seymour-Smith, Martin: *Robert Graves: His Life and Work*, London, 1982.

Thompson, E. J.: *Beyond Baghdad with the Leicestershires*, London, 1919; repr. as *Tigers along the Tigris*, 2007.

——: *Burmese Silver*, London, 1937.

——: *A Farewell to India*, London, 1931.

——: *100 Poems*, London, 1994.

——: *A Letter from India*, London, 1932.

——: *Robert Bridges*, London, 1944.

Tibawi, Abdul Latif: *American Interests in Syria 1800–1901*, Oxford, 1966.

Toynbee, Philip: *Friends Apart*, London, 1954.

Woolf, Virginia: *Diary*, ed. A. O. Bell and A. McNeillie, London 1977–84.

## Part Two: A Professional Murderer, 1939–43

Alpers, A.: *Katherine Mansfield: A Biography*, London, 1980.

Astor, Michael: *Tribal Feeling*, London, 1963.

Baker, Peter: *Confession of Faith*, London, 1946.

Cooper, Artemis: *Cairo in the War 1939–45*, London, 1989.

Hills, R. J.: *Phantom was There*, London, 1951.

Imperial War Museum: Martyn Highfield; ref. no. 26546, at No. 1 Officer Cadet Training Unit, Larkhill, 9/1939–12/1939, Barrington Bezant, ref. no. 29046 at officers' course at School of Artillery, Larkhill, 5/1940–6/1940.

LM [Leslie Moore]: *Katherine Mansfield: The Memories of LM*, London, 1971.

Lord, Graham: *The Authorised Biography of David Niven*, London, 2003.

Mark, Sir Robert: *In the Office of Constable*, London, 1978.

Mather, Carol: *When the Grass Stops Growing*, London, 1997.

Mayhew, Christopher: *Time to Explain*, London, 1987.

Niven, David: *The Moon's a Balloon*, London, 1972.

Seton-Watson, Christopher: *Dunkirk–Alamein–Bologna*, London, 1993.

Snyder, Timothy: 'Jews, Poles & Nazis: The Terrible History', *New York Review of Books*, 24 June 2010, pp. 44–6.

Warner, Philip: *Phantom*, London, 1982.

——: *Secret Forces of World War II*, London, 1985.

## Part Three: Beyond the Frontier, 1943–7

Bailey, Rod: *The Wildest Province: SOE in the Land of the Eagle*, London, 2008.

Barker, Elisabeth: *British Policy in South-East Europe in the Second World War*, London, 1976.

Boll, Michael: *Cold War in the Balkans: American Foreign Policy and the Emergence of Communist Bulgaria, 1943–1947*, Lexington, KY, 1985.

Davidson, Basil: *Partisan Picture*, Bedford, 1946.

——: *Special Operations Europe*, London, 1980.

Douglas, Keith: *Alamein to Zem Zem*, London, 1966, reprinted 1996.

——: *Collected Poems*, London, 1966.

Earle, John: *From Nile to Danube: A Wartime Memoir*, Trieste, 2010.

Foot, M. R. D.: *SOE in France*, London, 1966.

Graham, Desmond: *A Biography of Keith Douglas*, London, 1974.

Hamilton, Scott: *The Crisis of Theory: E. P. Thompson, the New Left and Postwar British Politics*, Manchester, 2011.

Hamson, Denys: *We Fell among Greeks*, London, 1946.

Henniker, John: *Painful Extractions*, Thornham Magna, Suffolk, 2002.

Imperial War Museum: the Chavasse papers (Captain E. F. J. Chavasse, ref. 06/23/1); Mostyn Davies's papers (Major M. L. Davies DSO, ref. 03/24/1).

Johnson, Stowers: *Agents Extraordinary*, London, 1975.

Kisch, Richard: *The Days of the Good Soldiers: Communists in the Armed Forces WWII*, London, 1985.

Lees, Michael: *The Rape of Serbia*, London, 1990.

Mackenzie, William: *The Secret History of SOE*, London, 2000.

Maclean, Fitzroy: *Eastern Approaches*, London, 1949.

National Archives: *SOE, Operations in the Balkans: A Guide to the Newly Released Records in the PRO*, London, n.d.

National Archives, Kew, HS [= SOE] files.

Palmer, Bryan D.: 'Homage to E. P. Thompson', *Labour/Le Travail*, pt 1 (vol. 32, 1993); pt 2 (vol. 33, 1994).

Rattenbury, A.: 'Convenient Death of a Hero', *London Review of Books*, 8 May 1997, pp. 12–13.

Sahgal, N. (ed.), *Before Freedom: Nehru's Letters to his Sister 1909–1947*, London, 2000.

Seton-Watson, Hugh: *The East European Revolution*, London, 1952.

Sweet-Escott, Bickham: *Baker Street Irregular*, London, 1965.

Thompson, E. P.: *The Heavy Dancers*, London, 1985 (ch. 4, 'The Liberation of Perugia').

Trŭnski, Slavchko: *Grateful Bulgaria*, Sofia, 1979.

Vukmanović-Tempo, Svetozar: *Struggle for the Balkans*, London, 1990.

Waugh, Evelyn: *Diaries*, ed. Michael Davie, London, 1976.

——: *Unconditional Surrender*, London, 1961.

West, Nigel: *Secret War*, London, 1992.

Wood, Neal: *Communism and British Intellectuals*, London, 1959.

Woodhouse, Monty: *Apple of Discord*, London, 1948.

Yanev, Kyril: *The Man from the Legend: A Life of Frank Thompson*, Sofia, 2001.

# Acknowledgements

In writing this book I've incurred many debts: to Michael Fishwick for understanding that this biography needed to explore Frank's family; to Dorothy Thompson for welcoming and supporting this, for sending around 60,000 words of family reminiscence and loaning many books and papers; to my agent Bill Hamilton for his encouragement and for suggesting what this biography's sub-title should be; and to Philippa Foot for believing in and backing the project.

John Dancy, Professor Freeman Dyson, Tony Forster, Lord Healey, Seymour Spencer, John Ounsted, John Willett and especially Professor M. R. D. Foot contributed stories about Frank at Winchester and/or Oxford, and Frank's first cousin Barbara Sloman (née Pilkington-Rogers) recalled Frank's and her childhoods. Rod Bailey helped me navigate the SOE files at the National Archives, pointed me to his discoveries in the Imperial War Museum and shared both his research and much expertise; Simon Kusseff offered early encouragement, a three-part Frank-related quarry and his interviews with Frank's friends; and Alan Ogden supplied some photographs. Robert Hutchison told me of the monument at Netley inscribed with words from Frank's best-known poem (and with some erroneous dates) and Suzanne Foster visited, took a photo and found that this is a D-Day memorial.

I am grateful to the Bodleian Library where I had special access to the Frank Thompson papers in the E. P. Thompson collection (accessed with the kind permission of the late Dorothy Thompson), a collection that is reserved and uncatalogued. Helen Langley, Becky Wall and Vicky Saywell rendered my visits there enjoyable and gave invaluable and prompt help. Gay Sturt, archivist at the Dragon school, Zoe Parsons at Kingswood, Suzanne Foster at Winchester College and Jennifer Thorp at New College Oxford each answered many queries as did the remarkable staff at the London Library (Country Orders), the

Manchester People's History Museum, the Imperial War Musuem and the National Archives at Kew.

In Bulgaria I am indebted to Professor Maria Stoicheva who in 1999 arranged for Professor Foot and me to meet with General Trŭnski and to visit Litakovo, and who later alerted me to and acquired a copy of Kyril Yanev's biography; to Professor Ludmila Kostova, Professor Roumen Genov, Kyril Yanev, Professor Evgenia Kalinova, Dr Nikolai Kotev and General Slavcho Trŭnski for their kind advice and to Biserka Anderson for translating Kyril Yanev's biography from the Bulgarian and for fielding sundry related enquiries.

In the UK Jane Jantet, Anne and Jim Roberts, Paddy Page and Daphne Turner helped explore many strange and interesting avenues and made some remarkable discoveries. I was also helped in various ways by Geoff Andrews, David Astor; John and Audi Bayley; David Bryers; Jeremy Catto; Colin Carritt, who allowed me to use his *The Oxford Carritts*; Tony and Jill Cockshut; Professor Robert Conquest; Deborah, Duchess of Devonshire; Harry Dickinson; John Earle; Val ffrench Blake; Dr Michael Gardner; Elizabeth, Lady Glenconner; Imogen Grundon; Helen Henry; David Holbrook; Cecil Hourani; Robert Hutchison; Donny Jones; Stuart Leasor; Priscilla Martin; Mary Midgley; Robin Murray; Sir Richard O' Brien; Sir Leo Pliatzky; Sim Rattenbury; David Reddaway; John Reddaway; David Sinclair-Loutit; Emma Tennant and Kate Thompson.

At Bloomsbury, where Anna Simpson ably and kindly steered the book through each phase of production, I also owe thanks to Peter James, Paul Nash, Jude Drake, Catherine Best and Alan Rutter.

Draft chapters were read by Jim Roberts, Paddy Page, John Earle, Professor R. T. Shannon, Rod Bailey, Jane Jantet, Jim O'Neill, Anne Roberts and David Schneider; and the whole by Anne Chisholm, who helped me rethink the prologue to the book, Juliet Gardiner, and Professor M. R. D. Foot, who wrote that it 'brings back the Frank I knew most vividly' and who taught me much; each of these made helpful suggestions.

My patient partner Jim O'Neill gave love and understanding and was, as always, extremely perceptive. Any remaining errors are my own responsibility.

# Index

## A NOTE ON THE AUTHOR

Peter J. Conradi became interested in Frank Thompson while researching his critically acclaimed *Iris Murdoch: A Life*, the authorised biography, and *A Writer at War: The Letters and Diaries of Iris Murdoch, 1938–1946*, which includes her correspondence with Frank. His critical studies of Dostoevsky, Angus Wilson and John Fowles were followed, more recently, by *Going Buddhist* and *At the Bright Hem of God*. He lives in London and Radnorshire where he gardens, walks, edits the *Radnorshire Transactions* and chairs the Bleddfa Trust. He was elected a Fellow of the Royal Society of Literature in 2011.